The UCAS Guide to getting into
ECONOMICS, FINANCE AND ACCOUNTANCY

For entry to university and college in 2013

Published by: UCAS Rosehill New Barn Lane Cheltenham GL52 3LZ

Produced in conjunction with GTI Media Ltd

© UCAS 2012

UCAS, a company limited by guarantee, is registered in England and Wales number: 2839815
Registered charity number: 1024741 (England and Wales) and SC038598 (Scotland)

UCAS reference number: PU032013
Publication reference: 12_043
ISBN: 978-1-908077-17-2
Price £15.99

Further copies available from UCAS (p&p charges apply):

Contact Publication Services PO Box 130 Cheltenham GL52 3ZF

email: publicationservices@ucas.ac.uk or fax: 01242 544806.

For further information about the UCAS application process go to www.ucas.com.

If you need to contact us, details can be found at www.ucas.com/about_us/contact_us.

UCAS QUALITY AWARDS

Foreword	5
Introducing economics	7
It could be you...	8
Introducing finance and accountancy	11
It could be you...	12
Why finance and accountancy?	14
A career in economics, finance and accountancy	17
Which economics degree?	18
A career in economics, finance and accountancy	20
Jargon buster	23
Which area?	26
The career for you?	35
Is economics, finance or accountancy for you?	36
Alternative economics, finance and accountancy careers	39
Professional bodies	41
Graduate destinations	43
Case studies	45
Entry routes	57
Routes to qualification	58
What others say...	63
Applicant journey	69
Six easy steps	70
Step 1 – Choosing courses	71
Planning your application for economics, finance or accountancy	71
Choosing courses	74
Choosing your institution	76
League tables	78
How will they choose you?	82
The cost of higher education	85
International students	88
Step 2 – Applying	92
How to apply	95
The personal statement	98
Step 3 – Offers	100
Extra	103
The Tariff	105
Step 4 – Results	116
Step 5 – Next steps	118
Step 6 – Starting university or college	120

378.41

Useful contacts   122

Essential reading   124

Courses   131
  Economics   135
  Finance   148
  Accountancy   156
  Economics and accountancy/accountancy and economics   166
  Finance and economics/economics and finance   171
  Accountancy and finance/finance and accountancy   175
  Banking combinations   185
  Business combinations   187
  Computing and computer science combinations   198
  Geography and geology combinations   202
  Language combinations   202
  Law combinations   213
  Management combinations   218
  Marketing combinations   227
  Mathematics and statistics combinations   230
  Politics combinations   240
  Science combinations   248
  Sociology and social science combinations   252
  Economics and other combinations   256
  Finance and other combinations   265
  Accountancy and other combinations   268

Foreword

THINKING ABOUT ECONOMICS, FINANCE OR ACCOUNTANCY?

Finding the course that's right for you at the right university or college can take time and it's important that you use all the resources available to you in making this key decision. We at UCAS have teamed up with **TARGETjobs.co.uk** to provide you with *The UCAS Guide to getting into Economics, Finance and Accountancy* to show you how you can progress from being a student to careers in economics, finance and accountancy. You will find information on what the subject includes, entry routes and real-life case studies showing how it worked out for others.

Once you know which subject area you might be interested in, you can use the listings of all the full-time higher education courses in economics, finance and accounting to see where you can study your subject. The course entry requirements are listed so you can check if getting in would be achievable for you. There's also advice on applying through UCAS, telling you what you need to know at each stage of the application process in just six easy steps to starting university or college.

We hope you find this publication helps you to choose and make your application to a course and university or college that is right for you.

On behalf of UCAS and **TARGETjobs.co.uk**, I wish you every success in your research.

Mary Curnock Cook, Chief Executive, UCAS

At TARGETjobs we champion paid work experience for UK university students. Find internships and placements across all sectors, plus take part in the TARGETjobs Undergraduate of the Year awards.

TARGETjobs.co.uk

the best possible start to your career

Introducing
economics

It could be you...

'Economics is not about things and tangible material objects: it is about men, their meanings and actions'
(Ludwig von Mises)

WHY ECONOMICS?

We all make economic decisions every day in our lives, from whether we have enough money to buy the latest CD to how much we need to save for a summer holiday with friends. In this way, economics shows us how to live our lives and, hopefully, how to make better economic decisions.

On a bigger scale, economics is all about the production, distribution and consumption of wealth, both on a small scale (eg individuals) and on a large scale (eg countries). Economics is also about comparing ways to use the limited resources that countries and individuals have, and how fair these are. Basically, economics gives us ways to think about the world so that we can make the best of what we already have. And it's not just about money (although of course finance plays a huge role in this area); it's also about how the choices we make impact on society. Who could ask for a more responsible and challenging potential career?

YOUR SKILLS

Not only will you have an interesting degree course if you study economics but you will also improve your future career prospects. Economics graduates are highly sought after in the world of work because of the variety of skills they can bring to a job. Equally, economists are needed in so many different fields that you are bound to find something that will satisfy both your interests and skills set.

It's all very well talking about skills but what exactly will you learn? The following are just examples:

SKILL	THE ABILITY TO...
Analysis and problem-solving	... develop strategic ways of thinking and devise effective frameworks to solve economic problems or issues
Communication	... explain complex information in a user-friendly way (often to clients in different work areas) and be able to summarise and apply difficult concepts
Self-management	... work efficiently on your own, managing often quite hectic work schedules and tight deadlines
Political and commercial awareness	... understand government policy, while shrewdly assessing economic performance
Teamworking	... work well within a team to achieve shared goals
Numeracy	... understand and confidently interpret numerical information, often by using various mathematical and statistical techniques

YOUR CAREER

Economics graduates are spoilt for choice when it comes to careers. The skills they learn as part of their undergraduate degree stand them in good stead for a wide range of high-level jobs, including:

- actuary
- market researcher
- insurance underwriter
- statistician
- management consultant
- economist
- retail banker
- investment banker
- chartered accountant
- political party research officer
- investment analyst
- trader (equities, bonds, shares).

WHAT WILL YOU EARN?

The average starting salary for graduates paid by The Association of Graduate Recruiters member organisations during 2010-11 was £25,000 (source: *The AGR Graduate Recruitment Survey 2012 – Winter Review)*. Due to their specific skills and knowledge, many economics graduates go into professions such as banking and investment, accountancy and taxation, and management consulting – all of which can offer substantially higher starting salaries as well as excellent long-term prospects. See page 22 for further information on graduate starting salaries.

WORKING AS AN ECONOMIST

Economists look at how society manages resources such as money, labour, businesses, services and raw materials. They study economic trends, produce economic forecasts and research issues such as interest rates, inflation, exchange rates, taxes, business cycles and employment levels. One of the key skills for an economist is the ability to present statistics and economic theories with clarity.

Economists can work for a range of organisations including government bodies, the media, charities and businesses.

OTHER CAREERS

For information on some of the financial jobs listed here, take a look at **Which area?** (starting on page 26) in the main finance and accountancy section, as well as the various **case studies** (starting on page 45).

Connect with us...

 www.facebook.com/ucasonline

 www.twitter.com/ucas_online

 www.youtube.com/ucasonline

Introducing finance and accountancy

It could be you...

... calculating losses arising from a flood or earthquake   – forensic accounting

... advising companies on mergers and acquisitions   – corporate finance

... rescuing troubled businesses   – corporate recovery

... making massive profits for clients   – markets

... helping clients make multibillion-euro acquisitions   – investment banking

... and lots more besides. Could a career in finance and accountancy be for you? The aim of this guide is to help you decide.

A CAREER IN FINANCE AND ACCOUNTANCY?

- Choose from a wide range of exciting career options. See **Which area?** starting on page 26.
- Learn about all the appropriate financial and technical language. See **Jargon buster** on page 23.
- Finance and accountancy professionals have good earnings potential. See how much in **A career in economics, finance and accountancy** on page 22.
- Make your UCAS application stand out from the crowd. Read **How will they choose you?** starting on page 82.

FINANCE AND ACCOUNTANCY IN CONTEXT

Mention a career in finance and accountancy to people outside the sector and, chances are, they will think you want to be an accountant. Worse still, thanks to unkind media portrayals, they may even stereotype accountants as grey-suit-wearing individuals with no sense of humour.

But who has the last laugh? **Accountancy** is far from dull. Nearly every business, whether an international conglomerate or a local handyman's company, needs an accountant to help with their business' planning and financial health. Someone somewhere will always need your expertise, with trainee accountants earning up to £29,000 per year and some senior accountants raking in well over £100,000.

But let's not forget the other business areas in this sector. The **banking and investment** business is all about making money work as hard as possible. It's borrowed and invested in a number of different ways but it's never allowed to sit still. The financial markets are open 24/7 and cross various time zones, from Hong Kong and Tokyo in the Far East, to Frankfurt and London in Europe and New York in the US – there is always something going on somewhere with money. London is a key player in the financial world because it straddles the working days of both the Far East and America. Key employers include investment banks, specialist finance houses and universal banks. And in spite of the recent financial crisis, the starting salaries

for graduates in investment banking in 2011 were well above the average graduate starting salary of £25,000.

Finally, you could opt for a career in **insurance and financial services**, a very fast-moving sector, driven by the very capable 'brains' that are behind it. Most jobs contain aspects of project and people management so you'll need to have a great combination of both analytical and people skills, plus, obviously, an ability to number-crunch. This sector particularly appeals to people who love reading the deals pages of the *FT* or who like to manage money. If you find yourself giving your parents advice on the best mortgage offers, this could be your dream area!

If you're interested in a possible career in finance and accountancy, then this guide can help point you further in the right direction. Read on to discover:

- the main roles on offer
- the skills and educational grades that employers in finance and accounting look for
- how to get into university and what you could do after graduating
- advice and personal experience stories from recent graduates working in finance and accountancy.

ARE YOU INTERESTED IN STUDYING ECONOMICS?

The careers outlined in the sections on finance and accountancy are open to students of economics who can, of course, also aim to work as economists. For more details please see the **Which economics degree?** section, starting on page 18.

Why finance and accountancy?

Choose a career that is...

VARIED

The people who work in finance and accountancy come from all walks of life and have studied all sorts of things. You needn't study a numerate subject as long as you have a strong interest in all things financial. Just think: you will be paid for helping to manage, invest, advise on or use other people's or companies' money, from a sole trader to a multinational organisation. Read **What do recent graduates say?** on the next page.

HIGHLY SKILLED

The chances of becoming professionally qualified in the accounting and financial management and the insurance and financial services sectors are excellent – and often essential to get ahead in your career. You can also study for a professional qualification linked to the banking and investment sector to add weight to your expertise. Such training not only helps you do your job more effectively but also makes you a very attractive potential employee either – in similar firms or in different career areas (where the transferable skills you gain can be used to great effect). Read **Routes to qualification** starting on page 58.

LUCRATIVE

Since your career is all about making money for other people, it's only fair that you should reap decent financial rewards. Finance and accountancy professionals can earn good salaries plus perks such as pension schemes, private healthcare and season ticket loans. It can be a work hard, play hard way of life. Check it out in **A career in economics, finance and accountancy** on page 22.

STIMULATING

Watching stock market changes in Tokyo and New York, managing cash flows, monitoring profits… All of these require a keen eye for detail and an interest in the financial status and health of both companies and individuals. Professionals in accounting and financial services work across a wide range of sectors, with a huge variety of companies, which means each day can bring a new challenge. Read **case studies** of graduates in the sector, starting on page 45.

INFLUENTIAL

It's true what they say: money does make the world go round. The fate of our economy, and of the industries within it, rests on the state of the country's (and the world's) financial status. Professionals in the finance and accounting arenas play a major role in determining a company's or an individual's financial future: ranging from advising on suitable investment opportunities to rescuing businesses in distress. Without this advice, companies couldn't function effectively and profitably, individuals might flounder with their tax returns and payments, and the country's economy would be in dire straits. Read **Which area?** on page 26 to see how you might be influencing future clients.

WHAT DO RECENT GRADUATES SAY?

'I had always enjoyed working with numbers and wanted to work in a business environment, so accounting seemed like a good choice for a degree.'
Katy Renshaw, auditor on an accounting and assurance placement, page 46

'I thoroughly enjoyed my MSc in health economics at the University of York; a particular highlight was undertaking my summer placement in New Zealand.'
Ramón Luengo-Fernandez, senior researcher in health economics, page 48

'I'd advise getting involved in any clubs and societies that allow you to work in and lead a team, as these are invaluable skills in any industry.'
Matthew Pullen, corporate graduate (group strategy & planning), page 50

'I enjoy the people, the work and the variety – basically working within a great team on lots of interesting projects. The work I'm doing is fun, challenging and diverse.'
Howard Thompson, audit assistant, page 52

'Studying a business and financial management degree has allowed me to do many things that other courses may not have, such as studying abroad and work experience opportunities.'
Hannah Newton, third-year business and financial management student, page 54

Focus your career with the TARGETjobs Careers Report.

Using biographical data, information about your interests and insightful psychometric testing, the Careers Report gives you a clear picture of jobs that match your skills and personality.

TARGETjobs.co.uk

the best possible start to your career

A career in economics, finance and accountancy

Which economics degree?

In 2012, there were over 1,400 economics-related courses on the UCAS website. How can you narrow those down to five?

SINGLE HONOURS

The first choice you will have to make is whether you would like to study economics on its own or as part of a combined degree. Since economics is a social science it links in well with other academic areas. Therefore, even if you opt for a straight single honours degree, you will almost certainly look at other related disciplines such as sociology, politics and international relations.

However, the mere fact that you have chosen to specialise in economics will mean that you'll cover the subject and its related areas in far greater detail than students on a joint honours degree. This is great if you are fascinated by economics and want to focus solely on it but if you want to keep your options open, you may be better off combining it with another subject.

JOINT HONOURS

Economics combines well with many other subjects, including history, business studies, human geography, maths, management, politics, psychology and languages. All of these share some common components with economics, while languages can add an international flavour to your studies.

HOW LONG DO COURSES LAST?

Economics courses typically last for three years, unless you combine them with a language, when you will normally be expected to spend either your second or third year abroad to develop your linguistic ability. In this case, courses will stretch to four years. Equally, some universities offer a joint degree of economics and engineering, which would typically mean a four-year course.

ECONOMICS YEAR BY YEAR

As with all higher education courses, your economics degree will differ in focus throughout each of the three years. This enables the university to teach you common principles that are key to all economics degrees, while allowing you to choose options at a later date that are more suited to your areas of interest. Broadly speaking, however, all undergraduate economics courses will be structured like this:

Year 1

In this year, tutors will give a general introduction to the subject: what it's all about, why it's relevant and how it applies to different aspects of our everyday life. This introduction not only gives students an idea of the different areas in which they can specialise, but also teaches them useful studying skills that they can use throughout the rest of their degree.

Year 2

The theme of year two is 'application'; you will, in effect, be applying the skills you learnt in year one to different fields of economics. You may cover areas such as industrial economics, international economics and political economy.

Year 3

The third year is all about specialising. After two years of intense study, you should be able to identify particular areas of economics that interest you – often culminating in a dissertation which provides you with an opportunity to develop economic ideas and theories.

A career in economics, finance and accountancy

Economics, finance and accounting degrees are hot topics at university, with thousands of students beginning degree courses in these areas every year. Careers in banking, accountancy and financial services offer graduates very attractive starting salaries, as you can see from the table on page 22. Equally encouraging for graduates in economics, accounting and finance is that these business sectors have a significant demand for graduates. Accounting firms and investment banks offered over 25% of the total of all graduate vacancies in 2011 *(The AGR Graduate Recruitment Survey 2012 – Winter Review)*.

WHERE THEY WORK

Where you work will depend on which business sector you choose. There are, broadly speaking, three main areas, which then break down into smaller sub-areas.

Banking and investment

Investment banks are global firms that carry out a full range of banking and investment services.

Specialist finance houses are smaller organisations that specialise in a particular area of work such as corporate finance.

Universal banks are financial services organisations that offer both corporate and investment banking.

Accounting and financial management

Professionals in these areas often work within general companies, or for specialist firms, providing a full range of advice and services in the following areas:

Assurance – the traditional side of financial work, involving auditing: independently reviewing a client's accounts and reassuring shareholders that a company's financial statements are accurate.

Corporate finance – advising companies on mergers and acquisitions, as well as financing for larger projects through loans or sales of assets.

Corporate recovery – saving ailing businesses, where possible, or putting them into liquidation if necessary.

Corporate treasury – managing a (normally large) company's cash flows, investing surpluses and controlling financial risk.

Forensic accounting – calculating losses arising from natural disasters such as floods and earthquakes, as well as thefts and accidents, helping with fraud allegations and assessing the financial impact of a disaster.

Tax – either advising companies and individuals on their tax liability and ways of minimising it, or working for HM Revenue & Customs in policy or as an inspector.

Insurance and financial services

Financial services providers – large employers (international companies with branches throughout the UK) offering a range of financial services (eg retail banking and savings accounts).

Large international corporates – businesses that have built their name in a different area but have diversified into financial services (such as food retailers).

Specialist firms – offer specialist services such as actuarial consulting, risk management, underwriting and reinsurance.

Regulation – the Financial Services Authority (FSA) regulates the industry and takes on graduates.

TRENDS

The 'credit crunch' and global recession have been the most significant trends in recent years. Banks, businesses and employment have been hard hit, with mergers and job losses frequently in the news. In spite of economic difficulties, however, banks, accounting and financial services firms are taking a strategic approach to the future and continuing to recruit top graduates who can prove their commitment to the industry. This means it's essential to keep up-to-date with current affairs and accrue as much relevant work experience as possible before and during university. It will stand you in good stead when it comes to applying for a permanent job.

FINANCE AND ACCOUNTANCY SALARY GUIDELINES

Median graduate starting salaries 2010-2011

Investment banks or fund managers	£38,250
Banking or financial services	£28,000
Consulting or business services firm	£23,000
Accountancy or professional services firm	£24,750

*paid by the Association of Graduate Recruiters member organisations

Share of graduate vacancies by type of occupation 2010-2011

Accountancy or professional services	21.4%
Banking or financial services	13.3%
Consulting or business services firms	11.1%
Investment bank or fund managers	6.8%

(Source: The AGR Graduate Recruitment Survey 2011 – Winter Review)

Jargon buster

There's a lot of specialist vocabulary in finance and accounting. We define some of the more common words you'll come across both here and elsewhere. Firstly it is worth noting that the terms 'accountancy' and 'accounting' and interchanged frequently.

ANALYST
A person who studies a number of different companies and makes buy-and-sell recommendations OR the entry position of someone starting their career in some investment banks.

BONDS
In simplest terms, an IOU! It is an agreement whereby a sum of money is repaid to an investor after a certain period of time, usually with interest.

BROKER
Either an intermediary between a buyer and a seller, receiving a commission typically based on the value of the transaction OR an insurance intermediary who advises clients and arranges their insurance or investments.

CAPITAL MARKET
The financial market in which investment products, such as stocks and bonds, are bought and sold.

CLAIM
A demand made by the insured, or the insured's beneficiary, for payment from a policy (eg insurance).

COMMODITIES

Commodities are goods such as oil, petrol, metal or grain traded on the commodity markets such as the London Metal Exchange.

DERIVATIVES

The group term for financial contracts between buyers and sellers of goods (commodities) or money (capital).

DUE DILIGENCE

An investigation into the true financial and commercial position of a company.

EQUITY

The risk-sharing part of a company's capital, usually referred to as ordinary shares.

FINANCIAL SERVICES AUTHORITY (FSA)

An independent, non-government body, which regulates the financial services industry in the UK.

FTSE 100/250 INDEX

The Financial Times Stock Exchange Index of the 100/250 companies with the largest market capitalisation on the UK stock market.

INDEMNITY

The legal principle that ensures that a policyholder is restored to the same financial position after a loss as he or she was in beforehand.

INDEPENDENT FINANCIAL ADVISER

A broker or other intermediary authorised to sell or advise on the policies of any life insurance company, as well as other financial products.

INSURANCE

A service that offers financial compensation for something that may or may not happen. Assurance is often used interchangeably for the same service.

INTEREST RATES

This is the 'rental' price for borrowing money and is charged to compensate for potential risk.

LIABILITY

Legal responsibility for injuring or damaging a person or their property.

LIQUIDATION

Selling a company's assets to pay off debts.

LIQUIDITY

The ease with which an asset or investment can be turned into money.

LLOYD'S OF LONDON

An insurance market, organised into syndicates, which underwrites most types of policy.

LONDON MARKET

A distinct, separate part of the UK insurance and reinsurance industry centred on the City of London, comprising insurance and reinsurance companies.

PERSONAL ACCIDENT INSURANCE

A policy that pays specified amounts of money if the policyholder is injured in an accident.

POLICY

A legal document confirming a contract between an insurer and a policyholder.

POLICYHOLDER

A person or organisation who takes out an insurance policy in cover of a particular risk.

PORTFOLIO

A collection of securities held by an investor.

PRIVATE EQUITY

High risk and high return investment in shares, which cannot easily be turned into cash, in new companies.

REINSURANCE

The cover insurance companies can purchase to protect themselves against large losses.

RISK MANAGEMENT

Evaluating and selecting alternative regulatory and non-regulatory responses to risk, normally through legal and economic considerations.

SECURITIES

This is a general term describing all types of bonds and shares.

SETTLEMENT

Once a deal has been made stock is transferred from seller to buyer to settle the deal.

STOCKS

A certificate of ownership in a company, rather like shares.

UNDERWRITER

A person who evaluates risks and decides whether or not to accept a risk. The underwriter also determines the rates and coverage that are associated with accepting a risk.

Which area?

Such is the range of career paths to choose from in this sector that finance and accounting students are spoilt for choice.

Those unfamiliar with the range of sectors within the finance and accounting worlds may think that the main work areas revolve around services offered by high street banks or accountancy firms. However, the situation is far more diverse and complex than that. There are many different disciplines to choose from, varying in location from a small town in the regions, to the City of London and beyond. We have summarised the main areas into which people are recruited to give you a flavour of what you might end up doing as a recent graduate.

BANKING AND INVESTMENT

Corporate banking
Managing financial flows for corporate customers

Corporate bankers help corporate customers, financial institutions and public-sector organisations to manage their daily financial flows. They are the 'bread and butter' winners of any corporate bank. They will provide advice on aspects such as a potential merger or acquisition, investments or fund management, and making payments to suppliers on time. The services corporate banks provide to customers are similar (but more complex) to those offered by high street banks to their retail customers.

Employees can expect early and high levels of responsibility and autonomy – with their own portfolio of junior products and client contact, and with opportunities for travel.

Inter-dealer broking

Buy and sell financial instruments for clients

Inter-dealer brokers act as intermediaries to help clients – normally corporations rather than individuals – buying and selling financial instruments including bonds and equities. Sometimes clients use inter-dealer brokers for the purpose of trading anonymously, in order to get the best price.

To succeed in the field you need good people skills and an outgoing personality, as well as a passion for financial markets.

Investment banking

Offering advice on finance and risk management to clients

Investment bankers provide advice on finance and risk management to a wide range of clients from corporate and financial institutions to government-related organisations. They analyse their financial needs and offer appropriate solutions. However, they do not force products onto their clients.

Long hours are common. Investment bankers normally start their careers by helping senior bankers with their work. The job can sometimes be routine, eg when collating and repackaging data, but you will soon move on to enjoying more direct contact with clients.

Investment management

Making and managing profits for clients

Investment managers try to select stock for a client's portfolio that will outperform both the wider market and their competitors, with the result that they will hopefully make their clients a tidy sum of money. They meet with senior managers from a wide range of companies to research both the businesses themselves and the markets in which they operate – before then investing money entrusted to them from pension funds or private investors.

Employees normally work towards the Chartered Financial Analyst qualification, while still undertaking their professional duties. Normally you will be given one or two sectors to research and it's your job to then pass on any buy-and-sell ideas to your investment manager, who will ultimately decide where the money is invested. Travel opportunities are good, both nationally and internationally, but expect long hours and an intense working environment.

Markets

Providing investment solutions for clients and profits for the firm

This sector provides both investment solutions for customers and profits for the firm, and covers three main areas: **sales** – providing a link between the firm and the Financial institutions that want to invest money; **trading** – investing the firm's capital, or making markets or providing liquidity on financial products for clients; and **structuring** – developing large financial products for clients.

Starters normally work in small teams of up to 10, designing presentations, working on spreadsheets and modelling: basically helping out wherever possible. Expect long working hours: 7am to 6pm is normal, as are 12 hour days during big deals.

Operations

Ensuring banks comply with financial and legal regulations

The main job of the operations department is to ensure that business activities within a bank are conducted in a controlled manner and comply with both banking and legal regulations. Roles in this area can have an accounting, settlement or risk-management bias.

Most people will be able to rotate around different operations groups for a couple of years to get an overview of the various jobs available. Not only does this give you excellent experience but it should also help you decide where you would like to base your career. Early responsibility and accountability is likely, and typical jobs include initiating the introduction of a new product on behalf of your team. Working hours depend on the markets you support and the activity within them, so can fluctuate from one day to the next.

Private banking
Also known as private wealth management
Private wealth management is about providing professional services to high net-worth clients to help them manage their finances to the best possible effect. Services offered firstly include advisory, where the private banker advises the client about investment opportunities and the client makes the final decision, and secondly discretionary, where, after an in-depth discussion, the bank manages the client's portfolio on their behalf.

Private banking tends to be an international business, so good language skills are invaluable. You also need to have excellent communication skills and a strong customer focus.

Risk management
Understanding and controlling trading risks
Risk management, or risk control, is the business function that ensures trading risks are understood by an organisation, which can then build a suitable strategy. Daily activities include running reports, analysing risks and communicating risk exposures to traders.

Graduates tend to join graduate training programmes. Numeracy and strong analytical skills are essential, and many graduates have a science or mathematics background.

Sales, trading and research
Trading and distributing financial assets
Financial markets are about trading and distributing financial assets and instruments. Work in sales, trading and research involves finding solutions for big clients such as governments or large corporations. It's a financially rewarding career but very hard work – traders, for example, tend to start the day at 6.30 or 7am when the markets open. Numeracy and analytical skills are required and a maths degree would be essential in some areas of work.

Specialist markets
Advising and structuring deals for specific sectors
Specialist market teams provide advice on mergers and acquisitions to clients from particular industry sectors, such as healthcare, the media and financial institutions. It's 'specialist' because you need an in-depth knowledge of your client's sector in order to effectively carry out transactions on your client's behalf, after you have made them aware of the different options available. You will also need to watch what is happening in their sector to both predict future transactions and approach clients with ideas.

You normally work in small teams of around four or five people and early responsibility is guaranteed. You will normally produce the financial analysis reports, prepare press materials, research the sector and oversee some aspects of a deal. Travel is common, depending on your clients' locations. Working hours tend to be long because of the project nature of the work.

Structured finance
Providing tailor-made financing solutions to clients
Specialists in this area use their in-depth knowledge of different industry sectors, such as telecommunications, gas and oil, and natural resources, to offer clients a variety of structured debt and equity products, while designing complex financing to meet their clients' requirements.

You will be involved with transactions from day one, as part of a small team. You will normally be responsible for tasks such as preparing pitch material, undertaking analysis and research, carrying out due diligence and helping to close a deal successfully. Since deals are becoming more complex, long days can be expected, often from 8am-8pm.

Technology
Providing innovative solutions to business
IT is crucial to facilitating and optimising the performance of investment and banking organisations, so it stands to reason that specialist IT professionals who are able to keep up with the rapid pace of technological change are in high demand. Some graduates take a postgraduate course but internships can be an equally good route into this area of work. A degree in IT isn't a necessity but an aptitude for working with technology and excellent communication skills are vital.

ACCOUNTING AND FINANCIAL MANAGEMENT

Assurance
Reviewing financial data and procedures
Assurance professionals review companies' financial data and procedures to ensure that the management is taking care of shareholders' money. It is impossible to check every single transaction, so it's important to assess areas that are considered higher risk. Clients vary from listed companies to small family businesses.

Everyone tends to work as part of a team in this area and a few weeks after joining, you would be heavily involved in all aspects of each process.

Business advisory
Offering clients a wide range of services
The main responsibility of people working in business advisory is to provide a high standard of service to clients based on the development of strong client relationships. The services provided range from audit, corporate and personal tax to corporate finance and business recovery.

Graduates in this area will normally work on projects as part of a small team. Opportunities for travel are huge, as are secondments to worldwide destinations on qualification.

Commercial finance
Analysing and improving performance
Commercial finance managers work in a variety of sectors including leisure, retail and fast-moving consumer goods to analyse the performances of their services or goods and recommend steps to maximise profits. The focus of analysis could be on one product or on broader strategic advice to drive a business forward. Pricing goods or services can fall within the remit of the commercial finance manager, who needs to find a balance between making a sufficient profit and being appealing to consumers.

Graduates can join a training programme in industry and commerce and gain a professional accountancy qualification. Commercial finance managers can move into a career in management, once they have acquired in-depth sector knowledge and an understanding of how businesses work.

Corporate finance
Add value to businesses in the process of change
Corporate finance involves adding value to businesses that are in the process of change, for example selling off a part of their business or acquiring a new one. There are three main areas of work: lead advisory (project management of a transaction), transaction support (including due diligence, valuations and business planning) and compliance work (regulatory work).

Graduates can gain professional qualifications in audit and accountancy or corporate finance. Excellent social skills are needed, as the role often involves communicating with senior business managers, as well as adaptability and the confidence to take on responsibility.

Corporate recovery

Assisting companies in financial distress

Professionals in this area provide services and advice to underperforming companies (mainly banks and private equity houses) and their stakeholders. Financial and restructuring solutions are normally offered, including restoring debt to reduce finance costs, improving cash management, and increasing operational performance. If it is too late in the day for the company to recover, insolvency is sometimes the only option.

Employees normally spend six months of a three-year training contract undertaking chartered accountancy exams. They will work mainly on insolvency assignments, helping an insolvent business continue to trade. Tasks include preparing financial projections and bank reports, dealing with a company's suppliers or debtors, or helping to sell the business.

Corporate treasury

Managing risks and looking forward

This involves, broadly speaking, managing financial risks, such as bank facilities and capital markets, cash investments, foreign exchange dealing, mergers and acquisitions, insurance and pensions.

The starting point is normally as a treasury dealer, which involves reviewing bank balances, proposing, executing and recording transactions, and ensuring compliance with internal controls. Hours tend to be long, especially when projects near completion.

Financial accounting

Communicating financial information with the outside world

Financial accountants record and report a company's results to the outside world, according to strict accounting rules. The work involves: analysing and reviewing business financial results; providing advice and support on accounting issues, deals and projects; consolidating and analysing financial results and reporting on them; external reporting and planning; and interpreting and communicating accounting developments to ensure open and accurate disclosure of financial information.

Forensic accounting

Putting together the accounting pieces

Forensic accountants provide expert reports on, or attend court to give oral evidence in, cases involving accountancy matters. They may also assess the effect of applying legal issues to a case, and assist with dispute resolution (trying to solve matters through arbitration or mediation instead of going to court). Specialists in this field also help clients to investigate accounting irregularities and fraud by looking at any evidence, such as witness interviews and paper and electronic sources.

Graduates are often offered a wealth of opportunities, including the chance to spend six months on secondment during training. A business understanding of corporate controls is normally gained by training in audit and then transferring to forensic accounting, enabling you to see a wider spectrum of businesses, not just the ones that are in conflict. Professionals normally work as part of a team, varying in size from two to 20 people, and new starters will normally be involved in research, analysis, evidence gathering and computer modelling.

Internal audit
Providing independent and objective financial opinions

Internal audit is all about providing an independent and objective appraisal of an organisation's operations, in order to assess the effectiveness of their internal administrative and accounting controls and to ensure that they conform to relevant policies. Internal auditors will normally do this by testing the internal controls that are already in place and drafting a subsequent report on their findings.

Those employed in this area may find themselves working for clients throughout the UK and possibly overseas. Team sizes vary from one individual working on their own to four or five auditors. The sheer variety of the clients served keeps the job stimulating and interesting.

Management accounting
Enabling effective decision-making

Management accountants work with company managers to help them make effective decisions about their business and how it is run. They provide financial interpretation and advice, report on financial performance within the company and give early warnings if underperformance is likely or suspected (and suitable plans of action if this is the case). They also help managers understand what drives the business and explain the financial consequences of their decisions.

Beginners normally support a management accountant team, often by covering a management accountant position. This carries with it a great deal of

responsibility, as you get to influence business decisions. The area is constantly changing and consequently is never dull: but you must be happy to accept frequent challenges.

Risk assessment
Protecting business from potential risks

Risk assessors help businesses to understand, prioritise and manage potential risks, thus avoiding future problems while making the most of opportunities. The role of the risk assessor is to identify and evaluate risks and then recommend appropriate strategies. It is an intellectually satisfying job but primarily advisory, which requires the ability to step back and let others make final decisions.

Graduates usually train in a broader area such as assurance, going on to specialise in risk assessment at a later stage, although some accountancy firms do employ graduates directly into risk assessment roles. Numerical and analytical skills are key, as are an ability to think logically and good interpersonal skills.

Tax
Offering tax advice to businesses and individual clients

Tax advisers are employed by businesses and highly paid individuals. This may be to find one-off solutions to a particular tax issue or on an ongoing basis, ensuring compliance with the law and cost-effective solutions to the business or individual client.

A good degree in a finance or economic discipline is helpful, while problem solving skills, a high level of numeracy, analytical ability and good communication skills are essential. Tax advisers often have to keep abreast of laws in several different countries simultaneously.

INSURANCE AND FINANCIAL SERVICES

Actuarial work
Advice, assessment and calculations
Three main business areas employ actuaries: pensions, insurance and investment. Actuaries advise clients on their schemes in each or any of these areas; this can be challenging as they have to explain quite technical information in layman's terms. Some of the typical tasks they undertake include working on risk-assessment models to set insurance premiums and monitoring the running and financial health of pension schemes. Not everyone working in an actuarial department is a qualified actuary; there are also IT, human resources and marketing experts.

Graduates will start off as trainee actuaries and will study, while working, for three to six years before taking their professional exams. Typical daily tasks include working on calculations and preparing papers for client meetings. Long hours should be expected when meeting client deadlines.

Insurance
Helping customers manage unforeseen risks
Insurance companies help individuals and organisations protect themselves against unforeseen circumstances in exchange for an annual premium. If anything unexpected happens, the insurance claim should help get them back on their feet again as quickly as possible.

You could be employed within the engineering or surveyors' departments, which assess damage to cars and property, or work as a team leader in a contact centre. Some specific areas include **strategy** – business planning and support; **underwriting** – setting policy terms and evaluating the risk an individual or company presents; and **relationship management** – managing relationships with client companies for whom

insurance schemes are provided and helping to develop new products for them.

Life assurance
Providing financial security for life
Companies in this area provide their customers with financial protection and money-management ideas. The main difference between general and life insurance is that this area is long term, providing three major product lines: **pensions** – financial protection at the end of your working life; **life assurance** – financial protection for your family if something unfortunate happens to you; and **investment** – life assurance companies invest their customers' premiums in the stock market, bonds and property.

Work in this area could be in one of many roles, including customer services, sales, marketing, risk management, finance, HR and IT.

Regulation and compliance
Setting regulations to protect consumers
Employers in this area fall into the following two main categories.
Regulatory bodies include the Financial Services Authority (FSA), which oversees the UK financial services industry, and the Office of Fair Trading (OFT), which ensures that markets work well for consumers.
Financial services providers employ compliance or risk officers to ensure their business and products meet with FSA regulations.

Professionals in this area are responsible for:

- making sure that each company's rules and regulations are financially trustworthy
- alerting consumers to the benefits and risks associated with different financial products
- looking into the type and level of risk associated with different investment products and transactions and

taking action to lower that risk

- ensuring that regulated businesses cannot easily be used to commit financial crime.

Those working for a regulatory body will have a broad introduction to regulation before specialising in a specific sector, eg insurance. Financial services providers normally recruit graduates into a more general finance scheme before offering the chance to specialise later.

Retail banking
Supplying financial products to a wide range of clients

This work not only involves front line sales staff and branch management but also covers jobs in human resources, marketing and finance – as is the case with any other retail business. Retail banks deal with a huge variety of clients, from individuals with personal accounts to multinational companies needing a range of financial services. This area is fast moving and exciting – requiring new initiatives to keep up-to-date with clients' needs.

There are opportunities for graduates in branch management, network support and project management. Many retail banks have an international element, so travel might be possible. Available training includes studying for relevant banking qualifications or a diploma in financial services.

Risk management
Protecting organisations against financial uncertainty

Risk managers act for financial services organisations to protect them against loss – ensuring companies stay within their business parameters and don't exceed their financial limits. Risks evaluated include fraud, market risks due to interest rate fluctuations, credit, liquidity, operational, and health and safety.

Degrees in economics, business, law or management are welcomed and evidence of work experience during undergraduate study is advantageous if not essential. Risk managers need to be good problem solvers with the ability to look ahead. Excellent numeracy, diplomacy and interpersonal skills are key to this role.

Want to see UCAS in action?
Visit www.ucas.tv to watch

case studies

how-to guides

UCAS

The career
for you?

Is economics, finance or accountancy for you?

Building a successful career in finance and accountancy requires more than a head for numbers.

A career in these sectors requires certain skills and personal qualities. To help you decide if this is the right working area for you we suggest you think about the following three areas:

- what you want from your future work
- what a finance or accounting course typically involves
- which skills and qualities admissions tutors in this field typically seek in new recruits.

WHAT DO YOU WANT FROM YOUR CAREER?

You may not have an instant answer for this but your current studies, work experience and even your hobbies can give you clues about the kind of work you enjoy and the skills you have already started to develop. Start with a blank sheet of paper and note down the answers to the following questions to help get you thinking. Be as honest with yourself as you can; don't write what you think will impress your teachers or parents. Just write what really matters to you and you'll start to see a pattern emerging.

WHAT REALLY MATTERS TO YOU

- When you think of your future, what kind of environment do you see yourself working in – eg in an office, outdoors, nine-to-five, relaxed or high-pressured?
- What are your favourite hobbies outside of school?
- What is it about them that you enjoy – eg the numerical challenges of a Sudoku puzzle or the strategies of a chess game?
- What are your favourite subjects in school and what is it about them that you enjoy most – eg being able to solve mathematical problems or working with people to arrive at solutions?
- What do you dislike about the other subjects you're studying?
- If you've had any work experience, which aspects have you most enjoyed?

WHAT DO FINANCE AND ACCOUNTING COURSES INVOLVE?

Unsurprisingly, the skills you'll require as a successful accountant or financial services professional will also be required at various stages of your studies. Therefore, it's important to know what typical finance and accounting courses entail before you apply, to be sure it's the kind of work you will enjoy. For example, most university courses will involve a mixture of practical knowledge, which can be applied and used in the modern workplace, and more theoretical study, often concentrating on both essential and advanced concepts of areas such as business, finance economics, accounting and management. Are you happy to undertake this type of in-depth analysis of your subject?

WHAT SKILLS WILL YOU NEED?

Despite the many different career options within the finance and accountancy sectors, the skills set they all require is broadly the same. Number one is **numerical ability**, which employers will mostly discern from your GCSEs, A levels and degree subject. Beyond this, other key skills required of any potential finance and accountancy professional are:

- **analytical ability** – to assess a situation or issue and identify key elements that need to be addressed in order to move on
- **commercial awareness** – a knowledge and understanding of the business issues that affect the sector you are interested in, as well as their external factors and internal structures
- **problem-solving** – finding an appropriate solution to a problem using the information and resources to hand
- **decision-making** – confidently choosing the best way forward for you and your client by assessing the various available options and the pros and cons of each

- **negotiation** – discussing an issue or problem either face-to-face or by telephone or, more rarely, by email. The aim is for both parties to come to a mutually satisfactory conclusion and this may involve compromise on one or both sides
- **self-confidence** – when dealing with often contentious and sensitive issues, you need to feel confident in yourself and your abilities to instil that belief in others to follow your recommendations
- **teamworking** – working with others to reach a desired goal: a key skill in virtually every working environment, finance-related or not
- **written communication** – an ability to make yourself clearly understood in text, whether in emails, letters or more formal documentation. With such large amounts of cash often at risk, it's vital people know where you're coming from
- **interpersonal skills** – since most roles in these sectors involve working in teams and dealing with clients, you need to be comfortable working with and relating to other people.

Alternative economics, finance and accountancy careers

If a career in finance and accountancy isn't for you, there are plenty of other interesting possibilities...

There are many career paths that can be linked directly, (or tenuously), to a degree in finance or accounting. The difficulty is choosing the right one. In broad terms, suitable career sectors include the law (particularly commercial law), management consulting, property and quantity surveying.

COMMERCIAL LAWYERS

Commercial solicitors work with investment bankers to get the best possible deal for their clients and to ensure that their contracts comply with the appropriate investment-related regulations. Typical employers range from large London-based firms that specialise in handling high-value and often international commercial transactions, to sole practitioners based in high street firms, undertaking work for local companies.

If working as a barrister appeals more to you, you will normally work on a self-employed basis, from a set of chambers, again probably situated in London. Typical tasks include defending or prosecuting cases of a commercial nature on behalf of a client in the commercial court.

If the legal route wins your vote you'll need to complete a one-year postgraduate law conversion course, (if your first degree subject isn't law). After that, if you want to become a solicitor you'll also need to study for the Legal Practice Course (LPC), followed by a two-year training contract with a firm.

Alternatively, if you want to become a barrister you'll need to continue on to the one year Bar Vocational Course (BVC), followed by a pupillage in a set or sets of chambers.

Further information

The Law Society of England and Wales, **www.lawsociety.org.uk**, for information on becoming a solicitor, or The Bar Council, **www.barcouncil.org.uk** for information on becoming a barrister.
Progression Series – Law
www.ucasbooks.com

MANAGEMENT CONSULTANTS

Management consultants provide organisations with strategies to improve their business. They identify potential problem areas and suggest, then implement, solutions. Employers range from the consultancy divisions of the four main accountancy firms (The Big Four: Deloitte Touche Tohmatsu, Ernst & Young, KPMG and PricewaterhouseCoopers) to specialist organisations that provide more specific advice on certain areas such as IT, healthcare, strategy, etc.

Further information

The Institute of Business Consulting, **www.iconsulting.org.uk**

CHARTERED SURVEYORS

Chartered surveyors advise clients on how to maximise the value of their property while **quantity surveyors** manage the cost of construction projects. In order to gain professional status, you will need to take a one-year full-time (or two-year part-time) conversion course, (if your first degree is not in quantity surveying), as well as completing the assessment of professional competence (APC), which is a two-year training scheme that all quantity surveyors undertake.

Property and quantity surveying are dominated by a few small international firms based both in London and regional centres and a larger number of smaller firms based throughout the UK.

Further information

The Royal Institution of Chartered Surveyors, **www.rics.org**

There are various industry associations and institutes that provide information for aspiring graduates. To check them out, visit **www.targetjobs.co.uk/career-sectors** and select 'Construction' or 'Property' from the list of options.

USING YOUR TRANSFERABLE SKILLS

While these three areas are great career matches for finance and accounting graduates, you don't have to limit yourself to these. The skills you will develop and hone as part of your degree are transferable to many other areas that require an ability with numbers, an analytical approach, an interest in financial processes and organisations, and an understanding of how companies work. Any business area would potentially benefit from the skills you'll develop through a finance or accounting-related degree, as would any roles that require financial research and advice, including those in politics and government and even in specialist publishing and media (eg financial broadcasting and journalism).

Professional bodies

Professional bodies are responsible for overseeing a particular profession or career area, ensuring that people who work in the area are fully trained and meet ethical guidelines. Professional bodies may be known as institutions, societies and associations. They generally have regulatory roles; they make sure that members of the profession are able to work successfully in their jobs without endangering lives or abusing their position.

Professional bodies are often involved in training and career development, so courses and workplace training may have to follow the body's guidelines. In order to be fully qualified and licensed to work in your profession of choice, you will have to follow the professional training route. In many areas of work, completion of the professional training results in gaining chartered status – and the addition of some extra letters after your name. Other institutions may award other types of

certification once certain criteria have been met. Chartered or certified members will usually need to take further courses and training to ensure their skills are kept up to date.

What professional bodies are there?
Not all career areas have professional bodies. Those jobs that require extensive learning and training are likely to have bodies with a regulatory focus. This includes careers such as engineering, law, construction, health and finance. If you want to work in one of these areas, it's important to make sure your degree course is accredited by the professional body – otherwise you may have to undertake further study or training later on.

Other bodies may play more of a supportive role – looking after the interests of people who work in the sector. This includes journalism, management and arts-based careers. Professional bodies may also be learned bodies, providing opportunities for further learning and promoting the development of knowledge in the field.

Can I join as a student?

Many professional bodies offer student membership – sometimes free or for reduced fees. Membership can be extremely valuable as a source of advice, information and resources. You'll have the opportunity to meet other students in the field, as well as experienced professionals. It will also look good on your CV, when you come to apply for jobs.

See below for a list of professional bodies in the fields of economics, finance and accountancy.

ECONOMICS

The Royal Economic Society
www.res.org.uk

Society of Business Economists
www.sbe.co.uk

FINANCE AND ACCOUNTANCY

The Actuarial Profession
www.actuaries.org.uk

The Association of Chartered Certified Accountants
www.acca.org.uk

Chartered Banker Institute (Chartered Institute of Bankers in Scotland)
www.charteredbanker.com

Chartered Institute of Management Accountants
www.cimaglobal.com

The Chartered Institute of Public Finance and Accountancy
www.cipfa.org.uk

Chartered Institute for Securities & Investment
www.cisi.org

Institute of Bankers in Ireland
www.bankers.ie

ICAEW
www.icaew.com

The Chartered Insurance Institute (CII)
www.cii.co.uk

Insurance Institute of London
www.iilondon.co.uk

Graduate destinations

Economics and Accountancy
HESA Destination of Leavers of Higher Education Survey

Each year, comprehensive statistics are collected on what graduates are doing six months after they complete their course. The survey is co-ordinated by the Higher Education Statistics Agency (HESA) and provides information about how many graduates move into employment (and what type of career) or further study and how many are believed to be unemployed.

The full results across all subject areas are published by the Higher Education Careers Service Unit (HECSU) and the Association of Graduate Careers Advisory Services (AGCAS) in *What Do Graduates Do?*, which is available from **www.ucasbooks.com**.

	Economics	Accountancy
In UK employment	50.9%	50.2%
In overseas employment	1.8%	0.8%
Working and studying	16.4%	20.7%
Studying in the UK for a higher degree	7.7%	4.2%
Studying in the UK for a teaching qualification	0.4%	0.4%
Undertaking other further study or training in the UK	3.6%	4.0%
Studying overseas	0.3%	0.1%
Assumed to be unemployed	10.5%	11.0%
Not available for employment, study or training	3.7%	3.3%
Other	4.7%	5.3%

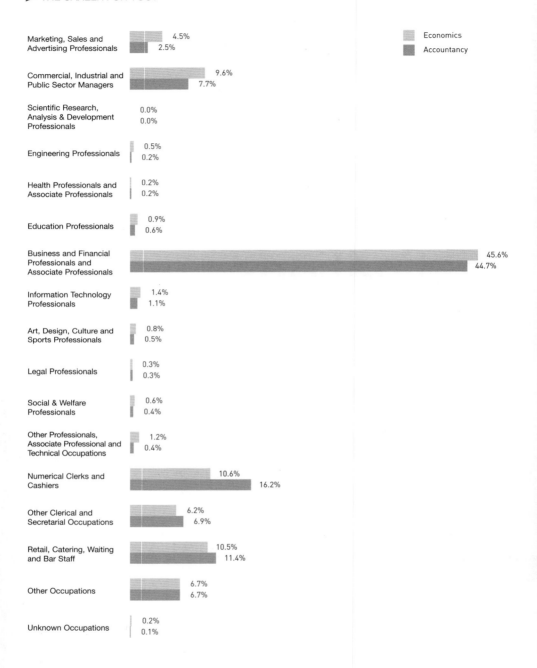

Economics
Accountancy

Occupation	Economics	Accountancy
Marketing, Sales and Advertising Professionals	4.5%	2.5%
Commercial, Industrial and Public Sector Managers	9.6%	7.7%
Scientific Research, Analysis & Development Professionals	0.0%	0.0%
Engineering Professionals	0.5%	0.2%
Health Professionals and Associate Professionals	0.2%	0.2%
Education Professionals	0.9%	0.6%
Business and Financial Professionals and Associate Professionals	45.6%	44.7%
Information Technology Professionals	1.4%	1.1%
Art, Design, Culture and Sports Professionals	0.8%	0.5%
Legal Professionals	0.3%	0.3%
Social & Welfare Professionals	0.6%	0.4%
Other Professionals, Associate Professional and Technical Occupations	1.2%	0.4%
Numerical Clerks and Cashiers	10.6%	16.2%
Other Clerical and Secretarial Occupations	6.2%	6.9%
Retail, Catering, Waiting and Bar Staff	10.5%	11.4%
Other Occupations	6.7%	6.7%
Unknown Occupations	0.2%	0.1%

Reproduced with the kind permission of HECSU/AGCAS, *What Do Graduates Do? 2010*.
All data comes from the HESA Destination of Leavers of Higher Education Survey 09/10

Case studies

HEAR IT FROM THE EXPERTS

Still not sure whether you want to work in finance or accountancy? Read the following profiles to see where the world of work has taken recent graduates in the financial professions and beyond!

Auditor on an accounting and assurance placement

working with a large selection of clients, including FTSE 100 companies

PricewaterhouseCoopers LLP

KATY RENSHAW

Route into accounting and finance:
A levels – maths, accounting, business studies, AS level sociology (2008);
BA accounting and finance, Kingston University (2013)

WHY ACCOUNTING?

I had always enjoyed working with numbers and wanted to work in a business environment, so accounting seemed like a good choice for a degree. Additionally, my long-term goal is to own my own business one day and I believe that an accounting background will be very helpful in understanding how businesses run.

My degree focuses on accounting and finance, with opportunities to study more general areas of business. In my first year, we looked at basic financial and management accounting and other general business areas. The second year was a lot more accounting-related, with a focus on management and financial accounting, finance, and law for accountants. Since the degree is quite numerical in nature, you really have to like working with numbers to enjoy it.

WHAT DID YOUR WORK PLACEMENT INVOLVE?

I am in the middle of my 11-month work placement with PricewaterhouseCoopers, and I undertake the same responsibilities as a graduate trainee. I am a junior team member and my responsibilities vary hugely. Most of my time is spent on year-end audits, which includes looking at different areas of clients' financial records and testing them for accuracy using various assurance procedures. I spend a lot of time helping others out with their work and I have also been on a few stock counts.

My working environment is busy and mainly client facing. I work a 35-hour week but it can be a lot more than that with the year-end work; it really depends on the project. I receive the same training as a graduate trainee – mainly an induction week, college and home study time for ACA qualification, four weeks of 'assurance fundamentals' training, and lots of coaching on the job. Basically because I am always doing something new, I am always learning.

HOW DID YOU GET YOUR WORK PLACEMENT?

I knew I wanted to work in professional services so I just applied. The selection process was fairly long and included an application form, written exercises, psychometric tests, verbal and numerical reasoning, telephone interview and assessment day – including partner interview. A lot of people applied so the competition was fairly fierce, and at times the selection process was quite stressful.

WHAT WOULD YOU SAY WAS THE BIGGEST CHALLENGE OF YOUR WORK PLACEMENT?

Professional exams are very challenging and the long hours can be tiring but all of this prepares you well for the real world, and I know I'll appreciate my schedule when I'm back at university. I have coped by revising hard, accepting that the long hours have to be worked and staying organised.

AND THE BEST BITS?

The whole experience has been great, especially the exposure to clients, the people I work with and the support. There have been lots of social events too. I know I'll be going back to university much more knowledgeable and with far greater experience than my peers.

KATY'S TOP TIPS

Show enthusiasm and a genuine interest in the area – employers want to know you are really interested in doing their job. Use your past experiences from working and student environments, and think about how these could be applied to working in the accounting and assurance area.

Senior researcher in health economics

University of Oxford

RAMÓN LUENGO-FERNANDEZ

Route into health economics:
A levels – Spanish, mathematics, physics, biology (1998); MA economics and European studies, Heriot-Watt University (2002); MSc health economics, University of York (2003); DPhil public health/health economics, University of Oxford (2009).

WHY HEALTH ECONOMICS?

Having a mother who is a nurse and an aunt who is a doctor, I have always been interested in health and medicine. Although economics might appear to be worlds apart from this, the healthcare system has to make 'economic decisions' – for example how best to put into use scarce and valuable resources such as hospitals, doctors and nurses to cover all of the health needs and demands of the population to achieve the greatest health possible.

HOW DID YOU GET TO WHERE YOU ARE TODAY?

In my fourth year at university, I found that the University of York offered a specialist MSc in health economics and, after discussing my options with my tutor, I decided to go for it because of the reputation of the course. I thoroughly enjoyed my MSc; a particular highlight was undertaking my summer placement in New Zealand. After graduating from York, I started a job as a junior health economist at the University of Oxford, during which time I also completed my DPhil thesis, looking at the costs and health outcomes of patients who have suffered a stroke. Thanks in part to completing my DPhil thesis successfully, I was promoted to senior researcher.

WHAT DOES YOUR JOB INVOLVE?

One of the purposes of health economics is to assess the costs and benefits of prevention and treatment and to decide whether a new health intervention represents good value for money. For the past seven years, I have been specialising in evaluating the costs, outcomes and quality of life for stroke patients. Such information is important to healthcare decision-makers and other researchers as they need to know the cost implications that strokes have on the NHS.

I spend most of my time in my office in front of the computer, analysing and interpreting the data and results of my study. In the past, I have also spent much time in hospital and general practices, reviewing the computerised records of patients in our study to see how they use healthcare resources.

The amount of time I have had to spend going through hospital and primary care records for over 1,000 patients, spanning five years of follow-up. This also generates a lot of information, which has to be analysed using complex statistical techniques, for example to test whether a particular patient characteristic might explain whether that patient is likely to incur higher healthcare costs than a patient without that characteristic. For this I have had to take numerous short courses on statistics, epidemiology and health economics.

AND THE BEST BITS?

Collaborating with people in many different healthcare fields, including consultants, nurses, statisticians, and other health economists; I get to know a lot of interesting people, and am not just confined to my area of work. I also enjoy presenting my work in publications or at conferences and hope that they will translate into better knowledge of that particular disease area to improve both patient care and efficiency within the healthcare.

RAMÓN'S TOP TIPS

To be a successful health economist you must be willing and able to work collaboratively with healthcare professionals and researchers in other fields, such as statisticians, qualitative researchers and epidemiologists.

Corporate graduate (Group Strategy & Planning)

Nationwide Building Society

MATTHEW PULLEN
Route into finance: A levels – economics, geography, critical thinking (2007); BSc economics with politics, Loughborough University (2011)

WHY FINANCE?

During my A levels I wasn't sure what career I wanted to pursue, but I knew I wanted to go to university as this would increase my choices for when I did decide. I chose a degree in economics with politics as it would be broad enough to allow me to pursue a career in many different areas, and would be considered academically rigorous in its analytical and numerical training. At university, I took several modules related to banking and the financial system, and I was specifically drawn to retail banking.

HOW DID YOU GET WHERE YOU ARE TODAY?

The single most important factor in me getting to where I am today was being a member of the University Officer Training Corps (UOTC) at university. We were trained to lead, take decisions under pressure, coordinate complex manoeuvres and exude confidence – all of which are important in my field of work. I applied for and secured my role before graduation, so in the time between university ending and my graduate scheme starting I went on holiday!

WHAT DOES YOUR JOB INVOLVE?

Nationwide Building Society is a member-owned organisation that provides personal banking and finance service to members and customers. The team I work in plans the future direction and strategic outlook of the organisation, coordinating internal strategic projects.

Much of my work consists of one-off projects, meeting with people from different areas of the business and bringing together information for projects or presentations for different audiences. I usually work in tandem with my line manager, which provides a lot of learning and development.

My responsibilities can vary depending on the task at hand, be it creating a presentation, collating information or reading reports. As the amount and pace of work can vary a lot, so do the working hours. A quiet week would be a 35 hours, whereas a busy week could be 50 to 60 hours.

Ours is a very 'face-to-face' organisation, meaning that often people prefer to meet in person rather than over the phone. As my job involves liaising with people throughout the business, I have the opportunity to meet a wide variety of individuals.

WHAT HAS BEEN THE BIGGEST CHALLENGE?

Producing a presentation for the executive directors, based on our third-quarter business assumptions, while my line manager was on holiday for two weeks. I had to coordinate submissions for a vast quantity of information from a large number of people and I had little understanding of the material myself. I succeeded in the end with the help of one of the senior managers, and a lot of perseverance.

AND THE BEST BITS?

The importance and nature of the work that I have been involved in – for example helping the CEO with an external presentation which resulted in a very positive outcome for us. In the future I see myself working in a retail banking capacity, with responsibility and a team of my own.

MATTHEW'S TOP TIPS

Choose a degree that has some numerical focus; this could range from maths to economics to geography. I'd also advise getting involved in any clubs and societies that allow you to work in and lead a team, as these are invaluable skills in any industry.

Audit assistant

KPMG

HOWARD THOMPSON

Route into auditing:

A levels – mathematics, fine art, biology and economics 2008; BSc economics and management, University of Bristol (2011)

WHY AUDITING?

I'd planned to be an artist until I did some work experience in the graphic design world and didn't enjoy it. I signed up for the Young Enterprise Award Scheme at school and loved the thrill of starting a business. I thought it would be good to study the theories behind business/the running of the world – so I studied economics. I was also attracted by the job security I would gain through having a professional qualification (ACA); this was something that was particularly lacking in the arts world.

HOW DID YOU GET TO WHERE YOU ARE TODAY?

I got along well with my tutor and a few of my lecturers at university and they helped me pick a career path based on my skills and abilities. I also did an internship at an accountancy firm and enjoyed my time with them.

During the first term of my final year, I focused on deciding what I wanted to do by asking a lot of questions and doing internet research into a mathematics-related career. I was offered my current job while still at university, which meant I had a fantastic summer travelling around India and Vietnam, knowing that I had a job starting in October.

WHAT DOES YOUR JOB INVOLVE?

The firm I work for provides professional services such as audit, tax and advisory. My job is to conduct external audits of firms to ensure that the accounts they produce give a true and fair reflection of their business activity.

What I do on a daily basis really depends on the time of the year. Since starting in October, I've spent a lot of time talking to clients, asking them questions about their business operations. I don't really spend much time 'counting' things, as many people outside the accountancy world might think. I have a lot of client interaction and have done my fair share of travelling up and down the UK on different engagements. My primary responsibility is to assist an audit senior in the testing of business operations in a firm.

My working hours vary depending on the client and department. Between January and March we work long hours, but it's not unmanageable. After March it's a pretty standard 9am to 5.30pm. I have a home office but the nature of the job means I have to travel to wherever the client is based – I've been as far north as Glasgow to down south in Bournemouth. As an auditor you'll move around a lot.

WHAT HAS BEEN YOUR BIGGEST CHALLENGE SO FAR?

Juggling studying and working at the same time. During the exam season, I was a little time pressurised but I kept focused, organised and always asked for help whenever I was stuck. My colleagues were always more than happy to help if required.

AND THE BEST BITS?

The people, the work and the variety – basically working within a great team on lots of interesting projects (not just counting numbers but actually travelling around to client sites and understanding their business operations). The work I'm doing is fun, challenging and diverse, and so long as it stays that way, I don't see any reason for moving!

HOWARD'S TOP TIPS

Make sure you know why you want to work in this area. Do your research and get industry work experience (every company has an accounts team). Then you'll be able to make a more informed decision. And, never be scared to ask questions... the life experiences in your network will be more diverse than you can probably imagine.

Third-year business and financial management student

University of Sunderland

HANNAH NEWTON

Route into business and financial management:
A levels – accounting, business studies, mathematics, economics (2009); BA business and financial management (third year), Sunderland University

WHY BUSINESS AND FINANCIAL MANAGEMENT?

I've also always enjoyed working with numbers. My degree has allowed me to gain a further understanding of business as well as working with financial problems, an aspect that I really enjoy.

WHAT HAS YOUR DEGREE INVOLVED SO FAR?

Studying for a degree is a lot more flexible than school and there are different ways of learning, from lectures where you meet a wide range of people doing your course to seminars, which develop what is taught in the lectures. During the first year, most of my modules were business related, which was a nice transition from college to university as nothing was too hard. I am responsible for making sure I do my work on time and there's lots of self-directed studying, but because I enjoy it so much it doesn't feel like too much.

My third year has consisted of mainly financial modules and a finance-related business research dissertation. It's required more work than in previous years but again I don't mind as it's so enjoyable. Lecturers are always around to offer help and advice and there are also many support groups, so it feels like a close and caring environment.

HAVE YOU BEEN ON A WORK PLACEMENT?

Instead of doing a work placement I opted to spend my second year on a study abroad placement. I went to Bond University (Gold Coast, Australia) and studied my usual modules, as well as some extra ones for fun. One of these was a law module which I really enjoyed as it was something different. I wanted to make the most of my time abroad; I had to find a middle ground between the social activities and study load.

WHAT HAS BEEN YOUR TOUGHEST CHALLENGE IN YOUR COURSE SO FAR?

Probably moving away from home to study abroad. I didn't know anyone in Australia and it was a totally new way of life but I had the most enjoyable year. On top of that, my dissertation is a challenge as it requires a lot of self-discipline, organisation and research. Since it's very broad, choosing a good topic to research has been interesting but tricky – I've changed my topic twice already.

AND THE BEST BITS?

Studying a business and financial management degree has allowed me to do many things that other courses may not have, such as studying abroad (the modules I study at the University of Sunderland are taught worldwide under the same regulations). There have also been work experience opportunities and I have accepted an internship at a hotel in Chicago, Illinois, after I graduate. Following this I intend to return to university to study a financial master's degree. I have no definite career goals at present; I may decide I want to continue to work in the hospitality industry after my internship. However, I recognise that a degree in business and financial management will open many windows of opportunities when I do decide.

HANNAH'S TOP TIPS

Buy a calculator. Take good notes and actively participate in class to ensure good grades. Buy the required textbooks, as they often provide a good source to study from when working towards the exams and they're recommended for a reason. Use them!

Organise your time effectively so you can find a balance between your social activities and study load.

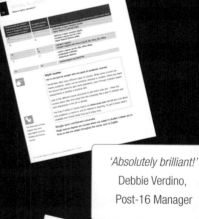

Entry routes

Routes to qualification

There are nearly 1,000 finance undergraduate courses on the UCAS Course Finder. With so much choice, how can you pick the best course for you?

UNDERGRADUATE QUALIFICATIONS

If you're interested in studying finance and/or accountancy at university, the first decision you need to make is whether to undertake a single honours degree (eg either finance or accountancy) or a combined honours degree (eg finance and accountancy together or one of these combined with another subject).

Remember that it's not essential to study a finance or accounting degree to work in these areas, although a finance or accounting degree will demonstrate your interest clearly.

SINGLE HONOURS VS...

Single honours accounting degrees will vary in content and focus from one university to the next. However, some basic principles apply. According to the Quality Assurance Agency for Higher Education, accounting degrees require students 'to study how the design, operation and validation of accounting systems affects, and is affected by, individuals, organisations, markets and society. This study is informed by perspectives from the social sciences... and may include, but is not restricted to, the behavioural, the economic, the political and the sociological.' In addition, a degree course should include study of the operation and design of financial systems, risk, financial structures and financial instruments.

The purpose of undergraduate finance degrees is to give students an in-depth knowledge of the decisions made by companies, investors and financial middlemen, as well as an understanding of complex modern-day financial markets. Studying finance is essential to understanding how financial markets, and the investments traded on these markets, affect the way in which companies operate.

With both finance and accounting single honours degrees, you can normally expect the first year to provide a more general introduction to the subject area, as well as to the methods and techniques employed by various financial and accountancy professionals in their jobs. The following two years allow for more specialisation within the individual subject, depending on where your current academic and future career aspirations lie. For example, you could choose from a wide variety of options such as public-sector accounting, corporate finance, auditing or business studies, or even related areas like business, law and banking.

JOINT HONOURS

Accountancy and finance can be studied together, as they complement each other very well in terms of subject matter and skills learnt. For example, you can learn about the stock exchange and financial markets as well as areas such as taxes and auditing, which could be of great use in your future career.

However, there is a vast array of other degree courses you can choose from to combine with your studies. You could either opt for a complementary subject – such as economics, entrepreneurship, computer science, law, marketing, management or business studies – or you could choose something completely different, such as creative writing, divinity, philosophy and even anthropology.

COURSE LENGTH

Whatever your decision, most finance and/or accounting courses last for three years, unless combined, for example, with a language, when you would be expected to spend your second or third year abroad to develop your linguistic skills.

ASSESSMENT

Undergraduate courses are normally graded according to the following structure: first class, upper second, lower second, and third, all of which carry (Hons) afterwards. Anything below this will not be graded as an honours degree.

Universities vary in how they award degree classifications to their students. Some rely on a totally examination-based method, in which you will sit 'finals' at the end of your third (or fourth, if relevant) year. This is often the case with more traditional universities, such as Oxford and Cambridge, although expect smaller examinations, often taken at the start of each term, as a revision aid too. Other universities will combine coursework and examinations to arrive at a final degree classification. You might like to think about this when choosing a university; after all, if you worry about your performance in examinations, you might want to consider doing a course where continuous assessment plays a feature in your final grade.

POSTGRADUATE AND PROFESSIONAL QUALIFICATIONS

If you have studied for an undergraduate degree unrelated to finance or accounting and are considering postgraduate study in a related subject, check out the UKPASS website (**www.ukpass.ac.uk**). This offers useful web-based tools to help you research and apply for postgraduate courses.

If, once you have completed your undergraduate degree, you are certain that you want a career in finance or accounting, you may need or want to undertake further study as part of your professional development. The financial advice sector is currently experiencing high levels of change and this also applies to the qualification requirements of its professionals.

The Financial Skills Partnership (FSP) is the employer-led body that sets performance standards for this sector – find out more about them on their website **www.financialskillspartnership.org.uk**.

On the following page there is a sample of the sort of professional qualifications you may need or want to gain as part of your continuous professional development.

PROFESSION	A SAMPLE OF PROFESSIONAL QUALIFICATIONS	MORE INFORMATION
Accountants	Need to complete a training contract (lasting 3–5 years) with an approved firm, involving external tutoring and home study	The Association of Chartered Certified Accountants **www.acca.org.uk**
	OR You can train outside of professional practice with the Chartered Institute of Management Accountants (CIMA) or the Chartered Institute of Public Finance and Accountancy (CIPFA)	The Chartered Institute of Management Accountants **www.cimaglobal.com**
		Chartered Institute of Public Finance and Accountancy **www.cipfa.org.uk**
		Institute of Chartered Accountants of England & Wales **www.icaew.com**
Actuaries	Need to become a Fellow of either the Faculty of Actuaries in Edinburgh or the Faculty and Institute of Actuaries in London and Oxford	The Actuarial Profession **www.actuaries.org.uk**
Retail bankers and financial advisers	Certificate in Financial Planning	The Chartered Insurance Institute **www.cii.co.uk**
	Certificate for Financial Advisers (CeFA)	ifs School of Finance **www.ifslearning.ac.uk**
	The Foundation Qualification – Introduction to Investment	Chartered Institute for Securities and Investment **www.cisi.org**
	International Certificate in Wealth Management	
	Certificate in Investment Planning (Chartered Institute of Bankers in Scotland – CIOBS)	The Chartered Banker Institute **www.charteredbanker.com**
Pension advisers	Fellow or Associate of the Pensions Management Institute	Pensions Management Institute **www.pensions-pmi.org.uk**
	Certificate in Life and Pensions	The Chartered Insurance Institute **www.cii.co.uk**
General business functions	Master of Business Administration (MBA) – a very popular choice among students and employers, the latter of whom will only offer funding if the student chooses one of the partner business schools	TOPMBA **www.topmba.com**
		Association of MBAs **www.mbaworld.com**

www.ucas.com

at the heart of connecting people to higher education

What others say....

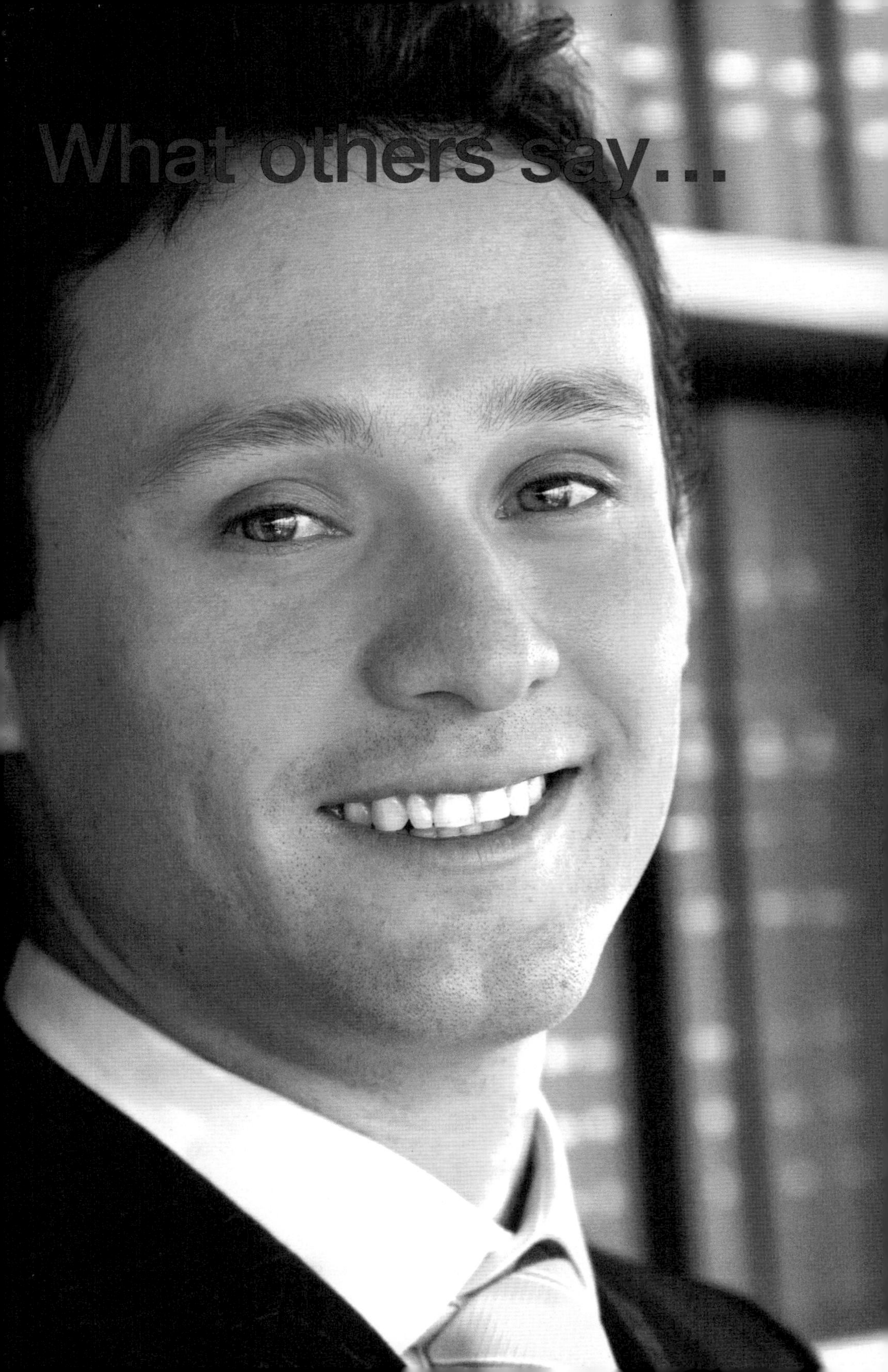

What others say...

These are extracts from case studies in previous editions of this book. They give some insights into the experiences and thoughts of people who were once in the same position as you.

GAURAV GANGULY – CHIEF ECONOMIST

After my first degree in business studies I fell into accountancy and qualified with one of the big London firms. It turned out not to be my thing, so I moved on to an investment bank in the City. While I was there, I decided to return to study economics and I ended up getting a doctorate in the field. Realising by the end of this that I did not want to work in academia, I looked for a job in industry. I was drawn to my current role as it was very wide-ranging with considerable flexibility.

Working with a company that has a very unusual product gives me the chance to think about a wide range of issues, from the impact of China's growth on international steel prices to the effect that the credit crisis has on demands for cars in the US. I find the environment very stimulating.

NATASHA CUBBIN – AUDIT TRAINEE

I wanted to build a career where it would be possible to see the inner workings of businesses and how they operate in their economic environments.

On a daily basis, I can either be at the client's premises or in my firm's offices. With clients, I perform control tests, run through their system's notes, or observe what controls they have in place to assess what risks certain financial statement areas hold. In the office, I may be completing the audit work that I started with the client or working on office-based audits – performing less analytical tests that do not require immediate client contact. During the final audit, I focus on testing various areas of the balance sheet.

My responsibilities vary per audit, but I am always responsible for representing the firm and all its values positively, honestly and professionally.

DAVID BAYLIFFE – CONSULTANCY DIRECTOR

I am still in the early stages of setting up my own company so I work from home, but this doesn't mean working any less than in an office; on the contrary, I tend to work at least 40 to 50 hours per week.

My work involves developing and improving financial models and monitoring what is happening in the markets, and letting my clients know of anything that my models cannot take account of. I forecast the returns of different asset classes (eg the equity market and the Government's interest rate – not individual equities or bonds) and combine them to help pension funds change their exposures, mainly to avoid big losses when some of the asset classes drop. The overall aim is to help companies pay their pensioners what they promised. I also produce reports with recommendations and reasons so the companies understand the thinking behind my advice.

I enjoy trying to piece together a realistic, rational approach to estimating what people should be doing, describing this mathematically and seeing what I can learn from the resulting models.

TIM MILLER – SENIOR RETAIL SALES AND DISTRIBUTION MANAGER

I knew I wanted to do a management training programme but I wasn't sure what kind of financial organisation would suit me. However, a paid summer job in a bank alerted me to the potential of a career in retail banking. What struck me in particular was that the business was very much about people; the combination of the human element with finance very much appealed to me.

Work experience will help you to get a better understanding of what you do and don't enjoy, and where your skills lie. Relevant experience will also give you knowledge of what recruiters are looking for, which will help in the applications process. Only pursue something that you believe you will enjoy. Find a company whose organisational culture you respect, and once you've decided what you want to do, throw yourself into it 100 per cent.

COLIN STREVENS – SENIOR ASSOCIATE AUDITOR

I studied accounting and finance at university. My studies entitled me to certain exemptions when I was working towards my professional qualifications on my training contract. It also helped me when I was applying for internships, partly because I had developed my understanding of business and built up commercial awareness, but also because it was clear that I was genuinely interested in the sector.

If you are interested in a career in accounting, it's important to develop your commercial awareness and keep up-to-date with the business news by reading websites and newspapers. This will help at interviews for any kind of business or finance-related university course you are applying for, and for jobs later on.

LUNA FADAYEL – ACTUARIAL CONSULTANT

I did three internships while I was at university [studying MMORSE – mathematics, operational research, statistics and economics]. During my first summer vacation I spent two months with a small reinsurance company; in my second year I worked on the trading floor for a large investment bank; and in my penultimate year I did an internship with Watson Wyatt, my current employer. Not only did I enjoy my final internship the most out of all three places, but it also led to a job offer. This meant that I was able to focus on my course work and exams in my final year rather than having to spend time applying for jobs.

Doing internships is a great way of trying out different work environments and can help you to see if a career is for you or not. It can be quite hard to secure an internship at university if you are not in your penultimate year; joining relevant societies is a useful way to make contacts, which means you can approach firms directly as well as making online applications.

RICHARD SPALTON – EQUITY RESEARCH ASSOCIATE

Equity research involves making judgements about the values of different companies' stocks and advising our portfolio managers accordingly. The recommendations I make are based on detailed research into how individual companies are managed and how they are performing in the context of current market conditions. It's vital to keep up-to-date with the news on individual companies and the market generally.

The current market environment is very challenging – because it is so volatile. There is a heightened level of uncertainty about how companies will perform. It's important to have conviction that your analysis will prove correct in the longer term, but it's also essential

to test your theories constantly. However, it's the unpredictability that makes the job so interesting!

ARTHUR CALLAGHAN – TAX AND CONSULTING WORK PLACEMENTS

I am now in the final year of my degree and when I finish I will be starting a graduate job within the restructuring division of Deloitte's corporate finance function. During my first three years I will also be studying for the ACA professional accounting qualification. I applied for my job once I had finished all my placements at the firm and was sure that I wanted to work there.

I was continually surprised by how friendly and open my colleagues were! I really enjoyed the chance to work on and learn about industries I was interested in but previously knew little about. Although I found it daunting at first to be treated the same as full-time graduate employees, I found that I loved being given so much responsibility during all my placements.

DOMINIC MAIER – EXECUTIVE

I chose a finance-oriented degree as I had always been more attracted to subjects related to numbers and logic at school. I was in the privileged position of having the opportunity to complete 18 months of paid placements at Ernst & Young, which gave me a real feel for what it would be like to work for a Big Four firm.

I currently work within the firm's assurance practice, as part of a team that performs financial statement audits. Our job is to independently verify that the financial statements published by a company for their shareholders are free from errors or uncertainties, and present a true and fair view of that company. My day-to-day job can be really varied. I am often working out of the office at a client's site, assisting with the planning of their audits and putting the knowledge gained from my professional accounting exams into practice.

The people are undoubtedly the highlight: meeting such a wide variety of individuals who are doing the same thing and who share similar values.

CHRIS ROE – MBA STUDENT

I chose my first degree in applied sports science because I was passionate about sport and wanted to understand more about the role science played in improving an individual's performance.

After graduation, I started as an intern with a social enterprise based in London, Zambia and Kenya. I worked my way up and ended up managing the business in Zambia, and it was there that I realised the role that business can play in development issues. I decided to do an MBA to understand the full scale of options available to me.

I wanted to study at the Saïd Business School because it has a focus on social entrepreneurship and, therefore, the group of students is more diverse than on other MBA programmes. My particular interest lies in the role that business can play in solving social problems and my MBA specialises in this.

I really enjoy the range of activities, lecture material and the high-calibre network of people available to us – it is a challenge at times but well worth it.

JAMES WADLEY – MARKET RISK MANAGEMENT – STRUCTURED CREDIT TRADING RISK OFFICE

At the end of my third year I got a Bank of America summer internship, which gave me a great insight into what market risk management entails day-to-day, and how an investment bank works and makes money.

During the internship I picked up key ideas behind risk management and became increasingly comfortable with speaking about technical subjects with colleagues. During my second internship I was placed in a slightly different team looking at different financial products, although still within market risk management.

After my gap year I joined the graduate programme. One of the best parts of the training was that it was in New York, with over 400 graduates from around the globe. As well as revising the basics of the banking world, I also made valuable contacts in different areas of the bank, in different parts of the world. This put me in good stead to start in my team in London.

STUART GOODMAN – TRAINEE CHARTERED ACCOUNTANT

I attended a large number of talks and open evenings hosted by finance-based companies while at university, which helped me understand the different graduate roles available.

When I started as a trainee, I worked on site at a client's office, assessing their business results for the year to ensure they were a true and fair representation. I progressed over the last two years and my current role has expanded to encompass planning jobs, leading teams of other trainees on site, attending meetings with senior clients and generally getting more involved in business advisory projects.

Day to day my workload is split between time in the office planning and finishing specific jobs and being responsible for all the work performed by the team, and time on site at clients' offices, managing teams and performing testing. On-site teams are normally made up of trainees, so it's quite a young vibe and can be great fun, especially when it involves trips abroad.

UCAS

Confused about courses?

Indecisive about institutions?

Stressed about student life?

Unsure about UCAS?

Frowning over finance?

Help is available at
www.ucasbooks.com

Applicant journey

SIX EASY STEPS TO UNIVERSITY AND COLLEGE

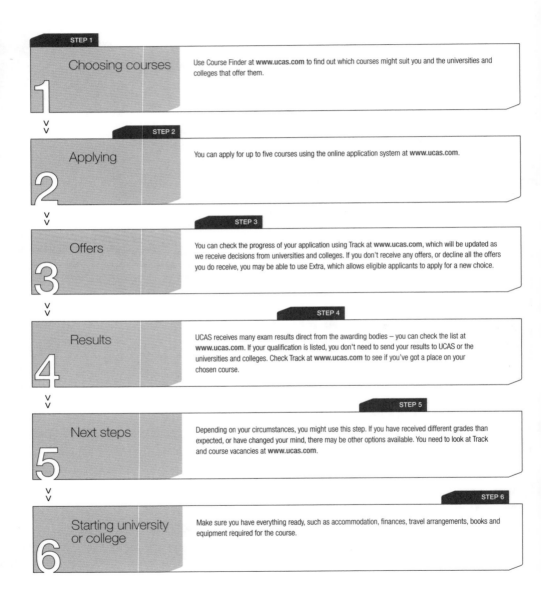

STEP 1

Choosing courses

1

Use Course Finder at **www.ucas.com** to find out which courses might suit you and the universities and colleges that offer them.

STEP 2

Applying

2

You can apply for up to five courses using the online application system at **www.ucas.com**.

STEP 3

Offers

3

You can check the progress of your application using Track at **www.ucas.com**, which will be updated as we receive decisions from universities and colleges. If you don't receive any offers, or decline all the offers you do receive, you may be able to use Extra, which allows eligible applicants to apply for a new choice.

STEP 4

Results

4

UCAS receives many exam results direct from the awarding bodies – you can check the list at **www.ucas.com**. If your qualification is listed, you don't need to send your results to UCAS or the universities and colleges. Check Track at **www.ucas.com** to see if you've got a place on your chosen course.

STEP 5

Next steps

5

Depending on your circumstances, you might use this step. If you have received different grades than expected, or have changed your mind, there may be other options available. You need to look at Track and course vacancies at **www.ucas.com**.

STEP 6

Starting university or college

6

Make sure you have everything ready, such as accommodation, finances, travel arrangements, books and equipment required for the course.

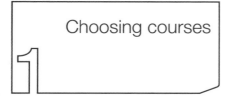

Choosing courses

Step 1 – Planning your application for economics, finance or accountancy

Planning your application is the start of your journey to finding a place at a university or college.

This section will help you decide what course to study and how to choose a university or college where you'll enjoy living and studying. Find out about qualifications, degree options, how they'll assess you, and coping with the cost of higher education.

WHICH SUBJECTS?

The good news is that most A level subjects are acceptable for economics, finance or accounting degrees. However, the more prestigious universities tend to prefer traditional subjects, such as English, maths, languages and sciences, over more modern vocational ones, such as business studies, sports studies, theatre studies or media studies. If an applicant offers a mixture of the two types with more emphasis on traditional subjects, this may be acceptable. It is worth bearing in mind that many universities do not normally consider general studies or key skills as suitable subjects for making an offer, although they may take them into account when looking at your application as a whole.

While A level economics is not normally a prerequisite for economics degrees (some universities such as

Kingston offer a special route for undergraduates without an economics background), mathematics A level is often desired, if not essential. Check with individual institutions for their entry requirements.

WHICH GRADES?

Economics, finance and accounting courses are intellectually demanding and high offers are often the norm to ensure you have the academic ability to cope.

These can range from AAB at the most popular and prestigious institutions to CCC elsewhere. Universities will usually ask for at least a GCSE in maths and English, often at grade C or above, as proof of your numeracy and language abilities.

HOW DO I FIND THE BEST COURSE FOR ME?

To find out what courses are on offer, for both single and joint honours, visit **www.ucas.com** and select Course Finder.

Applicants are advised to use various sources of information in order to make their choices for higher education, including the Course Finder facility at **www.ucas.com**. League tables might be a component of this research, but applicants should bear in mind that these tables attempt to rank institutions in an overall order, which reflects the interests, preoccupations and decisions of those who have produced and edited them. The ways in which they are compiled vary greatly and you need to look closely at the criteria that have been used.

UCAS CARD

At its simplest, the UCAS Card scheme is the start of your UCAS journey. It can save you a packet on the high street with exclusive offers to UCAS Card holders, as well as providing you with hints and tips about finding the best course at the right university or college. If that's not enough you'll also receive these benefits:

- frequent expert help from UCAS, with all the essential information you need on the application process
- free monthly newsletters providing advice, hints, tips and exclusive discounts
- tailored information on the universities and courses you're interested in
- and much more.

If you're in Year 12, S5 or equivalent and thinking about higher education for autumn 2013, sign up for your FREE UCAS Card today to receive all these benefits at **www.ucas.com/ucascard**.

Save with UCAS Card

If you're in Year 12, S5 or equivalent and thinking about higher education, sign up for the **FREE** UCAS Card to receive all these benefits:

- information about courses and unis
- expert advice from UCAS
- exclusive discounts for card holders

UCAS

Register today at
www.ucas.com/ucascard

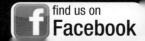

find us on
Facebook

Choosing courses

1

Choosing courses

USE COURSE FINDER AT WWW.UCAS.COM TO FIND OUT WHICH COURSES MIGHT SUIT YOU, AND THE UNIVERSITIES AND COLLEGES THAT OFFER THEM.

Start thinking about what you want to study and where you want to go. This section will help you, and see what courses are available where in the listings (starting on page 132). Check that the entry requirements required for each course meet your academic expectations.

Use the UCAS website – www.ucas.com has lots of advice on how to find a course. Go to the students' section of the website for the best advice or go straight to Course Finder to see a list of all the courses available through UCAS. Our map of the UK at www.ucas.com/students/choosingcourses/choosinguni/map/ shows you where all the universities and colleges are located.

Watch UCAStv – at www.ucas.tv there are videos on *How to choose your course*, *Attending events* and *Open Days* as well as case studies from students talking about their experiences of finding a course at university or college.

Attend UCAS conventions – UCAS conventions are held throughout the country. Universities and colleges have exhibition stands where their staff offer information about their courses and institutions. Details of when the conventions are happening, and a convention planner to help you prepare are shown at www.ucas.com/conventions.

Look at university and college websites and prospectuses – universities and colleges have prospectuses and course-specific leaflets on their undergraduate courses. Your school or college library may have copies or go to the university's website to download a copy, or you can ask them to send one to you.

Go to university and college open days – most institutions offer open days to anyone who wants to attend. See the lists of universities and colleges on **www.ucas.com** and the UCAS *Open Days* publication (**see the Essential reading chapter on page 124**) for information on when they are taking place. Aim to visit all of the universities and colleges you are interested in before you apply. It will help with your expectations of university life and make sure the course is the right one for you.

League tables – these can be helpful but bear in mind that they attempt to rank institutions in an overall order reflecting the views of those that produce them. They may not reflect your views and needs. Examples can be found at **www.thecompleteuniversityguide.co.uk**, **www.guardian.co.uk/education/universityguide**, **www.thetimes.co.uk** (subscription service) and **www.thesundaytimes.co.uk** (subscription service). See page 78 for more information about league tables.

Do your research – speak and refer to as many trusted sources as you can find. Talk to someone already doing the job you have in mind. The section on **Which area?** on page 26 will help you identify the different areas of economics, finance and accountancy you might want to enter.

DECIDING ON YOUR COURSE CHOICES

Through UCAS you can initially apply for up to five courses in total. How do you find out more information to make an informed decision?

Remember that you don't have to make five course choices. Only apply for a course if you're completely happy with both the course and the university or college and you would definitely be prepared to accept a place.

How do you narrow down your course choices? First of all, look up course details in this book or on Course Finder at **www.ucas.com**. This will give you an idea of the full range of courses and topics on offer. You may want to study economics, finance or accounting as single subjects, but there are also many courses which also include additional options, such as a modern

language (check out the degree subjects studied by our case studies). You'll quickly be able to eliminate institutions that don't offer the right course, or you can choose a 'hit list' of institutions first, and then see what they have to offer.

Once you've made a short(er) list, look at university or college websites, and generally find out as much as you can about the course, department and institution. Don't be afraid to contact them to ask for more information, request their prospectus or arrange an open day visit.

Choosing courses

1

Choosing your institution

Different people look for different things from their university or college course, but the checklist on the next page sets out the kinds of factors all prospective students should consider when choosing their university or college. Keep this list in mind on open days, when talking to friends about their experiences at various universities and colleges, or while reading prospectuses and websites.

WHAT TO CONSIDER WHEN CHOOSING YOUR ECONOMICS, FINANCE OR ACCOUNTING COURSE	
Location	Do you want to stay close to home? Would you prefer to study at a city or campus university?
Grades required	Use Course Finder on the UCAS website, **www.ucas.com**, to view entry requirements for courses you are interested in. Also, check out the university website or call up the admissions office. Some universities specify grades required, eg AAB, while others specify points required, eg 340. If they ask for points, it means they're using the UCAS Tariff system, which basically awards points to different types and levels of qualification. For example, an A grade at A level = 120 points; a B grade at A level = 100 points. The full Tariff tables are available on pages 107-114 and at **www.ucas.com**.
Employer links	Ask the course tutor and university careers office about links with employers such as banks, insurance companies, financial services providers, etc. Find out if the course involves visiting lecturers from the professional side of the industry and where they typically come from.
Graduate prospects	Ask the university department and careers office for their lists of graduate destinations.
Cost	Ask the admissions office about variable tuition fees and financial assistance.
Degree type	Think about whether you want to study finance or accounting on its own (single honours degree) or as a joint honours degree, eg with a language or with another subject such as legal studies or even geography.
Teaching style	How is the course taught? Ask about the number of lectures and seminars per week and whether the university runs a tutorial system.
Course assessment	How is your final degree classification reached? Is it completely exam-based (eg through finals) or is there an element of continuous assessment?
'Fit'	Even if all the above criteria meet your needs, this one relies on your instinct – visit the university and the individual departments that you are interested in and see if they 'fit' you. Open days can help with this; you will be able to get a good idea of the type and level of work the course produces by talking to tutors and finance and accounting undergraduates. Also ask about lecturers' own particular interests; many will have personal web pages somewhere on the departmental website.

Choosing courses

1

League tables

The information that follows has been provided by Dr Bernard Kingston of The Complete University Guide.

League tables are worth consulting early in your research and perhaps for confirmation later on. But never rely on them in isolation – always use them alongside other information sources available to you. Universities typically report that over a third of prospective students view league tables as important or very important in making their university choices. They give an insight into quality and are mainly based on data from the universities themselves. Somewhat confusingly, tables published in, say, 2012 are referred to as the 2013 tables because they are aimed at applicants going to university in that following year. The well known ones - *The Complete University Guide*, *The Guardian*, *The Times*, and *The Sunday Times* - rank the institutions and the subjects they teach using input measures (eg entry standards), throughput measures (eg student : staff ratios) and output measures (eg graduate prospects). Some tables are free to access whilst others are behind pay walls. All are interactive and enable users to create their own tables based on the measures important to them.

The universities are provided with their raw data for checking and are regularly consulted on methodology. But ultimately it is the compilers who decide what measures to use and what weights to put on them. They are competitors and rarely consult amongst themselves. So, for example, *The Times* tables differ significantly from *The Sunday Times* ones even though both newspapers belong to the same media proprietor.

Whilst the main university rankings tend to get the headlines, we would stress that the individual subject tables are as least as important, if not more so, when deciding where to study. All universities, regardless of their overall ranking, have some academic departments that rank highly in their subjects. Beware also giving much weight to an institution being a few places higher or lower in the tables – this is likely to be of little significance. This is particularly true in the lower half of the main table where overall scores show considerable bunching.

Most of the measures used to define quality come from hard factual data provided by the Higher Education Statistics Agency (HESA) but some, like student satisfaction and peer assessment, are derived from surveys of subjective impressions where you might wish to query sample size. We give a brief overview of the common measures here but please go to the individual websites for full details.

- **Student satisfaction** is derived from the annual National Student Survey (NSS) and is heavily used by *The Guardian* and *The Sunday Times.*
- **Research assessment** comes from a 2008 exercise (RAE) aimed at defining the quality of a university's research (excluded by *The Guardian*).
- **Entry standards** are based on the full UCAS Tariff scores obtained by new students.
- **Student : staff ratio** gives the number of students per member of academic staff.
- **Expenditure figures** show the costs of academic and student services.
- **Good honours** lists the proportion of graduates gaining a first or upper second honours degree.

- **Completion** indicates the proportion of students who successfully complete their studies.
- **Graduate prospects** usually reports the proportion of graduates who obtain a graduate job – not any job – or continue studying within six months of leaving.
- **Peer assessment** is used only by *The Sunday Times* which asks academics to rate other universities in their subjects.
- **Value added** is used only by *The Guardian* and compares entry standards with good honours.

All four main publishers of UK league tables (see Table 1) also publish university subject tables. *The Complete University Guide* and *The Times* are based on four measures: student satisfaction, research quality, entry standards and graduate destinations. *The Sunday Times* uses student satisfaction, entry standards, graduate destinations, graduate unemployment, good degrees and drop-out rate, while *The Guardian* uses student satisfaction (as three separate measures), entry standards, graduate destinations, student-staff ratio, spend per student and value added. This use of different measures is one reason why the different tables can yield different results (sometimes very different, especially in the case of *The Guardian* which has least in common with the other tables).

League tables compiled by *The Complete University Guide* (**www.thecompleteuniversityguide.co.uk**) and *The Guardian* (**www.guardian.co.uk**) are available in spring, those by *The Times* (**www.thetimes.co.uk**) and *The Sunday Times* (**www.thesundaytimes.co.uk**) in the summer.

Table 1 – measures used by the main publishers of UK league tables

	Universities	Measures	Subjects	Measures
The Complete University Guide	116	9	62	4
The Guardian	119	8	46	8
The Sunday Times	122	8	39	6
The Times	116	8	62	4

THINGS TO WATCH OUT FOR WHEN READING SUBJECT LEAGUE TABLES

- Finance and accountancy will usually be combined in the same table.
- The tables make no distinction between universities which offer courses that are accredited by one or more of the accountancy professional bodies and those which do not.

WHO PUBLISHES ECONOMICS, FINANCE AND ACCOUNTANCY LEAGUE TABLES?

The Complete University Guide	Accountancy and finance Economics
The Guardian	Economics
The Sunday Times	Economics Finance and Accountancy
The Times	Accountancy and finance Economics

www.ucas.com

at the heart of connecting people to higher education

Choosing courses

1

How will they choose you?

University departments receive thousands of applications each year for only a limited number of places. So how can you make your UCAS application stand out from the others?

ACADEMIC ABILITY

Many economics, finance and accounting degrees (and related subjects) are intellectually demanding. Not only will you possibly be learning about the basics of these disciplines for the very first time but you will also be expected to work on them in greater analytical depth than you have ever done before at GCSE and A level (or equivalent). Therefore, in order for admissions tutors to be certain that you have what it takes to cope with the course, you will have to show you have the academic ability to take on new ideas.

SELF-MOTIVATION AND SELF-DISCIPLINE

Studying at university is very different from school and sixth form. In those settings, you will have followed a set course, normally following a study pattern suggested by your teachers. The homework set for you will have ensured you studied regularly and on time.

At university, tutors and lecturers do not have the time to keep tabs on their students in the same way. Whereas at A level your teachers will have helped to motivate you to finish your work on time, university tutors will simply hand out reading lists and essay titles or problem sheets in advance and will expect you to complete them on time without constant reminders.

This can, understandably, be daunting for some people. Certainly, time management and self-motivation are skills you hone at university but it also helps if your referee can write about any instances where you have shown an ability to work well on your own, as this is how you will be studying throughout your undergraduate course.

DEVOTION TO YOUR CHOSEN SUBJECT

You might think that a degree in economics, finance or accounting will be the best way to earn a good salary as a graduate – but this motivation will not convince admissions tutors that you are devoted to their subject. In fact, it could put them off your application altogether if you cannot show any other commitment to their subject than what you will earn three or four years down the line.

The tutors who select students onto their courses want to see evidence that you have carefully considered what a degree in economics, finance or accounting will involve and why it appeals to you. After all, you don't need an economics, finance or accounting degree to get a job in the financial sector, so why have you chosen to specialise in this field earlier than some of your peers? Only you will know the reasons why you're fascinated by these subject areas, and it's your job to convey this enthusiasm to others in your UCAS application.

DO SOME READING

This is related to the above point. A good way to prove to potential admissions tutors that you have an interest in their field is to find out their specialist academic interests and do some reading into these, potentially from books that they have written. Additionally, contact the relevant department and ask for their first-year reading list, if this is not available online. You do not need to read everything on it, but if you choose two or three books that most appeal to you and read them in some depth it will show a commitment to both the subject and the relevant university's course.

Be warned, though – don't think that merely mentioning a few key books will automatically get you through. Admissions tutors will know if you're lying, so unless you can make a few valid points about why you enjoyed their books, don't bother: it could do more harm than good.

WORK EXPERIENCE

The value of work experience is the skillset it will give you, which in turn will help you produce better work during your course. Describing the work experience you've had, what you learned from it and the skills you gained, will also help convince admissions tutors of your commitment and insight into your chosen subject, and so help you stand out on your personal statement.

WHAT WORK EXPERIENCE COUNTS?

You will need to use your initiative to find work experience opportunities. Some formal schemes exist with larger financial organisations. Naturally, these tend to be very competitive. If you cannot manage to secure a formal opportunity, be proactive; contact local employers and ask family and friends if they know anyone who works in the field that interests you who might be able to help.

Work experience relevant to finance, accounting and economics courses includes:

- A few days or more spent volunteering or shadowing with an employer working within finance or accounting (eg an accounting firm, a professional services company, an economics research organisation), or within a department that handles the finance needs of a larger organisation
- A short placement at a local bank
- A one or two-day programme at an investment bank
- Any formal role (such as the treasurer) you have held

dealing with the accounting or finance side of an organisation, club or society – for example at school

- If you are interested in economics, any work experience in politics, such as helping out in a minister's parliamentary office or involvement in youth politics.

Admissions tutors recognise the value of the skills developed from other kinds of experience too, so even work experience that is not related to accounting, finance or economics can work in your favour. Any work experience, paid or voluntary, from a paper round to a stint helping out in an old people's home, can be a great way of building transferable skills, and showing that you are a reliable and hardworking individual. The trick is to identify and describe the professional and personal skills you developed: there are many of these, from teamworking and learning new skills quickly to communication skills and problem solving. Spend time thinking about what you learned and discovered about your skills during any work experience you have had, and use it in your personal statement.

YOUR PERSONAL STATEMENT

Your personal statement can really enhance your application. It is here that you can show evidence of all the above issues – academic attainment, self-discipline, work experience, a desire for your chosen subject. Most universities consider personal statements to be very important as this is where your own voice comes through, so make the most of it and use it to your advantage. Be honest but not over-friendly and give well-reasoned statements. And above all make sure it's free from mistakes and easy to read. There's nothing more offputting for an admissions tutor than applications and personal statements that have glaring grammatical errors and spelling mistakes, or are difficult to decipher.

As this is such an important part of your application, it's worth drafting it a few times before sending it to UCAS. Ask your family or friends and teacher to check it, not only for mistakes but also to see if you're leaving anything out that should be in, or equally if there's anything that should come out.

For more hints and tips about your personal statement, see page 98.

OTHER APPLICATION TESTS AND PROCEDURES

Most universities these days do not interview their students, preferring to select from their UCAS applications. However, some do use different procedures.

The University of Oxford and the University of Cambridge have an applications closing date of 15 October, which is earlier than other universities. If applying to the universities of Oxford or Cambridge, you will be asked to attend an interview and may also need to sit a test or submit some written work.

INTERVIEWS

Once they have sifted through the thousands of applications they receive, some universities will then invite shortlisted candidates for interview. This is normal at Oxford and Cambridge, and not uncommon at other prestigious institutions.

It may also be dependent on the subject you are applying to study; check individual institution websites for full information on their selection policies.

Interviews may sound daunting but they are actually a very effective way of helping admissions tutors to assess whether a candidate has what it takes to cope with the course and the university environment, and for the applicant to see if they like the course on offer, the tutors and the university as a whole.

Choosing courses

The cost of higher education

The information in this section was up-to-date when this book was published. You should visit the websites mentioned in this section for the very latest information.

THE COST OF STUDYING IN THE UK

As a student, you will usually have to pay for two things: tuition fees for your course, which for most students do not need to be paid for up front, and living costs such as rent, food, books, transport and entertainment. Fees charged vary between courses, between universities and colleges and also according to your normal country of residence, so it's important to check these before you apply. Course fee information is supplied to UCAS by the universities and is displayed in Course Finder at **www.ucas.com/coursefinder**.

STUDENT LOANS

The purpose of student loans from the Government is to help cover the costs of your tuition fees and basic living costs (rent, bills, food and so on). Two types are available: a tuition fee loan to cover the tuition charges and a maintenance loan to help with accommodation and other living costs. Both types of student loan are available to all students who meet the basic eligibility requirements. Interest will be charged at inflation plus a fixed percentage while you are studying. In addition, many other commercial loans are available to students studying at university or college but the interest rate can vary considerably. Loans to help with living costs will be available for all eligible students, irrespective of family income.

Find out more information from the relevant sites below:

England: Student Finance England –
www.direct.gov.uk/studentfinance
Northern Ireland: Student Finance Northern Ireland –
www.studentfinanceni.co.uk
Scotland: Student Awards Agency for Scotland –
www.saas.gov.uk
Wales: Student Finance Wales –
www.studentfinancewales.co.uk or
www.cyllidmyfyrwyrcymru.co.uk

BURSARIES AND SCHOLARSHIPS

- The National Scholarships Programme gives financial help to students studying in England. The scheme is designed to help students whose families have lower incomes.
- Students from families with lower incomes will be entitled to a non-repayable maintenance grant to help with living costs.
- Many universities and colleges also offer non-repayable scholarships and bursaries to help students cover tuition and living costs whilst studying.
- All eligible part-time undergraduates who study for at least 25% of their time will be able to apply for a loan to cover the costs of their tuition, which means they no longer have to pay up front.

There will be extra support for disabled students and students with child or adult dependants. For more information, visit the country-specific websites listed above.

wondering how much higher education costs?

need information about student finance?

Visit www.ucas.com/students/studentfinance and find sources for all the information on student money matters you need.

With access to up-to-date information on bursaries, scholarships and variable fees, plus our online budget calculator. Visit us today and get the full picture.

www.ucas.com/students/studentfinance

```
  ┌──────────────────────────┐
  │    Choosing courses      │
  ┌┐                         │
 ┌┘│                         │
┌┘ │                        ┌┘
└──┴────────────────────────┘
```

International students

APPLYING TO STUDY IN THE UK

Deciding to go to university or college in the UK is very exciting. You need to think about what course to do, where to study, and how much it will cost.
The decisions you make can have a huge effect on your future but UCAS is here to help.

HOW TO APPLY

Whatever your age or qualifications, if you want to apply for any of over 35,000 courses listed at 300 universities and colleges on the UCAS website, you must apply through UCAS at **www.ucas.com**. If you are unsure, your school, college, adviser, or local British Council office will be able to help. Further advice and a video guide for international students can be found on the non-UK students' section of the UCAS website at **www.ucas.com/international**.

Students may apply on their own or through their school, college, adviser, or local British Council if they are registered with UCAS to use Apply. If you choose to use an education agent's services, check with the British Council to see if they hold a list of certificated or registered agents in your country. Check also on any charges you may need to pay. UCAS charges only the application fee (see below) but agents may charge for additional services.

How much will my application cost?
If you choose to apply to more than one course, university or college you need to pay UCAS £23 GBP when you apply. If you only apply to one course at one university or college, you pay UCAS £12 GBP.

WHAT LEVEL OF ENGLISH?

UCAS provides a list of English language qualifications and grades that are acceptable to most UK universities and colleges, however you are advised to contact the institutions directly as each have their own entry requirement in English. For more information go to **www.ucas.com/students/wheretostart/ nonukstudents/englangprof**.

INTERNATIONAL STUDENT FEES

If you study in the UK, your fee status (whether you pay full-cost fees or a subsidised fee rate) will be decided by the UK university or college you plan to attend. Before you decide which university or college to attend, you need to be absolutely certain that you can pay the full cost of:

- your tuition fees (the amount is set by universities and colleges, so contact them for more information – visit their websites where many list their fees. Fee details will also be included on Course Finder at **www.ucas.com**
- the everyday living expenses for you (and your family) for the whole time that you are in the UK, including accommodation, food, gas and electricity bills, clothes, travel and leisure activities
- books and equipment for your course
- travel to and from your country.

You must include everything when you work out how much it will cost. You can get information to help you do this accurately from the international offices at universities and colleges, UKCISA (UK Council for International Student Affairs) and the British Council. There is a useful website tool to help you manage your money at university – **www.studentcalculator.org.uk**.

Scholarships and bursaries are offered at some universities and colleges and you should contact them for more information. In addition, you should check with your local British Council for additional scholarships available to students from your country who want to study in the UK.

LEGAL DOCUMENTS YOU WILL NEED

As you prepare to study in the UK, it is very important to think about the legal documents you will need to enter the country.

Everyone who comes to study in the UK needs a valid passport. If you do not have one, you should apply for one as soon as possible. People from certain countries also need visas before they come into the UK. They are known as 'visa nationals'. You can check if you require a visa to travel to the UK by visiting the UK Border Agency website and selecting 'Studying in the UK', at **www.ukba.homeoffice.gov.uk** for the most up-to-date guidance and information about the United Kingdom's visa requirements.

When you apply for your visa you need to make sure you have the following documents:

- A confirmation of acceptance for studies (CAS) number from the university or college where you are going to study. The institution must be on the UKBA Register of Sponsors in order to accept international students.
- A valid passport.
- Evidence that you have enough money to pay for your course and living costs.
- Certificates for all qualifications you have that are relevant to the course you have been accepted for and for any English language qualifications.

You will also have to give your biometric data.

Do check for further information from your local British Embassy or High Commission. Guidance information for international students is also available from UKCISA and from UKBA.

ADDITIONAL RESOURCES

There are a number of organisations that can provide further guidance and information to you as you prepare to study in the UK:

- British Council
  www.britishcouncil.org
- Education UK (British Council website dealing with educational matters)
  www.educationuk.org
- English UK (British Council accredited website listing English language courses in the UK)
  www.englishuk.com
- UK Border Agency (provides information on visa requirements and applications)
  www.ukba.homeoffice.gov.uk
- UKCISA (UK Council for International Student Affairs)
  www.ukcisa.org.uk
- Directgov (the official UK Government website)
  www.direct.gov.uk
- Prepare for success
  www.prepareforsuccess.org.uk.

www.ucas.com

at the heart of connecting people to higher education

Applying

2

Step 2 – Applying

You apply through UCAS using the online application system, called Apply, at **www.ucas.com**. You can apply for a maximum of five choices, but you don't have to use them all if you don't want to. If you apply for fewer than five choices, you can add more at a later date if you want to. But be aware of the course application deadlines (you can find these in Course Finder at **www.ucas.com**).

IMPORTANT DATES FOR 2012 ENTRY

Early June 2012	UCAS Apply opens for 2013 entry registration.
Mid-September 2012	Applications can be sent to UCAS.
15 October 2012	Application deadline for the receipt at UCAS of applications for all medicine, dentistry, veterinary medicine and veterinary science courses and for all courses at the universities of Oxford and Cambridge.
15 January 2013	Application deadline for the receipt at UCAS of applications for all courses except those listed above with a 15 October deadline, and some art and design courses with a 24 March deadline.
25 February 2013	Extra starts (see page 103 for more information about Extra).
24 March 2013	Application deadline for the receipt at UCAS of applications for art and design courses except those listed on Course Finder at **www.ucas.com** with a 15 January deadline.
31 March 2013	If you apply by 15 January, the universities and colleges should aim to have sent their decisions by this date (but they can take longer).
9 May 2013	If you apply by 15 January, universities and colleges need to send their decisions by this date. If they don't, UCAS will make any outstanding choices unsuccessful on their behalf.
30 June 2013	If you send your application to us by this date, we will send it to your chosen universities and colleges. Applications received after this date are entered into Clearing (see page 118 for more information about Clearing).
3 July 2013	Last date to apply through Extra.
August 2013 (date to be confirmed)	Scottish Qualifications Authority (SQA) results are published.
15 August 2013	GCE and Advanced Diploma results are published (often known as 'A level results day'). Adjustment opens for registration (see page 119 for more information about Adjustment).

DON'T FORGET...

Universities and colleges guarantee to consider your application only if we receive it by the appropriate deadline. Check application deadlines for your courses on Course Finder at **www.ucas.com**.

If you send it to UCAS after the deadline but before 30 June 2013, universities and colleges will consider your application only if they still have places available.

Connect with us...

 www.facebook.com/ucasonline

 www.twitter.com/ucas_online

 www.youtube.com/ucasonline

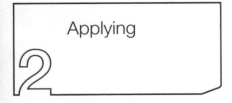

Applying

How to apply

You apply online at **www.ucas.com** through Apply – a secure, web-based application service that is designed for all our applicants, whether they are applying through a UCAS-registered centre or as an individual, anywhere in the world. Apply is:

- easy to access – all you need is an internet connection
- easy to use – you don't have to complete your application all in one go: you can save the sections as you complete them and come back to it later
- easy to monitor – once you've applied, you can use Track to check the progress of your application, including any decisions from universities or colleges. You can also reply to your offers using Track.

Watch the UCAStv guide to applying through UCAS at **www.ucas.tv.**

APPLICATION FEE

For 2013 entry the fee for applying through UCAS is £23 for two or more choices and £12 for one choice.

You can submit only one UCAS application in each year's application cycle.

DEFERRED ENTRY

If you want to apply for deferred entry in 2014, perhaps because you want to take a year out between school or college and higher education, you should check that the university or college will accept a deferred entry application. Occasionally, tutors are not happy to accept students who take a gap year, because it interrupts the flow of their learning. If you apply for deferred entry, you must meet the conditions of any offers by 31 August 2013 unless otherwise agreed by the university or college. If you accept a place for 2014 entry and then change your mind, you cannot reapply through us in the 2014 entry cycle unless you withdraw your original application.

APPLYING THROUGH YOUR SCHOOL OR COLLEGE

1 GET SCHOOL OR COLLEGE 'BUZZWORD'

Ask your UCAS application coordinator (may be your sixth form tutor) for your school or college UCAS 'buzzword'. This is a password for the school or college.

2 REGISTER

Go to **www.ucas.com/students/apply** and click on **Register/Log in to use Apply** and then **register**. After you have entered your registration details, the online system will automatically generate a username for you, but you'll have to come up with a password and answers to security questions.

3 COMPLETE SEVEN SECTIONS

Complete all the sections of the application. To access any section, click on the section name at the left of the screen and follow the instructions. The sections are:

Personal details – contact details, residential status, disability status

Additional information – only UK applicants need to complete this section

Student finance – UK students can share some of their application details with their student finance company. Finance information is provided for other EU and international applicants

Choices – which courses you'd like to apply for

Education – your education and qualifications

Employment – eg work experience, holiday jobs

Statement – see page 98 for personal statement advice.

Before you can send your application you need to go to the **View all details** screen and tick the **section completed** box.

4 PASS TO REFEREE

Once you've completed all the sections, send your application electronically to your referee (normally your form tutor). They'll check it, approve it and add their reference to it, and will then send it to UCAS on your behalf.

USEFUL INFORMATION ABOUT APPLY

- Important details like date of birth and course codes will be checked by Apply. It will alert you if they are not valid.
- We strongly recommend that the personal statement and reference are written in a word-processing package and pasted into Apply.
- If you want to, you can enter European characters into certain areas of Apply.
- You can change your application at any time before it is completed and sent to UCAS.
- You can print and preview your application at any time. Before you send it you need to go to the **View all details** screen and tick the **section completed** box.
- Your school, college or centre can choose different payment methods. For example, they may want us to bill them, or you may be able to pay online by debit or credit card.

NOT APPLYING THROUGH A SCHOOL OR COLLEGE

If you're not currently studying, you'll probably be applying as an independent applicant rather than through a school, college or other UCAS-registered centre. In this case you won't be able to provide a 'buzzword', but we'll ask you a few extra questions to check you are eligible to apply.

If you're not applying through a UCAS-registered centre, the procedure you use for obtaining a reference will depend on whether or not you want your reference to be provided through a registered centre. For information on the procedures for providing references, visit **www.ucas.com/students/applying/howtoapply/reference**.

INVISIBILITY OF CHOICES

Universities and colleges cannot see details of the other choices on your application until you reply to any offers or you are unsuccessful at all of your choices.

APPLICATION CHECKLIST

We want this to run smoothly for you and we also want to process your application as quickly as possible. You can help us to do this by remembering to do the following:

✓ check the closing dates for applications – see page 93
✓ check the student finance information at **www.ucas.com/students/studentfinance/** and course fees information in Course Finder at **www.ucas.com**
✓ start early and allow plenty of time for completing your application – including enough time for your referee to complete the reference section
✓ read the online instructions carefully before you start
✓ consider what each question is actually asking for – use the 'help'
✓ pay special attention to your personal statement (see page 98) and start drafting it early
✓ ask a teacher, parent, friend or careers adviser to review your draft application – particularly the personal statement
✓ if you get stuck, watch our videos on YouTube, where we answer your frequently asked questions on completing a UCAS application at **www.youtube.com/ucasonline**
✓ if you have extra information that will not fit on your application, send it direct to your chosen universities or colleges after we have sent you your Welcome letter with your Personal ID – don't send it to us
✓ print a copy of the final version of your application, in case you are asked questions on it at an interview.

Applying

2

The personal statement

Next to choosing your courses, this section of your application will be the most time-consuming. It is of immense importance as many colleges and universities rely solely on the information in the UCAS application, rather than interviews and admissions tests, when selecting students. The personal statement can be the deciding factor in whether or not they offer you a place. If it is an institution that interviews, it could be the deciding factor in whether you get called for interview.

Keep a copy of your personal statement – if you are called for interview, you will almost certainly be asked questions based on it.

Tutors will look carefully at your exam results, actual and predicted, your reference and your own personal statement. Remember, they are looking for reasons to offer you a place – try to give them every opportunity to do so!

A SALES DOCUMENT

The personal statement is your opportunity to sell yourself, so do so. The university or college admissions tutor who reads your personal statement wants to get a rounded picture of you to decide whether you will make an interesting member of the university or college, both academically and socially. They want to know more about you than the subjects you are studying at school.

HOW TO START

At **www.ucas.com** you'll find several tools to help you write a good personal statement:

- Personal statement timeline, to help you do all your research and plan your statement over several drafts and checks.
- Personal statement mind map, which gives you reminders and hints on preparation, content and

presentation, with extra hints for mature and international applicants.

- Personal statement worksheet, which gets you to start writing by asking relevant questions so that you include everything you need. You can also check your work against a list of dos and don'ts .

Include things like hobbies and work experience (see page 83), and try to link the skills you have gained to the type of course you are applying for. Describe your career plans and goals. Have you belonged to sports teams or orchestras or held positions of responsibility in the community? Try to give evidence of your ability to undertake higher level study successfully by showing your commitment and maturity. If you left full-time education a while ago, talk about the work you have done and the skills you have gathered or how you have juggled bringing up a family with other activities – that

is solid evidence of time management skills. Whoever you are, make sure you explain what appeals to you about the course you are applying for.

A good feel for numbers and enjoyment of analytical work will be important attributes to portray in a personal statement for economics, finance or accountancy. Make sure you demonstrate your interest, motivation and enthusiasm for the subject you're applying for. If you've not studied the subject before, it's especially important that you show your understanding of it.

Visit **www.ucas.tv** to view the video to help guide you through the process and address the most common fears and concerns about writing a personal statement.

WHAT ADMISSIONS TUTORS LOOK FOR	WHAT TO TELL THEM
- Your reasons for wanting to take this subject in general and this particular course. - Your communication skills – not only what you say but how you say it. Your grammar and spelling must be perfect. - Relevant experience – practical things you've done that are related to your choice of course. - Evidence of your teamworking ability, leadership capability, independence. - Evidence of your skills, for example: IT skills, empathy and people skills, debating and public speaking, research and analysis. - Other activities that show your dedication and ability to apply yourself and maintain your motivation.	- Why you want to do this subject – how you know it is the right subject for you. - What experience you already have in this field – for example work experience, school projects, hobbies, voluntary work. - The skills and qualities you have as a person that would make you a good student, for example anything that shows your dedication, communication ability, academic achievement, initiative. - Examples that show you can knuckle down and apply yourself, for example running a marathon or writing your Extended Project. - If you're taking a gap year, why you've chosen this and (if possible) what you're going to do during it. - About your other interests and activities away from studying – to show you're a rounded person. (But remember that it is mainly your suitability for the particular course that they're looking to judge.)

Offers

3

Step 3 – Offers

Once we have sent your application to your chosen universities and colleges, they will each consider it independently and tell us whether or not they can offer you a place. Some universities and colleges will take longer to make decisions than others. You may be asked to attend an interview, sit an additional test or provide a piece of work such as an essay before a decision can be made.

INTERVIEWS

Many universities (particularly the more popular ones, running competitive courses) use interviews as part of their selection process. Universities will want to find out why you want to study your chosen course at their institution, and they want to judge whether the course is suitable for you and your future career plans. Interviews also give you an opportunity to visit the university and ask any questions you may have about the course or

their institution.

If you are called for interview, the key areas they are likely to cover will be:

- evidence of your academic/financial ability
- your capacity to study hard
- your commitment to a career in economics, finance or accountancy, best shown by work experience
- your awareness of current issues in the news that may have an impact on your chosen field of study
- your logic and reasoning ability.

A lot of the interview will be based on information supplied on your application – especially your **personal statement** – see pages 98 and 99 for tips about the personal statement.

Whenever a university or college makes a decision about your application, we record it and let you know. You can check the progress of your application using Track at **www.ucas.com**. This is our secure online service which gives you access to your application using the same username and password you used when you applied. You use it to find out if you have been invited for interview or need to provide an additional piece of work, as well as check to see if you have received any offers. Whenever there is any change in your application status, we email you to advise you to check Track.

TYPES OF OFFER

Universities can make two types of offer: conditional or unconditional.

Conditional offer

A conditional offer means the university or college will offer you a place if you meet certain conditions – usually based on exam results. The conditions may be based on Tariff points (for example, 300 points from three A levels), or specify certain grades in named subjects (for example, A in economics, B in accounting, C in business studies).

Unconditional offer

If you've met all the academic requirements for the course and the university or college wants to accept you, they will make you an unconditional offer. If you accept this you'll have a definite place.

However, for both types of offer, there might be other requirements, such as medical or financial conditions, that you need to meet before you can start your course.

REPLYING TO OFFERS

When you have received decisions for all your choices, you must decide which offers you want to accept. You will be given a deadline in Track by which you have to make your replies. Before replying, get advice from family, friends or advisers, but remember that you're the one taking the course so it's your decision.

Firm acceptance

- Your firm acceptance is your first choice – this is your preferred choice out of all the offers you have received. You can only have one firm acceptance.
- If you accept an unconditional offer, you are entering a contract that you will attend the course, so you must decline any other offers.
- If you accept a conditional offer, you are entering a contract that you will attend the course at that university or college if you meet the conditions of the offer. You can accept another offer as an insurance choice.

Insurance acceptance

- If your firm acceptance is a conditional offer, you can accept another offer as an insurance choice. Your insurance choice can be conditional or unconditional and acts as a back-up, so if you don't meet the conditions for your firm choice but meet the conditions for your insurance, you will be committed to the insurance choice. You can only have one insurance choice.
- The conditions for your insurance choice would usually be lower than your firm choice.
- You don't have to accept an insurance choice if you don't want one: but if you do, you need to be certain that it is an offer you would accept.

For more information watch our video guides *How to use Track*, *Making sense of your offers*, and *How to reply to your offers* at **www.ucas.tv**.

WHAT IF YOU HAVE NO OFFERS?

If you have used all five choices on your application and either received no offers, or decided to turn down any offers you have received, you may be eligible to apply for another choice through Extra. Find out more about Extra on the next page.

If you are not eligible for Extra, in the summer you can contact universities and colleges with vacancies in Clearing. See page 118 for more information.

Offers

3

Extra

Extra allows you to make additional choices, one at a time, without having to wait for Clearing in July. It is completely optional and free, and is designed to encourage you to continue researching and choosing courses if you are holding no offers. The courses available through Extra will be highlighted on Course Finder, at **www.ucas.com**.

From 25 February – early July 2013
The Extra service is available to eligible applicants through Track at **www.ucas.com**.

WHO IS ELIGIBLE?

You will be eligible for Extra if you have already made five choices and:

- you have had unsuccessful or withdrawal decisions from all five of your choices, or

- you have cancelled your outstanding choices and hold no offers, or
- you have received decisions from all five choices and have declined all offers made to you.

HOW DOES IT WORK?

We contact you and explain what to do if you are eligible for Extra. If you are eligible a special Extra button will be available on your Track screen. If you want to use Extra you should:

- tick the 'Available in extra' box in the study options section when looking for courses on Course Finder
- choose a course that you would like to apply for and enter the details on your Track screen.

When you have chosen a course the university or college will be able to view your application and consider you for its course.

WHAT HAPPENS NEXT?

We give universities and colleges a maximum of 21 days to consider your Extra application. During this time, you cannot be considered by another university or college. If you have not heard after 21 days you can apply to a different university or college if you wish, but it is a good idea to ring the one currently considering you before doing so. If you are made an offer, you can choose whether or not to accept it.

If you accept an offer, conditional or unconditional, you will not be able to take any further part in Extra.

If you are currently studying for examinations, any offer that you receive is likely to be an offer conditional on exam grades. If you already have your examination results, it is possible that a university or college may make an unconditional offer. If you accept an unconditional offer, you will be placed.

If you decide to decline the offer, or the university or college decides they cannot make you an offer, you will be given another opportunity to use Extra, time permitting. Your Extra button on Track will be reactivated.

Once you have accepted an offer in Extra, you are committed to it in the same way as you would be with an offer through the main UCAS system. Conditional offers made through Extra will be treated in the same way as other conditional offers, when your examination results become available.

If your results do not meet the conditions and the university or college decides that they cannot confirm your Extra offer, you will automatically become eligible for Clearing if it is too late for you to be considered by another university or college in Extra.

If you are unsuccessful, decline an offer, or do not receive an offer, or 21 days have elapsed since choosing a course through Extra, you can use Extra to apply for another course, time permitting.

ADVICE

Do the same careful research and seek guidance on your Extra choice of university or college and course as you did for your initial choices. If you applied to high-demand courses and institutions in your original application and were unsuccessful, you could consider related or alternative subjects, or perhaps apply for the subject you want in combination with another. Your teachers or careers advisers or the universities and colleges themselves can provide useful guidance. Course Finder at **www.ucas.com/coursefinder** is another important source of information. Be flexible, that is the key to success. But you are the only one who knows how flexible you are prepared to be. Remember that even if you decide to take a degree course other than economics, finance or accountancy, you can take the postgraduate route into these professions.

Visit **www.ucas.tv** to watch the video guide on how to use Extra.

```
┌─────────────────────────────┐
│        Offers               │
│                             │
│ ⌐                           │
│ ⟨3⟩                         │
│ └                           │
└─────────────────────────────┘
```

Offers

3

The Tariff

Finding out what qualifications are needed for different higher education courses can be very confusing.

The UCAS Tariff is the system for allocating points to qualifications used for entry to higher education. Universities and colleges can use the UCAS Tariff to make comparisons between applicants with different qualifications. Tariff points are often used in entry requirements, although other factors are often taken into account. Information on Course Finder at **www.ucas.com** provides a fuller picture of what admissions tutors are seeking.

The tables on the following pages show the qualifications covered by the UCAS Tariff. There may have been changes to these tables since this book was printed. You should visit **www.ucas.com** to view the most up-to-date tables.

FURTHER INFORMATION?

Although Tariff points can be accumulated in a variety of ways, not all of these will necessarily be acceptable for entry to a particular higher education course. The achievement of a points score therefore does not give an automatic entitlement to entry, and many other factors are taken into account in the admissions process.

The Course Finder facility at **www.ucas.com** is the best source of reference to find out what qualifications are acceptable for entry to specific courses. Updates to the Tariff, including details on how new qualifications are added, can be found at **www.ucas.com/students/ucas_tariff/.**

HOW DOES THE TARIFF WORK?

- Students can collect Tariff points from a range of different qualifications, eg GCE A level with BTEC Nationals.
- There is no ceiling to the number of points that can be accumulated.
- There is no double counting. Certain qualifications within the Tariff build on qualifications in the same subject. In these cases only the qualification with the higher Tariff score will be counted. This principle applies to:
  - GCE Advanced Subsidiary level and GCE Advanced level
  - Scottish Highers and Advanced Highers
  - Speech, drama and music awards at grades 6, 7 and 8.
- Tariff points for the Advanced Diploma come from the Progression Diploma score plus the relevant Additional and Specialist Learning (ASL) Tariff points. Please see the appropriate qualification in the Tariff tables to calculate the ASL score.
- The Extended Project Tariff points are included within the Tariff points for Progression and Advanced Diplomas. Extended Project points represented in the Tariff only count when the qualification is taken outside of these Diplomas.
- Where the Tariff tables refer to specific awarding organisations, only qualifications from these awarding organisations attract Tariff points. Qualifications with a similar title, but from a different qualification awarding organisation do not attract Tariff points.

HOW DO UNIVERSITIES AND COLLEGES USE THE TARIFF?

The Tariff provides a facility to help universities and colleges when expressing entrance requirements and when making conditional offers. Entry requirements and conditional offers expressed as Tariff points will often require a minimum level of achievement in a specified subject (for example, '300 points to include grade A at A level chemistry', or '260 points including SQA Higher grade B in mathematics').

Use of the Tariff may also vary from department to department at any one institution, and may in some cases be dependent on the programme being offered.

In July 2010, UCAS announced plans to review the qualifications information provided to universities and colleges. You can read more about the review at **www.ucas.com/qireview**.

WHAT QUALIFICATIONS ARE INCLUDED IN THE TARIFF?

The following qualifications are included in the UCAS Tariff. See the number on the qualification title to find the relevant section of the Tariff table.

1   AAT NVQ Level 3 in Accounting
2   AAT Level 3 Diploma in Accounting (QCF)
3   Advanced Diploma
4   Advanced Extension Awards
5   Advanced Placement Programme (US and Canada)
6   Arts Award (Gold)
7   ASDAN Community Volunteering qualification
8   Asset Languages Advanced Stage
9   British Horse Society (Stage 3 Horse Knowledge & Care, Stage 3 Riding and Preliminary Teacher's Certificate)
10 BTEC Awards (NQF)
11 BTEC Certificates and Extended Certificates (NQF)
12 BTEC Diplomas (NQF)
13 BTEC National in Early Years (NQF)
14 BTEC Nationals (NQF)
15 BTEC QCF Qualifications (Suite known as Nationals)
16 BTEC Specialist Qualifications (QCF)
17 CACHE Award, Certificate and Diploma in Child Care and Education
18 CACHE Level 3 Extended Diploma for the Children and Young People's Workforce (QCF)
19 Cambridge ESOL Examinations
20 Cambridge Pre-U
21 Certificate of Personal Effectiveness (COPE)
22 CISI Introduction to Securities and Investment
23 City & Guilds Land Based Services Level 3 Qualifications
24 Graded Dance and Vocational Graded Dance
25 Diploma in Fashion Retail
26 Diploma in Foundation Studies (Art & Design; Art, Design & Media)
27 EDI Level 3 Certificate in Accounting, Certificate in Accounting (IAS)
28 Essential Skills (Northern Ireland)
29 Essential Skills Wales
30 Extended Project (stand alone)
31 Free-standing Mathematics
32 Functional skills
33 GCE (AS, AS Double Award, A level, A level Double Award and A level (with additional AS))
34 Hong Kong Diploma of Secondary Education (from 2012 entry onwards)
35 ifs School of Finance (Certificate and Diploma in Financial Studies)
36 iMedia (OCR level Certificate/Diploma for iMedia Professionals)
37 International Baccalaureate (IB) Diploma
38 International Baccalaureate (IB) Certificate
39 Irish Leaving Certificate (Higher and Ordinary levels)
40 IT Professionals (iPRO) (Certificate and Diploma)
41 Key Skills (Levels 2, 3 and 4)
42 Music examinations (grades 6, 7 and 8)
43 OCR Level 3 Certificate in Mathematics for Engineering
44 OCR Level 3 Certificate for Young Enterprise
45 OCR Nationals (National Certificate, National Diploma and National Extended Diploma)
46 Principal Learning Wales
47 Progression Diploma
48 Rockschool Music Practitioners Qualifications
49 Scottish Qualifications
50 Speech and Drama examinations (grades 6, 7 and 8 and Performance Studies)
51 Sports Leaders UK
52 Welsh Baccalaureate Advanced Diploma (Core)

Updates on the Tariff, including details on the incorporation of any new qualifications, are posted on **www.ucas.com.**

UCAS TARIFF TABLES

1

AAT NVQ LEVEL 3 IN ACCOUNTING

GRADE	TARIFF POINTS
PASS	160

2

AAT LEVEL 3 DIPLOMA IN ACCOUNTING

GRADE	TARIFF POINTS
PASS	160

3

ADVANCED DIPLOMA

Advanced Diploma = Progression Diploma plus Additional & Specialist Learning (ASL). Please see the appropriate qualification to calculate the ASL score. Please see the Progression Diploma (Table 47) for Tariff scores

4

ADVANCED EXTENSION AWARDS

GRADE	TARIFF POINTS
DISTINCTION	40
MERIT	20

Points for Advanced Extension Awards are over and above those gained from the A level grade

5

ADVANCED PLACEMENT PROGRAMME (US & CANADA)

GRADE	TARIFF POINTS
Group A	
5	120
4	90
3	60
Group B	
5	50
4	35
3	20

Details of the subjects covered by each group can be found at www.ucas.com/students/ucas_tariff/tarifftables

6

ARTS AWARD (GOLD)

GRADE	TARIFF POINTS
PASS	35

7

ASDAN COMMUNITY VOLUNTEERING QUALIFICATION

GRADE	TARIFF POINTS
CERTIFICATE	50
AWARD	30

8

ASSET LANGUAGES ADVANCED STAGE

GRADE	TARIFF POINTS	GRADE	TARIFF POINTS
Speaking		Listening	
GRADE 12	28	GRADE 12	25
GRADE 11	20	GRADE 11	18
GRADE 10	12	GRADE 10	11
Reading		Writing	
GRADE 12	25	GRADE 12	25
GRADE 11	18	GRADE 11	18
GRADE 10	11	GRADE 10	11

9

BRITISH HORSE SOCIETY

GRADE	TARIFF POINTS
Stage 3 Horse Knowledge & Care	
PASS	35
Stage 3 Riding	
PASS	35
Preliminary Teacher's Certificate	
PASS	35

Awarded by Equestrian Qualifications (GB) Ltd (EQL)

10

BTEC AWARDS (NQF) (EXCLUDING BTEC NATIONAL QUALIFICATIONS)

GRADE	TARIFF POINTS		
	Group A	Group B	Group C
DISTINCTION	20	30	40
MERIT	13	20	26
PASS	7	10	13

Details of the subjects covered by each group can be found at www.ucas.com/students/ucas_tariff/tarifftables

11

BTEC CERTIFICATES AND EXTENDED CERTIFICATES (NQF) (EXCLUDING BTEC NATIONAL QUALIFICATIONS)

GRADE	TARIFF POINTS				
	Group A	Group B	Group C	Group D	Extended Certificates
DISTINCTION	40	60	80	100	60
MERIT	26	40	52	65	40
PASS	13	20	26	35	20

Details of the subjects covered by each group can be found at www.ucas.com/students/ucas_tariff/tarifftables

12

BTEC DIPLOMAS (NQF) (EXCLUDING BTEC NATIONAL QUALIFICATIONS)

GRADE	TARIFF POINTS		
	Group A	Group B	Group C
DISTINCTION	80	100	120
MERIT	52	65	80
PASS	26	35	40

Details of the subjects covered by each group can be found at www.ucas.com/students/ucas_tariff/tarifftables

13

BTEC NATIONAL IN EARLY YEARS (NQF)					
GRADE	TARIFF POINTS	GRADE	TARIFF POINTS	GRADE	TARIFF POINTS
Theory				Practical	
Diploma		Certificate		D	120
DDD	320	DD	200	M	80
DDM	280	DM	160	P	40
DMM	240	MM	120		
MMM	220	MP	80		
MMP	160	PP	40		
MPP	120				
PPP	80				

Points apply to the following qualifications only: BTEC National Diploma in Early Years (100/1279/5); BTEC National Certificate in Early Years (100/1280/1)

14

BTEC NATIONALS (NQF)					
GRADE	TARIFF POINTS	GRADE	TARIFF POINTS	GRADE	TARIFF POINTS
Diploma		Certificate		Award	
DDD	360	DD	240	D	120
DDM	320	DM	200	M	80
DMM	280	MM	160	P	40
MMM	240	MP	120		
MMP	200	PP	80		
MPP	160				
PPP	120				

15

BTEC QUALIFICATIONS (QCF) (SUITE OF QUALIFICATIONS KNOWN AS NATIONALS)					
EXTENDED DIPLOMA	DIPLOMA	90 CREDIT DIPLOMA	SUBSIDIARY DIPLOMA	CERTIFICATE	TARIFF POINTS
D*D*D*					420
D*D*D					400
D*DD					380
DDD					360
DDM					320
DMM	D*D*				280
	D*D				260
MMM	DD				240
		D*D*			210
MMP	DM	D*D			200
		DD			180
MPP	MM	DM			160
			D*		140
PPP	MP	MM	D		120
		MP			100
	PP		M		80
				D*	70
		PP		D	60
			P	M	40
				P	20

16

BTEC SPECIALIST (QCF)			
GRADE	TARIFF POINTS		
	Diploma	Certificate	Award
DISTINCTION	120	60	20
MERIT	80	40	13
PASS	40	20	7

UCAS TARIFF TABLES

17

CACHE LEVEL 3 AWARD, CERTIFICATE AND DIPLOMA IN CHILD CARE & EDUCATION					
AWARD		CERTIFICATE		DIPLOMA	
GRADE	TARIFF POINTS	GRADE	TARIFF POINTS	GRADE	TARIFF POINTS
A	30	A	110	A	360
B	25	B	90	B	300
C	20	C	70	C	240
D	15	D	55	D	180
E	10	E	35	E	120

18

CACHE LEVEL 3 EXTENDED DIPLOMA FOR THE CHILDREN AND YOUNG PEOPLE'S WORKFORCE (QCF)	
GRADE	TARIFF POINTS
A*	420
A	340
B	290
C	240
D	140
E	80

19

CAMBRIDGE ESOL EXAMINATIONS	
GRADE	TARIFF POINTS
Certificate of Proficiency in English	
A	140
B	110
C	70
Certificate in Advanced English	
A	70

20

CAMBRIDGE PRE-U							
GRADE	TARIFF POINTS	GRADE	TARIFF POINTS	GRADE	TARIFF POINTS	GRADE	TARIFF POINTS
Principal Subject		Global Perspectives and Research		Short Course			
D1	TBC	D1	TBC	D1	TBC		
D2	145	D2	140	D2	TBC		
D3	130	D3	126	D3	60		
M1	115	M1	112	M1	53		
M2	101	M2	98	M2	46		
M3	87	M3	84	M3	39		
P1	73	P1	70	P1	32		
P2	59	P2	56	P2	26		
P3	46	P3	42	P3	20		

21

CERTIFICATE OF PERSONAL EFFECTIVENESS (COPE)	
GRADE	TARIFF POINTS
PASS	70

Points are awarded for the Certificate of Personal Effectiveness (CoPE) awarded by ASDAN and CCEA

22

CISI INTRODUCTION TO SECURITIES AND INVESTMENT	
GRADE	TARIFF POINTS
PASS WITH DISTINCTION	60
PASS WITH MERIT	40
PASS	20

23

CITY AND GUILDS LAND BASED SERVICES LEVEL 3 QUALIFICATIONS				
GRADE	TARIFF POINTS			
	EXTENDED DIPLOMA	DIPLOMA	SUBSIDIARY DIPLOMA	CERTIFICATE
DISTINCTION*	420	280	140	70
DISTINCTION	360	240	120	60
MERIT	240	160	80	40
PASS	120	80	40	20

24

GRADED DANCE AND VOCATIONAL GRADED DANCE					
GRADE	TARIFF POINTS	GRADE	TARIFF POINTS	GRADE	TARIFF POINTS
Graded Dance					
Grade 8		Grade 7		Grade 6	
DISTINCTION	65	DISTINCTION	55	DISTINCTION	40
MERIT	55	MERIT	45	MERIT	35
PASS	45	PASS	35	PASS	30
Vocational Graded Dance					
Advanced Foundation		Intermediate			
DISTINCTION	70	DISTINCTION	65		
MERIT	55	MERIT	50		
PASS	45	PASS	40		

25

DIPLOMA IN FASHION RETAIL	
GRADE	TARIFF POINTS
DISTINCTION	160
MERIT	120
PASS	80

Applies to the NQF and QCF versions of the qualifications awarded by ABC Awards

UCAS TARIFF TABLES

26

DIPLOMA IN FOUNDATION STUDIES (ART & DESIGN AND ART, DESIGN & MEDIA)	
GRADE	TARIFF POINTS
DISTINCTION	285
MERIT	225
PASS	165

Awarded by ABC, Edexcel, UAL and WJEC

27

EDI LEVEL 3 CERTIFICATE IN ACCOUNTING, CERTIFICATE IN ACCOUNTING (IAS)	
GRADE	TARIFF POINTS
DISTINCTION	120
MERIT	90
PASS	70

28

ESSENTIAL SKILLS (NORTHERN IRELAND)	
GRADE	TARIFF POINTS
LEVEL 2	10

Only allocated at level 2 if studied as part of a wider composite qualification such as 14-19 Diploma or Welsh Baccalaureate

29

ESSENTIAL SKILLS WALES	
GRADE	TARIFF POINTS
LEVEL 4	30
LEVEL 3	20
LEVEL 2	10

Only allocated at level 2 if studied as part of a wider composite qualification such as 14-19 Diploma or Welsh Baccalaureate

30

EXTENDED PROJECT (STAND ALONE)	
GRADE	TARIFF POINTS
A*	70
A	60
B	50
C	40
D	30
E	20

Points for the Extended Project cannot be counted if taken as part of Progression/Advanced Diploma

31

FREE-STANDING MATHEMATICS	
GRADE	TARIFF POINTS
A	20
B	17
C	13
D	10
E	7

Covers free-standing Mathematics - Additional Maths, Using and Applying Statistics, Working with Algebraic and Graphical Techniques, Modelling with Calculus

32

FUNCTIONAL SKILLS	
GRADE	TARIFF POINTS
LEVEL 2	10

Only allocated if studied as part of a wider composite qualification such as 14-19 Diploma or Welsh Baccalaureate

33

GCE AND VCE									
GRADE	TARIFF POINTS	GRADE	TARIFF POINTS	GRADE	TARIFF POINTS	GRADE	TARIFF POINTS	GRADE	TARIFF POINTS
GCE & AVCE Double Award		GCE A level with additional AS (9 units)		GCE A level & AVCE		GCE AS Double Award		GCE AS & AS VCE	
A*A*	280	A*A	200	A*	140	AA	120	A	60
A*A	260	AA	180	A	120	AB	110	B	50
AA	240	AB	170	B	100	BB	100	C	40
AB	220	BB	150	C	80	BC	90	D	30
BB	200	BC	140	D	60	CC	80	E	20
BC	180	CC	120	E	40	CD	70		
CC	160	CD	110			DD	60		
CD	140	DD	90			DE	50		
DD	120	DE	80			EE	40		
DE	100	EE	60						
EE	80								

34

HONG KONG DIPLOMA OF SECONDARY EDUCATION					
GRADE	TARIFF POINTS	GRADE	TARIFF POINTS	GRADE	TARIFF POINTS
All subjects except mathematics		Mathematics compulsory component		Mathematics optional components	
5**	No value	5**	No value	5**	No value
5*	130	5*	60	5*	70
5	120	5	45	5	60
4	80	4	35	4	50
3	40	3	25	3	40

No value for 5** pending receipt of candidate evidence (post 2012)

UCAS TARIFF TABLES

35

IFS SCHOOL OF FINANCE (NQF & QCF)			
GRADE	TARIFF POINTS	GRADE	TARIFF POINTS
Certificate in Financial Studies (CeFS)		Diploma in Financial Studies (DipFS)	
A	60	A	120
B	50	B	100
C	40	C	80
D	30	D	60
E	20	E	40

Applicants with the ifs Diploma cannot also count points allocated to the ifs Certificate. Completion of both qualifications will result in a maximum of 120 UCAS Tariff points

36

LEVEL 3 CERTIFICATE / DIPLOMA FOR iMEDIA USERS (iMEDIA)	
GRADE	TARIFF POINTS
DIPLOMA	66
CERTIFICATE	40

Awarded by OCR

37

INTERNATIONAL BACCALAUREATE (IB) DIPLOMA			
GRADE	TARIFF POINTS	GRADE	TARIFF POINTS
45	720	34	479
44	698	33	457
43	676	32	435
42	654	31	413
41	632	30	392
40	611	29	370
39	589	28	348
38	567	27	326
37	545	26	304
36	523	25	282
35	501	24	260

38

INTERNATIONAL BACCALAUREATE (IB) CERTIFICATE					
GRADE	TARIFF POINTS	GRADE	TARIFF POINTS	GRADE	TARIFF POINTS
Higher Level		Standard Level		Core	
7	130	7	70	3	120
6	110	6	59	2	80
5	80	5	43	1	40
4	50	4	27	0	10
3	20	3	11		

39

IRISH LEAVING CERTIFICATE			
GRADE	TARIFF POINTS	GRADE	TARIFF POINTS
Higher		Ordinary	
A1	90	A1	39
A2	77	A2	26
B1	71	B1	20
B2	64	B2	14
B3	58	B3	7
C1	52		
C2	45		
C3	39		
D1	33		
D2	26		
D3	20		

40

IT PROFESSIONALS (iPRO)	
GRADE	TARIFF POINTS
DIPLOMA	100
CERTIFICATE	80

Awarded by OCR

41

KEY SKILLS	
GRADE	TARIFF POINTS
LEVEL 4	30
LEVEL 3	20
LEVEL 2	10

Only allocated at level 2 if studied as part of a wider composite qualification such as 14-19 Diploma or Welsh Baccalaureate

UCAS TARIFF TABLES

42

MUSIC EXAMINATIONS					
GRADE	TARIFF POINTS	GRADE	TARIFF POINTS	GRADE	TARIFF POINTS
Practical					
Grade 8		Grade 7		Grade 6	
DISTINCTION	75	DISTINCTION	60	DISTINCTION	45
MERIT	70	MERIT	55	MERIT	40
PASS	55	PASS	40	PASS	25
Theory					
Grade 8		Grade 7		Grade 6	
DISTINCTION	30	DISTINCTION	20	DISTINCTION	15
MERIT	25	MERIT	15	MERIT	10
PASS	20	PASS	10	PASS	5

Points shown are for the ABRSM, LCMM/University of West London, Rockschool and Trinity Guildhall/Trinity College London Advanced Level music examinations

43

OCR LEVEL 3 CERTIFICATE IN MATHEMATICS FOR ENGINEERING	
GRADE	TARIFF POINTS
A*	TBC
A	90
B	75
C	60
D	45
E	30

44

OCR LEVEL 3 CERTIFICATE FOR YOUNG ENTERPRISE	
GRADE	TARIFF POINTS
DISTINCTION	40
MERIT	30
PASS	20

45

OCR NATIONALS					
GRADE	TARIFF POINTS	GRADE	TARIFF POINTS	GRADE	TARIFF POINTS
National Extended Diploma		National Diploma		National Certificate	
D1	360	D	240	D	120
D2/M1	320	M1	200	M	80
M2	280	M2/P1	160	P	40
M3	240	P2	120		
P1	200	P3	80		
P2	160				
P3	120				

46

PRINCIPAL LEARNING WALES	
GRADE	TARIFF POINTS
A*	210
A	180
B	150
C	120
D	90
E	60

47

PROGRESSION DIPLOMA	
GRADE	TARIFF POINTS
A*	350
A	300
B	250
C	200
D	150
E	100

Advanced Diploma = Progression Diploma plus Additional & Specialist Learning (ASL). Please see the appropriate qualification to calculate the ASL score

48

	ROCKSCHOOL MUSIC PRACTITIONERS QUALIFICATIONS				
GRADE	TARIFF POINTS				
	Extended Diploma	Diploma	Subsidiary Diploma	Extended Certificate	Certificate
DISTINCTION	240	180	120	60	30
MERIT	160	120	80	40	20
PASS	80	60	40	20	10

49

	SCOTTISH QUALIFICATIONS						
GRADE	TARIFF POINTS	GRADE	TARIFF POINTS	GRADE	TARIFF POINTS	GROUP	TARIFF POINTS
Advanced Higher		Higher		Scottish Interdisciplinary Project		Scottish National Certificates	
A	130	A	80	A	65	C	125
B	110	B	65	B	55	B	100
C	90	C	50	C	45	A	75
D	72	D	36				
Ungraded Higher		NPA PC Passport					
PASS	45	PASS	45				
		Core Skills					
		HIGHER	20				

Details of the subjects covered by each Scottish National Certificate can be found at www.ucas.com/students/ucas_tariff/tarifftables

50

	SPEECH AND DRAMA EXAMINATIONS						
GRADE	TARIFF POINTS	GRADE	TARIFF POINTS	GRADE	TARIFF POINTS	GRADE	TARIFF POINTS
PCertLAM		Grade 8		Grade 7		Grade 6	
DISTINCTION	90	DISTINCTION	65	DISTINCTION	55	DISTINCTION	40
MERIT	80	MERIT	60	MERIT	50	MERIT	35
PASS	60	PASS	45	PASS	35	PASS	20

Details of the Speech and Drama Qualifications covered by the Tariff can be found at www.ucas.com/students/ucas_tariff/tarifftables

51

SPORTS LEADERS UK	
GRADE	TARIFF POINTS
PASS	30

These points are awarded to Higher Sports Leader Award and Level 3 Certificate in Higher Sports Leadership (QCF)

52

WELSH BACCALAUREATE ADVANCED DIPLOMA (CORE)	
GRADE	TARIFF POINTS
PASS	120

These points are awarded only when a candidate achieves the Welsh Baccalaureate Advanced Diploma

www.ucas.com

at the heart of connecting people to higher education

Results

4

Step 4 – Results

You should arrange your holidays so that you are at home when your exam results are published, because if there are any issues to discuss, admissions tutors will need to speak to you in person.

We receive many UK exam results direct from the exam boards – check the list at **www.ucas.com**.

If your qualification is listed, we send your results to the universities and colleges that you have accepted as your firm and insurance choices. If your qualification is not listed, you must send your exam results to the universities and colleges where you are holding offers.

After you have received your exam results check Track to find out if you have a place on your chosen course.

If you have met all the conditions for your firm choice, the university or college will confirm that you have a place. Occasionally, they may still confirm you have a place even if you have not quite met all the offer conditions; or they may offer you a place on a similar course.

If you have not met the conditions of your firm choice and the university or college has not confirmed your place, but you have met all the conditions of your insurance offer, your insurance university or college will confirm that you have a place.

When a university or college tells us that you have a place, we send you confirmation by letter.

RE-MARKED EXAMS

If you ask for any of your exams to be re-marked, you must tell the universities or colleges where you're holding offers. If a university or college cannot confirm your place based on the initial results, you should ask them if they would be able to reconsider their decision after the re-mark. They are under no obligation have to reconsider their position even if your re-mark results in higher grades. Don't forget that re-marks may also result in lower grades.

The exam boards tell us about any re-marks that result in grade changes. We then send the revised grades to the universities or colleges where you're holding offers. As soon as you know about any grade changes, you should also tell them.

'CASHING IN' A LEVEL RESULTS

If you have taken A levels, your school or college must certificate or 'cash in' all your unit scores before the exam board can award final grades. If when you collect your A level results you have to add up your unit scores to find out your final grades, this means your school or college has not 'cashed in' your results.

We only receive cashed in results from the exam boards, so if your school or college has not cashed in your results, you must ask them to send a 'cash in' request to the exam board. You also need to tell the universities or colleges where you're holding offers that there'll be a delay in receiving your results and call our Customer Service Unit to find out when your results have been received.

When we receive your 'cashed in' results from the exam board we send them straight away to the universities or colleges where you're holding offers.

WHAT IF YOU DON'T HAVE A PLACE?

If you have not met the conditions of either your firm or insurance choice, and your chosen universities or colleges have not confirmed your place, you are eligible for Clearing. In Clearing you can apply for any courses that still have vacancies (but remember that admissions tutors will still be reading your original personal statement). Clearing operates from mid-July to late September 2013 (page 118).

BETTER RESULTS THAN EXPECTED?

If you obtain exam results that meet and exceed the conditions of the offer for your firm choice, you can for a short period use a process called Adjustment to look for an alternative place, whilst still keeping your original firm choice. See page 119 for information about Adjustment.

Next steps

5

Step 5 – Next steps

You might find yourself with different exam results than you were expecting, or you may change your mind about what you want to do. If so, there may be other options open to you.

CLEARING

Clearing is a service that helps people without a place find suitable course vacancies. It runs from mid-July until the end of September, but most people use it after the exam results are published in August.

You could consider related or alternative subjects or perhaps combining your original choice of subject with another. Your teachers or careers adviser, or the universities and colleges themselves, can provide useful guidance.

Course vacancies are listed at **www.ucas.com** and in the national media following the publication of exam results in August. **Once you have your exam results**, if you're in Clearing you need to look at the vacancy listings and then contact any university or college you are interested in.

Talk to the institutions; don't be afraid to call them. Make sure you have your Personal ID and Clearing Number ready and prepare notes on what you will say to them about:

- why you want to study the course
- why you want to study at their university or college
- any relevant employment or activities you have done that relate to the course
- your grades.

Accepting an offer – you can contact as many universities and colleges as you like through Clearing, and you may informally be offered more than one place. If this happens, you will need to decide which offer you want to accept. If you're offered a place you want to be formally considered for, you enter the course details in Track, and the university or college will then let you know if they're accepting you.

ADJUSTMENT

If you receive better results than expected, and meet and exceed the conditions of your conditional firm choice, you have the opportunity to reconsider what and where you want to study. This process is called Adjustment.

Adjustment runs from A level results day on 15 August 2013 until the end of August. Your individual Adjustment period starts on A level results day or when your conditional firm choice changes to unconditional firm, whichever is the later. You then have a maximum of five calendar days to register and secure an alternative course, if you decide you want to do this. If you want to try to find an alternative course you must register in Track to use Adjustment, so universities and colleges can view your application.

There are no vacancy listings for Adjustment, so you'll need to talk to the institutions. When you contact a university or college make it clear that you are applying through Adjustment, not Clearing. If they want to consider you they will ask for your Personal ID, so they can view your application.

If you don't find an alternative place then you remain accepted at your original firm choice.

Adjustment is entirely optional; remember that nothing really beats the careful research you carried out to find the right courses before you made your UCAS application. Talk to a careers adviser at your school, college or local careers office, as they can help you decide if registering to use Adjustment is right for you.

More information about Adjustment and Clearing is available at **www.ucas.com**. You can also view UCAStv video guides on how to use Adjustment and Clearing at **www.ucas.tv**.

IF YOU ARE STILL WITHOUT A PLACE TO STUDY

If you haven't found a suitable place, or changed your mind about what you want to do, there are lots of other options. Ask for advice from your school, college or careers office. Here are some suggestions you might want to consider:

- studying a part-time course (there's a part-time course search at **www.ucas.com** from July until September)
- studying a foundation degree
- re-sitting your exams
- getting some work experience
- studying in another country
- reapplying next year to university or college through UCAS
- taking a gap year
- doing an apprenticeship (you'll find a vacancy search on the National Apprenticeship Service (NAS) website at **www.apprenticeships.org.uk**)
- finding a job
- starting a business.

More advice and links to other organisations can be found on the UCAS website at **www.ucas.com/ students/nextsteps/advice**.

Starting university or college

6

Step 6 – Starting university or college

Congratulations! Now that you have confirmed your place at university or college you will need to finalise your plans on how to get there, where to live and how to finance it. Make lists of things to do with deadlines and start contacting people whose help you can call on. Will you travel independently or call on your parents or relatives to help with transport? If you are keeping a car at uni, have you checked out parking facilities and told your insurance company?

Make sure you have everything organised, including travel arrangements, essential documents and paperwork, books and equipment required for the course. The university will send you joining information – contact the Admissions Office or the Students' Union if you have questions about anything to do with starting your course.

Freshers' week will help you settle in and make friends, but don't forget you are there to study. You may find the teaching methods rather alien at first, but remember there are plenty of sources of help, including your tutors, other students or student mentors, and the Students' Union.

Where to live – unless you are planning to live at home, your university or college will usually be able to provide you with guidance on finding somewhere to live. The earlier you contact them the better your chance of finding a suitable range of options, from halls to private landlords. Find out what facilities are available at the different types of accommodation and check whether it fits within your budget. Check also what you need to bring with you and what is supplied. Don't leave it all to the last minute – especially things like arranging a bank account, checking what proof of identity you might need, gathering together a few essentials like a mug and supplies of coffee, insurance cover, TV licence etc.

Student finance – you will need to budget for living costs, accommodation, travel and books (and tuition fees if you're paying them up front). Learn about budgeting by visiting **www.ucas.com** where you will find further links to useful resources to help you manage your money. Remember that if you do get into financial difficulties the welfare office at the university will help you change tack and manage better in future, but it is always better to live within your means from the outset, and if you need help, find it before the situation gets stressful.

Useful contacts

CONNECTING WITH UCAS

You can follow UCAS on Twitter at
www.twitter.com/ucas_online, and ask a question or
see what others are asking on Facebook at
www.facebook.com/ucasonline. You can also watch
videos of UCAS advisers answering frequently asked
questions on YouTube at
www.youtube.com/ucasonline.

There are many UCAStv video guides to help with your
journey into higher education, such as *How to choose
your courses, Attending events, Open days,* and
How to apply. These can all be viewed at
www.ucas.tv or in the relevant section of
www.ucas.com.

If you need to speak to UCAS, please contact the
Customer Service Unit on 0871 468 0 468 or 0044
871 468 0 468 from outside the UK. Calls from BT

landlines within the UK will cost no more than 9p per
minute. The cost of calls from mobiles and other
networks may vary.

If you have hearing difficulties, you can call the Text
Relay service on 18001 0871 468 0 468 (outside the
UK 0044 151 494 1260). Calls are charged at normal
rates.

CAREERS ADVICE

The Directgov Careers Helpline for Young People is for you if you live in England, are aged 13 to 19 and want advice on getting to where you want to be in life.

Careers advisers can give you information, advice and practical help with all sorts of things, like choosing subjects at school or mapping out your future career options. They can help you with anything that might be affecting you at school, college, work or in your personal or family life.

Contact a careers adviser at **www.direct.gov.uk/en/youngpeople/index.htm**.

Skills Development Scotland provides a starting point for anyone looking for careers information, advice or guidance.
www.myworldofwork.co.uk.

Careers Wales – Wales' national all-age careers guidance service.
www.careerswales.com or **www.gyrfacymru.com**.

Northern Ireland Careers Service website for the new, all-age careers guidance service in Northern Ireland.
www.nidirect.gov.uk/careers.

If you're not sure what job you want or you need help to decide which course to do, give learndirect a call on 0800 101 901 or visit
www.learndirect.co.uk.

GENERAL HIGHER EDUCATION ADVICE

National Union of Students (NUS) is the national voice of students, helping them to campaign, get cheap student discounts and provide advice on living student life to the full – **www.nus.org.uk**.

STUDENTS WITH DISABILITIES

If you have a disability or specific learning difficulty, you are strongly encouraged to make early direct contact with individual institutions before submitting your application. Most universities and colleges have disability coordinators or advisers. You can find their contact details and further advice on the Disability Rights UK website – **www.disabilityalliance.org**.

There is financial help for students with disabilities, known as Disabled Students' Allowances (DSAs). More information is available on the Directgov website at
www.direct.gov.uk/disabledstudents.

YEAR OUT

For useful information on taking a year out, see
www.gap-year.com.

The Year Out Group website is packed with information and guidance for young people and their parents and advisers. **www.yearoutgroup.org**.

Essential reading

UCAS has brought together the best books and resources you need to make the important decisions regarding entry to higher education. With guidance on choosing courses, finding the right institution, information about student finance, admissions tests, gap years and lots more, you can find the most trusted guides at **www.ucasbooks.com**.

The publications listed on the following pages and many others are available through **www.ucasbooks.com** or from UCAS Publication Services unless otherwise stated.

UCAS PUBLICATION SERVICES

UCAS Publication Services
PO Box 130, Cheltenham, Gloucestershire GL52 3ZF

f: 01242 544 806
e: publicationservices@ucas.ac.uk
// www.ucasbooks.com

ENTIRE RESEARCH AND APPLICATION PROCESS EXPLAINED

The UCAS Guide to getting into University and College

This guide contains advice and up-to-date information about the entire research and application process, and brings together the expertise of UCAS staff, along with insights and tips from well known universities including Oxford and Cambridge, and students who are involved with or have experienced the process first-hand.

The book clearly sets out the information you need in an easy-to-read format, with myth busters, tips from students, checklists and much more; this book will be a companion for applicants throughout their entire journey into higher education.

Published by UCAS
Price £11.99
Publication date January 2011

NEED HELP COMPLETING YOUR APPLICATION?

How to Complete your UCAS Application 2013

A must for anyone applying through UCAS. Contains advice on the preparation needed, a step-by-step guide to filling out the UCAS application, information on the UCAS process and useful tips for completing the personal statement.

Published by Trotman

Price £12.99

Publication date May 2012

Insider's Guide to Applying to University

Full of honest insights, this is a thorough guide to the application process. It reveals advice from careers advisers and current students, guidance on making sense of university information and choosing courses. Also includes tips for the personal statement, interviews, admissions tests, UCAS Extra and Clearing.

Published by Trotman

Price £12.99

Publication date June 2011

How to Write a Winning UCAS Personal Statement

The personal statement is your chance to stand out from the crowd. Based on information from admissions tutors, this book will help you sell yourself. It includes specific guidance for over 30 popular subjects, common mistakes to avoid, information on what admissions tutors look for, and much more.

Published by Trotman

Price £12.99

Publication date March 2010

CHOOSING COURSES

Progression Series 2013 entry

The 'UCAS Guide to getting into…' titles are designed to help you access good quality, useful information on some of the most competitive subject areas. The books cover advice on applying through UCAS, routes to qualifications, course details, job prospects, case studies and career advice.

New for 2013: information on the pros and cons of league tables and how to read them.

The UCAS Guide to getting into…

Art and Design

Economics, Finance and Accountancy

Engineering and Mathematics

Journalism, Broadcasting, Media Production and
  Performing Arts

Law

Medicine, Dentistry and Optometry

Nursing, Healthcare and Social Work

Psychology

Sports Science and Physiotherapy

Teaching and Education

Published by UCAS

Price £15.99 each

Publication date June 2012

UCAS Parent Guide

Free of charge.

Order online at **www.ucas.com/parents**.

Publication date February 2012

Open Days 2012

Attending open days, taster courses and higher education conventions is an important part of the application process. This publication makes planning attendance at these events quick and easy.

Published annually by UCAS.

Price £3.50

Publication date January 2012

Heap 2013: University Degree Course Offers

An independent, reliable guide to selecting university degree courses in the UK.

The guide lists degree courses available at universities and colleges throughout the UK and the grades, UCAS points or equivalent that you need to achieve to get on to each course listed.

Published by Trotman

Price £32.99

Publication date May 2012

ESSENTIAL READING

Choosing Your Degree Course & University

With so many universities and courses to choose from, it is not an easy decision for students embarking on their journey to higher education. This guide will offer expert guidance on the questions students need to ask when considering the opportunities available.

Published by Trotman

Price £24.99

Publication date April 2012

Degree Course Descriptions

Providing details of the nature of degree courses, the descriptions in this book are written by heads of departments and senior lecturers at major universities. Each description contains an overview of the course area, details of course structures, career opportunities and more.

Published by COA

Price £12.99

Publication date September 2011

CHOOSING WHERE TO STUDY

The Virgin Guide to British Universities

An insider's guide to choosing a university or college. Written by students and using independent statistics, this guide evaluates what you get from a higher education institution.

Published by Virgin

Price £15.99

Publication date May 2011

Times Good University Guide 2013

How do you find the best university for the subject you wish to study? You need a guide that evaluates the quality of what is available, giving facts, figures and comparative assessments of universities. The rankings provide hard data, analysed, interpreted and presented by a team of experts.

Published by Harper Collins

Price £16.99

Publication date June 2012

A Parent's Guide to Graduate Jobs

A must-have guide for any parent who is worried about their child's job prospects when they graduate.

In this guide, the graduate careers guru, Paul Redmond, advises parents how to help their son or daughter:

- increase their employability
- boost their earning potential
- acquire essential work skills
- use their own contacts to get them ahead
- gain the right work experience.

Published by Trotman
Price £12.99
Publication date January 2012

Which Uni?

One person's perfect uni might be hell for someone else. Picking the right one will give you the best chance of future happiness, academic success and brighter job prospects. This guide is packed with tables from a variety of sources, rating universities on everything from the quality of teaching to the make-up of the student population and much more.

Published by Trotman
Price £14.99
Publication date September 2011

Getting into the UK's Best Universities and Courses

This book is for those who set their goals high and dream of studying on a highly regarded course at a good university. It provides information on selecting the best courses for a subject, the application and personal statement, interviews, results day, timescales for applications and much more.

Published by Trotman
Price £12.99
Publication date June 2011

FINANCIAL INFORMATION

Student Finance - e-book

All students need to know about tuition fees, loans, grants, bursaries and much more. Covering all forms of income and expenditure, this comprehensive guide is produced in association with UCAS and offers great value for money.

Published by Constable Robinson
Price £4.99
Publication date May 2012

CAREERS PLANNING

A-Z of Careers and Jobs

It is vital to be well informed about career decisions and this guide will help you make the right choice. It provides full details of the wide range of opportunities on the market, the personal qualities and skills needed for each job, entry qualifications and training, realistic salary expectations and useful contact details.

Published by Kogan Page
Price £16.99
Publication date March 2012

The Careers Directory

An indispensable resource for anyone seeking careers information, covering over 350 careers. It presents up-to-date information in an innovative double-page format. Ideal for students in years 10 to 13 who are considering their futures and for other careers professionals.

Published by COA
Price £14.99
Publication date September 2011

Careers with a Science Degree

Over 100 jobs and areas of work for graduates of biological, chemical and physical sciences are described in this guide.

Whether you have yet to choose your degree subject and want to know where the various choices could lead, or are struggling for ideas about what to do with your science degree, this book will guide and inspire you. The title includes: nature of the work and potential employers, qualifications required for entry, including personal qualities and skills; training routes and opportunities for career development and postgraduate study options.
Published by Lifetime Publishing
Price £12.99
Publication date September 2010

Careers with an Arts and Humanities Degree

Covers careers and graduate opportunities related to these degrees.

The book describes over 100 jobs and areas of work suitable for graduates from a range of disciplines including: English and modern languages, history and geography, music and the fine arts. The guide highlights: graduate opportunities, training routes, postgraduate study options and entry requirements.
Published by Lifetime Publishing
Price £12.99
Publication date September 2010

'Getting into…' guides

Clear and concise guides to help applicants secure places. They include qualifications required, advice on applying, tests, interviews and case studies. The guides give an honest view and discuss current issues and careers.

Getting into Oxford and Cambridge
Publication date April 2011
Getting into Veterinary School
Publication date February 2011
Published by Trotman
Price £12.99 each

DEFERRING ENTRY

Gap Years: The Essential Guide

The essential book for all young people planning a gap year before continuing with their education. This up-to-date guide provides essential information on specialist gap year programmes, as well as the vast range of jobs and voluntary opportunities available to young people around the world.
Published by Crimson Publishing
Price £9.99
Publication date April 2012

Gap Year Guidebook 2012

This thorough and easy-to-use guide contains everything you need to know before taking a gap year. It includes real-life traveller tips, hundreds of contact details, realistic advice on everything from preparing, learning and working abroad, coping with coming home and much more.
Published by John Catt Education
Price £14.99
Publication date November 2011

Summer Jobs Worldwide 2012

This unique and specialist guide contains over 40,000 jobs for all ages. No other book includes such a variety and wealth of summer work opportunities in Britain and aboard. Anything from horse trainer in Iceland, to a guide for nature walks in Peru, to a yoga centre helper in Greece, to an animal keeper for London Zoo, can be found.

Published by Crimson Publishing

Price £14.99

Publication date November 2011

Please note all publications incur a postage and packing charge. All information was correct at the time of printing.

For a full list of publications, please visit **www.ucasbooks.com**.

Courses

Courses

Keen to get started on your career in economics, finance or accountancy? This section contains details of the various courses available at UK institutions.

EXPLAINING THE LIST OF COURSES

The list of courses has been divided into subject categories (see page 132). We list the universities and colleges by their UCAS institution codes. Within each institution, courses are listed first by award type (such as BA, BSc, FdA, HND, MA and many others), then alphabetically by course title.

You might find some courses showing an award type '(Mod)', which indicates a combined degree that might be modular in design. A small number of courses have award type '(FYr)'. This indicates a 12-month foundation course, after which students can choose to apply for a degree course. In either case, you should contact the university or college for further details.

Generally speaking, when a course comprises two or more subjects, the word used to connect the subjects indicates the make-up of the award: 'Subject A and Subject B' is a joint award, where both subjects carry equal weight; 'Subject A with Subject B' is a major/minor award, where Subject A accounts for at least 60% of your study. If the title shows 'Subject A/Subject B', it may indicate that students can decide on the weighting of the subjects at the end of the first year. You should check with the university or college for full details.

Each entry shows the UCAS course code and the duration of the course. Where known, the entry contains details of the minimum qualification requirements for the course, as supplied to UCAS by the universities and colleges. Bear in mind that possessing the minimum qualifications does not guarantee acceptance to the course: there may be far more applicants than places. You may be asked to attend an interview, present a portfolio or sit an admissions test.

Courses with entry requirements that require applicants to disclose information about spent and unspent convictions and may require a Criminal Records Bureau (CRB) check, are marked '**CRB Check:** Required'.

Before applying for any course, you are advised to contact the university or college to check any changes in entry requirements and to see if any new courses have come on stream since the data was approved for publication. To make this easy, each institution's entry starts with their address, email, phone and fax details, as well as their website address.

LIST OF SUBJECT CATEGORIES

The list of courses in this section has been divided into the following subject categories

Economics	135
Finance	148
Accountancy	156
Economics and accountancy/accountancy and economics	166
Finance and economics/economics and finance	171
Accountancy and finance/finance and accountancy	175
Banking combinations	185
Business combinations	187
Computing and computer science combinations	198
Geography and geology combinations	202
Language combinations	202
Law combinations	213
Management combinations	218
Marketing combinations	227
Mathematics and statistics combinations	230
Politics combinations	240
Science combinations	248
Sociology and social science combinations	252
Economics and other combinations	256
Finance and other combinations	265
Accountancy and other combinations	268

ECONOMICS

A20 THE UNIVERSITY OF ABERDEEN
UNIVERSITY OFFICE
KING'S COLLEGE
ABERDEEN AB24 3FX
t: +44 (0) 1224 273504 f: +44 (0) 1224 272034
e: sras@abdn.ac.uk
// www.abdn.ac.uk/sras

L100 MA Economics
Duration: 4FT Hon
Entry Requirements: *GCE:* BBB. *SQAH:* BBBB. *IB:* 30.

A40 ABERYSTWYTH UNIVERSITY
ABERYSTWYTH UNIVERSITY, WELCOME CENTRE
PENGLAIS CAMPUS
ABERYSTWYTH
CEREDIGION SY23 3FB
t: 01970 622021 f: 01970 627410
e: ug-admissions@aber.ac.uk
// www.aber.ac.uk

L113 BScEcon Business Economics
Duration: 3FT Hon
Entry Requirements: *GCE:* 300. *IB:* 27.

L100 BScEcon Economics
Duration: 3FT Hon
Entry Requirements: *GCE:* 300. *IB:* 30.

A60 ANGLIA RUSKIN UNIVERSITY
BISHOP HALL LANE
CHELMSFORD
ESSEX CM1 1SQ
t: 0845 271 3333 f: 01245 251789
e: answers@anglia.ac.uk
// www.anglia.ac.uk

L100 BSc Business Economics
Duration: 3FT Hon
Entry Requirements: *GCE:* 200-240. *IB:* 24. *OCR ND:* D *OCR NED:* M3

B06 BANGOR UNIVERSITY
BANGOR UNIVERSITY
BANGOR
GWYNEDD LL57 2DG
t: 01248 388484 f: 01248 370451
e: admissions@bangor.ac.uk
// www.bangor.ac.uk

L114 BA Business Economics
Duration: 3FT Hon
Entry Requirements: *GCE:* 260-300. *IB:* 28.

L190 BSc Business Economics
Duration: 3FT Hon
Entry Requirements: *GCE:* 260-300. *IB:* 28.

L111 BSc Financial Economics
Duration: 3FT Hon
Entry Requirements: Contact the institution for details.

B16 UNIVERSITY OF BATH
CLAVERTON DOWN
BATH BA2 7AY
t: 01225 383019 f: 01225 386366
e: admissions@bath.ac.uk
// www.bath.ac.uk

L100 BSc Economics
Duration: 3FT Hon
Entry Requirements: *GCE:* A*AA. *SQAAH:* AAB. *IB:* 38.

L101 BSc Economics (Sandwich)
Duration: 4SW Hon
Entry Requirements: *GCE:* A*AA. *SQAAH:* AAB. *IB:* 38.

B24 BIRKBECK, UNIVERSITY OF LONDON
MALET STREET
LONDON WC1E 7HX
t: 020 7631 6316
e: webform: www.bbk.ac.uk/ask
// www.bbk.ac.uk/ask

L111 BSc Financial Economics
Duration: 3FT Hon
Entry Requirements: *GCE:* AAB. *SQAH:* AAAA-AABB. *IB:* 36.
Admissions Test required.

B32 THE UNIVERSITY OF BIRMINGHAM
EDGBASTON
BIRMINGHAM B15 2TT
t: 0121 415 8900 f: 0121 414 7159
e: admissions@bham.ac.uk
// www.birmingham.ac.uk

L150 BA Political Economy
Duration: 3FT Hon
Entry Requirements: *GCE:* AAA-AAB. *SQAH:* AAABB-AABBB. *SQAAH:* AA.

L100 BSc Economics
Duration: 3FT Hon
Entry Requirements: *GCE:* AAA. *SQAH:* AAABB. *SQAAH:* AA.

B50 BOURNEMOUTH UNIVERSITY
TALBOT CAMPUS
FERN BARROW
POOLE
DORSET BH12 5BB
t: 01202 524111
// www.bournemouth.ac.uk

L100 BA Economics
Duration: 3FT/4SW Hon
Entry Requirements: *GCE:* 320. *IB:* 32. *BTEC SubDip:* D. *BTEC Dip:* DD. *BTEC ExtDip:* DDM.

B56 THE UNIVERSITY OF BRADFORD
RICHMOND ROAD
BRADFORD
WEST YORKSHIRE BD7 1DP
t: 0800 073 1225 f: 01274 235585
e: course-enquiries@bradford.ac.uk
// www.bradford.ac.uk

L161 BA Global Trade and Finance
Duration: 1FT Hon
Entry Requirements: HND required.

L101 BSc Business Economics
Duration: 3FT Hon
Entry Requirements: GCE: 260-300. IB: 25.

L100 BSc Economics
Duration: 3FT Hon
Entry Requirements: GCE: 260-300. IB: 25.

L111 BSc Financial Economics
Duration: 3FT Hon
Entry Requirements: GCE: 260-300. IB: 25.

B78 UNIVERSITY OF BRISTOL
UNDERGRADUATE ADMISSIONS OFFICE
SENATE HOUSE
TYNDALL AVENUE
BRISTOL BS8 1TH
t: 0117 928 9000 f: 0117 331 7391
e: ug-admissions@bristol.ac.uk
// www.bristol.ac.uk

L100 BSc Economics
Duration: 3FT Hon
Entry Requirements: GCE: A*AA-AAA. SQAH: AAAA. SQAAH: AA.
IB: 38.

L140 BSc Economics and Econometrics
Duration: 3FT Hon
Entry Requirements: GCE: A*AA-AAA. SQAH: AAAA. SQAAH: AA.
IB: 38.

L101 BSc Economics with Study in Continental Europe (4 years)
Duration: 4FT Hon
Entry Requirements: GCE: A*AA-AAA. SQAH: AAAA. SQAAH: AA.
IB: 38.

B80 UNIVERSITY OF THE WEST OF ENGLAND, BRISTOL
FRENCHAY CAMPUS
COLDHARBOUR LANE
BRISTOL BS16 1QY
t: +44 (0)117 32 83333 f: +44 (0)117 32 82810
e: admissions@uwe.ac.uk
// www.uwe.ac.uk

L100 BA Economics
Duration: 3FT/4SW Hon
Entry Requirements: GCE: 300.

B84 BRUNEL UNIVERSITY
UXBRIDGE
MIDDLESEX UB8 3PH
t: 01895 265265 f: 01895 269790
e: admissions@brunel.ac.uk
// www.brunel.ac.uk

L101 BSc Economics
Duration: 3FT Hon
Entry Requirements: GCE: ABB. SQAAH: ABB. IB: 33. BTEC
ExtDip: D*DD.

L106 BSc Economics (4 year Thick SW)
Duration: 4SW Hon
Entry Requirements: GCE: ABB. SQAAH: ABB. IB: 33. BTEC
ExtDip: D*DD.

B90 THE UNIVERSITY OF BUCKINGHAM
YEOMANRY HOUSE
HUNTER STREET
BUCKINGHAM MK18 1EG
t: 01280 820313 f: 01280 822245
e: info@buckingham.ac.uk
// www.buckingham.ac.uk

L112 BScEcon Business Economics
Duration: 2FT Hon
Entry Requirements: GCE: BBB. SQAH: ABBB. SQAAH: BBB. IB: 34.

L100 BScEcon Economics
Duration: 2FT/3FT Hon
Entry Requirements: GCE: BBB. SQAH: ABBB. SQAAH: BBB. IB: 34.

C05 UNIVERSITY OF CAMBRIDGE
CAMBRIDGE ADMISSIONS OFFICE
FITZWILLIAM HOUSE
32 TRUMPINGTON STREET
CAMBRIDGE CB2 1QY
t: 01223 333 308 f: 01223 746 868
e: admissions@cam.ac.uk
// www.study.cam.ac.uk/undergraduate/

L100 BA Economics
Duration: 3FT Hon
Entry Requirements: GCE: A*AA. SQAAH: AAA-AAB. Interview required.

C15 CARDIFF UNIVERSITY
PO BOX 927
30-36 NEWPORT ROAD
CARDIFF CF24 0DE
t: 029 2087 9999 f: 029 2087 6138
e: admissions@cardiff.ac.uk
// www.cardiff.ac.uk

L160 BSc Economics with a European Language (French)
Duration: 4FT Hon
Entry Requirements: *GCE:* AAB. *SQAH:* AAABB. *SQAAH:* AAB. *IB:* 35. *OCR NED:* D1 Interview required.

L114 BScEcon Business Economics
Duration: 3FT Hon
Entry Requirements: *GCE:* AAB. *SQAH:* AAABB. *SQAAH:* AAB. *IB:* 35. *OCR NED:* D1 Interview required.

L100 BScEcon Economics
Duration: 3FT Hon
Entry Requirements: *GCE:* AAB. *SQAH:* AAABB. *SQAAH:* AAB. *IB:* 35. *OCR NED:* D1 Interview required.

C20 CARDIFF METROPOLITAN UNIVERSITY (UWIC)
ADMISSIONS UNIT
LLANDAFF CAMPUS
WESTERN AVENUE
CARDIFF CF5 2YB
t: 029 2041 6070 f: 029 2041 6286
e: admissions@cardiffmet.ac.uk
// www.cardiffmet.ac.uk

L101 BA Business Economics
Duration: 3FT/4SW Hon
Entry Requirements: *GCE:* 300. *IB:* 26. *BTEC ExtDip:* DDM. *OCR NED:* M1

L100 BSc Economics
Duration: 3FT/4SW Hon
Entry Requirements: *GCE:* 300. *IB:* 26. *BTEC ExtDip:* DDM. *OCR NED:* M1

C30 UNIVERSITY OF CENTRAL LANCASHIRE
PRESTON
LANCS PR1 2HE
t: 01772 201201 f: 01772 894954
e: uadmissions@uclan.ac.uk
// www.uclan.ac.uk

L110 BA Business Economics
Duration: 3FT Hon
Entry Requirements: *GCE:* 260-300. *SQAH:* AABB-BBBC. *IB:* 28. *OCR ND:* D

L100 BA Economics
Duration: 3FT Hon
Entry Requirements: *GCE:* 260-300. *SQAH:* AABB-BBBC. *IB:* 28. *OCR ND:* D

L101 BSc Economics
Duration: 3FT Hon
Entry Requirements: *GCE:* 260-300. *SQAH:* AABB-BBBC. *IB:* 28. *OCR ND:* D

C60 CITY UNIVERSITY
NORTHAMPTON SQUARE
LONDON EC1V 0HB
t: 020 7040 5060 f: 020 7040 8995
e: ugadmissions@city.ac.uk
// www.city.ac.uk

L100 BSc Economics
Duration: 3FT Hon
Entry Requirements: *GCE:* AAA. *SQAH:* BBBBC. *IB:* 35.

L111 BSc Financial Economics
Duration: 3FT Hon
Entry Requirements: *GCE:* AAA. *SQAH:* BBBBB. *IB:* 35.

L101 Cert International Foundation (Economics)
Duration: 1FT FYr
Entry Requirements: Contact the institution for details.

C85 COVENTRY UNIVERSITY
THE STUDENT CENTRE
COVENTRY UNIVERSITY
1 GULSON RD
COVENTRY CV1 2JH
t: 024 7615 2222 f: 024 7615 2223
e: studentenquiries@coventry.ac.uk
// www.coventry.ac.uk

L112 BA Business Economics
Duration: 3FT/4SW Hon
Entry Requirements: *GCE:* BBB. *SQAH:* BBBBC. *IB:* 30. *BTEC ExtDip:* DDM. *OCR NED:* M1

L100 BA Economics
Duration: 3FT/4SW Hon
Entry Requirements: *GCE:* BBB. *SQAH:* BBBBC. *IB:* 30. *BTEC ExtDip:* DDM. *OCR NED:* M1

L111 BA Financial Economics
Duration: 3FT/4SW Hon
Entry Requirements: *GCE:* BBB. *SQAH:* BBBBC. *IB:* 30. *BTEC ExtDip:* DDM. *OCR NED:* M1

D39 UNIVERSITY OF DERBY
KEDLESTON ROAD
DERBY DE22 1GB
t: 01332 591167 f: 01332 597724
e: askadmissions@derby.ac.uk
// www.derby.ac.uk

L160 BA International Business and Finance (top-up)
Duration: 1FT Hon
Entry Requirements: HND required.

D65 UNIVERSITY OF DUNDEE
NETHERGATE
DUNDEE DD1 4HN
t: 01382 383838 f: 01382 388150
e: contactus@dundee.ac.uk
// www.dundee.ac.uk/admissions/
undergraduate/

L101 BSc Economics
Duration: 4FT Hon
Entry Requirements: *GCE:* BCC. *SQAH:* ABBB. *IB:* 30.

L111 BSc Financial Economics
Duration: 4FT Hon
Entry Requirements: *GCE:* BCC. *SQAH:* ABBB. *IB:* 30.

L100 MA Economics
Duration: 4FT Hon
Entry Requirements: *GCE:* BCC. *SQAH:* ABBB. *IB:* 30.

L114 MA Financial Economics
Duration: 4FT Hon
Entry Requirements: *GCE:* BCC. *SQAH:* ABBB. *IB:* 30.

D86 DURHAM UNIVERSITY
DURHAM UNIVERSITY
UNIVERSITY OFFICE
DURHAM DH1 3HP
t: 0191 334 2000 f: 0191 334 6055
e: admissions@durham.ac.uk
// www.durham.ac.uk

L112 BA Business Economics
Duration: 3FT Hon
Entry Requirements: *GCE:* A*AA. *SQAH:* AAAAA. *SQAAH:* AAA. *IB:* 38.

L100 BA Economics
Duration: 3FT Hon
Entry Requirements: *GCE:* A*AA. *SQAH:* AAAAA. *SQAAH:* AAA. *IB:* 38.

E14 UNIVERSITY OF EAST ANGLIA
NORWICH NR4 7TJ
t: 01603 591515 f: 01603 591523
e: admissions@uea.ac.uk
// www.uea.ac.uk

L111 BSc Business Economics
Duration: 3FT Hon   CRB Check: Required
Entry Requirements: *GCE:* ABB. *SQAAH:* ABB. *IB:* 32. *BTEC ExtDip:* DDM. Interview required.

L100 BSc Economics
Duration: 3FT Hon   CRB Check: Required
Entry Requirements: *GCE:* ABB. *SQAAH:* ABB. *IB:* 32. *BTEC ExtDip:* DDM. Interview required.

E28 UNIVERSITY OF EAST LONDON
DOCKLANDS CAMPUS
UNIVERSITY WAY
LONDON E16 2RD
t: 020 8223 3333 f: 020 8223 2978
e: study@uel.ac.uk
// www.uel.ac.uk

L190 BSc Business Economics
Duration: 3FT Hon
Entry Requirements: *GCE:* 240. *IB:* 24.

E56 THE UNIVERSITY OF EDINBURGH
STUDENT RECRUITMENT & ADMISSIONS
57 GEORGE SQUARE
EDINBURGH EH8 9JU
t: 0131 650 4360 f: 0131 651 1236
e: sra.enquiries@ed.ac.uk
// www.ed.ac.uk/studying/undergraduate/

L100 MA Economics
Duration: 4FT Hon
Entry Requirements: *GCE:* AAA-BBB. *SQAH:* AAAA-BBBB. *IB:* 34.

E70 THE UNIVERSITY OF ESSEX
WIVENHOE PARK
COLCHESTER
ESSEX CO4 3SQ
t: 01206 873666 f: 01206 874477
e: admit@essex.ac.uk
// www.essex.ac.uk

L100 BA Economics
Duration: 3FT Hon
Entry Requirements: *GCE:* ABB. *SQAH:* AAAB.

L106 BA Economics (Including Year Abroad)
Duration: 4FT Hon
Entry Requirements: *GCE:* ABB. *SQAH:* AAAB.

L102 BA Economics (including Foundation Year)
Duration: 4FT Hon
Entry Requirements: *GCE:* 180. *SQAH:* CCCD. *IB:* 24.

L111 BA Financial Economics
Duration: 3FT Hon
Entry Requirements: *GCE:* ABB. *SQAH:* AAAB.

L118 BA Financial Economics (Including Foundation Year)
Duration: 4FT Hon
Entry Requirements: *GCE:* 180. *SQAH:* CCCD. *IB:* 24.

L195 BA Financial Economics (Including Year Abroad)
Duration: 4FT Hon
Entry Requirements: *GCE:* ABB. *SQAH:* AAAB.

L115 BA International Economics
Duration: 3FT Hon
Entry Requirements: *GCE:* ABB. *SQAH:* AAAB.

L160 BA International Economics (Including Foundation Year)
Duration: 4FT Hon
Entry Requirements: *GCE:* 180. *SQAH:* CCCD. *IB:* 24.

L163 BA International Economics (Including Year Abroad)
Duration: 4FT Hon
Entry Requirements: *GCE:* ABB. *SQAH:* AAAB.

L108 BA Management Economics
Duration: 3FT Hon
Entry Requirements: *GCE:* ABB. *SQAH:* AAAB.

L190 BA Management Economics (Including Foundation Year)
Duration: 4FT Hon
Entry Requirements: *GCE:* 180. *SQAH:* CCCD. *IB:* 24.

L192 BA Management Economics (Including Year Abroad)
Duration: 4FT Hon
Entry Requirements: *GCE:* ABB. *SQAH:* AAAB.

L101 BSc Economics
Duration: 3FT Hon
Entry Requirements: *GCE:* ABB. *SQAH:* AAAB.

L107 BSc Economics (Including Year Abroad)
Duration: 4FT Hon
Entry Requirements: *GCE:* ABB. *SQAH:* AAAB.

L103 BSc Economics (including Foundation Year)
Duration: 4FT Hon
Entry Requirements: *GCE:* 180. *SQAH:* CCCD. *IB:* 24.

L114 BSc Financial Economics
Duration: 3FT Hon
Entry Requirements: *GCE:* ABB. *SQAH:* AAAB.

L117 BSc Financial Economics (Including Foundation Year)
Duration: 4FT Hon
Entry Requirements: *GCE:* 180. *SQAH:* CCCD. *IB:* 24.

L194 BSc Financial Economics (Including Year Abroad)
Duration: 4FT Hon
Entry Requirements: *GCE:* ABB. *SQAH:* AAAB.

L116 BSc International Economics
Duration: 3FT Hon
Entry Requirements: *GCE:* ABB. *SQAH:* AAAB.

L161 BSc International Economics (Including Foundation Year)
Duration: 4FT Hon
Entry Requirements: *GCE:* 180. *SQAH:* CCCD. *IB:* 24.

L162 BSc International Economics (Including Year Abroad)
Duration: 4FT Hon
Entry Requirements: *GCE:* ABB. *SQAH:* AAAB.

L109 BSc Management Economics
Duration: 3FT Hon
Entry Requirements: *GCE:* ABB. *SQAH:* AAAB.

L191 BSc Management Economics (Including Foundation Year)
Duration: 4FT Hon
Entry Requirements: *GCE:* 180. *SQAH:* CCCD. *IB:* 24.

L193 BSc Management Economics (Including Year Abroad)
Duration: 4FT Hon
Entry Requirements: *GCE:* ABB. *SQAH:* AAAB.

E84 UNIVERSITY OF EXETER
LAVER BUILDING
NORTH PARK ROAD
EXETER
DEVON EX4 4QE
t: 01392 723044 f: 01392 722479
e: admissions@exeter.ac.uk
// www.exeter.ac.uk

L112 BA Business Economics
Duration: 3FT Hon
Entry Requirements: *GCE:* A*AA-AAB. *SQAH:* AAAAA-AAABB. *SQAAH:* AAA-ABB.

L115 BA Business Economics with European Study (4 years)
Duration: 4FT Hon
Entry Requirements: *GCE:* A*AA-AAB. *SQAH:* AAAAA-AAABB. *SQAAH:* AAA-ABB.

L192 BA Business Economics with Industrial Experience (4 years)
Duration: 4FT Hon
Entry Requirements: *GCE:* A*AA-AAB. *SQAH:* AAAAA-AAABB. *SQAAH:* AAA-ABB.

L194 BA Business Economics with International Study (4 years)
Duration: 4FT Hon
Entry Requirements: *GCE:* A*AA-AAB. *SQAH:* AAAAA-AAABB. *SQAAH:* AAA-ABB.

L100 BA Economics
Duration: 3FT Hon
Entry Requirements: *GCE:* A*AA-AAB. *SQAH:* AAAAA-AAABB. *SQAAH:* AAA-ABB.

L195 BA Economics with Econometrics with International Study (4 years)
Duration: 4FT Hon
Entry Requirements: *GCE:* A*AA-AAB. *SQAH:* AAAAA-AAABB. *SQAAH:* AAA-ABB.

L101 BA Economics with European Study (4 years)
Duration: 4FT Hon
Entry Requirements: *GCE:* A*AA-AAB. *SQAH:* AAAAA-AAABB. *SQAAH:* AAA-ABB.

L102 BA Economics with Industrial Experience (4 years)
Duration: 4FT Hon
Entry Requirements: *GCE:* A*AA-AAB. *SQAH:* AAAAA-AAABB. *SQAAH:* AAA-ABB.

L103 BA Economics with International Study (4 years)
Duration: 4FT Hon
Entry Requirements: *GCE:* A*AA-AAB. *SQAH:* AAAAA-AAABB. *SQAAH:* AAA-ABB.

G28 UNIVERSITY OF GLASGOW
71 SOUTHPARK AVENUE
UNIVERSITY OF GLASGOW
GLASGOW G12 8QQ
t: 0141 330 6062 f: 0141 330 2961
e: student.recruitment@glasgow.ac.uk
// www.glasgow.ac.uk

L112 MA Business Economics
Duration: 4FT Hon
Entry Requirements: *GCE:* ABB. *SQAH:* AAAA-AABB. *IB:* 36.

L150 MA Economics
Duration: 4FT Hon
Entry Requirements: *GCE:* ABB. *SQAH:* AAAA-AABB. *IB:* 36.

G70 UNIVERSITY OF GREENWICH
GREENWICH CAMPUS
OLD ROYAL NAVAL COLLEGE
PARK ROW
LONDON SE10 9LS
t: 020 8331 9000 f: 020 8331 8145
e: courseinfo@gre.ac.uk
// www.gre.ac.uk

L112 BA Business Economics
Duration: 3FT Hon
Entry Requirements: *GCE:* 260. *IB:* 24.

L100 BSc Economics
Duration: 3FT/4SW Hon
Entry Requirements: *GCE:* 280. *IB:* 24.

G74 GREENWICH SCHOOL OF MANAGEMENT
MERIDIAN HOUSE
ROYAL HILL
GREENWICH
LONDON SE10 8RD
t: +44(0)20 8516 7800 f: +44(0)20 8516 7801
e: admissions@greenwich-college.ac.uk
// www.greenwich-college.ac.uk/?utm_source=UCAS&utm_medium=Profil

L102 BSc Economics
Duration: 3FT Hon
Entry Requirements: *GCE:* 80-120. *SQAH:* A-B. *IB:* 24. *OCR ND:* P3 *OCR NED:* P3 Interview required.

L101 BSc Economics (Accelerated with Foundation Year)
Duration: 3FT Hon
Entry Requirements: *OCR ND:* P3 Interview required.

L100 BSc Economics (Accelerated)
Duration: 2FT Hon
Entry Requirements: *GCE:* 80-120. *SQAH:* A-B. *IB:* 24. *OCR ND:* P3 *OCR NED:* P3 Interview required.

L103 BSc Economics (with Foundation Year)
Duration: 4FT Hon
Entry Requirements: *OCR ND:* P3 Interview required.

H24 HERIOT-WATT UNIVERSITY, EDINBURGH
EDINBURGH CAMPUS
EDINBURGH EH14 4AS
t: 0131 449 5111 f: 0131 451 3630
e: ugadmissions@hw.ac.uk
// www.hw.ac.uk

L100 MA Economics
Duration: 4FT Hon
Entry Requirements: *GCE:* BBB. *SQAH:* AAAB-BBBBC. *SQAAH:* BB. *IB:* 29.

H36 UNIVERSITY OF HERTFORDSHIRE
UNIVERSITY ADMISSIONS SERVICE
COLLEGE LANE
HATFIELD
HERTS AL10 9AB
t: 01707 284800
// www.herts.ac.uk

L112 BA Business Economics
Duration: 3FT/4SW Hon
Entry Requirements: *GCE:* 260. *IB:* 26.

L101 BA Economics
Duration: 3FT/4SW Hon
Entry Requirements: *GCE:* 260. *IB:* 26.

H72 THE UNIVERSITY OF HULL
THE UNIVERSITY OF HULL
COTTINGHAM ROAD
HULL HU6 7RX
t: 01482 466100 f: 01482 442290
e: admissions@hull.ac.uk
// www.hull.ac.uk

L112 BA Business Economics
Duration: 3FT Hon
Entry Requirements: **GCE:** 300. **IB:** 30. **BTEC ExtDip:** DMM.

L160 BA Business Economics (International) (4 years)
Duration: 4FT Hon
Entry Requirements: **GCE:** 300. **IB:** 30. **BTEC ExtDip:** DMM.

L101 BA Business Economics (with Professional Experience) (4 years)
Duration: 4FT Hon
Entry Requirements: **GCE:** 300. **IB:** 30. **BTEC ExtDip:** DMM.

L100 BScEcon Economics
Duration: 3FT Hon
Entry Requirements: **GCE:** 320. **IB:** 30. **BTEC ExtDip:** DMM.

L161 BScEcon Economics (International) (4 years)
Duration: 4FT Hon
Entry Requirements: **GCE:** 320. **IB:** 30. **BTEC ExtDip:** DMM.

L102 BScEcon Economics (with Professional Experience) (4 years)
Duration: 4FT Hon
Entry Requirements: **GCE:** 320. **IB:** 30. **BTEC ExtDip:** DMM.

K24 THE UNIVERSITY OF KENT
RECRUITMENT & ADMISSIONS OFFICE
REGISTRY
UNIVERSITY OF KENT
CANTERBURY, KENT CT2 7NZ
t: 01227 827272 f: 01227 827077
e: information@kent.ac.uk
// www.kent.ac.uk

L100 BSc Economics
Duration: 3FT Hon
Entry Requirements: **GCE:** ABB. **SQAH:** AABBB. **SQAAH:** ABB. **IB:** 33. **OCR ND:** D **OCR NED:** D2

L141 BSc Economics with Econometrics
Duration: 3FT Hon
Entry Requirements: **GCE:** ABB. **SQAH:** AABBB. **SQAAH:** ABB. **IB:** 33. **OCR ND:** M1 **OCR NED:** M3

L102 BSc Economics with a Year in Industry
Duration: 4SW Hon
Entry Requirements: **GCE:** ABB. **SQAH:** AABBB. **SQAAH:** ABB. **IB:** 33. **OCR ND:** D **OCR NED:** D2

L171 BSc European Economics (4 years)
Duration: 4FT Hon
Entry Requirements: **GCE:** ABB. **SQAH:** AABBB. **SQAAH:** ABB. **IB:** 33. **OCR ND:** D **OCR NED:** D2

L176 BSc European Economics (French) (4 years)
Duration: 4FT Hon
Entry Requirements: **GCE:** ABB. **SQAH:** AABBB. **SQAAH:** ABB. **IB:** 33. **OCR ND:** D **OCR NED:** D2

L174 BSc European Economics (German) (4 years)
Duration: 4FT Hon
Entry Requirements: **GCE:** ABB. **SQAH:** AABBB. **SQAAH:** ABB. **IB:** 33. **OCR ND:** M1 **OCR NED:** M3

L177 BSc European Economics (Spanish) (4 years)
Duration: 4FT Hon
Entry Requirements: **GCE:** ABB. **SQAH:** AABBB. **SQAAH:** ABB. **IB:** 33. **OCR ND:** D **OCR NED:** D2

L111 BSc Financial Economics
Duration: 3FT Hon
Entry Requirements: **GCE:** ABB. **SQAH:** AABBB. **SQAAH:** ABB. **IB:** 33. **OCR ND:** D **OCR NED:** D2

L142 BSc Financial Economics (with Econometrics)
Duration: 3FT Hon
Entry Requirements: **GCE:** ABB. **SQAH:** AABBB. **SQAAH:** ABB. **IB:** 33. **OCR ND:** M1 **OCR NED:** M3

K84 KINGSTON UNIVERSITY
STUDENT INFORMATION & ADVICE CENTRE
COOPER HOUSE
40-46 SURBITON ROAD
KINGSTON UPON THAMES KT1 2HX
t: 0844 8552177 f: 020 8547 7080
e: aps@kingston.ac.uk
// www.kingston.ac.uk

L110 BA Applied Economics
Duration: 3FT Hon
Entry Requirements: **GCE:** 260.

L100 BSc Economics
Duration: 3FT Hon
Entry Requirements: **GCE:** 260. **IB:** 24.

L111 BSc Financial Economics
Duration: 3FT Hon
Entry Requirements: **GCE:** 280. **IB:** 30.

L14 LANCASTER UNIVERSITY
THE UNIVERSITY
LANCASTER
LANCASHIRE LA1 4YW
t: 01524 592029 f: 01524 846243
e: ugadmissions@lancaster.ac.uk
// www.lancs.ac.uk

L102 BA Business Economics
Duration: 3FT Hon
Entry Requirements: *GCE:* AAB. *SQAH:* ABBBB. *SQAAH:* AAB. *IB:* 35.

L103 BA Business Economics (Study Abroad)
Duration: 3FT Hon
Entry Requirements: *GCE:* AAA. *SQAH:* AAABB. *SQAAH:* AAA. *IB:* 36.

L100 BSc Economics
Duration: 3FT Hon
Entry Requirements: *GCE:* AAB. *SQAH:* ABBBB. *SQAAH:* AAB. *IB:* 35.

L101 BSc Economics (Study Abroad)
Duration: 3FT Hon
Entry Requirements: *GCE:* AAA. *SQAH:* AAABB. *SQAAH:* AAA. *IB:* 36.

L23 UNIVERSITY OF LEEDS
THE UNIVERSITY OF LEEDS
WOODHOUSE LANE
LEEDS LS2 9JT
t: 0113 343 3999
e: admissions@leeds.ac.uk
// www.leeds.ac.uk

L112 BSc Business Economics
Duration: 3FT Hon
Entry Requirements: *GCE:* AAA. *SQAH:* AAAAA. *SQAAH:* AAA. *IB:* 36. Interview required.

L100 BSc Economics
Duration: 3FT Hon
Entry Requirements: *GCE:* AAA. *SQAH:* AAAAA. *SQAAH:* AAA. *IB:* 36. Interview required.

L27 LEEDS METROPOLITAN UNIVERSITY
COURSE ENQUIRIES OFFICE
CITY CAMPUS
LEEDS LS1 3HE
t: 0113 81 23113 f: 0113 81 23129
// www.leedsmet.ac.uk

L110 BA Economics for Business
Duration: 3FT/4SW Hon
Entry Requirements: *GCE:* 240. *IB:* 24.

L34 UNIVERSITY OF LEICESTER
UNIVERSITY ROAD
LEICESTER LE1 7RH
t: 0116 252 5281 f: 0116 252 2447
e: admissions@le.ac.uk
// www.le.ac.uk

L112 BA Business Economics
Duration: 3FT Hon
Entry Requirements: *GCE:* AAB. *SQAH:* AAAAB-AAABB. *SQAAH:* AAB. *IB:* 34.

L100 BA Economics
Duration: 3FT Hon
Entry Requirements: *GCE:* AAB. *SQAH:* AAAAB-AAABB. *SQAAH:* AAB. *IB:* 34.

L111 BA Financial Economics
Duration: 3FT Hon
Entry Requirements: *GCE:* AAB. *SQAH:* AAAAB-AAABB. *SQAAH:* AAB. *IB:* 34.

L115 BSc Financial Economics
Duration: 3FT Hon
Entry Requirements: *GCE:* AAB. *SQAH:* AAAAB-AAABB. *SQAAH:* AAB. *IB:* 34.

L113 BScEcon Business Economics
Duration: 3FT Hon
Entry Requirements: *GCE:* AAB. *SQAH:* AAAAB-AAABB. *SQAAH:* AAB. *IB:* 34.

L102 BScEcon Economics
Duration: 3FT Hon
Entry Requirements: *GCE:* AAB. *SQAH:* AAAAB-AAABB. *SQAAH:* AAB. *IB:* 34.

L41 THE UNIVERSITY OF LIVERPOOL
THE FOUNDATION BUILDING
BROWNLOW HILL
LIVERPOOL L69 7ZX
t: 0151 794 2000 f: 0151 708 6502
e: ugrecruitment@liv.ac.uk
// www.liv.ac.uk

L100 BSc Economics
Duration: 3FT Hon
Entry Requirements: *GCE:* AAB. *SQAH:* AAABB. *SQAAH:* AAB. *IB:* 35.

L68 LONDON METROPOLITAN UNIVERSITY
166-220 HOLLOWAY ROAD
LONDON N7 8DB
t: 020 7133 4200
e: admissions@londonmet.ac.uk
// www.londonmet.ac.uk

L103 BA Business Economics
Duration: 3FT Hon
Entry Requirements: *GCE:* 240. *IB:* 28.

L100 BA Economics
Duration: 3FT Hon
Entry Requirements: **GCE:** 240. **IB:** 28.

L102 BSc Business Economics and Finance
Duration: 3FT Hon
Entry Requirements: **GCE:** 240. **IB:** 28.

L72 LONDON SCHOOL OF ECONOMICS AND POLITICAL SCIENCE (UNIVERSITY OF LONDON)
HOUGHTON STREET
LONDON WC2A 2AE
t: 020 7955 7125 f: 020 7955 6001
e: ug.admissions@lse.ac.uk
// www.lse.ac.uk

L140 BSc Econometrics & Mathematical Economics
Duration: 3FT Hon
Entry Requirements: **GCE:** A*AA. **SQAH:** AAAAA. **SQAAH:** AAA. **IB:** 38.

L101 BSc Economics
Duration: 3FT Hon
Entry Requirements: **GCE:** A*AA. **SQAH:** AAAAA. **SQAAH:** AAA. **IB:** 38.

L79 LOUGHBOROUGH UNIVERSITY
LOUGHBOROUGH
LEICESTERSHIRE LE11 3TU
t: 01509 223522 f: 01509 223905
e: admissions@lboro.ac.uk
// www.lboro.ac.uk

L100 BSc Economics
Duration: 3FT Hon
Entry Requirements: **GCE:** AAB. **SQAH:** AABBB. **SQAAH:** AB. **IB:** 34. **BTEC ExtDip:** DDD.

L115 BSc International Economics
Duration: 3FT Hon
Entry Requirements: **GCE:** AAB. **SQAH:** AABBB. **SQAAH:** AB. **IB:** 34. **BTEC ExtDip:** DDD.

M20 THE UNIVERSITY OF MANCHESTER
RUTHERFORD BUILDING
OXFORD ROAD
MANCHESTER M13 9PL
t: 0161 275 2077 f: 0161 275 2106
e: ug-admissions@manchester.ac.uk
// www.manchester.ac.uk

L100 BAEcon Economics
Duration: 3FT Hon
Entry Requirements: **GCE:** AAB. **SQAH:** AAABB. **SQAAH:** AAB. **IB:** 35.

L102 BEconSc Economics
Duration: 3FT Hon
Entry Requirements: **GCE:** AAA. **SQAH:** AAAAA. **SQAAH:** AAA. **IB:** 36.

M40 THE MANCHESTER METROPOLITAN UNIVERSITY
ADMISSIONS OFFICE
ALL SAINTS (GMS)
ALL SAINTS
MANCHESTER M15 6BH
t: 0161 247 2000
// www.mmu.ac.uk

L112 BA Business Economics
Duration: 3FT Hon
Entry Requirements: **IB:** 29.

L114 BA Business Economics (Foundation)
Duration: 4FT Hon
Entry Requirements: **GCE:** 160. **IB:** 24. **BTEC Dip:** MM. **BTEC ExtDip:** MPP.

L100 BA Economics
Duration: 3FT Hon
Entry Requirements: **IB:** 29.

M80 MIDDLESEX UNIVERSITY
MIDDLESEX UNIVERSITY
THE BURROUGHS
LONDON NW4 4BT
t: 020 8411 5555 f: 020 8411 5649
e: enquiries@mdx.ac.uk
// www.mdx.ac.uk

L110 BSc Business Economics
Duration: 3FT/4SW Hon
Entry Requirements: **GCE:** 200-300. **IB:** 28.

N21 NEWCASTLE UNIVERSITY
KING'S GATE
NEWCASTLE UPON TYNE NE1 7RU
t: 01912083333
// www.ncl.ac.uk

L100 BSc Economics
Duration: 3FT Hon
Entry Requirements: **GCE:** AAB. **SQAH:** AAABB. **IB:** 35. **BTEC ExtDip:** DDD.

L161 BSc Financial and Business Economics
Duration: 3FT Hon
Entry Requirements: **GCE:** AAB. **SQAH:** AAABB. **IB:** 35. **BTEC ExtDip:** DDD.

N38 UNIVERSITY OF NORTHAMPTON
PARK CAMPUS
BOUGHTON GREEN ROAD
NORTHAMPTON NN2 7AL
t: 0800 358 2232 f: 01604 722083
e: admissions@northampton.ac.uk
// www.northampton.ac.uk

L101 BA Economics
Duration: 3FT Hon
Entry Requirements: *GCE:* 260-300. *SQAH:* ABBB. *IB:* 25. *BTEC Dip:* DD. *BTEC ExtDip:* DMM. *OCR ND:* D *OCR NED:* M2

N84 THE UNIVERSITY OF NOTTINGHAM
THE ADMISSIONS OFFICE
THE UNIVERSITY OF NOTTINGHAM
UNIVERSITY PARK
NOTTINGHAM NG7 2RD
t: 0115 951 5151 f: 0115 951 4668
// www.nottingham.ac.uk

L1N2 BA Industrial Economics
Duration: 3FT Hon
Entry Requirements: *GCE:* AAB. *SQAAH:* AAB. *IB:* 34.

L1N3 BA Industrial Economics with Insurance
Duration: 3FT Hon
Entry Requirements: *GCE:* AAB. *SQAAH:* AAB. *IB:* 34.

L100 BA/BSc Economics
Duration: 3FT Hon
Entry Requirements: *GCE:* A*AA-AABB. *SQAAH:* AAA. *IB:* 38.

L140 BSc Economics and Econometrics
Duration: 3FT Hon
Entry Requirements: *GCE:* A*AA-AABB. *SQAAH:* AAA. *IB:* 38.

N91 NOTTINGHAM TRENT UNIVERSITY
DRYDEN BUILDING
BURTON STREET
NOTTINGHAM NG1 4BU
t: +44 (0) 115 848 4200 f: +44 (0) 115 848 8869
e: applications@ntu.ac.uk
// www.ntu.ac.uk

L101 BA Business Economics
Duration: 3FT Hon
Entry Requirements: *GCE:* 300. *BTEC ExtDip:* DDM. *OCR NED:* D2

L110 BA Business Economics
Duration: 4SW Hon
Entry Requirements: *GCE:* 300. *BTEC ExtDip:* DDM. *OCR NED:* D2

L100 BA Economics
Duration: 3FT Hon
Entry Requirements: *GCE:* 300. *BTEC ExtDip:* DDM. *OCR NED:* D2

L10C BA Economics
Duration: 4SW Hon
Entry Requirements: *GCE:* 300. *BTEC ExtDip:* DDM. *OCR NED:* D2

P60 PLYMOUTH UNIVERSITY
DRAKE CIRCUS
PLYMOUTH PL4 8AA
t: 01752 585858 f: 01752 588055
e: admissions@plymouth.ac.uk
// www.plymouth.ac.uk

L112 BSc Business Economics
Duration: 3FT/4SW Hon
Entry Requirements: *GCE:* 240. *IB:* 24.

L101 BSc Economics
Duration: 3FT/4SW Hon
Entry Requirements: *GCE:* 240. *IB:* 24.

L111 BSc Financial Economics
Duration: 3FT/4SW Hon
Entry Requirements: *GCE:* 240. *IB:* 24.

L160 BSc International Business Economics
Duration: 3FT/4SW Hon
Entry Requirements: *GCE:* 240. *IB:* 24.

P80 UNIVERSITY OF PORTSMOUTH
ACADEMIC REGISTRY
UNIVERSITY HOUSE
WINSTON CHURCHILL AVENUE
PORTSMOUTH PO1 2UP
t: 023 9284 8484 f: 023 9284 3082
e: admissions@port.ac.uk
// www.port.ac.uk

L112 BSc Business Economics
Duration: 3FT/4SW Hon
Entry Requirements: *GCE:* 260-300. *IB:* 27. *BTEC Dip:* D*D. *BTEC ExtDip:* DMM.

L100 BSc Economics
Duration: 3FT/4SW Hon
Entry Requirements: *GCE:* 280-320. *IB:* 28. *BTEC Dip:* D*D*. *BTEC ExtDip:* DMM.

Q50 QUEEN MARY, UNIVERSITY OF LONDON
QUEEN MARY, UNIVERSITY OF LONDON
MILE END ROAD
LONDON E1 4NS
t: 020 7882 5555 f: 020 7882 5500
e: admissions@qmul.ac.uk
// www.qmul.ac.uk

L100 BScEcon Economics
Duration: 3FT Hon
Entry Requirements: *GCE:* AAB. *SQAAH:* AAB. *IB:* 36.

Q75 QUEEN'S UNIVERSITY BELFAST
UNIVERSITY ROAD
BELFAST BT7 1NN
t: 028 9097 3838 f: 028 9097 5151
e: admissions@qub.ac.uk
// www.qub.ac.uk

L110 BSc Business Economics
Duration: 3FT Hon
Entry Requirements: *GCE:* ABB-BBBb. *SQAH:* ABBBB. *SQAAH:* ABB. *IB:* 33.

L100 BSc Economics
Duration: 3FT Hon
Entry Requirements: *GCE:* ABB-BBBb. *SQAH:* ABBBB. *SQAAH:* ABB. *IB:* 33.

R12 THE UNIVERSITY OF READING
THE UNIVERSITY OF READING
PO BOX 217
READING RG6 6AH
t: 0118 378 8619 f: 0118 378 8924
e: student.recruitment@reading.ac.uk
// www.reading.ac.uk

L114 BA Business Economics
Duration: 3FT Hon
Entry Requirements: *GCE:* ABB. *SQAH:* ABBBB. *SQAAH:* ABB. *BTEC Dip:* DM. *BTEC ExtDip:* DDM.

L101 BA Economics
Duration: 3FT Hon
Entry Requirements: *GCE:* ABB. *SQAH:* ABBBB. *SQAAH:* ABB. *BTEC Dip:* DM. *BTEC ExtDip:* DDM.

L113 BSc Business Economics
Duration: 3FT Hon
Entry Requirements: *GCE:* ABB. *SQAH:* ABBBB. *SQAAH:* ABB. *BTEC Dip:* DM. *BTEC ExtDip:* DDM.

L100 BSc Economics
Duration: 3FT Hon
Entry Requirements: *GCE:* ABB. *SQAH:* ABBBB. *SQAAH:* ABB. *BTEC Dip:* DM. *BTEC ExtDip:* DDM.

L140 BSc Economics and Econometrics
Duration: 3FT Hon
Entry Requirements: *GCE:* ABB. *SQAH:* ABBBB. *SQAAH:* ABB. *BTEC Dip:* DM. *BTEC ExtDip:* DDM.

R20 RICHMOND, THE AMERICAN INTERNATIONAL UNIVERSITY IN LONDON
QUEENS ROAD
RICHMOND
SURREY TW10 6JP
t: 020 8332 9000 f: 020 8332 1596
e: enroll@richmond.ac.uk
// www.richmond.ac.uk

L100 BA Economics
Duration: 3FT/4FT Hon
Entry Requirements: *GCE:* 260. *IB:* 33.

L101 BA International and Development Economics
Duration: 3FT/4FT Hon
Entry Requirements: Contact the institution for details.

R48 ROEHAMPTON UNIVERSITY
ROEHAMPTON LANE
LONDON SW15 5PU
t: 020 8392 3232 f: 020 8392 3470
e: enquiries@roehampton.ac.uk
// www.roehampton.ac.uk

L100 BSc Business Management and Economics
Duration: 3FT Hon
Entry Requirements: *GCE:* 320. *IB:* 27. *BTEC ExtDip:* DDM. *OCR NED:* D2 Interview required.

R72 ROYAL HOLLOWAY, UNIVERSITY OF LONDON
ROYAL HOLLOWAY, UNIVERSITY OF LONDON
EGHAM
SURREY TW20 0EX
t: 01784 414944 f: 01784 473662
e: Admissions@rhul.ac.uk
// www.rhul.ac.uk

L101 BSc Economics
Duration: 3FT Hon
Entry Requirements: *GCE:* AAA-ABB. *SQAH:* AAAAA-AABBB. *SQAAH:* AAA-ABB. *IB:* 32.

L111 BSc Financial and Business Economics
Duration: 3FT Hon
Entry Requirements: *GCE:* AAA-ABB. *SQAH:* AAAAA-AABBB. *SQAAH:* AAA-ABB. *IB:* 32.

S09 SCHOOL OF ORIENTAL AND AFRICAN STUDIES (UNIVERSITY OF LONDON)
THORNHAUGH STREET
RUSSELL SQUARE
LONDON WC1H 0XG
t: 020 7898 4301 f: 020 7898 4039
e: undergradadmissions@soas.ac.uk
// www.soas.ac.uk

L170 BSc Development Economics
Duration: 3FT Hon
Entry Requirements: *GCE:* AAA.

L100 BSc Economics
Duration: 3FT Hon
Entry Requirements: *GCE:* AAA.

S18 THE UNIVERSITY OF SHEFFIELD
THE UNIVERSITY OF SHEFFIELD
LEVEL 2, ARTS TOWER
WESTERN BANK
SHEFFIELD S10 2TN
t: 0114 222 8030 f: 0114 222 8032
// www.sheffield.ac.uk

L100 BA Economics
Duration: 3FT Hon
Entry Requirements: *GCE:* AAB. *SQAH:* AAABB. *SQAAH:* AB. *IB:* 35. *BTEC ExtDip:* DDD.

L101 BSc Economics
Duration: 3FT Hon
Entry Requirements: *GCE:* AAB. *SQAH:* AAABB. *SQAAH:* AB. *IB:* 35. *BTEC Dip:* DD. *BTEC ExtDip:* DDD.

S21 SHEFFIELD HALLAM UNIVERSITY
CITY CAMPUS
HOWARD STREET
SHEFFIELD S1 1WB
t: 0114 225 5555 f: 0114 225 2167
e: admissions@shu.ac.uk
// www.shu.ac.uk

L100 BA Business Economics
Duration: 3FT/4SW Hon
Entry Requirements: *GCE:* 300.

S27 UNIVERSITY OF SOUTHAMPTON
HIGHFIELD
SOUTHAMPTON SO17 1BJ
t: 023 8059 4732 f: 023 8059 3037
e: admissions@soton.ac.uk
// www.southampton.ac.uk

L100 BSc Economics
Duration: 3FT Hon
Entry Requirements: *GCE:* AAA-AABB. *SQAH:* AAAA. *SQAAH:* AA. *IB:* 36.

L112 BSc Economics and Management Sciences
Duration: 3FT Hon
Entry Requirements: *GCE:* AAA-AABB. *SQAH:* AAAA. *SQAAH:* AA. *IB:* 36.

L101 MEcon Master of Economics
Duration: 4FT Hon
Entry Requirements: *GCE:* AAA. *SQAH:* AAAA. *SQAAH:* AA. *IB:* 36.

S36 UNIVERSITY OF ST ANDREWS
ST KATHARINE'S WEST
16 THE SCORES
ST ANDREWS
FIFE KY16 9AX
t: 01334 462150 f: 01334 463330
e: admissions@st-andrews.ac.uk
// www.st-andrews.ac.uk

L112 BSc Applied Economics
Duration: 4FT Hon
Entry Requirements: *GCE:* AAA. *SQAH:* AAAB. *IB:* 38.

L102 BSc Economics
Duration: 4FT Hon
Entry Requirements: *GCE:* AAA. *SQAH:* AAAB. *IB:* 38.

L161 BSc Financial Economics
Duration: 4FT Hon
Entry Requirements: *GCE:* AAA. *SQAH:* AAAB. *IB:* 38.

L110 MA Applied Economics
Duration: 4FT Hon
Entry Requirements: *GCE:* AAA. *SQAH:* AAAB. *IB:* 38.

L100 MA Economics
Duration: 4FT Hon
Entry Requirements: *GCE:* AAA. *SQAH:* AAAB. *IB:* 38.

L111 MA Financial Economics
Duration: 4FT Hon
Entry Requirements: *GCE:* AAA. *SQAH:* AAAB. *IB:* 38.

S75 THE UNIVERSITY OF STIRLING
STUDENT RECRUITMENT & ADMISSIONS SERVICE
UNIVERSITY OF STIRLING
STIRLING
SCOTLAND FK9 4LA
t: 01786 467044 f: 01786 466800
e: admissions@stir.ac.uk
// www.stir.ac.uk

L100 BA Economics
Duration: 4FT Hon
Entry Requirements: *GCE:* BBC. *SQAH:* BBBB. *SQAAH:* AAA-CCC. *IB:* 32. *BTEC ExtDip:* DMM.

S78 THE UNIVERSITY OF STRATHCLYDE
GLASGOW G1 1XQ
t: 0141 552 4400 f: 0141 552 0775
// www.strath.ac.uk

L100 BA Economics
Duration: 4FT Hon
Entry Requirements: *GCE:* AAB. *SQAH:* AAAABB-AAAB. *IB:* 36.

S85 UNIVERSITY OF SURREY
STAG HILL
GUILDFORD
SURREY GU2 7XH
t: +44(0)1483 689305 f: +44(0)1483 689388
e: ugteam@surrey.ac.uk
// www.surrey.ac.uk

L100 BSc Economics (3 or 4 years)
Duration: 3FT/4SW Hon
Entry Requirements: *GCE:* AAA-AAB. *SQAH:* AAAAA-AAABB. *SQAAH:* AAA-AAB.

L111 BSc Economics and Finance
Duration: 3FT/4SW Hon
Entry Requirements: *GCE:* AAA-AAB. *SQAH:* AAAAA-AAABB. *SQAAH:* AAA-AAB.

S90 UNIVERSITY OF SUSSEX
UNDERGRADUATE ADMISSIONS
SUSSEX HOUSE
UNIVERSITY OF SUSSEX
BRIGHTON BN1 9RH
t: 01273 678416 f: 01273 678545
e: ug.applicants@sussex.ac.uk
// www.sussex.ac.uk

L100 BA Economics
Duration: 3FT Hon
Entry Requirements: *GCE:* AAB. *SQAH:* AAABB. *IB:* 35. *BTEC SubDip:* D. *BTEC Dip:* DD. *BTEC ExtDip:* DDD. *OCR ND:* D *OCR NED:* D1

L102 BSc Economics
Duration: 3FT Hon
Entry Requirements: *GCE:* AAB. *SQAH:* AAABB. *IB:* 35. *BTEC SubDip:* D. *BTEC Dip:* DD. *BTEC ExtDip:* DDD. *OCR ND:* D *OCR NED:* D1

S93 SWANSEA UNIVERSITY
SINGLETON PARK
SWANSEA SA2 8PP
t: 01792 295111 f: 01792 295110
e: admissions@swansea.ac.uk
// www.swansea.ac.uk

L113 BA Business Economics
Duration: 3FT Hon
Entry Requirements: *GCE:* BBB. *IB:* 33.

L115 BA Business Economics (with a Year Abroad)
Duration: 4FT Hon
Entry Requirements: *GCE:* ABB. *IB:* 34.

L104 BA Economics
Duration: 3FT Hon
Entry Requirements: *GCE:* BBB. *IB:* 33.

L105 BA Economics with a Year Abroad
Duration: 4FT Hon
Entry Requirements: *GCE:* ABB. *IB:* 34.

L112 BSc Business Economics
Duration: 3FT Hon
Entry Requirements: *GCE:* BBB. *IB:* 33.

L114 BSc Business Economics (with a Year Abroad)
Duration: 4FT Hon
Entry Requirements: *GCE:* ABB. *IB:* 34.

L100 BSc Economics
Duration: 3FT Hon
Entry Requirements: *GCE:* BBB. *IB:* 33.

L101 BSc Economics With A Year Abroad
Duration: 4FT Hon
Entry Requirements: *GCE:* ABB. *IB:* 34.

L111 BSc Financial Economics
Duration: 3FT Hon
Entry Requirements: *GCE:* BBB. *IB:* 33.

L160 BSc International Business Economics
Duration: 3FT Hon
Entry Requirements: *GCE:* BBB. *IB:* 33.

U80 UNIVERSITY COLLEGE LONDON (UNIVERSITY OF LONDON)
GOWER STREET
LONDON WC1E 6BT
t: 020 7679 3000 f: 020 7679 3001
// www.ucl.ac.uk

L101 BSc (Econ) Economics with a Year Abroad
Duration: 4FT Hon
Entry Requirements: *GCE:* A*AAe. *SQAAH:* AAA. *IB:* 39.

L100 BScEcon Economics
Duration: 3FT Hon
Entry Requirements: *GCE:* A*AAe. *SQAAH:* AAA. *IB:* 39.

W20 THE UNIVERSITY OF WARWICK
COVENTRY CV4 8UW
t: 024 7652 3723 f: 024 7652 4649
e: ugadmissions@warwick.ac.uk
// www.warwick.ac.uk

L100 BSc Economics
Duration: 3FT Hon
Entry Requirements: *GCE:* A*AAB-A*AAa. *SQAAH:* AA. *IB:* 38.

L112 BSc Economics and Industrial Organization
Duration: 3FT Hon
Entry Requirements: *GCE:* A*AAB-A*AAa. *SQAAH:* AA. *IB:* 38.

W50 UNIVERSITY OF WESTMINSTER
2ND FLOOR, CAVENDISH HOUSE
101 NEW CAVENDISH STREET,
LONDON W1W 6XH
t: 020 7915 5511
e: course-enquiries@westminster.ac.uk
// www.westminster.ac.uk

L114 BSc Business Economics
Duration: 3FT/4SW Hon
Entry Requirements: *GCE:* BBB. *SQAH:* BBBBB. *SQAAH:* BBB. *IB:* 28.

Y50 THE UNIVERSITY OF YORK
STUDENT RECRUITMENT AND ADMISSIONS
UNIVERSITY OF YORK
HESLINGTON
YORK YO10 5DD
t: 01904 324000 f: 01904 323538
e: ug-admissions@york.ac.uk
// www.york.ac.uk

L144 BA/BSc Economics/Econometrics (Equal)
Duration: 3FT Hon
Entry Requirements: *GCE:* AAA-AAB. *SQAH:* AAAAA-AAAAB. *SQAAH:* AA-AB. *IB:* 36. *BTEC ExtDip:* DDD.

L100 BSc Economics
Duration: 3FT Hon
Entry Requirements: *GCE:* AAA-AAB. *SQAH:* AAAAA-AAAAB. *SQAAH:* AA-AB. *IB:* 36. *BTEC ExtDip:* DDD.

L112 BSc Economics and Finance
Duration: 3FT Hon
Entry Requirements: *GCE:* AAA-AAB. *SQAH:* AAAAA-AAAAB. *SQAAH:* AA-AB. *IB:* 36. *BTEC ExtDip:* DDD.

FINANCE

A20 THE UNIVERSITY OF ABERDEEN
UNIVERSITY OFFICE
KING'S COLLEGE
ABERDEEN AB24 3FX
t: +44 (0) 1224 273504 f: +44 (0) 1224 272034
e: sras@abdn.ac.uk
// www.abdn.ac.uk/sras

N300 MA Finance
Duration: 4FT Hon
Entry Requirements: *GCE:* BBB. *SQAH:* BBBB. *IB:* 30.

A30 UNIVERSITY OF ABERTAY DUNDEE
BELL STREET
DUNDEE DD1 1HG
t: 01382 308080 f: 01382 308081
e: sro@abertay.ac.uk
// www.abertay.ac.uk

N100 BA Business Studies option - Finance
Duration: 4SW Hon
Entry Requirements: *GCE:* CCD. *SQAH:* BBB. *IB:* 24.

A40 ABERYSTWYTH UNIVERSITY
ABERYSTWYTH UNIVERSITY, WELCOME CENTRE
PENGLAIS CAMPUS
ABERYSTWYTH
CEREDIGION SY23 3FB
t: 01970 622021 f: 01970 627410
e: ug-admissions@aber.ac.uk
// www.aber.ac.uk

N310 BScEcon Business Finance
Duration: 3FT Hon
Entry Requirements: *GCE:* 300. *IB:* 27.

A80 ASTON UNIVERSITY, BIRMINGHAM
ASTON TRIANGLE
BIRMINGHAM B4 7ET
t: 0121 204 4444 f: 0121 204 3696
e: admissions@aston.ac.uk   (automatic response)
// www.aston.ac.uk/prospective-students/ug

N300 BSc Finance
Duration: 4SW Hon
Entry Requirements: *GCE:* AAA-AAB. *SQAH:* AAAAA-AAAAB. *SQAAH:* AAA-AAB. *IB:* 35. *OCR NED:* D1

B22 UNIVERSITY OF BEDFORDSHIRE
PARK SQUARE
LUTON
BEDS LU1 3JU
t: 0844 8482234 f: 01582 489323
e: admissions@beds.ac.uk
// www.beds.ac.uk

N300 BA Business Studies (Finance)
Duration: 3FT Hon
Entry Requirements: *Foundation:* Pass. *GCE:* 200. *SQAH:* BCC. *SQAAH:* BCC. *IB:* 24. *OCR ND:* M1 *OCR NED:* P1

N390 BSc International Finance
Duration: 3FT Hon
Entry Requirements: *Foundation:* Pass. *GCE:* 200. *SQAH:* BCC. *SQAAH:* BCC. *IB:* 24. *OCR ND:* M1 *OCR NED:* P1

N392 BSc International Finance and Banking
Duration: 3FT Hon
Entry Requirements: Contact the institution for details.

B25 BIRMINGHAM CITY UNIVERSITY
PERRY BARR
BIRMINGHAM B42 2SU
t: 0121 331 5595 f: 0121 331 7994
// www.bcu.ac.uk

N390 BA International Finance (1 year top-up)
Duration: 1FT Hon
Entry Requirements: Contact the institution for details.

B32 THE UNIVERSITY OF BIRMINGHAM
EDGBASTON
BIRMINGHAM B15 2TT
t: 0121 415 8900 f: 0121 414 7159
e: admissions@bham.ac.uk
// www.birmingham.ac.uk

N300 BSc Money, Banking and Finance
Duration: 3FT Hon
Entry Requirements: *GCE:* AAA. *SQAH:* AAABB. *SQAAH:* AA.

B40 BLACKBURN COLLEGE
FEILDEN STREET
BLACKBURN BB2 1LH
t: 01254 292594 f: 01254 679647
e: he-admissions@blackburn.ac.uk
// www.blackburn.ac.uk

N300 BA Financial Services (Top-Up)
Duration: 1FT Hon
Entry Requirements: Contact the institution for details.

NM31 FdA Financial Services
Duration: 2FT Fdg
Entry Requirements: *GCE:* 80.

B50 BOURNEMOUTH UNIVERSITY
TALBOT CAMPUS
FERN BARROW
POOLE
DORSET BH12 5BB
t: 01202 524111
// www.bournemouth.ac.uk

N390 BA International Finance (Top Up)
Duration: 1FT Hon
Entry Requirements: Contact the institution for details.

B56 THE UNIVERSITY OF BRADFORD
RICHMOND ROAD
BRADFORD
WEST YORKSHIRE BD7 1DP
t: 0800 073 1225 f: 01274 235585
e: course-enquiries@bradford.ac.uk
// www.bradford.ac.uk

N390 BSc Financial Planning
Duration: 4SW Hon
Entry Requirements: *GCE:* 320. *IB:* 26.

B60 BRADFORD COLLEGE: AN ASSOCIATE COLLEGE OF LEEDS METROPOLITAN UNIVERSITY
GREAT HORTON ROAD
BRADFORD
WEST YORKSHIRE BD7 1AY
t: 01274 433008 f: 01274 431652
e: heregistry@bradfordcollege.ac.uk
// www.bradfordcollege.ac.uk/university-centre

N300 BA Financial Services
Duration: 3FT Hon
Entry Requirements: *GCE:* 100-140.

C10 CANTERBURY CHRIST CHURCH UNIVERSITY
NORTH HOLMES ROAD
CANTERBURY
KENT CT1 1QU
t: 01227 782900 f: 01227 782888
e: admissions@canterbury.ac.uk
// www.canterbury.ac.uk

N300 BSc Business Finance
Duration: 3FT Hon
Entry Requirements: *GCE:* 240. *IB:* 24.

C15 CARDIFF UNIVERSITY
PO BOX 927
30-36 NEWPORT ROAD
CARDIFF CF24 0DE
t: 029 2087 9999 f: 029 2087 6138
e: admissions@cardiff.ac.uk
// www.cardiff.ac.uk

N300 BScEcon Banking and Finance
Duration: 3FT Hon
Entry Requirements: *GCE:* AAB. *SQAH:* AAABB. *SQAAH:* AAB. *IB:* 35. *OCR NED:* D1 Interview required.

C60 CITY UNIVERSITY
NORTHAMPTON SQUARE
LONDON EC1V 0HB
t: 020 7040 5060 f: 020 7040 8995
e: ugadmissions@city.ac.uk
// www.city.ac.uk

N302 BSc Banking and International Finance (3 years or 4 year SW)
Duration: 3FT Hon
Entry Requirements: *GCE:* AAA. *SQAH:* AAA-BB. *IB:* 35.

N390 BSc Investment and Financial Risk Management (3 years or 4 year SW)
Duration: 3FT/4SW Hon
Entry Requirements: *GCE:* AAA. *SQAH:* AAA-BB. *IB:* 35.

C85 COVENTRY UNIVERSITY
THE STUDENT CENTRE
COVENTRY UNIVERSITY
1 GULSON RD
COVENTRY CV1 2JH
t: 024 7615 2222 f: 024 7615 2223
e: studentenquiries@coventry.ac.uk
// www.coventry.ac.uk

N341 BA Finance and Investment
Duration: 3FT/4SW Hon
Entry Requirements: *GCE:* BBC. *SQAH:* BBCCC. *IB:* 29. *BTEC ExtDip:* DDM. *OCR NED:* M1

N321 BA Investment Operations
Duration: 3FT Hon
Entry Requirements: *GCE:* 260. *IB:* 28. *BTEC Dip:* DD. *BTEC ExtDip:* MMM. *OCR ND:* D *OCR NED:* M3

N322 BSc Insurance and Risk Management
Duration: 3FT Hon
Entry Requirements: *GCE:* 260. *IB:* 28. *BTEC Dip:* DD. *BTEC ExtDip:* MMM. *OCR ND:* D *OCR NED:* M3

22HN HNC Insurance and Risk Management
Duration: 1FT HNC
Entry Requirements: *GCE:* 160. *IB:* 24. *BTEC Dip:* MM. *BTEC ExtDip:* MPP. *OCR ND:* P1 *OCR NED:* P2

123N HNC Investment Advice
Duration: 1FT HNC
Entry Requirements: *GCE:* 160. *IB:* 24. *BTEC Dip:* MM. *BTEC ExtDip:* MPP. *OCR ND:* P1 *OCR NED:* P2

223N HND Insurance and Risk Management
Duration: 2FT HND
Entry Requirements: *GCE:* 200. *IB:* 24. *BTEC Dip:* DM. *BTEC ExtDip:* MMP. *OCR ND:* M1 *OCR NED:* P1

D26 DE MONTFORT UNIVERSITY
THE GATEWAY
LEICESTER LE1 9BH
t: 0116 255 1551 f: 0116 250 6204
e: enquiries@dmu.ac.uk
// www.dmu.ac.uk

N300 BSc Finance (with an Optional Year in Industry)
Duration: 3FT/4SW Hon
Entry Requirements: *GCE:* 300. *IB:* 30. *BTEC ExtDip:* DDM. Interview required.

D65 UNIVERSITY OF DUNDEE
NETHERGATE
DUNDEE DD1 4HN
t: 01382 383838 f: 01382 388150
e: contactus@dundee.ac.uk
// www.dundee.ac.uk/admissions/undergraduate/

N300 BFin Finance
Duration: 4FT Hon
Entry Requirements: *GCE:* BCC. *SQAH:* ABBB. *IB:* 30.

N390 BIFin International Finance
Duration: 4FT Hon
Entry Requirements: *GCE:* BCC. *SQAH:* ABBB. *IB:* 30.

D86 DURHAM UNIVERSITY
DURHAM UNIVERSITY
UNIVERSITY OFFICE
DURHAM DH1 3HP
t: 0191 334 2000 f: 0191 334 6055
e: admissions@durham.ac.uk
// www.durham.ac.uk

N390 BA Business Finance with Foundation
Duration: 4FT Hon
Entry Requirements: Interview required.

E14 UNIVERSITY OF EAST ANGLIA
NORWICH NR4 7TJ
t: 01603 591515 f: 01603 591523
e: admissions@uea.ac.uk
// www.uea.ac.uk

N323 BSc Actuarial Science with a Year in Industry
Duration: 4FT Hon   CRB Check: Required
Entry Requirements: *GCE:* AAA. *SQAH:* AAAAA. *SQAAH:* AAA. *IB:* 34. *BTEC ExtDip:* DDD. Interview required.

N324 BSc Actuarial Sciences
Duration: 3FT Hon   CRB Check: Required
Entry Requirements: *GCE:* AAA. *SQAH:* AAAAA. *SQAAH:* AAA. *IB:* 34. *BTEC ExtDip:* DDD. Interview required.

E28 UNIVERSITY OF EAST LONDON
DOCKLANDS CAMPUS
UNIVERSITY WAY
LONDON E16 2RD
t: 020 8223 3333 f: 020 8223 2978
e: study@uel.ac.uk
// www.uel.ac.uk

N301 BA Finance
Duration: 3FT Hon
Entry Requirements: *GCE:* 240. *IB:* 24.

E59 EDINBURGH NAPIER UNIVERSITY
CRAIGLOCKHART CAMPUS
EDINBURGH EH14 1DJ
t: +44 (0)8452 60 60 40 f: 0131 455 6464
e: info@napier.ac.uk
// www.napier.ac.uk

N340 BA Financial Services Management
Duration: 3FT/4FT Ord/Hon
Entry Requirements: *GCE:* 230.

E70 THE UNIVERSITY OF ESSEX
WIVENHOE PARK
COLCHESTER
ESSEX CO4 3SQ
t: 01206 873666 f: 01206 874477
e: admit@essex.ac.uk
// www.essex.ac.uk

N323 BSc Actuarial Science
Duration: 3FT Hon
Entry Requirements: *GCE:* AAB-ABB. *SQAH:* AAAA-AAAB. *IB:* 36.
BTEC ExtDip: DDD. *OCR ND:* M1

N300 BSc Finance
Duration: 3FT Hon
Entry Requirements: *GCE:* ABB. *SQAH:* AAAB. *IB:* 34.

N301 BSc Finance (Including Foundation Year)
Duration: 4FT Hon
Entry Requirements: *GCE:* 180. *SQAH:* CCCD. *IB:* 24.

N302 BSc Finance (Including Year Abroad)
Duration: 4FT Hon
Entry Requirements: *GCE:* ABB. *SQAH:* AAAB. *IB:* 34.

N340 BSc Financial Management
Duration: 3FT Hon
Entry Requirements: *GCE:* ABB. *SQAH:* AAAB. *IB:* 34.

N341 BSc Financial Management (Including Foundation Year)
Duration: 4FT Hon
Entry Requirements: *GCE:* 180. *SQAH:* CCCD. *IB:* 24.

NH40 BSc Financial Management (Including Year Abroad)
Duration: 4FT Hon
Entry Requirements: *GCE:* ABB. *SQAH:* AAAB. *IB:* 34.

E78 EUROPEAN SCHOOL OF ECONOMICS
8/9 GROSVENOR PLACE
BELGRAVIA
LONDON SW1X 7SH
t: 020 7245 6148 f: 020 7245 6164
e: admissions@eselondon.ac.uk
// www.eselondon.ac.uk

N300 BBA Finance
Duration: 3FT Hon
Entry Requirements: *GCE:* A-C. Interview required.

G14 UNIVERSITY OF GLAMORGAN, CARDIFF AND PONTYPRIDD
ENQUIRIES AND ADMISSIONS UNIT
PONTYPRIDD CF37 1DL
t: 08456 434030 f: 01443 654050
e: enquiries@glam.ac.uk
// www.glam.ac.uk

N301 BSc Finance (Top-Up)
Duration: 1FT Hon
Entry Requirements: Contact the institution for details.

N300 FdA Finance (Financial Planning)
Duration: 2FT Fdg
Entry Requirements: Contact the institution for details.

G70 UNIVERSITY OF GREENWICH
GREENWICH CAMPUS
OLD ROYAL NAVAL COLLEGE
PARK ROW
LONDON SE10 9LS
t: 020 8331 9000 f: 020 8331 8145
e: courseinfo@gre.ac.uk
// www.gre.ac.uk

N390 BSc Financial Mathematics
Duration: 3FT Hon
Entry Requirements: *GCE:* 260. *IB:* 24.

H24 HERIOT-WATT UNIVERSITY, EDINBURGH
EDINBURGH CAMPUS
EDINBURGH EH14 4AS
t: 0131 449 5111 f: 0131 451 3630
e: ugadmissions@hw.ac.uk
// www.hw.ac.uk

N300 MA Finance
Duration: 4FT Hon
Entry Requirements: *GCE:* BBB. *SQAH:* AAAB-BBBBC. *SQAAH:* BB. *IB:* 29.

H36 UNIVERSITY OF HERTFORDSHIRE
UNIVERSITY ADMISSIONS SERVICE
COLLEGE LANE
HATFIELD
HERTS AL10 9AB
t: 01707 284800
// www.herts.ac.uk

N300 BA Finance
Duration: 3FT/4SW Hon
Entry Requirements: *GCE:* 260.

H72 THE UNIVERSITY OF HULL
THE UNIVERSITY OF HULL
COTTINGHAM ROAD
HULL HU6 7RX
t: 01482 466100 f: 01482 442290
e: admissions@hull.ac.uk
// www.hull.ac.uk

N340 BSc Financial Management
Duration: 3FT Hon
Entry Requirements: *GCE:* 300. *IB:* 30. *BTEC ExtDip:* DMM.

N341 BSc Financial Management (International) (4 years)
Duration: 4FT Hon
Entry Requirements: *GCE:* 300. *IB:* 30. *BTEC ExtDip:* DMM.

N342 BSc Financial Management (with Professional Experience) (4 years)
Duration: 4FT Hon
Entry Requirements: *GCE:* 300. *IB:* 30. *BTEC ExtDip:* DMM.

I55 IFS SCHOOL OF FINANCE
PENINSULAR HOUSE
36 MONUMENT STREET
LONDON EC3R 8LJ
t: 01227 829499
e: enquiries@ifslearning.ac.uk
// www.ifslearning.ac.uk

N300 BSc Finance, Investment and Risk
Duration: 3FT Hon
Entry Requirements: *GCE:* 360.

K12 KEELE UNIVERSITY
KEELE UNIVERSITY
STAFFORDSHIRE ST5 5BG
t: 01782 734005 f: 01782 632343
e: undergraduate@keele.ac.uk
// www.keele.ac.uk

N323 BSc Actuarial Science
Duration: 3FT Hon
Entry Requirements: *GCE:* AAB. *SQAAH:* AAB.

NL33 BSc Actuarial Science with Social Science Foundation Year
Duration: 4FT Hon
Entry Requirements: *GCE:* CC.

K24 THE UNIVERSITY OF KENT
RECRUITMENT & ADMISSIONS OFFICE
REGISTRY
UNIVERSITY OF KENT
CANTERBURY, KENT CT2 7NZ
t: 01227 827272 f: 01227 827077
e: information@kent.ac.uk
// www.kent.ac.uk

N323 BSc Actuarial Science
Duration: 3FT Hon
Entry Requirements: *GCE:* AAA-AAB. *SQAH:* AAAAA. *SQAAH:* AAA. *IB:* 33. *OCR ND:* D *OCR NED:* M1

N324 BSc Actuarial Science with a year in Industry
Duration: 4FT Hon
Entry Requirements: *GCE:* AAA-AAB. *SQAH:* AAAAA. *SQAAH:* AAA. *IB:* 33. *OCR ND:* D *OCR NED:* M1

K84 KINGSTON UNIVERSITY
STUDENT INFORMATION & ADVICE CENTRE
COOPER HOUSE
40-46 SURBITON ROAD
KINGSTON UPON THAMES KT1 2HX
t: 0844 8552177 f: 020 8547 7080
e: aps@kingston.ac.uk
// www.kingston.ac.uk

N323 BSc Actuarial Science
Duration: 4SW Hon
Entry Requirements: *GCE:* 300.

N324 BSc Actuarial Science
Duration: 3FT Hon
Entry Requirements: *GCE:* 300.

L14 LANCASTER UNIVERSITY
THE UNIVERSITY
LANCASTER
LANCASHIRE LA1 4YW
t: 01524 592029 f: 01524 846243
e: ugadmissions@lancaster.ac.uk
// www.lancs.ac.uk

N300 BSc Finance
Duration: 3FT Hon
Entry Requirements: *GCE:* AAA-AAB. *SQAH:* AAABB-ABBBB. *SQAAH:* AAA-AAB.

L27 LEEDS METROPOLITAN UNIVERSITY
COURSE ENQUIRIES OFFICE
CITY CAMPUS
LEEDS LS1 3HE
t: 0113 81 23113 f: 0113 81 23129
// www.leedsmet.ac.uk

N301 BA Financial Services
Duration: 1FT Hon
Entry Requirements: Contact the institution for details.

L34 UNIVERSITY OF LEICESTER
UNIVERSITY ROAD
LEICESTER LE1 7RH
t: 0116 252 5281 f: 0116 252 2447
e: admissions@le.ac.uk
// www.le.ac.uk

N340 BA Management Studies (Finance)
Duration: 3FT Hon
Entry Requirements: *GCE:* ABB. *SQAH:* AABBB. *SQAAH:* ABB. *IB:* 32.

L41 THE UNIVERSITY OF LIVERPOOL
THE FOUNDATION BUILDING
BROWNLOW HILL
LIVERPOOL L69 7ZX
t: 0151 794 2000 f: 0151 708 6502
e: ugrecruitment@liv.ac.uk
// www.liv.ac.uk

N300 BSc e-Finance
Duration: 3FT Hon
Entry Requirements: *GCE:* AAB. *SQAAH:* AAB. *IB:* 33.

L68 LONDON METROPOLITAN UNIVERSITY
166-220 HOLLOWAY ROAD
LONDON N7 8DB
t: 020 7133 4200
e: admissions@londonmet.ac.uk
// www.londonmet.ac.uk

N300 BA Banking and Finance (with Integrated Professional Training)
Duration: 4SW Hon
Entry Requirements: *GCE:* 240. *IB:* 28.

N301 BSc Finance
Duration: 3FT Hon
Entry Requirements: *GCE:* 240. *IB:* 28.

N390 BSc International Financial Services (Top-Up)
Duration: 1FT Hon
Entry Requirements: HND required.

L71 LONDON SCHOOL OF SCIENCE AND TECHNOLOGY
12 ALPERTON HOUSE
WEMBLEY
MIDDLESEX HA0 1EH
t: 020 8795 3863 f: 020 8795 3864
e: admissions@lsst.com
// www.lsst.com

103N HNC Business Finance
Duration: 1FT HNC
Entry Requirements: Contact the institution for details.

003N HND Business Finance
Duration: 1FT HND
Entry Requirements: Contact the institution for details.

L72 LONDON SCHOOL OF ECONOMICS AND POLITICAL SCIENCE (UNIVERSITY OF LONDON)
HOUGHTON STREET
LONDON WC2A 2AE
t: 020 7955 7125 f: 020 7955 6001
e: ug.admissions@lse.ac.uk
// www.lse.ac.uk

N321 BSc Actuarial Science
Duration: 3FT Hon
Entry Requirements: *GCE:* AAA. *SQAH:* AAAAA. *SQAAH:* AAA. *IB:* 38.

L79 LOUGHBOROUGH UNIVERSITY
LOUGHBOROUGH
LEICESTERSHIRE LE11 3TU
t: 01509 223522 f: 01509 223905
e: admissions@lboro.ac.uk
// www.lboro.ac.uk

N301 BSc Banking Finance and Management
Duration: 4SW Hon
Entry Requirements: *GCE:* AAA-AAB. *IB:* 36. *BTEC ExtDip:* DDD.

M10 THE MANCHESTER COLLEGE
OPENSHAW CAMPUS
ASHTON OLD ROAD
OPENSHAW
MANCHESTER M11 2WH
t: 0800 068 8585 f: 0161 920 4103
e: enquiries@themanchestercollege.ac.uk
// www.themanchestercollege.ac.uk

N340 BSc Financial Management
Duration: 1FT Hon
Entry Requirements: Contact the institution for details.

M20 THE UNIVERSITY OF MANCHESTER
RUTHERFORD BUILDING
OXFORD ROAD
MANCHESTER M13 9PL
t: 0161 275 2077 f: 0161 275 2106
e: ug-admissions@manchester.ac.uk
// www.manchester.ac.uk

N300 BAEcon Finance
Duration: 3FT Hon
Entry Requirements: *GCE:* AAB. *SQAH:* AAABB. *SQAAH:* AAB.

M40 THE MANCHESTER METROPOLITAN UNIVERSITY
ADMISSIONS OFFICE
ALL SAINTS (GMS)
ALL SAINTS
MANCHESTER M15 6BH
t: 0161 247 2000
// www.mmu.ac.uk

N341 BA Financial Services, Planning and Management
Duration: 3FT Hon
Entry Requirements: *IB:* 29.

N342 BA Financial Services, Planning and Management
Duration: 4SW Hon
Entry Requirements: *IB:* 29.

N300 BA Financial Studies
Duration: 1FT Hon
Entry Requirements: Contact the institution for details.

M80 MIDDLESEX UNIVERSITY
MIDDLESEX UNIVERSITY
THE BURROUGHS
LONDON NW4 4BT
t: 020 8411 5555 f: 020 8411 5649
e: enquiries@mdx.ac.uk
// www.mdx.ac.uk

N301 BA Financial Services (Top-Up)
Duration: 1FT Hon
Entry Requirements: Contact the institution for details.

N38 UNIVERSITY OF NORTHAMPTON
PARK CAMPUS
BOUGHTON GREEN ROAD
NORTHAMPTON NN2 7AL
t: 0800 358 2232 f: 01604 722083
e: admissions@northampton.ac.uk
// www.northampton.ac.uk

N390 BSc Banking and Financial Planning
Duration: 4FT Hon
Entry Requirements: *GCE:* 260-280. *SQAH:* AAA-BBBB. *IB:* 24.
BTEC Dip: DD. *BTEC ExtDip:* DMM. *OCR ND:* D *OCR NED:* M2

N34A BSc Banking and Financial Planning (Top-Up)
Duration: 1FT Hon
Entry Requirements: Contact the institution for details.

N91 NOTTINGHAM TRENT UNIVERSITY
DRYDEN BUILDING
BURTON STREET
NOTTINGHAM NG1 4BU
t: +44 (0) 115 848 4200 f: +44 (0) 115 848 8869
e: applications@ntu.ac.uk
// www.ntu.ac.uk

N300 BA (Hons) Business Finance (Top-Up)
Duration: 1FT Hon
Entry Requirements: HND required.

P60 PLYMOUTH UNIVERSITY
DRAKE CIRCUS
PLYMOUTH PL4 8AA
t: 01752 585858 f: 01752 588055
e: admissions@plymouth.ac.uk
// www.plymouth.ac.uk

N304 BA International Finance
Duration: 1FT Hon
Entry Requirements: Contact the institution for details.

N303 FdA Financial Services
Duration: 2FT Fdg
Entry Requirements: *GCE:* 60. *OCR ND:* P *OCR NED:* M

P80 UNIVERSITY OF PORTSMOUTH
ACADEMIC REGISTRY
UNIVERSITY HOUSE
WINSTON CHURCHILL AVENUE
PORTSMOUTH PO1 2UP
t: 023 9284 8484 f: 023 9284 3082
e: admissions@port.ac.uk
// www.port.ac.uk

N350 BA International Finance and Trade
Duration: 3FT/4SW Hon
Entry Requirements: *GCE:* 280. *IB:* 28. *BTEC Dip:* D*D*. *BTEC ExtDip:* DMM.

N300 BSc Finance
Duration: 3FT/4SW Hon
Entry Requirements: *GCE:* 280. *IB:* 28. *BTEC Dip:* D*D*. *BTEC ExtDip:* DMM.

Q75 QUEEN'S UNIVERSITY BELFAST
UNIVERSITY ROAD
BELFAST BT7 1NN
t: 028 9097 3838 f: 028 9097 5151
e: admissions@qub.ac.uk
// www.qub.ac.uk

N300 BSc Finance (with a Year in Industry)
Duration: 4SW Hon
Entry Requirements: *GCE:* ABB-BBBb. *SQAH:* ABBBB. *SQAAH:* ABB. *IB:* 32.

R12 THE UNIVERSITY OF READING
THE UNIVERSITY OF READING
PO BOX 217
READING RG6 6AH
t: 0118 378 8619 f: 0118 378 8924
e: student.recruitment@reading.ac.uk
// www.reading.ac.uk

N380 BSc Investment and Finance in Property
Duration: 3FT Hon
Entry Requirements: *GCE:* AAB-ABBb. *SQAH:* AAABB. *SQAAH:* AAB. *BTEC Dip:* DD. *BTEC ExtDip:* DDD.

R18 REGENT'S COLLEGE, LONDON (INCORPORATING REGENT'S BUSINESS SCHOOL, LONDON)
INNER CIRCLE, REGENT'S COLLEGE
REGENT'S PARK
LONDON NW1 4NS
t: +44(0)20 7487 7505 f: +44(0)20 7487 7425
e: exrel@regents.ac.uk
// www.regents.ac.uk/

N342 BA Global Financial Management
Duration: 3FT Hon
Entry Requirements: *GCE:* 240-300.

R20 RICHMOND, THE AMERICAN INTERNATIONAL UNIVERSITY IN LONDON
QUEENS ROAD
RICHMOND
SURREY TW10 6JP
t: 020 8332 9000 f: 020 8332 1596
e: enroll@richmond.ac.uk
// www.richmond.ac.uk

N300 BA Financial Economics
Duration: 3FT/4FT Hon
Entry Requirements: Contact the institution for details.

S21 SHEFFIELD HALLAM UNIVERSITY
CITY CAMPUS
HOWARD STREET
SHEFFIELD S1 1WB
t: 0114 225 5555 f: 0114 225 2167
e: admissions@shu.ac.uk
// www.shu.ac.uk

N390 BA International Finance and Banking
Duration: 3FT/4SW Hon
Entry Requirements: *GCE:* 300.

S75 THE UNIVERSITY OF STIRLING
STUDENT RECRUITMENT & ADMISSIONS SERVICE
UNIVERSITY OF STIRLING
STIRLING
SCOTLAND FK9 4LA
t: 01786 467044 f: 01786 466800
e: admissions@stir.ac.uk
// www.stir.ac.uk

N300 BA Finance
Duration: 4FT Hon
Entry Requirements: *GCE:* BBC. *SQAH:* BBBB. *SQAAH:* AAA-CCC. *IB:* 32. *BTEC ExtDip:* DMM.

S78 THE UNIVERSITY OF STRATHCLYDE
GLASGOW G1 1XQ
t: 0141 552 4400 f: 0141 552 0775
// www.strath.ac.uk

N300 BA Finance
Duration: 4FT Hon
Entry Requirements: *GCE:* AAB. *SQAH:* AAAABB-AAAB. *IB:* 36.

S85 UNIVERSITY OF SURREY
STAG HILL
GUILDFORD
SURREY GU2 7XH
t: +44(0)1483 689305 f: +44(0)1483 689388
e: ugteam@surrey.ac.uk
// www.surrey.ac.uk

N300 BSc Financial Mathematics (3 years)
Duration: 3FT Hon
Entry Requirements: *GCE:* AAB-ABB. Interview required.

N301 BSc Financial Mathematics (4 years)
Duration: 4SW Hon
Entry Requirements: *GCE:* AAB-ABB. Interview required.

S96 SWANSEA METROPOLITAN UNIVERSITY
MOUNT PLEASANT CAMPUS
SWANSEA SA1 6ED
t: 01792 481000 f: 01792 481061
e: gemma.green@smu.ac.uk
// www.smu.ac.uk

N300 BA Financial Services
Duration: 3FT Hon
Entry Requirements: *GCE:* 160-360. *IB:* 24. Interview required.

T20 TEESSIDE UNIVERSITY
MIDDLESBROUGH TS1 3BA
t: 01642 218121 f: 01642 384201
e: registry@tees.ac.uk
// www.tees.ac.uk

N390 BA Business Finance
Duration: 3FT/4SW Hon
Entry Requirements: Contact the institution for details.

U20 UNIVERSITY OF ULSTER
COLERAINE
CO. LONDONDERRY
NORTHERN IRELAND BT52 1SA
t: 028 7012 4221 f: 028 7012 4908
e: online@ulster.ac.uk
// www.ulster.ac.uk

N321 BSc Finance and Investment Analysis
Duration: 3FT/4SW Hon
Entry Requirements: *GCE:* 300. *IB:* 25.

W80 UNIVERSITY OF WORCESTER
HENWICK GROVE
WORCESTER WR2 6AJ
t: 01905 855111 f: 01905 855377
e: admissions@worc.ac.uk
// www.worcester.ac.uk

N390 BA International Finance
Duration: 1FT Hon
Entry Requirements: HND required.

ACCOUNTANCY

A20 THE UNIVERSITY OF ABERDEEN
UNIVERSITY OFFICE
KING'S COLLEGE
ABERDEEN AB24 3FX
t: +44 (0) 1224 273504 f: +44 (0) 1224 272034
e: sras@abdn.ac.uk
// www.abdn.ac.uk/sras

N400 MA Accountancy
Duration: 4FT Hon
Entry Requirements: *GCE:* BBB. *SQAH:* BBBB. *IB:* 30.

A80 ASTON UNIVERSITY, BIRMINGHAM
ASTON TRIANGLE
BIRMINGHAM B4 7ET
t: 0121 204 4444 f: 0121 204 3696
e: admissions@aston.ac.uk (automatic response)
// www.aston.ac.uk/prospective-students/ug

N420 BSc Accounting for Management
Duration: 4SW Hon
Entry Requirements: *GCE:* AAA-AAB. *SQAH:* AAAAA-AAAAB. *SQAAH:* AAA-AAB. *IB:* 35. *OCR NED:* D1

B22 UNIVERSITY OF BEDFORDSHIRE
PARK SQUARE
LUTON
BEDS LU1 3JU
t: 0844 8482234 f: 01582 489323
e: admissions@beds.ac.uk
// www.beds.ac.uk

N403 BA Accounting
Duration: 4SW Hon
Entry Requirements: *Foundation:* Merit. *GCE:* 200. *SQAH:* BBB. *SQAAH:* BC. *IB:* 24. *BTEC Dip:* DM. *OCR ND:* M1 *OCR NED:* P1

N420 BA Accounting
Duration: 3FT Hon
Entry Requirements: *GCE:* 200. *SQAH:* BCC. *SQAAH:* BB. *IB:* 30.

B24 BIRKBECK, UNIVERSITY OF LONDON
MALET STREET
LONDON WC1E 7HX
t: 020 7631 6316
e: webform: www.bbk.ac.uk/ask
// www.bbk.ac.uk/ask

N400 BSc Accounting
Duration: 3FT Hon
Entry Requirements: *GCE:* BCC. *SQAH:* AAAA-AABB. *IB:* 36.
Admissions Test required.

B25 BIRMINGHAM CITY UNIVERSITY
PERRY BARR
BIRMINGHAM B42 2SU
t: 0121 331 5595 f: 0121 331 7994
// www.bcu.ac.uk

N400 BA Accountancy
Duration: 3FT/4SW Hon
Entry Requirements: *GCE:* 280. *IB:* 32. *OCR ND:* D *OCR NED:* M2

B40 BLACKBURN COLLEGE
FEILDEN STREET
BLACKBURN BB2 1LH
t: 01254 292594 f: 01254 679647
e: he-admissions@blackburn.ac.uk
// www.blackburn.ac.uk

N400 BA Business Accounting
Duration: 3FT Hon
Entry Requirements: *GCE:* 120.

N401 FdA Accounting
Duration: 2FT Fdg
Entry Requirements: *GCE:* 80.

B41 BLACKPOOL AND THE FYLDE COLLEGE AN ASSOCIATE COLLEGE OF LANCASTER UNIVERSITY
ASHFIELD ROAD
BISPHAM
BLACKPOOL
LANCS FY2 0HB
t: 01253 504346 f: 01253 504198
e: admissions@blackpool.ac.uk
// www.blackpool.ac.uk

N400 FdA Accounting
Duration: 2FT Fdg
Entry Requirements: Interview required.

B44 UNIVERSITY OF BOLTON
DEANE ROAD
BOLTON BL3 5AB
t: 01204 903903 f: 01204 399074
e: enquiries@bolton.ac.uk
// www.bolton.ac.uk

N400 BA Accountancy
Duration: 3FT Hon
Entry Requirements: *GCE:* 260. Interview required.

B50 BOURNEMOUTH UNIVERSITY
TALBOT CAMPUS
FERN BARROW
POOLE
DORSET BH12 5BB
t: 01202 524111
// www.bournemouth.ac.uk

N420 BA Accounting and Finance
Duration: 3FT Hon
Entry Requirements: *GCE:* 320. *IB:* 32. *BTEC SubDip:* D. *BTEC Dip:* DD. *BTEC ExtDip:* DDM.

B54 BPP UNIVERSITY COLLEGE OF PROFESSIONAL STUDIES LIMITED
142-144 UXBRIDGE ROAD
LONDON W12 8AW
t: 02031 312 298
e: admissions@bpp.com
// undergraduate.bpp.com/

N400 BSc Professional Accounting
Duration: 3FT Hon
Entry Requirements: Contact the institution for details.

N401 BSc Professional Accounting (Accelerated)
Duration: 2FT Hon
Entry Requirements: Contact the institution for details.

B56 THE UNIVERSITY OF BRADFORD
RICHMOND ROAD
BRADFORD
WEST YORKSHIRE BD7 1DP
t: 0800 073 1225 f: 01274 235585
e: course-enquiries@bradford.ac.uk
// www.bradford.ac.uk

N420 BSc Accounting and Finance
Duration: 3FT Hon
Entry Requirements: *GCE:* 340. *IB:* 27.

N421 BSc Accounting and Finance (4 years)
Duration: 4SW Hon
Entry Requirements: *GCE:* 340. *IB:* 27.

B60 BRADFORD COLLEGE: AN ASSOCIATE COLLEGE OF LEEDS METROPOLITAN UNIVERSITY
GREAT HORTON ROAD
BRADFORD
WEST YORKSHIRE BD7 1AY
t: 01274 433008 f: 01274 431652
e: heregistry@bradfordcollege.ac.uk
// www.bradfordcollege.ac.uk/
university-centre

N410 BA Accountancy
Duration: 3FT Hon
Entry Requirements: *GCE:* 180.

B72 UNIVERSITY OF BRIGHTON
MITHRAS HOUSE 211
LEWES ROAD
BRIGHTON BN2 4AT
t: 01273 644644 f: 01273 642607
e: admissions@brighton.ac.uk
// www.brighton.ac.uk

N420 BSc Accounting and Finance
Duration: 3FT/4SW Hon
Entry Requirements: *GCE:* BBB. *IB:* 30.

B80 UNIVERSITY OF THE WEST OF ENGLAND, BRISTOL
FRENCHAY CAMPUS
COLDHARBOUR LANE
BRISTOL BS16 1QY
t: +44 (0)117 32 83333 f: +44 (0)117 32 82810
e: admissions@uwe.ac.uk
// www.uwe.ac.uk

N420 BA Accounting and Finance
Duration: 3FT/4SW Hon
Entry Requirements: *GCE:* 300.

C15 CARDIFF UNIVERSITY
PO BOX 927
30-36 NEWPORT ROAD
CARDIFF CF24 0DE
t: 029 2087 9999 f: 029 2087 6138
e: admissions@cardiff.ac.uk
// www.cardiff.ac.uk

N400 BSc Accounting
Duration: 3FT Hon
Entry Requirements: *GCE:* AAB. *SQAH:* AAABB. *SQAAH:* AAB. *IB:* 35. *OCR NED:* D1 Interview required.

N490 BSc Accounting and Finance
Duration: 3FT Hon
Entry Requirements: *GCE:* AAB. *SQAH:* AAABB. *SQAAH:* AAB. *IB:* 35. *OCR NED:* D1 Interview required.

N410 BSc Accounting with a European Language (French)
Duration: 4FT Hon
Entry Requirements: *GCE:* AAB. *SQAH:* AAABB. *SQAAH:* AAB. *IB:* 35. *OCR NED:* D1 Interview required.

C20 CARDIFF METROPOLITAN UNIVERSITY (UWIC)
ADMISSIONS UNIT
LLANDAFF CAMPUS
WESTERN AVENUE
CARDIFF CF5 2YB
t: 029 2041 6070 f: 029 2041 6286
e: admissions@cardiffmet.ac.uk
// www.cardiffmet.ac.uk

N400 BA Accounting
Duration: 3FT/4SW Hon
Entry Requirements: *GCE:* 300. *IB:* 26. *BTEC ExtDip:* DDM. *OCR NED:* M1

C30 UNIVERSITY OF CENTRAL LANCASHIRE
PRESTON
LANCS PR1 2HE
t: 01772 201201 f: 01772 894954
e: uadmissions@uclan.ac.uk
// www.uclan.ac.uk

N400 BA Accounting
Duration: 3FT/4SW Hon
Entry Requirements: *SQAH:* AAAB-AABB. *IB:* 28.

N420 BA Accounting and Financial Studies
Duration: 3FT/4SW Hon
Entry Requirements: *SQAH:* AAAB-AABB. *IB:* 28.

N421 BA Accounting and Financial Studies (Year 2 entry)
Duration: 2FT Hon
Entry Requirements: *GCE:* 260-280. *SQAH:* AABB-BBBB. *IB:* 28. *OCR ND:* D

C85 COVENTRY UNIVERSITY
THE STUDENT CENTRE
COVENTRY UNIVERSITY
1 GULSON RD
COVENTRY CV1 2JH
t: 024 7615 2222 f: 024 7615 2223
e: studentenquiries@coventry.ac.uk
// www.coventry.ac.uk

N410 BA Accountancy
Duration: 3FT/4SW Hon
Entry Requirements: *GCE:* BBB. *SQAH:* BBBBC. *IB:* 30. *BTEC ExtDip:* DDM. *OCR NED:* M1

N401 FYr Accounting (Foundation Year)
Duration: 1FT FYr
Entry Requirements: *GCE:* 160. *IB:* 24. *BTEC Dip:* MM. *BTEC ExtDip:* MPP. *OCR ND:* P1 *OCR NED:* P2

N400 HNC Accounting Technician
Duration: 1FT HNC
Entry Requirements: *GCE:* 200. *IB:* 24. *BTEC Dip:* DM. *BTEC ExtDip:* MMP. *OCR ND:* M1 *OCR NED:* P1

004N HND Business Accounting
Duration: 2FT HND
Entry Requirements: *GCE:* 200. *IB:* 24. *BTEC Dip:* DM. *BTEC ExtDip:* MMP. *OCR ND:* M1 *OCR NED:* P1

D26 DE MONTFORT UNIVERSITY
THE GATEWAY
LEICESTER LE1 9BH
t: 0116 255 1551 f: 0116 250 6204
e: enquiries@dmu.ac.uk
// www.dmu.ac.uk

N420 BA Accounting and Finance
Duration: 3FT/4SW Hon
Entry Requirements: *GCE:* 320. *IB:* 30. *BTEC ExtDip:* DDM. *OCR NED:* D2 Interview required.

D39 UNIVERSITY OF DERBY
KEDLESTON ROAD
DERBY DE22 1GB
t: 01332 591167 f: 01332 597724
e: askadmissions@derby.ac.uk
// www.derby.ac.uk

N400 BA Accounting and Finance
Duration: 3FT/4SW Hon
Entry Requirements: *Foundation:* Distinction. *GCE:* 280. *IB:* 28. *BTEC Dip:* D*D*. *BTEC ExtDip:* DMM. *OCR NED:* M2

D65 UNIVERSITY OF DUNDEE
NETHERGATE
DUNDEE DD1 4HN
t: 01382 383838 f: 01382 388150
e: contactus@dundee.ac.uk
// www.dundee.ac.uk/admissions/undergraduate/

N400 BAcc Accountancy
Duration: 4FT Hon
Entry Requirements: *GCE:* BCC. *SQAH:* ABBB. *IB:* 30.

N410 BAcc Accountancy
Duration: 3FT Ord
Entry Requirements: *GCE:* BCC. *SQAH:* ABBB. *IB:* 30.

D86 DURHAM UNIVERSITY
DURHAM UNIVERSITY
UNIVERSITY OFFICE
DURHAM DH1 3HP
t: 0191 334 2000 f: 0191 334 6055
e: admissions@durham.ac.uk
// www.durham.ac.uk

N420 BA Business Finance
Duration: 3FT/4SW Hon
Entry Requirements: *GCE:* ABB. *SQAH:* AABBB. *SQAAH:* ABB. *IB:* 34.

N402 MAcc Financial Accounting
Duration: 4FT Hon
Entry Requirements: *GCE:* ABB. *SQAH:* AABBB. *SQAAH:* ABB. *IB:* 34.

N401 MAcc Management Accounting
Duration: 4FT Hon
Entry Requirements: *GCE:* ABB. *SQAH:* AABBB. *SQAAH:* ABB. *IB:* 34.

E14 UNIVERSITY OF EAST ANGLIA
NORWICH NR4 7TJ
t: 01603 591515 f: 01603 591523
e: admissions@uea.ac.uk
// www.uea.ac.uk

N400 BSc Accounting and Finance
Duration: 3FT Hon   CRB Check: Required
Entry Requirements: *GCE:* ABB. *SQAAH:* ABB. *IB:* 32. *BTEC ExtDip:* DDM. Interview required.

E28 UNIVERSITY OF EAST LONDON
DOCKLANDS CAMPUS
UNIVERSITY WAY
LONDON E16 2RD
t: 020 8223 3333 f: 020 8223 2978
e: study@uel.ac.uk
// www.uel.ac.uk

N420 BA Accounting and Finance
Duration: 3FT Hon
Entry Requirements: *GCE:* 240. *IB:* 24.

E42 EDGE HILL UNIVERSITY
ORMSKIRK
LANCASHIRE L39 4QP
t: 01695 657000 f: 01695 584355
e: study@edgehill.ac.uk
// www.edgehill.ac.uk

N410 BSc Accountancy
Duration: 3FT Hon
Entry Requirements: *GCE:* 280. *IB:* 26. *OCR ND:* D *OCR NED:* M2

E59 EDINBURGH NAPIER UNIVERSITY
CRAIGLOCKHART CAMPUS
EDINBURGH EH14 1DJ
t: +44 (0)8452 60 60 40 f: 0131 455 6464
e: info@napier.ac.uk
// www.napier.ac.uk

N400 BA Accounting
Duration: 3FT/4FT Deg/Hon
Entry Requirements: *GCE:* 230.

E70 THE UNIVERSITY OF ESSEX
WIVENHOE PARK
COLCHESTER
ESSEX CO4 3SQ
t: 01206 873666 f: 01206 874477
e: admit@essex.ac.uk
// www.essex.ac.uk

N400 BA Accounting
Duration: 3FT Hon
Entry Requirements: *GCE:* ABB. *SQAH:* AAAB. *IB:* 34.

N402 BA Accounting (Including Year Abroad)
Duration: 4FT Hon
Entry Requirements: *GCE:* ABB. *SQAH:* AAAB. *IB:* 34.

N401 BA Accounting (including Foundation Year)
Duration: 4FT Hon
Entry Requirements: *GCE:* 180. *SQAH:* CCCD. *IB:* 24.

N420 BA Accounting and Finance
Duration: 3FT Hon
Entry Requirements: *GCE:* ABB. *SQAH:* AAAB. *IB:* 34.

E84 UNIVERSITY OF EXETER
LAVER BUILDING
NORTH PARK ROAD
EXETER
DEVON EX4 4QE
t: 01392 723044 f: 01392 722479
e: admissions@exeter.ac.uk
// www.exeter.ac.uk

N422 BA Accounting and Finance
Duration: 3FT Hon
Entry Requirements: *GCE:* AAA-AAB. *SQAH:* AAAAB-AAABB. *SQAAH:* AAB-ABB.

N423 BA Accounting and Finance with European Study (4 years)
Duration: 4FT Hon
Entry Requirements: *GCE:* AAA-AAB. *SQAH:* AAAAB-AAABB. *SQAAH:* AAB-ABB. *BTEC ExtDip:* DDD.

F66 FARNBOROUGH COLLEGE OF TECHNOLOGY
BOUNDARY ROAD
FARNBOROUGH
HAMPSHIRE GU14 6SB
t: 01252 407028 f: 01252 407041
e: admissions@farn-ct.ac.uk
// www.farn-ct.ac.uk

N400 BA Accounting
Duration: 3FT Hon
Entry Requirements: Contact the institution for details.

G14 UNIVERSITY OF GLAMORGAN, CARDIFF AND PONTYPRIDD
ENQUIRIES AND ADMISSIONS UNIT
PONTYPRIDD CF37 1DL
t: 08456 434030 f: 01443 654050
e: enquiries@glam.ac.uk
// www.glam.ac.uk

N420 BA Accounting and Finance
Duration: 3FT Hon
Entry Requirements: *GCE:* BBC. *IB:* 25. *BTEC SubDip:* M. *BTEC Dip:* D*D*. *BTEC ExtDip:* DMM. *OCR NED:* M2

N421 BA Accounting and Finance
Duration: 4SW Hon
Entry Requirements: *GCE:* BBC. *IB:* 25. *BTEC SubDip:* M. *BTEC Dip:* D*D*. *BTEC ExtDip:* DMM. *OCR NED:* M2

N490 BA Forensic Accounting
Duration: 3FT Hon
Entry Requirements: *GCE:* BBC. *IB:* 25. *BTEC SubDip:* M. *BTEC Dip:* D*D*. *BTEC ExtDip:* DMM. *OCR NED:* M2

N491 BA Forensic Accounting
Duration: 4SW Hon
Entry Requirements: *GCE:* BBC. *IB:* 25. *BTEC SubDip:* M. *BTEC Dip:* D*D*. *BTEC ExtDip:* DMM. *OCR NED:* M2

N401 BA International Accounting
Duration: 3FT Hon
Entry Requirements: *GCE:* BBC. *IB:* 25. *BTEC SubDip:* M. *BTEC Dip:* D*D*. *BTEC ExtDip:* DMM. *OCR NED:* M2

N402 BA International Accounting
Duration: 4SW Hon
Entry Requirements: *GCE:* BBC. *IB:* 25. *BTEC SubDip:* M. *BTEC Dip:* D*D*. *BTEC ExtDip:* DMM. *OCR NED:* M2

004N HND Accounting
Duration: 2FT HND
Entry Requirements: Interview required.

G28 UNIVERSITY OF GLASGOW
71 SOUTHPARK AVENUE
UNIVERSITY OF GLASGOW
GLASGOW G12 8QQ
t: 0141 330 6062 f: 0141 330 2961
e: student.recruitment@glasgow.ac.uk
// www.glasgow.ac.uk

N400 BAcc Accountancy
Duration: 4FT Hon
Entry Requirements: *GCE:* A*AB-AAA. *SQAH:* AAAABB-AAABB. *IB:* 36.

N401 BAcc Accountancy with International Accounting
Duration: 4FT Hon
Entry Requirements: *GCE:* A*AB-AAA. *SQAH:* AAAABB-AAABB. *IB:* 36.

G42 GLASGOW CALEDONIAN UNIVERSITY
STUDENT RECRUITMENT & ADMISSIONS SERVICE
CITY CAMPUS
COWCADDENS ROAD
GLASGOW G4 0BA
t: 0141 331 3000 f: 0141 331 8676
e: undergraduate@gcu.ac.uk
// www.gcu.ac.uk

N400 BA Accountancy
Duration: 4FT Hon
Entry Requirements: *GCE:* BCC. *SQAH:* BBBB-BBBC. *IB:* 24.

G50 THE UNIVERSITY OF GLOUCESTERSHIRE
PARK CAMPUS
THE PARK
CHELTENHAM GL50 2RH
t: 01242 714501 f: 01242 714869
e: admissions@glos.ac.uk
// www.glos.ac.uk

N400 BA Accounting and Financial Management Studies
Duration: 3FT Hon
Entry Requirements: *GCE:* 260-300.

G70 UNIVERSITY OF GREENWICH
GREENWICH CAMPUS
OLD ROYAL NAVAL COLLEGE
PARK ROW
LONDON SE10 9LS
t: 020 8331 9000 f: 020 8331 8145
e: courseinfo@gre.ac.uk
// www.gre.ac.uk

N400 BA Accounting and Finance
Duration: 3FT/4SW Hon
Entry Requirements: *GCE:* 300. *IB:* 30.

H36 UNIVERSITY OF HERTFORDSHIRE
UNIVERSITY ADMISSIONS SERVICE
COLLEGE LANE
HATFIELD
HERTS AL10 9AB
t: 01707 284800
// www.herts.ac.uk

N400 BA Accounting
Duration: 3FT/4SW Hon
Entry Requirements: *GCE:* 280. *IB:* 28.

H49 UNIVERSITY OF THE HIGHLANDS AND ISLANDS
UHI EXECUTIVE OFFICE
NESS WALK
INVERNESS
SCOTLAND IV3 5SQ
t: 01463 279000 f: 01463 279001
e: info@uhi.ac.uk
// www.uhi.ac.uk

104N HNC Accounting
Duration: 1FT HNC
Entry Requirements: *GCE:* D. *SQAH:* C.

004N HND Accounting
Duration: 2FT HND
Entry Requirements: *GCE:* C. *SQAH:* CC.

H50 HOLBORN COLLEGE
WOOLWICH ROAD
LONDON SE7 8LN
t: 020 8317 6000 f: 020 8317 6001
e: UKAdmissions@kaplan.co.uk
// www.holborncollege.ac.uk

N400 BA Accountancy
Duration: 3FT Hon
Entry Requirements: *GCE:* 120. *IB:* 24.

N410 BA Accountancy (with Foundation Year)
Duration: 4FT Hon
Entry Requirements: Contact the institution for details.

H60 THE UNIVERSITY OF HUDDERSFIELD
QUEENSGATE
HUDDERSFIELD HD1 3DH
t: 01484 473969 f: 01484 472765
e: admissionsandrecords@hud.ac.uk
// www.hud.ac.uk

N410 BA Accountancy
Duration: 3FT/4SW Hon
Entry Requirements: *GCE:* 300.

N420 BA Accountancy and Finance
Duration: 3FT/4SW Hon
Entry Requirements: *GCE:* 300.

N414 BA International Accountancy (Top-up)
Duration: 1FT Hon
Entry Requirements: Contact the institution for details.

H72 THE UNIVERSITY OF HULL
THE UNIVERSITY OF HULL
COTTINGHAM ROAD
HULL HU6 7RX
t: 01482 466100 f: 01482 442290
e: admissions@hull.ac.uk
// www.hull.ac.uk

N400 BSc Accounting
Duration: 3FT Hon
Entry Requirements: *GCE:* 300. *IB:* 30. *BTEC ExtDip:* DMM.

N401 BSc Accounting (International) (4 years)
Duration: 4FT Hon
Entry Requirements: *GCE:* 300. *IB:* 30. *BTEC ExtDip:* DMM.

N402 BSc Accounting (with Professional Experience) (4 years)
Duration: 4SW Hon
Entry Requirements: *GCE:* 300. *IB:* 30. *BTEC ExtDip:* DMM.

K12 KEELE UNIVERSITY
KEELE UNIVERSITY
STAFFORDSHIRE ST5 5BG
t: 01782 734005 f: 01782 632343
e: undergraduate@keele.ac.uk
// www.keele.ac.uk

NL43 BA Accounting with Social Science Foundation Year
Duration: 4FT FYr
Entry Requirements: *GCE:* CC.

K24 THE UNIVERSITY OF KENT
RECRUITMENT & ADMISSIONS OFFICE
REGISTRY
UNIVERSITY OF KENT
CANTERBURY, KENT CT2 7NZ
t: 01227 827272 f: 01227 827077
e: information@kent.ac.uk
// www.kent.ac.uk

N400 BA Accounting & Finance
Duration: 3FT Hon
Entry Requirements: *GCE:* 320. *IB:* 33. *OCR ND:* D *OCR NED:* M1

N404 BSc Accounting & Finance with a year in Industry
Duration: 4SW Hon
Entry Requirements: *GCE:* 320. *IB:* 33. *OCR ND:* D *OCR NED:* M1

K84 KINGSTON UNIVERSITY
STUDENT INFORMATION & ADVICE CENTRE
COOPER HOUSE
40-46 SURBITON ROAD
KINGSTON UPON THAMES KT1 2HX
t: 0844 8552177 f: 020 8547 7080
e: aps@kingston.ac.uk
// www.kingston.ac.uk

N420 BA Accounting & Finance
Duration: 3FT Hon
Entry Requirements: *GCE:* 320. *IB:* 27.

L14 LANCASTER UNIVERSITY
THE UNIVERSITY
LANCASTER
LANCASHIRE LA1 4YW
t: 01524 592029 f: 01524 846243
e: ugadmissions@lancaster.ac.uk
// www.lancs.ac.uk

N400 BSc Accounting and Finance
Duration: 3FT Hon
Entry Requirements: *GCE:* AAA-AAB. *SQAH:* AAABB-ABBBB.
SQAAH: AAA-AAB.

L23 UNIVERSITY OF LEEDS
THE UNIVERSITY OF LEEDS
WOODHOUSE LANE
LEEDS LS2 9JT
t: 0113 343 3999
e: admissions@leeds.ac.uk
// www.leeds.ac.uk

N420 BSc Accounting and Finance
Duration: 3FT Hon
Entry Requirements: *GCE:* AAA. *SQAH:* AAAAA. *SQAAH:* AAA. *IB:* 36. Interview required.

L27 LEEDS METROPOLITAN UNIVERSITY
COURSE ENQUIRIES OFFICE
CITY CAMPUS
LEEDS LS1 3HE
t: 0113 81 23113 f: 0113 81 23129
// www.leedsmet.ac.uk

N420 BA Accounting and Finance
Duration: 3FT/4SW Hon
Entry Requirements: *GCE:* 220. *IB:* 24.

L41 THE UNIVERSITY OF LIVERPOOL
THE FOUNDATION BUILDING
BROWNLOW HILL
LIVERPOOL L69 7ZX
t: 0151 794 2000 f: 0151 708 6502
e: ugrecruitment@liv.ac.uk
// www.liv.ac.uk

N400 BA Accounting and Finance
Duration: 3FT Hon
Entry Requirements: *GCE:* AAB. *SQAAH:* AAB. *IB:* 35.

L46 LIVERPOOL HOPE UNIVERSITY
HOPE PARK
LIVERPOOL L16 9JD
t: 0151 291 3331 f: 0151 291 3434
e: administration@hope.ac.uk
// www.hope.ac.uk

N400 BA Accounting
Duration: 3FT Hon
Entry Requirements: *GCE:* 300-320. *IB:* 25.

L51 LIVERPOOL JOHN MOORES UNIVERSITY
KINGSWAY HOUSE
HATTON GARDEN
LIVERPOOL L3 2AJ
t: 0151 231 5090 f: 0151 904 6368
e: courses@ljmu.ac.uk
// www.ljmu.ac.uk

N420 BSc Accounting and Finance
Duration: 3FT/4SW Hon
Entry Requirements: *GCE:* 280. *IB:* 28.

L68 LONDON METROPOLITAN UNIVERSITY
166-220 HOLLOWAY ROAD
LONDON N7 8DB
t: 020 7133 4200
e: admissions@londonmet.ac.uk
// www.londonmet.ac.uk

N400 BA Accounting and Finance
Duration: 3FT Hon
Entry Requirements: *GCE:* 240. *IB:* 28.

L70 LONDON SCHOOL OF COMMERCE
CHAUCER HOUSE
WHITE HART YARD
LONDON SE1 1NX
t: 020 7357 0077 f: 020 7403 1163
e: contactus@lsclondon.co.uk
// www.lsclondon.co.uk

N400 BSc Accounting
Duration: 2FT Hon
Entry Requirements: Contact the institution for details.

N401 BSc (Hons) Accounting
Duration: 2FT Hon
Entry Requirements: Contact the institution for details.

L75 LONDON SOUTH BANK UNIVERSITY
ADMISSIONS AND RECRUITMENT CENTRE
90 LONDON ROAD
LONDON SE1 6LN
t: 0800 923 8888 f: 020 7815 8273
e: course.enquiry@lsbu.ac.uk
// www.lsbu.ac.uk

N420 BA Accounting and Finance
Duration: 3FT Hon
Entry Requirements: *GCE:* 280. *IB:* 25.

N400 FdA Accounting
Duration: 2FT Fdg
Entry Requirements: *GCE:* 180. *IB:* 24.

M20 THE UNIVERSITY OF MANCHESTER
RUTHERFORD BUILDING
OXFORD ROAD
MANCHESTER M13 9PL
t: 0161 275 2077 f: 0161 275 2106
e: ug-admissions@manchester.ac.uk
// www.manchester.ac.uk

N400 BSc Accounting
Duration: 3FT/4FT Hon
Entry Requirements: *GCE:* AAA. *SQAAH:* AAA. *IB:* 37.

M40 THE MANCHESTER METROPOLITAN UNIVERSITY
ADMISSIONS OFFICE
ALL SAINTS (GMS)
ALL SAINTS
MANCHESTER M15 6BH
t: 0161 247 2000
// www.mmu.ac.uk

N420 BA Accounting and Finance
Duration: 3FT Hon
Entry Requirements: *IB:* 29.

N423 BA Accounting and Finance (Foundation)
Duration: 4FT/5SW Hon
Entry Requirements: *GCE:* 160. *IB:* 24. *BTEC Dip:* MM. *BTEC ExtDip:* MPP.

M80 MIDDLESEX UNIVERSITY
MIDDLESEX UNIVERSITY
THE BURROUGHS
LONDON NW4 4BT
t: 020 8411 5555 f: 020 8411 5649
e: enquiries@mdx.ac.uk
// www.mdx.ac.uk

N420 BA Accounting and Finance
Duration: 3FT/4SW Hon
Entry Requirements: *GCE:* 200-300. *IB:* 28.

N490 BA Business Accounting
Duration: 3FT Hon
Entry Requirements: *GCE:* 200-300. *IB:* 28.

N21 NEWCASTLE UNIVERSITY
KING'S GATE
NEWCASTLE UPON TYNE NE1 7RU
t: 01912083333
// www.ncl.ac.uk

N400 BA Accounting and Finance
Duration: 3FT Hon
Entry Requirements: *GCE:* AAB. *SQAH:* AAABB. *IB:* 35. *BTEC ExtDip:* DDD.

N37 UNIVERSITY OF WALES, NEWPORT
ADMISSIONS
LODGE ROAD
CAERLEON
NEWPORT NP18 3QT
t: 01633 432030 f: 01633 432850
e: admissions@newport.ac.uk
// www.newport.ac.uk

N401 BSc Accounting
Duration: 3FT Hon
Entry Requirements: *GCE:* 240. *IB:* 24.

N38 UNIVERSITY OF NORTHAMPTON
PARK CAMPUS
BOUGHTON GREEN ROAD
NORTHAMPTON NN2 7AL
t: 0800 358 2232 f: 01604 722083
e: admissions@northampton.ac.uk
// www.northampton.ac.uk

N491 BA International Accounting (top-up)
Duration: 1FT Hon
Entry Requirements: HND required.

N420 BSc Accounting and Finance
Duration: 3FT Hon
Entry Requirements: *GCE:* 260-300. *SQAH:* ABBB. *IB:* 25. *BTEC Dip:* DD. *BTEC ExtDip:* DMM. *OCR ND:* D *OCR NED:* M2

N77 NORTHUMBRIA UNIVERSITY
TRINITY BUILDING
NORTHUMBERLAND ROAD
NEWCASTLE UPON TYNE NE1 8ST
t: 0191 243 7420 f: 0191 227 4561
e: er.admissions@northumbria.ac.uk
// www.northumbria.ac.uk

N400 BA Accounting
Duration: 3FT Hon
Entry Requirements: *GCE:* 320. *SQAH:* BBBBB. *SQAAH:* BBB. *IB:* 27. *BTEC ExtDip:* DDM. *OCR NED:* D2

N420 BA Accounting and Finance (Top-up)
Duration: 1FT Hon
Entry Requirements: HND required.

P60 PLYMOUTH UNIVERSITY
DRAKE CIRCUS
PLYMOUTH PL4 8AA
t: 01752 585858 f: 01752 588055
e: admissions@plymouth.ac.uk
// www.plymouth.ac.uk

N420 BA Accounting and Finance
Duration: 3FT/4SW Hon
Entry Requirements: *GCE:* 240. *IB:* 24.

N401 FdA Accounting and Finance
Duration: 2FT Fdg
Entry Requirements: *GCE:* 120-180. *IB:* 24.

P80 UNIVERSITY OF PORTSMOUTH
ACADEMIC REGISTRY
UNIVERSITY HOUSE
WINSTON CHURCHILL AVENUE
PORTSMOUTH PO1 2UP
t: 023 9284 8484 f: 023 9284 3082
e: admissions@port.ac.uk
// www.port.ac.uk

N420 BA Accountancy Studies
Duration: 2FT Hon
Entry Requirements: Contact the institution for details.

N400 BA Accounting
Duration: 3FT/4SW Hon
Entry Requirements: *GCE:* 300. *IB:* 29. *BTEC ExtDip:* DDM.

Q75 QUEEN'S UNIVERSITY BELFAST
UNIVERSITY ROAD
BELFAST BT7 1NN
t: 028 9097 3838 f: 028 9097 5151
e: admissions@qub.ac.uk
// www.qub.ac.uk

N400 BSc Accounting
Duration: 3FT Hon
Entry Requirements: *GCE:* AAB-ABBa. *SQAH:* AAAA-AAABB. *SQAAH:* AAB. *IB:* 34.

R36 ROBERT GORDON UNIVERSITY
ROBERT GORDON UNIVERSITY
SCHOOLHILL
ABERDEEN
SCOTLAND AB10 1FR
t: 01224 26 27 28 f: 01224 26 21 47
e: UGOffice@rgu.ac.uk
// www.rgu.ac.uk

N420 BA Accounting and Finance
Duration: 4FT Hon
Entry Requirements: *GCE:* BCC. *SQAH:* BBBB. *IB:* 28.

S18 THE UNIVERSITY OF SHEFFIELD
THE UNIVERSITY OF SHEFFIELD
LEVEL 2, ARTS TOWER
WESTERN BANK
SHEFFIELD S10 2TN
t: 0114 222 8030 f: 0114 222 8032
// www.sheffield.ac.uk

N420 BA Accounting & Financial Management
Duration: 3FT Hon
Entry Requirements: *GCE:* AAB. *SQAH:* AAAAB. *IB:* 35. *BTEC ExtDip:* DDD.

S21 SHEFFIELD HALLAM UNIVERSITY
CITY CAMPUS
HOWARD STREET
SHEFFIELD S1 1WB
t: 0114 225 5555 f: 0114 225 2167
e: admissions@shu.ac.uk
// www.shu.ac.uk

N490 BA Forensic Accounting
Duration: 3FT/4SW Hon
Entry Requirements: *GCE:* 300.

S30 SOUTHAMPTON SOLENT UNIVERSITY
EAST PARK TERRACE
SOUTHAMPTON
HAMPSHIRE SO14 0RT
t: +44 (0) 23 8031 9039 f: + 44 (0)23 8022 2259
e: admissions@solent.ac.uk
// www.solent.ac.uk/

N400 BA Accountancy
Duration: 3FT Hon
Entry Requirements: *GCE:* 220.

S75 THE UNIVERSITY OF STIRLING
STUDENT RECRUITMENT & ADMISSIONS SERVICE
UNIVERSITY OF STIRLING
STIRLING
SCOTLAND FK9 4LA
t: 01786 467044 f: 01786 466800
e: admissions@stir.ac.uk
// www.stir.ac.uk

N400 BAcc Accountancy
Duration: 4FT Hon
Entry Requirements: *GCE:* BBC. *SQAH:* BBBB. *SQAAH:* AAA-CCC. *IB:* 32. *BTEC ExtDip:* DMM.

S78 THE UNIVERSITY OF STRATHCLYDE
GLASGOW G1 1XQ
t: 0141 552 4400 f: 0141 552 0775
// www.strath.ac.uk

N400 BA Accounting
Duration: 4FT Hon
Entry Requirements: *GCE:* AAA. *SQAH:* AAAAAB-AAAA. *IB:* 36.

S84 UNIVERSITY OF SUNDERLAND
STUDENT HELPLINE
THE STUDENT GATEWAY
CHESTER ROAD
SUNDERLAND SR1 3SD
t: 0191 515 3000 f: 0191 515 3805
e: student.helpline@sunderland.ac.uk
// www.sunderland.ac.uk

NN41 BA Accounting and Finance
Duration: 3FT Hon
Entry Requirements: *OCR ND:* D *OCR NED:* M3

S96 SWANSEA METROPOLITAN UNIVERSITY
MOUNT PLEASANT CAMPUS
SWANSEA SA1 6ED
t: 01792 481000 f: 01792 481061
e: gemma.green@smu.ac.uk
// www.smu.ac.uk

N400 BA Accounting
Duration: 3FT/4SW Hon
Entry Requirements: *GCE:* 160-360. *IB:* 24. Interview required.

T20 TEESSIDE UNIVERSITY
MIDDLESBROUGH TS1 3BA
t: 01642 218121 f: 01642 384201
e: registry@tees.ac.uk
// www.tees.ac.uk

N420 BA Accounting & Finance
Duration: 3FT/4SW Hon
Entry Requirements: *GCE:* 240. *IB:* 30. *BTEC Dip:* DD. *BTEC ExtDip:* MMM. *OCR ND:* D *OCR NED:* M3

N400 BA Applied Accounting
Duration: 1FT Hon
Entry Requirements: HND required.

U20 UNIVERSITY OF ULSTER
COLERAINE
CO. LONDONDERRY
NORTHERN IRELAND BT52 1SA
t: 028 7012 4221 f: 028 7012 4908
e: online@ulster.ac.uk
// www.ulster.ac.uk

N400 BSc Accounting
Duration: 3FT Hon
Entry Requirements: *GCE:* 340-360. *IB:* 27.

U40 UNIVERSITY OF THE WEST OF SCOTLAND
PAISLEY
RENFREWSHIRE
SCOTLAND PA1 2BE
t: 0141 848 3727 f: 0141 848 3623
e: admissions@uws.ac.uk
// www.uws.ac.uk

N400 BAcc Accountancy
Duration: 3FT/4FT/5SW Ord/Hon
Entry Requirements: *GCE:* CCC. *SQAH:* BBBC.

W05 THE UNIVERSITY OF WEST LONDON
ST MARY'S ROAD
EALING
LONDON W5 5RF
t: 0800 036 8888 f: 020 8566 1353
e: learning.advice@uwl.ac.uk
// www.uwl.ac.uk

N420 BA Accounting and Finance
Duration: 3FT Hon
Entry Requirements: *GCE:* 200. *IB:* 28. Interview required.

W52 WESTMINSTER KINGSWAY COLLEGE
VICTORIA CENTRE
VINCENT SQUARE
LONDON SW1P 2PD
t: 0870 060 9800 f: 020 7931 6969
e: courseinfo@westking.ac.uk
// www.westking.ac.uk

N401 FdA Accounting
Duration: 2FT Fdg
Entry Requirements: Contact the institution for details.

W75 UNIVERSITY OF WOLVERHAMPTON
ADMISSIONS UNIT
MX207, CAMP STREET
WOLVERHAMPTON
WEST MIDLANDS WV1 1AD
t: 01902 321000 f: 01902 321896
e: admissions@wlv.ac.uk
// www.wlv.ac.uk

N400 BA Accounting and Finance
Duration: 3FT/4SW Hon
Entry Requirements: *GCE:* 220. *IB:* 28.

W80 UNIVERSITY OF WORCESTER
HENWICK GROVE
WORCESTER WR2 6AJ
t: 01905 855111 f: 01905 855377
e: admissions@worc.ac.uk
// www.worcester.ac.uk

N400 BA Accounting
Duration: 3FT/4SW Hon
Entry Requirements: *GCE:* 280. *IB:* 25. *OCR ND:* D *OCR NED:* M3

ECONOMICS AND
ACCOUNTANCY/ACCOUNTANCY AND
ECONOMICS

A20 THE UNIVERSITY OF ABERDEEN
UNIVERSITY OFFICE
KING'S COLLEGE
ABERDEEN AB24 3FX
t: +44 (0) 1224 273504 f: +44 (0) 1224 272034
e: sras@abdn.ac.uk
// www.abdn.ac.uk/sras

NL41 MA Accountancy and Economics
Duration: 4FT Hon
Entry Requirements: *GCE:* BBB. *SQAH:* BBBB. *IB:* 30.

B06 BANGOR UNIVERSITY
BANGOR UNIVERSITY
BANGOR
GWYNEDD LL57 2DG
t: 01248 388484 f: 01248 370451
e: admissions@bangor.ac.uk
// www.bangor.ac.uk

LN14 BA Economics/Accounting
Duration: 3FT Hon
Entry Requirements: *GCE:* 260-300. *IB:* 28.

NL41 BSc Accounting and Economics
Duration: 3FT Hon
Entry Requirements: *GCE:* 260-300. *IB:* 28.

www.ucas.com

at the heart of connecting people to higher education

B24 BIRKBECK, UNIVERSITY OF LONDON
MALET STREET
LONDON WC1E 7HX
t: 020 7631 6316
e: webform: www.bbk.ac.uk/ask
// **www.bbk.ac.uk/ask**

L1N4 BSc Financial Economics with Accounting
Duration: 3FT Hon
Entry Requirements: *GCE:* AAB. *SQAH:* AAAA-AABB. *IB:* 36.
Admissions Test required.

B78 UNIVERSITY OF BRISTOL
UNDERGRADUATE ADMISSIONS OFFICE
SENATE HOUSE
TYNDALL AVENUE
BRISTOL BS8 1TH
t: 0117 928 9000 f: 0117 331 7391
e: ug-admissions@bristol.ac.uk
// **www.bristol.ac.uk**

LN14 BSc Economics and Accounting
Duration: 3FT Hon
Entry Requirements: *GCE:* AAA-AAB. *SQAH:* AAAA. *SQAAH:* AA-AB.

B84 BRUNEL UNIVERSITY
UXBRIDGE
MIDDLESEX UB8 3PH
t: 01895 265265 f: 01895 269790
e: admissions@brunel.ac.uk
// **www.brunel.ac.uk**

LN14 BSc Economics and Accounting
Duration: 3FT Hon
Entry Requirements: *GCE:* AAB. *SQAAH:* AAB. *IB:* 35. *BTEC ExtDip:* D*D*D.

NL41 BSc Economics and Accounting (Thick SW)
Duration: 4SW Hon
Entry Requirements: *GCE:* AAB. *SQAAH:* AAB. *IB:* 35. *BTEC ExtDip:* D*D*D.

C15 CARDIFF UNIVERSITY
PO BOX 927
30-36 NEWPORT ROAD
CARDIFF CF24 0DE
t: 029 2087 9999 f: 029 2087 6138
e: admissions@cardiff.ac.uk
// **www.cardiff.ac.uk**

LN14 BScEcon Accounting and Economics
Duration: 3FT Hon
Entry Requirements: *GCE:* AAB. *SQAH:* AAABB. *SQAAH:* AAB. *IB:* 35. *OCR NED:* D1 Interview required.

C30 UNIVERSITY OF CENTRAL LANCASHIRE
PRESTON
LANCS PR1 2HE
t: 01772 201201 f: 01772 894954
e: uadmissions@uclan.ac.uk
// **www.uclan.ac.uk**

LNC4 BA Accounting and Economics
Duration: 3FT Hon
Entry Requirements: *GCE:* 240-280. *SQAH:* AABB-BBBC. *IB:* 28. *OCR ND:* D

LN14 BA Economics and Accounting
Duration: 3FT Hon
Entry Requirements: *GCE:* 240-280. *SQAH:* AABB-BBBC. *IB:* 28. *OCR ND:* D

C60 CITY UNIVERSITY
NORTHAMPTON SQUARE
LONDON EC1V 0HB
t: 020 7040 5060 f: 020 7040 8995
e: ugadmissions@city.ac.uk
// **www.city.ac.uk**

LN14 BSc Economics/Accountancy
Duration: 3FT Hon
Entry Requirements: *GCE:* AAA. *SQAH:* BBBBB. *IB:* 35.

D26 DE MONTFORT UNIVERSITY
THE GATEWAY
LEICESTER LE1 9BH
t: 0116 255 1551 f: 0116 250 6204
e: enquiries@dmu.ac.uk
// **www.dmu.ac.uk**

NL41 BA Accounting and Economics
Duration: 3FT Hon
Entry Requirements: *GCE:* 280. *IB:* 28. *BTEC Dip:* D*D*. *BTEC ExtDip:* DMM. *OCR NED:* M2 Interview required.

E14 UNIVERSITY OF EAST ANGLIA
NORWICH NR4 7TJ
t: 01603 591515 f: 01603 591523
e: admissions@uea.ac.uk
// **www.uea.ac.uk**

NL41 BSc Business Finance and Economics
Duration: 3FT Hon CRB Check: Required
Entry Requirements: *GCE:* ABB. *SQAAH:* ABB. *IB:* 32. *BTEC ExtDip:* DDM. Interview required.

L1N4 BSc Economics with Accountancy
Duration: 3FT Hon CRB Check: Required
Entry Requirements: *GCE:* ABB. *SQAAH:* ABB. *IB:* 32. *BTEC ExtDip:* DDM. Interview required.

E56 THE UNIVERSITY OF EDINBURGH
STUDENT RECRUITMENT & ADMISSIONS
57 GEORGE SQUARE
EDINBURGH EH8 9JU
t: 0131 650 4360 f: 0131 651 1236
e: sra.enquiries@ed.ac.uk
// www.ed.ac.uk/studying/undergraduate/

LN14 MA Economics and Accounting
Duration: 4FT Hon
Entry Requirements: *GCE:* AAA-BBB. *SQAH:* AAAA-BBBB. *IB:* 34.

E59 EDINBURGH NAPIER UNIVERSITY
CRAIGLOCKHART CAMPUS
EDINBURGH EH14 1DJ
t: +44 (0)8452 60 60 40 f: 0131 455 6464
e: info@napier.ac.uk
// www.napier.ac.uk

N4L1 BA Accounting with Economics
Duration: 3FT/4FT Ord/Hon
Entry Requirements: *GCE:* 230.

E70 THE UNIVERSITY OF ESSEX
WIVENHOE PARK
COLCHESTER
ESSEX CO4 3SQ
t: 01206 873666 f: 01206 874477
e: admit@essex.ac.uk
// www.essex.ac.uk

NL41 BA Accounting with Economics
Duration: 3FT Hon
Entry Requirements: *GCE:* ABB. *SQAH:* AAAB. *IB:* 34.

NKL1 BA Accounting with Economics (Including Year Abroad)
Duration: 4FT Hon
Entry Requirements: *GCE:* ABB. *SQAH:* AAAB. *IB:* 34.

N4L1 BA Accounting with Economics (including Foundation Year)
Duration: 4FT Hon
Entry Requirements: *GCE:* 180. *SQAH:* CCCD. *IB:* 24.

G28 UNIVERSITY OF GLASGOW
71 SOUTHPARK AVENUE
UNIVERSITY OF GLASGOW
GLASGOW G12 8QQ
t: 0141 330 6062 f: 0141 330 2961
e: student.recruitment@glasgow.ac.uk
// www.glasgow.ac.uk

LN14 BAcc Accountancy/Economics
Duration: 4FT Hon
Entry Requirements: *GCE:* A*AB-AAA. *SQAH:* AAAABB-AAABB. *IB:* 36.

H24 HERIOT-WATT UNIVERSITY, EDINBURGH
EDINBURGH CAMPUS
EDINBURGH EH14 4AS
t: 0131 449 5111 f: 0131 451 3630
e: ugadmissions@hw.ac.uk
// www.hw.ac.uk

LN14 MA Economics and Accountancy
Duration: 4FT Hon
Entry Requirements: *GCE:* BBB. *SQAH:* AAAB-BBBBC. *SQAAH:* BB. *IB:* 29.

H36 UNIVERSITY OF HERTFORDSHIRE
UNIVERSITY ADMISSIONS SERVICE
COLLEGE LANE
HATFIELD
HERTS AL10 9AB
t: 01707 284800
// www.herts.ac.uk

NL41 BA Accounting/Economics
Duration: 3FT/4SW Hon
Entry Requirements: *GCE:* 300. *IB:* 30.

H72 THE UNIVERSITY OF HULL
THE UNIVERSITY OF HULL
COTTINGHAM ROAD
HULL HU6 7RX
t: 01482 466100 f: 01482 442290
e: admissions@hull.ac.uk
// www.hull.ac.uk

LN14 BSc Accounting and Business Economics
Duration: 3FT Hon
Entry Requirements: *GCE:* 300. *IB:* 30. *BTEC ExtDip:* DMM.

LNC4 BSc Accounting and Business Economics (International) (4 years)
Duration: 4FT Hon
Entry Requirements: *GCE:* 300. *IB:* 30. *BTEC ExtDip:* DMM.

LND4 BSc Accounting and Business Economics (with Professional Experience) (4 years)
Duration: 4FT Hon
Entry Requirements: *GCE:* 300. *IB:* 30. *BTEC ExtDip:* DMM.

K24 THE UNIVERSITY OF KENT
RECRUITMENT & ADMISSIONS OFFICE
REGISTRY
UNIVERSITY OF KENT
CANTERBURY, KENT CT2 7NZ
t: 01227 827272 f: 01227 827077
e: information@kent.ac.uk
// www.kent.ac.uk

LN14 BA Accounting & Finance and Economics
Duration: 3FT Hon
Entry Requirements: *GCE:* 320. *IB:* 33. *OCR ND:* D *OCR NED:* M1

L14 LANCASTER UNIVERSITY
THE UNIVERSITY
LANCASTER
LANCASHIRE LA1 4YW
t: 01524 592029 f: 01524 846243
e: ugadmissions@lancaster.ac.uk
// www.lancs.ac.uk

NL41 BA Accounting and Economics
Duration: 3FT Hon
Entry Requirements: *GCE:* AAA-AAB. *SQAH:* AAABB-ABBBB. *SQAAH:* AAA-AAB.

L79 LOUGHBOROUGH UNIVERSITY
LOUGHBOROUGH
LEICESTERSHIRE LE11 3TU
t: 01509 223522 f: 01509 223905
e: admissions@lboro.ac.uk
// www.lboro.ac.uk

L1NK BSc Business Economics and Finance
Duration: 3FT Hon
Entry Requirements: *GCE:* AAB. *SQAH:* AABBB. *SQAAH:* AB. *IB:* 34. *BTEC ExtDip:* DDD.

L1N4 BSc Economics with Accounting
Duration: 3FT Hon
Entry Requirements: *GCE:* AAB. *SQAH:* AABBB. *SQAAH:* AB. *IB:* 34. *BTEC ExtDip:* DDD.

N37 UNIVERSITY OF WALES, NEWPORT
ADMISSIONS
LODGE ROAD
CAERLEON
NEWPORT NP18 3QT
t: 01633 432030 f: 01633 432850
e: admissions@newport.ac.uk
// www.newport.ac.uk

LN14 BSc Accounting and Economics
Duration: 3FT Hon
Entry Requirements: *GCE:* 240. *IB:* 24.

N38 UNIVERSITY OF NORTHAMPTON
PARK CAMPUS
BOUGHTON GREEN ROAD
NORTHAMPTON NN2 7AL
t: 0800 358 2232 f: 01604 722083
e: admissions@northampton.ac.uk
// www.northampton.ac.uk

N4L1 BA Accounting/Economics
Duration: 3FT Hon
Entry Requirements: *GCE:* 260-280. *SQAH:* AAA-BBBB. *IB:* 24. *BTEC Dip:* DD. *BTEC ExtDip:* DMM. *OCR ND:* D *OCR NED:* M2

L1N4 BA Economics/Accounting
Duration: 3FT Hon
Entry Requirements: *GCE:* 260-280. *SQAH:* AAA-BBBB. *IB:* 24. *BTEC Dip:* DD. *BTEC ExtDip:* DMM. *OCR ND:* D *OCR NED:* M2

P60 PLYMOUTH UNIVERSITY
DRAKE CIRCUS
PLYMOUTH PL4 8AA
t: 01752 585858 f: 01752 588055
e: admissions@plymouth.ac.uk
// www.plymouth.ac.uk

L1NK BSc Business Economics with Accounting
Duration: 3FT/4SW Hon
Entry Requirements: *GCE:* 240. *IB:* 24.

Q75 QUEEN'S UNIVERSITY BELFAST
UNIVERSITY ROAD
BELFAST BT7 1NN
t: 028 9097 3838 f: 028 9097 5151
e: admissions@qub.ac.uk
// www.qub.ac.uk

LN14 BSc Economics and Accounting
Duration: 3FT Hon
Entry Requirements: *GCE:* ABB-BBBb. *SQAH:* ABBBB. *SQAAH:* ABB. *IB:* 33.

R12 THE UNIVERSITY OF READING
THE UNIVERSITY OF READING
PO BOX 217
READING RG6 6AH
t: 0118 378 8619 f: 0118 378 8924
e: student.recruitment@reading.ac.uk
// www.reading.ac.uk

NL41 BA Accounting and Economics
Duration: 3FT/4SW Hon
Entry Requirements: *GCE:* AAB. *SQAH:* AAABB. *SQAAH:* AAB. *BTEC Dip:* DD. *BTEC ExtDip:* DDD.

LN14 BSc Accounting and Economics
Duration: 3FT/4SW Hon
Entry Requirements: *GCE:* AAB. *SQAH:* AAABB. *SQAAH:* AAB. *BTEC Dip:* DD. *BTEC ExtDip:* DDD.

S18 THE UNIVERSITY OF SHEFFIELD
THE UNIVERSITY OF SHEFFIELD
LEVEL 2, ARTS TOWER
WESTERN BANK
SHEFFIELD S10 2TN
t: 0114 222 8030 f: 0114 222 8032
// www.sheffield.ac.uk

NL41 BA Accounting & Financial Management and Economics
Duration: 3FT Hon
Entry Requirements: *GCE:* AAB. *SQAH:* AAABB. *SQAAH:* AB. *IB:*
35. *BTEC ExtDip:* DDD.

S27 UNIVERSITY OF SOUTHAMPTON
HIGHFIELD
SOUTHAMPTON SO17 1BJ
t: 023 8059 4732 f: 023 8059 3037
e: admissions@soton.ac.uk
// www.southampton.ac.uk

NL41 BSc Accounting and Economics
Duration: 3FT Hon
Entry Requirements: *GCE:* AAA-AABB. *SQAH:* AAAA. *SQAAH:* AA.
IB: 36.

S75 THE UNIVERSITY OF STIRLING
STUDENT RECRUITMENT & ADMISSIONS SERVICE
UNIVERSITY OF STIRLING
STIRLING
SCOTLAND FK9 4LA
t: 01786 467044 f: 01786 466800
e: admissions@stir.ac.uk
// www.stir.ac.uk

LN14 BAcc Accountancy and Economics
Duration: 4FT Hon
Entry Requirements: *GCE:* BBC. *SQAH:* BBBB. *SQAAH:* AAA-CCC.
IB: 32. *BTEC ExtDip:* DMM.

S78 THE UNIVERSITY OF STRATHCLYDE
GLASGOW G1 1XQ
t: 0141 552 4400 f: 0141 552 0775
// www.strath.ac.uk

NL41 BA Accounting and Economics
Duration: 4FT Hon
Entry Requirements: *GCE:* AAA. *SQAH:* AAAAAB-AAAA. *IB:* 36.

S93 SWANSEA UNIVERSITY
SINGLETON PARK
SWANSEA SA2 8PP
t: 01792 295111 f: 01792 295110
e: admissions@swansea.ac.uk
// www.swansea.ac.uk

L1N4 BA Business Economics with Accounting
Duration: 3FT Hon
Entry Requirements: *GCE:* BBB. *IB:* 33.

L1NK BSc Financial Economics with Accounting
Duration: 3FT Hon
Entry Requirements: *GCE:* BBB. *IB:* 33.

FINANCE AND ECONOMICS/ECONOMICS AND FINANCE

A20 THE UNIVERSITY OF ABERDEEN
UNIVERSITY OFFICE
KING'S COLLEGE
ABERDEEN AB24 3FX
t: +44 (0) 1224 273504 f: +44 (0) 1224 272034
e: sras@abdn.ac.uk
// www.abdn.ac.uk/sras

LN13 MA Economics and Finance
Duration: 4FT Hon
Entry Requirements: *GCE:* BBB. *SQAH:* BBBB. *IB:* 30.

B25 BIRMINGHAM CITY UNIVERSITY
PERRY BARR
BIRMINGHAM B42 2SU
t: 0121 331 5595 f: 0121 331 7994
// www.bcu.ac.uk

LN13 BA Economics and Finance
Duration: 3FT/4SW Hon
Entry Requirements: *GCE:* 280. *IB:* 32. *OCR ND:* D *OCR NED:* M2

B50 BOURNEMOUTH UNIVERSITY
TALBOT CAMPUS
FERN BARROW
POOLE
DORSET BH12 5BB
t: 01202 524111
// www.bournemouth.ac.uk

NL31 BA Finance and Economics
Duration: 3FT/4SW Hon
Entry Requirements: *GCE:* 320. *IB:* 32. *BTEC SubDip:* D. *BTEC Dip:* DD. *BTEC ExtDip:* DDM.

B78 UNIVERSITY OF BRISTOL
UNDERGRADUATE ADMISSIONS OFFICE
SENATE HOUSE
TYNDALL AVENUE
BRISTOL BS8 1TH
t: 0117 928 9000 f: 0117 331 7391
e: ug-admissions@bristol.ac.uk
// www.bristol.ac.uk

LN13 BSc Economics and Finance
Duration: 3FT Hon
Entry Requirements: *GCE:* A*AA-AAA. *SQAH:* AAAA. *SQAAH:* AA.
IB: 38.

B84 BRUNEL UNIVERSITY
UXBRIDGE
MIDDLESEX UB8 3PH
t: 01895 265265 f: 01895 269790
e: admissions@brunel.ac.uk
// www.brunel.ac.uk

LND3 BSc Economics and Business Finance
Duration: 3FT Hon
Entry Requirements: GCE: ABB. SQAAH: ABB. IB: 33. BTEC ExtDip: D*DD.

LNC3 BSc Economics and Business Finance (4 year Thick SW)
Duration: 4SW Hon
Entry Requirements: GCE: ABB. SQAAH: ABB. IB: 33. BTEC ExtDip: D*DD.

C15 CARDIFF UNIVERSITY
PO BOX 927
30-36 NEWPORT ROAD
CARDIFF CF24 0DE
t: 029 2087 9999 f: 029 2087 6138
e: admissions@cardiff.ac.uk
// www.cardiff.ac.uk

LN13 BSc Econ Economics and Finance
Duration: 3FT Hon
Entry Requirements: GCE: AAB. SQAH: AAABB. SQAAH: AAB. IB: 35. OCR NED: D1 Interview required.

C20 CARDIFF METROPOLITAN UNIVERSITY (UWIC)
ADMISSIONS UNIT
LLANDAFF CAMPUS
WESTERN AVENUE
CARDIFF CF5 2YB
t: 029 2041 6070 f: 029 2041 6286
e: admissions@cardiffmet.ac.uk
// www.cardiffmet.ac.uk

LN13 BScEcon International Economics and Finance
Duration: 3FT/4SW Hon
Entry Requirements: GCE: 300. IB: 26. BTEC ExtDip: DDM. OCR NED: M1

D26 DE MONTFORT UNIVERSITY
THE GATEWAY
LEICESTER LE1 9BH
t: 0116 255 1551 f: 0116 250 6204
e: enquiries@dmu.ac.uk
// www.dmu.ac.uk

LN13 BSc Economics and Finance
Duration: 3FT/4SW Hon
Entry Requirements: GCE: 280. IB: 28. BTEC Dip: D*D*. BTEC ExtDip: DMM. OCR NED: M2 Interview required.

E28 UNIVERSITY OF EAST LONDON
DOCKLANDS CAMPUS
UNIVERSITY WAY
LONDON E16 2RD
t: 020 8223 3333 f: 020 8223 2978
e: study@uel.ac.uk
// www.uel.ac.uk

LN13 BSc Economics and Financial Institutions
Duration: 3FT Hon
Entry Requirements: GCE: 240. IB: 24.

E56 THE UNIVERSITY OF EDINBURGH
STUDENT RECRUITMENT & ADMISSIONS
57 GEORGE SQUARE
EDINBURGH EH8 9JU
t: 0131 650 4360 f: 0131 651 1236
e: sra.enquiries@ed.ac.uk
// www.ed.ac.uk/studying/undergraduate/

L1N3 MA Economics with Finance
Duration: 4FT Hon
Entry Requirements: GCE: AAA-BBB. SQAH: AAAA-BBBB. IB: 34.

E84 UNIVERSITY OF EXETER
LAVER BUILDING
NORTH PARK ROAD
EXETER
DEVON EX4 4QE
t: 01392 723044 f: 01392 722479
e: admissions@exeter.ac.uk
// www.exeter.ac.uk

LN13 BA Economics and Finance
Duration: 3FT Hon
Entry Requirements: GCE: A*AA-AAB. SQAH: AAAAA-AAABB. SQAAH: AAA-ABB.

LNC3 BA Economics and Finance with European Study (4 years)
Duration: 4FT Hon
Entry Requirements: GCE: A*AA-AAB. SQAH: AAAAA-AAABB. SQAAH: AAA-ABB.

LND3 BA Economics and Finance with Industrial Experience (4 years)
Duration: 4FT Hon
Entry Requirements: GCE: A*AA-AAB. SQAH: AAAAA-AAABB. SQAAH: AAA-ABB.

LN1J BA Economics and Finance with International Study (4 years)
Duration: 4FT Hon
Entry Requirements: GCE: A*AA-AAB. SQAH: AAAAA-AAABB. SQAAH: AAA-ABB.

G70 UNIVERSITY OF GREENWICH
GREENWICH CAMPUS
OLD ROYAL NAVAL COLLEGE
PARK ROW
LONDON SE10 9LS
t: 020 8331 9000 f: 020 8331 8145
e: courseinfo@gre.ac.uk
// www.gre.ac.uk

L1NH BSc Economics with Banking
Duration: 3FT Hon
Entry Requirements: *GCE:* 280. *IB:* 24.

H24 HERIOT-WATT UNIVERSITY, EDINBURGH
EDINBURGH CAMPUS
EDINBURGH EH14 4AS
t: 0131 449 5111 f: 0131 451 3630
e: ugadmissions@hw.ac.uk
// www.hw.ac.uk

LN13 MA Economics and Finance
Duration: 4FT Hon
Entry Requirements: *GCE:* BBB. *SQAH:* AAAB-BBBBC. *SQAAH:* BB. *IB:* 29.

H36 UNIVERSITY OF HERTFORDSHIRE
UNIVERSITY ADMISSIONS SERVICE
COLLEGE LANE
HATFIELD
HERTS AL10 9AB
t: 01707 284800
// www.herts.ac.uk

L1N3 BA Economics with Finance
Duration: 3FT/4SW Hon
Entry Requirements: *GCE:* 260. *IB:* 30.

H72 THE UNIVERSITY OF HULL
THE UNIVERSITY OF HULL
COTTINGHAM ROAD
HULL HU6 7RX
t: 01482 466100 f: 01482 442290
e: admissions@hull.ac.uk
// www.hull.ac.uk

LN13 BA Business Economics and Financial Management
Duration: 3FT Hon
Entry Requirements: *GCE:* 300. *IB:* 30. *BTEC ExtDip:* DMM.

LN1H BA Business Economics and Financial Management (International) (4 years)
Duration: 4FT Hon
Entry Requirements: *GCE:* 300. *IB:* 30. *BTEC ExtDip:* DMM.

LNC3 BA Business Economics and Financial Management (with Prof Experience) (4 years)
Duration: 4FT Hon
Entry Requirements: *GCE:* 300. *IB:* 30. *BTEC ExtDip:* DMM.

K12 KEELE UNIVERSITY
KEELE UNIVERSITY
STAFFORDSHIRE ST5 5BG
t: 01782 734005 f: 01782 632343
e: undergraduate@keele.ac.uk
// www.keele.ac.uk

LNC3 BA Business Economics
Duration: 3FT Hon
Entry Requirements: *GCE:* AAB.

LN13 BA Economics and Finance
Duration: 3FT Hon
Entry Requirements: *GCE:* ABB.

L14 LANCASTER UNIVERSITY
THE UNIVERSITY
LANCASTER
LANCASHIRE LA1 4YW
t: 01524 592029 f: 01524 846243
e: ugadmissions@lancaster.ac.uk
// www.lancs.ac.uk

NL31 BSc Finance and Economics
Duration: 3FT Hon
Entry Requirements: *GCE:* AAA-AAB. *SQAH:* AAABB-ABBBB. *SQAAH:* AAA-AAB.

L23 UNIVERSITY OF LEEDS
THE UNIVERSITY OF LEEDS
WOODHOUSE LANE
LEEDS LS2 9JT
t: 0113 343 3999
e: admissions@leeds.ac.uk
// www.leeds.ac.uk

LN13 BSc Economics and Finance
Duration: 3FT Hon
Entry Requirements: *GCE:* AAA. *SQAH:* AAAAA. *SQAAH:* AAA. *IB:* 36. Interview required.

L34 UNIVERSITY OF LEICESTER
UNIVERSITY ROAD
LEICESTER LE1 7RH
t: 0116 252 5281 f: 0116 252 2447
e: admissions@le.ac.uk
// www.le.ac.uk

LN13 BA Banking and Finance
Duration: 3FT Hon
Entry Requirements: *GCE:* AAB. *SQAH:* AAAAB-AAABB. *SQAAH:* AAB. *IB:* 34.

NL31 BSc Banking and Finance
Duration: 3FT Hon
Entry Requirements: *GCE:* AAB. *SQAH:* AAAAB-AAABB. *SQAAH:* AAB. *IB:* 34.

L68 LONDON METROPOLITAN UNIVERSITY
166-220 HOLLOWAY ROAD
LONDON N7 8DB
t: 020 7133 4200
e: admissions@londonmet.ac.uk
// www.londonmet.ac.uk

LN1J BSc Economics and Finance
Duration: 3FT Hon
Entry Requirements: Contact the institution for details.

M20 THE UNIVERSITY OF MANCHESTER
RUTHERFORD BUILDING
OXFORD ROAD
MANCHESTER M13 9PL
t: 0161 275 2077 f: 0161 275 2106
e: ug-admissions@manchester.ac.uk
// www.manchester.ac.uk

LN13 BA Economics and Finance
Duration: 3FT Hon
Entry Requirements: *GCE:* AAB. *SQAH:* AAABB. *SQAAH:* AAB. *IB:* 35.

N91 NOTTINGHAM TRENT UNIVERSITY
DRYDEN BUILDING
BURTON STREET
NOTTINGHAM NG1 4BU
t: +44 (0) 115 848 4200 f: +44 (0) 115 848 8869
e: applications@ntu.ac.uk
// www.ntu.ac.uk

LN13 BA Economics, Finance and Banking
Duration: 4SW Hon
Entry Requirements: *GCE:* 300. *BTEC ExtDip:* DDM. *OCR NED:* D2

LN1H BA Economics, Finance and Banking
Duration: 3FT Hon
Entry Requirements: *GCE:* 300. *BTEC ExtDip:* DDM. *OCR NED:* D2

P80 UNIVERSITY OF PORTSMOUTH
ACADEMIC REGISTRY
UNIVERSITY HOUSE
WINSTON CHURCHILL AVENUE
PORTSMOUTH PO1 2UP
t: 023 9284 8484 f: 023 9284 3082
e: admissions@port.ac.uk
// www.port.ac.uk

LN13 BSc Economics, Finance and Banking
Duration: 3FT/4SW Hon
Entry Requirements: *GCE:* 260-300. *IB:* 27. *BTEC Dip:* D*D. *BTEC ExtDip:* DMM.

Q50 QUEEN MARY, UNIVERSITY OF LONDON
QUEEN MARY, UNIVERSITY OF LONDON
MILE END ROAD
LONDON E1 4NS
t: 020 7882 5555 f: 020 7882 5500
e: admissions@qmul.ac.uk
// www.qmul.ac.uk

LN13 BScEcon Economics and Finance
Duration: 3FT Hon
Entry Requirements: *GCE:* AAB. *SQAAH:* AAB. *IB:* 36.

Q75 QUEEN'S UNIVERSITY BELFAST
UNIVERSITY ROAD
BELFAST BT7 1NN
t: 028 9097 3838 f: 028 9097 5151
e: admissions@qub.ac.uk
// www.qub.ac.uk

L1N3 BSc Economics with Finance
Duration: 3FT Hon
Entry Requirements: *GCE:* ABB-BBBb. *SQAH:* ABBBB. *SQAAH:* ABB. *IB:* 33.

S18 THE UNIVERSITY OF SHEFFIELD
THE UNIVERSITY OF SHEFFIELD
LEVEL 2, ARTS TOWER
WESTERN BANK
SHEFFIELD S10 2TN
t: 0114 222 8030 f: 0114 222 8032
// www.sheffield.ac.uk

L1N3 BSc Economics with Finance
Duration: 3FT Hon
Entry Requirements: *GCE:* AAA. *SQAH:* AAAAB. *SQAAH:* AA. *IB:* 37. *BTEC Dip:* DD. *BTEC ExtDip:* DDD.

S21 SHEFFIELD HALLAM UNIVERSITY
CITY CAMPUS
HOWARD STREET
SHEFFIELD S1 1WB
t: 0114 225 5555 f: 0114 225 2167
e: admissions@shu.ac.uk
// www.shu.ac.uk

NL31 BA International Finance and Economics
Duration: 3FT/4SW Hon
Entry Requirements: *GCE:* 300.

S27 UNIVERSITY OF SOUTHAMPTON
HIGHFIELD
SOUTHAMPTON SO17 1BJ
t: 023 8059 4732 f: 023 8059 3037
e: admissions@soton.ac.uk
// www.southampton.ac.uk

L1N3 BSc Economics and Actuarial Science
Duration: 3FT Hon
Entry Requirements: *GCE:* AAA-AABB. *SQAH:* AAAA. *SQAAH:* AA.
IB: 36.

L1NH BSc Economics and Finance
Duration: 3FT Hon
Entry Requirements: *GCE:* AAA. *SQAH:* AAAA. *SQAAH:* AA. *IB:* 36.

S75 THE UNIVERSITY OF STIRLING
STUDENT RECRUITMENT & ADMISSIONS SERVICE
UNIVERSITY OF STIRLING
STIRLING
SCOTLAND FK9 4LA
t: 01786 467044 f: 01786 466800
e: admissions@stir.ac.uk
// www.stir.ac.uk

LN13 BA Economics and Finance
Duration: 4FT Hon
Entry Requirements: *GCE:* BBC. *SQAH:* BBBB. *SQAAH:* AAA-CCC.
IB: 32. *BTEC ExtDip:* DMM.

S78 THE UNIVERSITY OF STRATHCLYDE
GLASGOW G1 1XQ
t: 0141 552 4400 f: 0141 552 0775
// www.strath.ac.uk

LN13 BA Economics and Finance
Duration: 4FT Hon
Entry Requirements: *GCE:* AAB. *SQAH:* AAAABB-AAAB. *IB:* 36.

Y50 THE UNIVERSITY OF YORK
STUDENT RECRUITMENT AND ADMISSIONS
UNIVERSITY OF YORK
HESLINGTON
YORK YO10 5DD
t: 01904 324000 f: 01904 323538
e: ug-admissions@york.ac.uk
// www.york.ac.uk

L124 BA/BSc Economics, Econometrics and Finance
Duration: 3FT Hon
Entry Requirements: *GCE:* AAA-AAB. *SQAH:* AAAAA-AAAAB.
SQAAH: AA-AB. *IB:* 36. *BTEC ExtDip:* DDD.

ACCOUNTANCY AND FINANCE/FINANCE AND
ACCOUNTANCY

A20 THE UNIVERSITY OF ABERDEEN
UNIVERSITY OFFICE
KING'S COLLEGE
ABERDEEN AB24 3FX
t: +44 (0) 1224 273504 f: +44 (0) 1224 272034
e: sras@abdn.ac.uk
// www.abdn.ac.uk/sras

NN34 MA Accountancy and Finance
Duration: 4FT Hon
Entry Requirements: *GCE:* BBB. *SQAH:* BBBB. *IB:* 30.

A30 UNIVERSITY OF ABERTAY DUNDEE
BELL STREET
DUNDEE DD1 1HG
t: 01382 308080 f: 01382 308081
e: sro@abertay.ac.uk
// www.abertay.ac.uk

N4N3 BA Accounting with Finance
Duration: 3FT Hon
Entry Requirements: *GCE:* BBC. *SQAAH:* BBC.

A40 ABERYSTWYTH UNIVERSITY
ABERYSTWYTH UNIVERSITY, WELCOME CENTRE
PENGLAIS CAMPUS
ABERYSTWYTH
CEREDIGION SY23 3FB
t: 01970 622021 f: 01970 627410
e: ug-admissions@aber.ac.uk
// www.aber.ac.uk

N400 BScEcon Accounting and Finance
Duration: 3FT Hon
Entry Requirements: *GCE:* 300. *IB:* 30.

A60 ANGLIA RUSKIN UNIVERSITY
BISHOP HALL LANE
CHELMSFORD
ESSEX CM1 1SQ
t: 0845 271 3333 f: 01245 251789
e: answers@anglia.ac.uk
// www.anglia.ac.uk

N421 BSc Accounting and Finance
Duration: 3FT Hon
Entry Requirements: *GCE:* 200-240. *SQAH:* BCCC. *SQAAH:* CC.
IB: 24.

B06 BANGOR UNIVERSITY
BANGOR UNIVERSITY
BANGOR
GWYNEDD LL57 2DG
t: 01248 388484 f: 01248 370451
e: admissions@bangor.ac.uk
// www.bangor.ac.uk

N400 BA Accounting and Finance
Duration: 3FT Hon
Entry Requirements: *GCE:* 260-300. *IB:* 28.

NN34 BA Banking/Accounting
Duration: 3FT Hon
Entry Requirements: *GCE:* 260-300. *IB:* 28.

NN43 BSc Accounting and Banking
Duration: 3FT Hon
Entry Requirements: *GCE:* 260-300. *IB:* 28.

NN4H BSc Accounting and Finance
Duration: 3FT Hon
Entry Requirements: *GCE:* 260-300. *IB:* 28.

B16 UNIVERSITY OF BATH
CLAVERTON DOWN
BATH BA2 7AY
t: 01225 383019 f: 01225 386366
e: admissions@bath.ac.uk
// www.bath.ac.uk

NN34 BSc Accounting and Finance
Duration: 3FT Hon
Entry Requirements: *GCE:* AAA. *SQAAH:* AAA. *IB:* 38.

NN43 BSc Accounting and Finance (Sandwich)
Duration: 4SW Hon
Entry Requirements: *GCE:* AAA-AAB. *SQAAH:* AAA. *IB:* 38.

B22 UNIVERSITY OF BEDFORDSHIRE
PARK SQUARE
LUTON
BEDS LU1 3JU
t: 0844 8482234 f: 01582 489323
e: admissions@beds.ac.uk
// www.beds.ac.uk

N391 BA Accounting and Finance
Duration: 3FT Hon
Entry Requirements: *GCE:* 200.

B24 BIRKBECK, UNIVERSITY OF LONDON
MALET STREET
LONDON WC1E 7HX
t: 020 7631 6316
e: webform: www.bbk.ac.uk/ask
// www.bbk.ac.uk/ask

NN43 BA Accounting and Management
Duration: 3FT Hon
Entry Requirements: *GCE:* BCC. *SQAH:* AAAA-AABB. *IB:* 36.
Admissions Test required.

B25 BIRMINGHAM CITY UNIVERSITY
PERRY BARR
BIRMINGHAM B42 2SU
t: 0121 331 5595 f: 0121 331 7994
// www.bcu.ac.uk

NN43 BA Accounting and Finance
Duration: 3FT/4SW Hon
Entry Requirements: *GCE:* 280. *IB:* 32. *OCR ND:* D *OCR NED:* M2

B32 THE UNIVERSITY OF BIRMINGHAM
EDGBASTON
BIRMINGHAM B15 2TT
t: 0121 415 8900 f: 0121 414 7159
e: admissions@bham.ac.uk
// www.birmingham.ac.uk

N400 BSc Accounting and Finance
Duration: 3FT Hon
Entry Requirements: *GCE:* AAB. *SQAAH:* AAB. *IB:* 35. *BTEC SubDip:* D. *BTEC Dip:* DD. *BTEC ExtDip:* D*DD.

B50 BOURNEMOUTH UNIVERSITY
TALBOT CAMPUS
FERN BARROW
POOLE
DORSET BH12 5BB
t: 01202 524111
// www.bournemouth.ac.uk

NN43 BA Accounting and Taxation
Duration: 3FT/4SW Hon
Entry Requirements: *GCE:* 320. *IB:* 32. *BTEC SubDip:* D. *BTEC Dip:* DD. *BTEC ExtDip:* DDM.

B78 UNIVERSITY OF BRISTOL
UNDERGRADUATE ADMISSIONS OFFICE
SENATE HOUSE
TYNDALL AVENUE
BRISTOL BS8 1TH
t: 0117 928 9000 f: 0117 331 7391
e: ug-admissions@bristol.ac.uk
// www.bristol.ac.uk

NN43 BSc Accounting and Finance
Duration: 3FT Hon
Entry Requirements: *GCE:* AAA-AAB. *SQAH:* AAAA. *SQAAH:* AA-AB.

NN34 BSc Accounting and Finance with Study in Continental Europe
Duration: 4FT Hon
Entry Requirements: *GCE:* AAA-AAB. *SQAH:* AAAA. *SQAAH:* AA-AB. *IB:* 38.

B84 BRUNEL UNIVERSITY
UXBRIDGE
MIDDLESEX UB8 3PH
t: 01895 265265 f: 01895 269790
e: admissions@brunel.ac.uk
// www.brunel.ac.uk

NN34 BSc Finance and Accounting
Duration: 3FT Hon
Entry Requirements: *GCE:* AAB. *SQAAH:* AAB. *IB:* 35. *BTEC ExtDip:* D*D*D.

NN3K BSc Finance and Accounting (4 year Thick SW)
Duration: 4SW Hon
Entry Requirements: *GCE:* AAB. *SQAAH:* AAB. *IB:* 35. *BTEC ExtDip:* D*D*D.

B90 THE UNIVERSITY OF BUCKINGHAM
YEOMANRY HOUSE
HUNTER STREET
BUCKINGHAM MK18 1EG
t: 01280 820313 f: 01280 822245
e: info@buckingham.ac.uk
// www.buckingham.ac.uk

NN43 BSc Accounting and Financial Management
Duration: 2FT Hon
Entry Requirements: *GCE:* BBB-BCC. *SQAH:* ABBB-BBBC. *SQAAH:* BBB-BCC. *IB:* 34.

B94 BUCKINGHAMSHIRE NEW UNIVERSITY
QUEEN ALEXANDRA ROAD
HIGH WYCOMBE
BUCKINGHAMSHIRE HP11 2JZ
t: 0800 0565 660 f: 01494 605 023
e: admissions@bucks.ac.uk
// bucks.ac.uk

NN43 BSc Accounting and Finance
Duration: 3FT Hon
Entry Requirements: *GCE:* 200-240. *IB:* 24. *OCR ND:* M1 *OCR NED:* M3

C10 CANTERBURY CHRIST CHURCH UNIVERSITY
NORTH HOLMES ROAD
CANTERBURY
KENT CT1 1QU
t: 01227 782900 f: 01227 782888
e: admissions@canterbury.ac.uk
// www.canterbury.ac.uk

NN43 BSc Accounting and Finance
Duration: 3FT Hon
Entry Requirements: *GCE:* 240. *IB:* 24.

NN4H BSc Accounting and Finance 'International only'
Duration: 4FT Hon
Entry Requirements: Interview required.

C20 CARDIFF METROPOLITAN UNIVERSITY (UWIC)
ADMISSIONS UNIT
LLANDAFF CAMPUS
WESTERN AVENUE
CARDIFF CF5 2YB
t: 029 2041 6070 f: 029 2041 6286
e: admissions@cardiffmet.ac.uk
// www.cardiffmet.ac.uk

NN43 BA Accounting & Finance
Duration: 3FT/4SW Hon
Entry Requirements: *GCE:* 300. *IB:* 26. *BTEC ExtDip:* DDM. *OCR NED:* M1

C30 UNIVERSITY OF CENTRAL LANCASHIRE
PRESTON
LANCS PR1 2HE
t: 01772 201201 f: 01772 894954
e: uadmissions@uclan.ac.uk
// www.uclan.ac.uk

N4N3 BA Accounting and Finance
Duration: 3FT Hon
Entry Requirements: *SQAH:* AAAB-AABB. *IB:* 28.

NN34 BA Accounting and Financial Management
Duration: 3FT Hon
Entry Requirements: *SQAH:* AAAB-AABB. *IB:* 28.

NN43 FdA Accounting and Financial Studies
Duration: 2FT Fdg
Entry Requirements: *GCE:* 80-120.

C55 UNIVERSITY OF CHESTER
PARKGATE ROAD
CHESTER CH1 4BJ
t: 01244 511000 f: 01244 511300
e: enquiries@chester.ac.uk
// www.chester.ac.uk

NN4H BSc Accounting and Finance (3 year)
Duration: 3FT Hon
Entry Requirements: *GCE:* 240-280. *SQAH:* BBBB. *IB:* 26.

NN4J BSc Accounting and Finance (4 year)
Duration: 4FT Hon
Entry Requirements: *GCE:* 240-280. *SQAH:* BBBB. *IB:* 26.

C58 UNIVERSITY OF CHICHESTER
BISHOP OTTER CAMPUS
COLLEGE LANE
CHICHESTER
WEST SUSSEX PO19 6PE
t: 01243 816002 f: 01243 816161
e: admissions@chi.ac.uk
// www.chiuni.ac.uk

NN43 BA Accounting and Finance
Duration: 3FT Hon
Entry Requirements: *GCE:* BCD-CCC. *SQAAH:* CCC. *IB:* 28. *BTEC SubDip:* M. *BTEC Dip:* DD.

NN4H BA Accounting and Finance - Professional Placement
Duration: 4SW Hon
Entry Requirements: *GCE:* BCD-CCC. *SQAAH:* CCC. *IB:* 28. *BTEC SubDip:* M. *BTEC Dip:* DD.

C60 CITY UNIVERSITY
NORTHAMPTON SQUARE
LONDON EC1V 0HB
t: 020 7040 5060 f: 020 7040 8995
e: ugadmissions@city.ac.uk
// www.city.ac.uk

NN43 BSc Accounting and Finance
Duration: 3FT Hon
Entry Requirements: *GCE:* A*AA. *IB:* 35.

C85 COVENTRY UNIVERSITY
THE STUDENT CENTRE
COVENTRY UNIVERSITY
1 GULSON RD
COVENTRY CV1 2JH
t: 024 7615 2222 f: 024 7615 2223
e: studentenquiries@coventry.ac.uk
// www.coventry.ac.uk

NN34 BA Accounting and Finance
Duration: 3FT/4SW Hon
Entry Requirements: *GCE:* BBC. *SQAH:* BBCCC. *IB:* 29. *BTEC ExtDip:* DDM. *OCR NED:* M1

NN3L BA International Finance and Accounting
Duration: 3FT/4SW Hon
Entry Requirements: *GCE:* BBB. *SQAH:* BBBBC. *IB:* 29. *BTEC ExtDip:* DDM. *OCR NED:* M1

D86 DURHAM UNIVERSITY
DURHAM UNIVERSITY
UNIVERSITY OFFICE
DURHAM DH1 3HP
t: 0191 334 2000 f: 0191 334 6055
e: admissions@durham.ac.uk
// www.durham.ac.uk

NN43 BA Accounting and Finance
Duration: 3FT/4SW Hon
Entry Requirements: *GCE:* ABB. *SQAH:* AABBB. *SQAAH:* ABB. *IB:* 34.

NN4H BA Accounting and Finance with Foundation
Duration: 4FT Hon
Entry Requirements: Interview required.

E56 THE UNIVERSITY OF EDINBURGH
STUDENT RECRUITMENT & ADMISSIONS
57 GEORGE SQUARE
EDINBURGH EH8 9JU
t: 0131 650 4360 f: 0131 651 1236
e: sra.enquiries@ed.ac.uk
// www.ed.ac.uk/studying/undergraduate/

NN43 MA Accounting and Finance
Duration: 4FT Hon
Entry Requirements: *GCE:* AAA-BBB. *SQAH:* AAAA-BBBB. *IB:* 34.

E59 EDINBURGH NAPIER UNIVERSITY
CRAIGLOCKHART CAMPUS
EDINBURGH EH14 1DJ
t: +44 (0)8452 60 60 40 f: 0131 455 6464
e: info@napier.ac.uk
// www.napier.ac.uk

NN43 BA Accounting and Finance
Duration: 1FT/2FT Ord/Hon
Entry Requirements: Contact the institution for details.

N4N3 BA Accounting with Corporate Finance
Duration: 3FT/4FT Ord/Hon
Entry Requirements: *GCE:* 230.

E70 THE UNIVERSITY OF ESSEX
WIVENHOE PARK
COLCHESTER
ESSEX CO4 3SQ
t: 01206 873666 f: 01206 874477
e: admit@essex.ac.uk
// www.essex.ac.uk

NNK3 BA Accounting and Finance (Including Year Abroad)
Duration: 4FT Hon
Entry Requirements: *GCE:* ABB. *SQAH:* AAAB. *IB:* 34.

NN43 BA Accounting and Finance (including Foundation Year)
Duration: 4FT Hon
Entry Requirements: *GCE:* 180. *SQAH:* CCCD. *IB:* 24.

E84 UNIVERSITY OF EXETER
LAVER BUILDING
NORTH PARK ROAD
EXETER
DEVON EX4 4QE
t: 01392 723044 f: 01392 722479
e: admissions@exeter.ac.uk
// www.exeter.ac.uk

NN43 BA Accounting and Finance with Industrial Experience (4 years)
Duration: 4FT Hon
Entry Requirements: *GCE:* AAA-AAB. *SQAH:* AAAAB-AAABB. *SQAAH:* AAB-ABB.

NN4H BA Accounting and Finance with International Study (4 years)
Duration: 4FT Hon
Entry Requirements: *GCE:* AAA-AAB. *SQAH:* AAAAB-AAABB. *SQAAH:* AAB-ABB. *BTEC ExtDip:* DDD.

G28 UNIVERSITY OF GLASGOW
71 SOUTHPARK AVENUE
UNIVERSITY OF GLASGOW
GLASGOW G12 8QQ
t: 0141 330 6062 f: 0141 330 2961
e: student.recruitment@glasgow.ac.uk
// www.glasgow.ac.uk

N4N3 BAcc Accountancy with Finance
Duration: 4FT Hon
Entry Requirements: *GCE:* A*AB-AAA. *SQAH:* AAAABB-AAABB. *IB:* 36.

G50 THE UNIVERSITY OF GLOUCESTERSHIRE
PARK CAMPUS
THE PARK
CHELTENHAM GL50 2RH
t: 01242 714501 f: 01242 714869
e: admissions@glos.ac.uk
// www.glos.ac.uk

NN34 BA Accounting and Financial Management
Duration: 4SW Hon
Entry Requirements: *GCE:* 260-300.

NN43 BA Accounting and Financial Management
Duration: 3FT Hon
Entry Requirements: *GCE:* 280-300.

G70 UNIVERSITY OF GREENWICH
GREENWICH CAMPUS
OLD ROYAL NAVAL COLLEGE
PARK ROW
LONDON SE10 9LS
t: 020 8331 9000 f: 020 8331 8145
e: courseinfo@gre.ac.uk
// www.gre.ac.uk

NN43 BA Accounting and Financial Information Systems
Duration: 3FT/4SW Hon
Entry Requirements: *GCE:* 260. *IB:* 24.

G74 GREENWICH SCHOOL OF MANAGEMENT
MERIDIAN HOUSE
ROYAL HILL
GREENWICH
LONDON SE10 8RD
t: +44(0)20 8516 7800 f: +44(0)20 8516 7801
e: admissions@greenwich-college.ac.uk
// www.greenwich-college.ac.uk/
?utm_source=UCAS&utm_medium=Profil

NN4H BA Accounting and Finance
Duration: 3FT Hon
Entry Requirements: *GCE:* 80-120. *SQAH:* A-B. *IB:* 24. *OCR ND:* P3 *OCR NED:* P3 Interview required.

2435 BA Accounting and Finance (Accelerated with Foundation Year)
Duration: 3FT Hon
Entry Requirements: Contact the institution for details.

NNK3 BA Accounting and Finance (Accelerated)
Duration: 2FT Hon
Entry Requirements: *GCE:* 80-120. *SQAH:* A-B. *IB:* 24. *OCR ND:* P3 *OCR NED:* P3 Interview required.

NN4J BA Accounting and Finance (with Foundation Year)
Duration: 4FT Hon
Entry Requirements: *OCR ND:* P3 Interview required.

NNKJ BSc Accounting and Finance
Duration: 3FT Hon
Entry Requirements: *GCE:* 80-120. *SQAH:* A-B. *IB:* 24. *OCR ND:* P3 *OCR NED:* P3 Interview required.

NNL3 BSc Accounting and Finance (Accelerated with Foundation Year)
Duration: 3FT Hon
Entry Requirements: *OCR ND:* P3 Interview required.

NN43 BSc Accounting and Finance (Accelerated)
Duration: 2FT Hon
Entry Requirements: *GCE:* 80-120. *SQAH:* A-B. *IB:* 24. *OCR ND:* P3 *OCR NED:* P3 Interview required.

NNKH BSc Accounting and Finance (with Foundation Year)
Duration: 4FT Hon
Entry Requirements: *OCR ND:* P3 Interview required.

H24 HERIOT-WATT UNIVERSITY, EDINBURGH
EDINBURGH CAMPUS
EDINBURGH EH14 4AS
t: 0131 449 5111 f: 0131 451 3630
e: ugadmissions@hw.ac.uk
// www.hw.ac.uk

NN34 MA Accountancy and Finance
Duration: 4FT Hon
Entry Requirements: *GCE:* BBB. *SQAH:* AAAB-BBBBC. *SQAAH:* BB. *IB:* 29.

H36 UNIVERSITY OF HERTFORDSHIRE
UNIVERSITY ADMISSIONS SERVICE
COLLEGE LANE
HATFIELD
HERTS AL10 9AB
t: 01707 284800
// www.herts.ac.uk

NN43 BA Accounting and Finance
Duration: 3FT/4SW Hon
Entry Requirements: *GCE:* 280. *IB:* 28.

H60 THE UNIVERSITY OF HUDDERSFIELD
QUEENSGATE
HUDDERSFIELD HD1 3DH
t: 01484 473969 f: 01484 472765
e: admissionsandrecords@hud.ac.uk
// www.hud.ac.uk

N4N3 BA Accountancy with Financial Services
Duration: 3FT/4SW Hon
Entry Requirements: *GCE:* 300.

H72 THE UNIVERSITY OF HULL
THE UNIVERSITY OF HULL
COTTINGHAM ROAD
HULL HU6 7RX
t: 01482 466100 f: 01482 442290
e: admissions@hull.ac.uk
// www.hull.ac.uk

NN43 BSc Accounting and Financial Management
Duration: 3FT Hon
Entry Requirements: *GCE:* 300. *IB:* 30. *BTEC ExtDip:* DMM.

NN4H BSc Accounting and Financial Management (International) (4 years)
Duration: 4FT Hon
Entry Requirements: *GCE:* 300. *IB:* 30. *BTEC ExtDip:* DMM.

NN4J BSc Accounting and Financial Management (with Professional Experience) (4 years)
Duration: 4FT Hon
Entry Requirements: *GCE:* 300. *IB:* 30. *BTEC ExtDip:* DMM.

I55 IFS SCHOOL OF FINANCE
PENINSULAR HOUSE
36 MONUMENT STREET
LONDON EC3R 8LJ
t: 01227 829499
e: enquiries@ifslearning.ac.uk
// www.ifslearning.ac.uk

NN34 BSc Finance and Accounting for Financial Services
Duration: 3FT Hon
Entry Requirements: *GCE:* 300.

K12 KEELE UNIVERSITY
KEELE UNIVERSITY
STAFFORDSHIRE ST5 5BG
t: 01782 734005 f: 01782 632343
e: undergraduate@keele.ac.uk
// www.keele.ac.uk

NN34 BA Accounting & Finance
Duration: 3FT Hon
Entry Requirements: *GCE:* ABB.

N4L0 BA Accounting & Finance with Social Sciences Foundation Year
Duration: 4FT Hon
Entry Requirements: *GCE:* CC.

K84 KINGSTON UNIVERSITY
STUDENT INFORMATION & ADVICE CENTRE
COOPER HOUSE
40-46 SURBITON ROAD
KINGSTON UPON THAMES KT1 2HX
t: 0844 8552177 f: 020 8547 7080
e: aps@kingston.ac.uk
// www.kingston.ac.uk

NN43 BA Accounting & Finance
Duration: 4SW Hon
Entry Requirements: *GCE:* 320. *IB:* 27.

NN4H BA Accounting and Finance
Duration: 4FT Hon
Entry Requirements: *GCE:* 320. *IB:* 27.

L14 LANCASTER UNIVERSITY
THE UNIVERSITY
LANCASTER
LANCASHIRE LA1 4YW
t: 01524 592029 f: 01524 846243
e: ugadmissions@lancaster.ac.uk
// www.lancs.ac.uk

NN43 BSc Accounting, Auditing and Finance
Duration: 4SW Hon
Entry Requirements: *GCE:* AAA-AAB. *SQAH:* AAABB-ABBBB.
SQAAH: AAA-AAB. Admissions Test required.

L39 UNIVERSITY OF LINCOLN
ADMISSIONS
BRAYFORD POOL
LINCOLN LN6 7TS
t: 01522 886097 f: 01522 886146
e: admissions@lincoln.ac.uk
// www.lincoln.ac.uk

N400 BA Accountancy and Finance
Duration: 3FT Hon
Entry Requirements: *GCE:* 280.

L53 COLEG LLANDRILLO CYMRU
LLANDUDNO ROAD
RHOS-ON-SEA
COLWYN BAY
NORTH WALES LL28 4HZ
t: 01492 542338/339 f: 01492 543052
e: degrees@llandrillo.ac.uk
// www.llandrillo.ac.uk

NN43 FdA Accounting and Finance
Duration: 2FT Fdg
Entry Requirements: Contact the institution for details.

L63 LCA BUSINESS SCHOOL, LONDON
19 CHARTERHOUSE STREET
LONDON EC1N 6RA
t: 020 7400 6789
e: info@lcabusinessschool.com
// www.lcabusinessschool.com

NN43 BSc Finance and Accounting
Duration: 2FT/3FT Hon
Entry Requirements: *GCE:* 260. *SQAH:* BBCCC. *IB:* 24. *OCR ND:*
D *OCR NED:* M2 Interview required.

L68 LONDON METROPOLITAN UNIVERSITY
166-220 HOLLOWAY ROAD
LONDON N7 8DB
t: 020 7133 4200
e: admissions@londonmet.ac.uk
// www.londonmet.ac.uk

NN43 BA Accounting and Banking
Duration: 3FT Hon
Entry Requirements: *GCE:* 240. *IB:* 28.

L72 LONDON SCHOOL OF ECONOMICS AND POLITICAL SCIENCE (UNIVERSITY OF LONDON)
HOUGHTON STREET
LONDON WC2A 2AE
t: 020 7955 7125 f: 020 7955 6001
e: ug.admissions@lse.ac.uk
// www.lse.ac.uk

NN34 BSc Accounting & Finance
Duration: 3FT Hon
Entry Requirements: *GCE:* AAA. *SQAH:* AAAAA. *SQAAH:* AAA. *IB:* 38.

L79 LOUGHBOROUGH UNIVERSITY
LOUGHBOROUGH
LEICESTERSHIRE LE11 3TU
t: 01509 223522 f: 01509 223905
e: admissions@lboro.ac.uk
// www.lboro.ac.uk

NN34 BSc Accounting and Financial Management
Duration: 4SW Hon
Entry Requirements: *GCE:* AAA-AAB. *IB:* 36. *BTEC ExtDip:* DDD.

M10 THE MANCHESTER COLLEGE
OPENSHAW CAMPUS
ASHTON OLD ROAD
OPENSHAW
MANCHESTER M11 2WH
t: 0800 068 8585 f: 0161 920 4103
e: enquiries@themanchestercollege.ac.uk
// www.themanchestercollege.ac.uk

NN43 BSC Accounting and Finance
Duration: 1FT Hon
Entry Requirements: Interview required. HND required.

N3N4 BSc Accounting and Finance
Duration: 2FT Hon
Entry Requirements: Contact the institution for details.

M20 THE UNIVERSITY OF MANCHESTER
RUTHERFORD BUILDING
OXFORD ROAD
MANCHESTER M13 9PL
t: 0161 275 2077 f: 0161 275 2106
e: ug-admissions@manchester.ac.uk
// www.manchester.ac.uk

NN43 BA Accounting and Finance
Duration: 3FT Hon
Entry Requirements: *GCE:* AAB. *SQAH:* AAABB. *SQAAH:* AAB. *IB:* 35.

M40 THE MANCHESTER METROPOLITAN UNIVERSITY
ADMISSIONS OFFICE
ALL SAINTS (GMS)
ALL SAINTS
MANCHESTER M15 6BH
t: 0161 247 2000
// www.mmu.ac.uk

NN34 BA Accounting and Finance (Sandwich)
Duration: 4SW Hon
Entry Requirements: *IB:* 29.

N84 THE UNIVERSITY OF NOTTINGHAM
THE ADMISSIONS OFFICE
THE UNIVERSITY OF NOTTINGHAM
UNIVERSITY PARK
NOTTINGHAM NG7 2RD
t: 0115 951 5151 f: 0115 951 4668
// www.nottingham.ac.uk

NN34 BA Finance, Accounting and Management
Duration: 3FT Hon
Entry Requirements: *GCE:* AAB. *SQAAH:* AAB. *IB:* 34.

N91 NOTTINGHAM TRENT UNIVERSITY
DRYDEN BUILDING
BURTON STREET
NOTTINGHAM NG1 4BU
t: +44 (0) 115 848 4200 f: +44 (0) 115 848 8869
e: applications@ntu.ac.uk
// www.ntu.ac.uk

NN43 BA Accounting & Finance
Duration: 4SW Hon
Entry Requirements: *GCE:* 300. *BTEC ExtDip:* DDM. *OCR NED:* D2

NN4H BA Accounting & Finance
Duration: 3FT Hon
Entry Requirements: *GCE:* 300. *BTEC ExtDip:* DDM. *OCR NED:* D2

O66 OXFORD BROOKES UNIVERSITY
ADMISSIONS OFFICE
HEADINGTON CAMPUS
GIPSY LANE
OXFORD OX3 0BP
t: 01865 483040 f: 01865 483983
e: admissions@brookes.ac.uk
// www.brookes.ac.uk

NN43 BSc Accounting and Finance
Duration: 3FT/4SW Hon
Entry Requirements: *GCE:* BBB. *IB:* 31. *BTEC ExtDip:* DDM.

P56 UNIVERSITY CENTRE PETERBOROUGH
PARK CRESCENT
PETERBOROUGH PE1 4DZ
t: 0845 1965750 f: 01733 767986
e: UCPenquiries@anglia.ac.uk
// www.anglia.ac.uk/ucp

NN43 BSc Accounting and Finance
Duration: 3FT Hon
Entry Requirements: *GCE:* 200.

P80 UNIVERSITY OF PORTSMOUTH
ACADEMIC REGISTRY
UNIVERSITY HOUSE
WINSTON CHURCHILL AVENUE
PORTSMOUTH PO1 2UP
t: 023 9284 8484 f: 023 9284 3082
e: admissions@port.ac.uk
// www.port.ac.uk

NN34 BA Accountancy and Financial Management
Duration: 2FT Hon
Entry Requirements: Contact the institution for details.

N4N3 BA Accounting with Finance
Duration: 3FT/4SW Hon
Entry Requirements: *GCE:* 280. *IB:* 28. *BTEC Dip:* D*D*. *BTEC ExtDip:* DMM.

S03 THE UNIVERSITY OF SALFORD
SALFORD M5 4WT
t: 0161 295 4545 f: 0161 295 4646
e: ug-admissions@salford.ac.uk
// www.salford.ac.uk

NN34 BSc Finance and Accounting
Duration: 3FT Hon
Entry Requirements: *GCE:* 300. *IB:* 29. *BTEC ExtDip:* DDM. *OCR ND:* D *OCR NED:* M2

NN3K BSc Finance and Accounting with Professional Experience
Duration: 4SW Hon
Entry Requirements: *GCE:* 320. *IB:* 30. *OCR NED:* D2

S27 UNIVERSITY OF SOUTHAMPTON
HIGHFIELD
SOUTHAMPTON SO17 1BJ
t: 023 8059 4732 f: 023 8059 3037
e: admissions@soton.ac.uk
// www.southampton.ac.uk

N400 BSc Accounting and Finance
Duration: 3FT Hon
Entry Requirements: *GCE:* AAB. *SQAH:* AAABB. *SQAAH:* AB. *IB:* 34.

S30 SOUTHAMPTON SOLENT UNIVERSITY
EAST PARK TERRACE
SOUTHAMPTON
HAMPSHIRE SO14 0RT
t: +44 (0) 23 8031 9039 f: + 44 (0)23 8022 2259
e: admissions@solent.ac.uk
// www.solent.ac.uk/

NN34 BA Accountancy and Finance
Duration: 3FT Hon
Entry Requirements: *GCE:* 200.

NN3K BA Accountancy and Finance (with foundation)
Duration: 4FT Hon
Entry Requirements: *GCE:* 80.

S72 STAFFORDSHIRE UNIVERSITY
COLLEGE ROAD
STOKE ON TRENT ST4 2DE
t: 01782 292753 f: 01782 292740
e: admissions@staffs.ac.uk
// www.staffs.ac.uk

NN43 BA Accounting and Finance
Duration: 3FT Hon
Entry Requirements: *GCE:* BB-BCC. *IB:* 24. *BTEC Dip:* DD. *BTEC ExtDip:* MMM. Interview required.

NN34 BA Accounting and Finance (2 year award)
Duration: 2FT Hon
Entry Requirements: *GCE:* BB-BCC. *IB:* 24. *BTEC Dip:* DD. *BTEC ExtDip:* MMM. Interview required.

S75 THE UNIVERSITY OF STIRLING
STUDENT RECRUITMENT & ADMISSIONS SERVICE
UNIVERSITY OF STIRLING
STIRLING
SCOTLAND FK9 4LA
t: 01786 467044 f: 01786 466800
e: admissions@stir.ac.uk
// www.stir.ac.uk

NN43 BAcc Accountancy and Finance
Duration: 4FT Hon
Entry Requirements: *GCE:* BBC. *SQAH:* BBBB. *SQAAH:* AAA-CCC. *IB:* 32. *BTEC ExtDip:* DMM.

S78 THE UNIVERSITY OF STRATHCLYDE
GLASGOW G1 1XQ
t: 0141 552 4400 f: 0141 552 0775
// www.strath.ac.uk

NN43 BA Accounting and Finance
Duration: 4FT Hon
Entry Requirements: *GCE:* AAA. *SQAH:* AAAAAB-AAAA. *IB:* 36.

S84 UNIVERSITY OF SUNDERLAND
STUDENT HELPLINE
THE STUDENT GATEWAY
CHESTER ROAD
SUNDERLAND SR1 3SD
t: 0191 515 3000 f: 0191 515 3805
e: student.helpline@sunderland.ac.uk
// www.sunderland.ac.uk

NN43 BA Accounting and Financial Management
Duration: 1FT Hon
Entry Requirements: HND required.

S85 UNIVERSITY OF SURREY
STAG HILL
GUILDFORD
SURREY GU2 7XH
t: +44(0)1483 689305 f: +44(0)1483 689388
e: ugteam@surrey.ac.uk
// www.surrey.ac.uk

NN34 BSc Accounting and Finance (3 or 4 years)
Duration: 3FT/4SW Hon
Entry Requirements: *GCE:* AAB. *SQAH:* AAAB-AABB. *IB:* 35.
Interview required.

S90 UNIVERSITY OF SUSSEX
UNDERGRADUATE ADMISSIONS
SUSSEX HOUSE
UNIVERSITY OF SUSSEX
BRIGHTON BN1 9RH
t: 01273 678416 f: 01273 678545
e: ug.applicants@sussex.ac.uk
// www.sussex.ac.uk

NN43 BSc Accounting and Finance
Duration: 3FT Hon
Entry Requirements: *GCE:* AAB. *SQAH:* AAABB. *IB:* 35. *BTEC SubDip:* D. *BTEC Dip:* DD. *BTEC ExtDip:* DDD. *OCR ND:* D *OCR NED:* D1

NN4H BSc Accounting and Finance (with a professional placement year)
Duration: 4SW Hon
Entry Requirements: *GCE:* AAB. *SQAH:* AAABB. *IB:* 35. *BTEC SubDip:* D. *BTEC Dip:* DD. *BTEC ExtDip:* DDD. *OCR ND:* D *OCR NED:* D1

S93 SWANSEA UNIVERSITY
SINGLETON PARK
SWANSEA SA2 8PP
t: 01792 295111 f: 01792 295110
e: admissions@swansea.ac.uk
// www.swansea.ac.uk

NN43 BSc Accounting and Finance
Duration: 3FT Hon
Entry Requirements: *GCE:* ABB. *IB:* 33.

NN4H BSc Accounting and Finance (with a Year Abroad)
Duration: 4FT Hon
Entry Requirements: *GCE:* ABB. *IB:* 33.

U20 UNIVERSITY OF ULSTER
COLERAINE
CO. LONDONDERRY
NORTHERN IRELAND BT52 1SA
t: 028 7012 4221 f: 028 7012 4908
e: online@ulster.ac.uk
// www.ulster.ac.uk

NN43 BSc Accounting and Managerial Finance
Duration: 4SW Hon
Entry Requirements: *GCE:* AAB. *IB:* 33.

U40 UNIVERSITY OF THE WEST OF SCOTLAND
PAISLEY
RENFREWSHIRE
SCOTLAND PA1 2BE
t: 0141 848 3727 f: 0141 848 3623
e: admissions@uws.ac.uk
// www.uws.ac.uk

NN34 BA International Finance and Accounting
Duration: 1FT Ord
Entry Requirements: Contact the institution for details.

W05 THE UNIVERSITY OF WEST LONDON
ST MARY'S ROAD
EALING
LONDON W5 5RF
t: 0800 036 8888 f: 020 8566 1353
e: learning.advice@uwl.ac.uk
// www.uwl.ac.uk

NN3K BA Accounting and Finance with Internship
Duration: 4SW Hon
Entry Requirements: *GCE:* 200. *IB:* 28. Interview required.

W20 THE UNIVERSITY OF WARWICK
COVENTRY CV4 8UW
t: 024 7652 3723 f: 024 7652 4649
e: ugadmissions@warwick.ac.uk
// www.warwick.ac.uk

NN34 BSc Accounting and Finance
Duration: 3FT Hon
Entry Requirements: *GCE:* A*AA-AAAb. *SQAH:* AAB. *SQAAH:* AA.
IB: 38.

W76 UNIVERSITY OF WINCHESTER
WINCHESTER
HANTS SO22 4NR
t: 01962 827234 f: 01962 827288
e: course.enquiries@winchester.ac.uk
// www.winchester.ac.uk

NN34 BA Accounting & Finance
Duration: 3FT Hon
Entry Requirements: *Foundation:* Distinction. *GCE:* 260-300. *IB:*
25. *OCR ND:* D *OCR NED:* M2

BANKING COMBINATIONS

B06 BANGOR UNIVERSITY
BANGOR UNIVERSITY
BANGOR
GWYNEDD LL57 2DG
t: 01248 388484 f: 01248 370451
e: admissions@bangor.ac.uk
// www.bangor.ac.uk

N322 BA Banking and Finance
Duration: 3FT Hon
Entry Requirements: *GCE:* 260-300. *IB:* 28.

NR33 BA Banking/Italian (4 years)
Duration: 4FT Hon
Entry Requirements: *GCE:* 240-260. *IB:* 28.

NR34 BA Banking/Spanish (4 years)
Duration: 4FT Hon
Entry Requirements: *GCE:* 240-260. *IB:* 28.

NR31 BA French/Banking (4 years)
Duration: 4FT Hon
Entry Requirements: *GCE:* 240-260. *IB:* 28.

NR32 BA German/Banking (4 years)
Duration: 4FT Hon
Entry Requirements: *GCE:* 240-260. *IB:* 28.

N2N3 BA Management with Banking & Finance
Duration: 3FT Hon
Entry Requirements: *GCE:* 260-300. *IB:* 28.

N391 BSc Banking and Finance
Duration: 3FT Hon
Entry Requirements: *GCE:* 260-300. *IB:* 28.

N2NH BSc Management with Banking & Finance
Duration: 3FT Hon
Entry Requirements: *GCE:* 260-300. *IB:* 28.

B54 BPP UNIVERSITY COLLEGE OF PROFESSIONAL STUDIES LIMITED
142-144 UXBRIDGE ROAD
LONDON W12 8AW
t: 02031 312 298
e: admissions@bpp.com
// undergraduate.bpp.com/

N390 BSc Banking and Finance
Duration: 3FT Hon
Entry Requirements: Contact the institution for details.

N392 BSc Banking and Finance (Extended)
Duration: 4FT Hon
Entry Requirements: Contact the institution for details.

B80 UNIVERSITY OF THE WEST OF ENGLAND, BRISTOL
FRENCHAY CAMPUS
COLDHARBOUR LANE
BRISTOL BS16 1QY
t: +44 (0)117 32 83333 f: +44 (0)117 32 82810
e: admissions@uwe.ac.uk
// www.uwe.ac.uk

N300 BA Banking and Finance
Duration: 4SW Hon
Entry Requirements: Contact the institution for details.

C15 CARDIFF UNIVERSITY
PO BOX 927
30-36 NEWPORT ROAD
CARDIFF CF24 0DE
t: 029 2087 9999 f: 029 2087 6138
e: admissions@cardiff.ac.uk
// www.cardiff.ac.uk

N3R9 BSc Banking and Finance with a European Language (French)
Duration: 4FT Hon
Entry Requirements: *GCE:* AAB. *SQAH:* AAABB. *SQAAH:* AAB. *IB:*
35. *OCR NED:* D1 Interview required.

N3R2 BSc Banking and Finance with a European Language (German)
Duration: 4FT Hon
Entry Requirements: *GCE:* AAB. *SQAH:* AAABB. *SQAAH:* AAB. *IB:*
35. *OCR NED:* D1 Interview required.

N3R4 BSc Banking and Finance with a European Language (Spanish)
Duration: 4FT Hon
Entry Requirements: *GCE:* AAB. *SQAH:* AAABB. *SQAAH:* AAB. *IB:*
35. *OCR NED:* D1 Interview required.

C85 COVENTRY UNIVERSITY
THE STUDENT CENTRE
COVENTRY UNIVERSITY
1 GULSON RD
COVENTRY CV1 2JH
t: 024 7615 2222 f: 024 7615 2223
e: studentenquiries@coventry.ac.uk
// www.coventry.ac.uk

N391 BA Banking and Insurance
Duration: 3FT Hon
Entry Requirements: Contact the institution for details.

N310 FYr Banking (Foundation Year)
Duration: 1FT FYr
Entry Requirements: *GCE:* 100. *IB:* 24. *BTEC Dip:* MP. *BTEC ExtDip:* PPP. *OCR ND:* P2 *OCR NED:* P3

093N HNC Banking and Insurance
Duration: 1FT HNC
Entry Requirements: *GCE:* 160. *IB:* 24. *BTEC Dip:* MM. *BTEC ExtDip:* MPP. *OCR ND:* P1 *OCR NED:* P2

193N HND Banking and Insurance
Duration: 2FT HND
Entry Requirements: *GCE:* 260. *IB:* 28. *BTEC Dip:* DD. *BTEC ExtDip:* MMM. *OCR ND:* D *OCR NED:* M3

E70 THE UNIVERSITY OF ESSEX
WIVENHOE PARK
COLCHESTER
ESSEX CO4 3SQ
t: 01206 873666 f: 01206 874477
e: admit@essex.ac.uk
// www.essex.ac.uk

N390 BSc Banking and Finance
Duration: 3FT Hon
Entry Requirements: *GCE:* ABB. *SQAH:* AAAB. *IB:* 34.

NH90 BSc Banking and Finance (Including Year Abroad)
Duration: 4FT Hon
Entry Requirements: *GCE:* ABB. *SQAH:* AAAB. *IB:* 34.

NRH9 BSc Banking, Finance and Modern Languages
Duration: 4FT Hon
Entry Requirements: *GCE:* ABB. *SQAH:* AAAB. *IB:* 34.

I55 IFS SCHOOL OF FINANCE
PENINSULAR HOUSE
36 MONUMENT STREET
LONDON EC3R 8LJ
t: 01227 829499
e: enquiries@ifslearning.ac.uk
// www.ifslearning.ac.uk

N310 BSc Banking Practice and Management
Duration: 3FT Hon
Entry Requirements: *GCE:* 300.

L68 LONDON METROPOLITAN UNIVERSITY
166-220 HOLLOWAY ROAD
LONDON N7 8DB
t: 020 7133 4200
e: admissions@londonmet.ac.uk
// www.londonmet.ac.uk

N340 BA Banking and Finance
Duration: 3FT Hon
Entry Requirements: *GCE:* 240. *IB:* 28.

M80 MIDDLESEX UNIVERSITY
MIDDLESEX UNIVERSITY
THE BURROUGHS
LONDON NW4 4BT
t: 020 8411 5555 f: 020 8411 5649
e: enquiries@mdx.ac.uk
// www.mdx.ac.uk

N390 BSc Banking and Finance
Duration: 3FT Hon
Entry Requirements: *GCE:* 200-280.

S84 UNIVERSITY OF SUNDERLAND
STUDENT HELPLINE
THE STUDENT GATEWAY
CHESTER ROAD
SUNDERLAND SR1 3SD
t: 0191 515 3000 f: 0191 515 3805
e: student.helpline@sunderland.ac.uk
// www.sunderland.ac.uk

NN31 BA (Hons) Banking and Finance
Duration: 1FT Hon
Entry Requirements: Contact the institution for details.

BUSINESS COMBINATIONS

A30 UNIVERSITY OF ABERTAY DUNDEE
BELL STREET
DUNDEE DD1 1HG
t: 01382 308080 f: 01382 308081
e: sro@abertay.ac.uk
// www.abertay.ac.uk

NN13 BA Finance and Business
Duration: 4FT Hon
Entry Requirements: *GCE:* CCD. *SQAH:* BBB. *IB:* 24.

LN11 BA International Economics and Management
Duration: 2FT Hon
Entry Requirements: HND required.

A80 ASTON UNIVERSITY, BIRMINGHAM
ASTON TRIANGLE
BIRMINGHAM B4 7ET
t: 0121 204 4444 f: 0121 204 3696
e: admissions@aston.ac.uk (automatic response)
// www.aston.ac.uk/prospective-students/ug

LNC1 BSc International Business and Economics
Duration: 4SW Hon
Entry Requirements: *GCE:* AAA-AAB. *SQAH:* AAAAA-AAAAB. *SQAAH:* AAA-AAB. *IB:* 35. *OCR NED:* D1

B06 BANGOR UNIVERSITY
BANGOR UNIVERSITY
BANGOR
GWYNEDD LL57 2DG
t: 01248 388484 f: 01248 370451
e: admissions@bangor.ac.uk
// www.bangor.ac.uk

NN13 BA Business Studies and Finance
Duration: 3FT Hon
Entry Requirements: *GCE:* 260-300. *IB:* 28.

NN1H BSc Business Studies and Finance
Duration: 3FT Hon
Entry Requirements: *GCE:* 260-300. *IB:* 28.

B25 BIRMINGHAM CITY UNIVERSITY
PERRY BARR
BIRMINGHAM B42 2SU
t: 0121 331 5595 f: 0121 331 7994
// www.bcu.ac.uk

NN41 BA Accountancy and Business
Duration: 3FT/4SW Hon
Entry Requirements: *GCE:* 280. *IB:* 32. *OCR ND:* D *OCR NED:* M2

NL11 BA Business and Economics
Duration: 3FT/4SW Hon
Entry Requirements: *GCE:* 280. *IB:* 32. *OCR ND:* D *OCR NED:* M2

NN13 BA Business and Finance
Duration: 3FT/4SW Hon
Entry Requirements: *GCE:* 280. *IB:* 32. *OCR ND:* D *OCR NED:* M2

B50 BOURNEMOUTH UNIVERSITY
TALBOT CAMPUS
FERN BARROW
POOLE
DORSET BH12 5BB
t: 01202 524111
// www.bournemouth.ac.uk

NN41 BA Accounting and Business
Duration: 3FT/4SW Hon
Entry Requirements: *GCE:* 320. *IB:* 32. *BTEC Dip:* DD. *BTEC ExtDip:* DDM.

NN13 BA Finance and Business
Duration: 4SW Hon
Entry Requirements: *GCE:* 320. *IB:* 32. *BTEC SubDip:* D. *BTEC Dip:* DD. *BTEC ExtDip:* DDM.

B56 THE UNIVERSITY OF BRADFORD
RICHMOND ROAD
BRADFORD
WEST YORKSHIRE BD7 1DP
t: 0800 073 1225 f: 01274 235585
e: course-enquiries@bradford.ac.uk
// www.bradford.ac.uk

NL11 BSc International Business Economics
Duration: 1FT Hon
Entry Requirements: HND required.

B72 UNIVERSITY OF BRIGHTON
MITHRAS HOUSE 211
LEWES ROAD
BRIGHTON BN2 4AT
t: 01273 644644 f: 01273 642607
e: admissions@brighton.ac.uk
// www.brighton.ac.uk

NL11 BSc Business Management with Economics
Duration: 3SW Hon
Entry Requirements: *GCE:* BBB. *IB:* 32.

N1L1 BSc Business with Economics
Duration: 3FT Hon
Entry Requirements: Contact the institution for details.

NN13 BSc Business with Finance
Duration: 3FT Hon
Entry Requirements: Contact the institution for details.

B80 UNIVERSITY OF THE WEST OF ENGLAND, BRISTOL
FRENCHAY CAMPUS
COLDHARBOUR LANE
BRISTOL BS16 1QY
t: +44 (0)117 32 83333 f: +44 (0)117 32 82810
e: admissions@uwe.ac.uk
// www.uwe.ac.uk

N1N4 BA Business Studies with Accounting & Finance
Duration: 3FT/4SW Hon
Entry Requirements: *GCE:* 300.

N1L1 BA Business Studies with Economics
Duration: 3FT/4SW Hon
Entry Requirements: *GCE:* 300.

B84 BRUNEL UNIVERSITY
UXBRIDGE
MIDDLESEX UB8 3PH
t: 01895 265265 f: 01895 269790
e: admissions@brunel.ac.uk
// www.brunel.ac.uk

NN14 BSc Business and Management (Accounting)
Duration: 3FT Hon
Entry Requirements: *GCE:* AAB. *SQAAH:* AAB. *IB:* 35. *BTEC Dip:* D*D*. *BTEC ExtDip:* D*D*D. *OCR NED:* D1

B94 BUCKINGHAMSHIRE NEW UNIVERSITY
QUEEN ALEXANDRA ROAD
HIGH WYCOMBE
BUCKINGHAMSHIRE HP11 2JZ
t: 0800 0565 660 f: 01494 605 023
e: admissions@bucks.ac.uk
// bucks.ac.uk

NN13 BA Business and Finance
Duration: 3FT Hon
Entry Requirements: *GCE:* 200-240. *IB:* 24. *OCR ND:* M1 *OCR NED:* M3

C10 CANTERBURY CHRIST CHURCH UNIVERSITY
NORTH HOLMES ROAD
CANTERBURY
KENT CT1 1QU
t: 01227 782900 f: 01227 782888
e: admissions@canterbury.ac.uk
// www.canterbury.ac.uk

N1NL BSc Business Studies with Accounting 'International Only'
Duration: 4FT Hon
Entry Requirements: Interview required.

C20 CARDIFF METROPOLITAN UNIVERSITY (UWIC)
ADMISSIONS UNIT
LLANDAFF CAMPUS
WESTERN AVENUE
CARDIFF CF5 2YB
t: 029 2041 6070 f: 029 2041 6286
e: admissions@cardiffmet.ac.uk
// www.cardiffmet.ac.uk

N1N3 BA Business & Management Studies with Finance
Duration: 3FT/4SW Hon
Entry Requirements: *GCE:* 300. *IB:* 26. *BTEC ExtDip:* DDM. *OCR NED:* M1

C30 UNIVERSITY OF CENTRAL LANCASHIRE
PRESTON
LANCS PR1 2HE
t: 01772 201201 f: 01772 894954
e: uadmissions@uclan.ac.uk
// www.uclan.ac.uk

NN14 BA Accounting and Business
Duration: 3FT Hon
Entry Requirements: *GCE:* 240-280. *SQAH:* AABB-BBBC. *IB:* 28. *OCR ND:* D

NNC4 BA Business and Accounting
Duration: 3FT Hon
Entry Requirements: *GCE:* 240-280. *SQAH:* AABB-BBBC. *IB:* 28. *OCR ND:* D

NN41 BA International Business and Accounting
Duration: 3FT Hon
Entry Requirements: *GCE:* 240-280. *SQAH:* AABB-BBBC. *IB:* 28. *OCR ND:* D

C58 UNIVERSITY OF CHICHESTER
BISHOP OTTER CAMPUS
COLLEGE LANE
CHICHESTER
WEST SUSSEX PO19 6PE
t: 01243 816002 f: 01243 816161
e: admissions@chi.ac.uk
// www.chiuni.ac.uk

NN13 BA Business Studies and Finance
Duration: 3FT Hon
Entry Requirements: *GCE:* BCD-CCC. *SQAAH:* CCC. *IB:* 28. *BTEC SubDip:* M. *BTEC Dip:* DD.

NN1H BA Business Studies and Finance - Placement
Duration: 4FT Hon
Entry Requirements: *GCE:* BCD-CCC. *SQAAH:* CCC. *IB:* 28. *BTEC SubDip:* M. *BTEC Dip:* DD.

C85 COVENTRY UNIVERSITY
THE STUDENT CENTRE
COVENTRY UNIVERSITY
1 GULSON RD
COVENTRY CV1 2JH
t: 024 7615 2222 f: 024 7615 2223
e: studentenquiries@coventry.ac.uk
// www.coventry.ac.uk

N900 BA Accounting and Finance for International Business (Top-Up)
Duration: 1FT Hon
Entry Requirements: Contact the institution for details.

LN11 BA International Economics and Trade
Duration: 3FT/4SW Hon
Entry Requirements: *GCE:* BBB. *SQAH:* BBBBC. *IB:* 30. *BTEC ExtDip:* DDM. *OCR NED:* M1

NN1K BA Management and Professional Accounting
Duration: 3FT Hon
Entry Requirements: *GCE:* 260. *IB:* 28. *BTEC Dip:* DD. *BTEC ExtDip:* MMM. *OCR ND:* D *OCR NED:* M3

D26 DE MONTFORT UNIVERSITY
THE GATEWAY
LEICESTER LE1 9BH
t: 0116 255 1551 f: 0116 250 6204
e: enquiries@dmu.ac.uk
// www.dmu.ac.uk

NN14 BA Accounting and Business
Duration: 3FT/4SW Hon
Entry Requirements: *GCE:* 280. *IB:* 28. *BTEC Dip:* D*D*. *BTEC ExtDip:* DMM. *OCR NED:* M2 Interview required.

NN31 BA Business and Finance
Duration: 3FT/4SW Hon
Entry Requirements: *GCE:* 280. *IB:* 28. *BTEC Dip:* D*D*. *BTEC ExtDip:* DMM. *OCR NED:* M2 Interview required.

D65 UNIVERSITY OF DUNDEE
NETHERGATE
DUNDEE DD1 4HN
t: 01382 383838 f: 01382 388150
e: contactus@dundee.ac.uk
// www.dundee.ac.uk/admissions/ undergraduate/

N1N3 BSc International Business with Financial Management
Duration: 4FT Hon
Entry Requirements: *GCE:* BCC. *SQAH:* ABBB. *IB:* 30.

NN1H MA International Business and Finance
Duration: 4FT Hon
Entry Requirements: *GCE:* BCC. *SQAH:* ABBB. *IB:* 30.

E28 UNIVERSITY OF EAST LONDON
DOCKLANDS CAMPUS
UNIVERSITY WAY
LONDON E16 2RD
t: 020 8223 3333 f: 020 8223 2978
e: study@uel.ac.uk
// www.uel.ac.uk

N122 BSc (Hons) International Business Finance
Duration: 1FT Hon
Entry Requirements: Contact the institution for details.

E56 THE UNIVERSITY OF EDINBURGH
STUDENT RECRUITMENT & ADMISSIONS
57 GEORGE SQUARE
EDINBURGH EH8 9JU
t: 0131 650 4360 f: 0131 651 1236
e: sra.enquiries@ed.ac.uk
// www.ed.ac.uk/studying/undergraduate/

NN14 MA Business Studies and Accounting
Duration: 4FT Hon
Entry Requirements: *GCE:* AAA-BBB. *SQAH:* AAAA-BBBB. *IB:* 34.

NL11 MA Business Studies and Economics
Duration: 4FT Hon
Entry Requirements: *GCE:* AAA-BBB. *SQAH:* AAAA-BBBB. *IB:* 34.

E59 EDINBURGH NAPIER UNIVERSITY
CRAIGLOCKHART CAMPUS
EDINBURGH EH14 1DJ
t: +44 (0)8452 60 60 40 f: 0131 455 6464
e: info@napier.ac.uk
// www.napier.ac.uk

N1N3 BA Business Studies with Finance
Duration: 3FT/4FT Ord/Hon
Entry Requirements: *GCE:* 230.

E70 THE UNIVERSITY OF ESSEX
WIVENHOE PARK
COLCHESTER
ESSEX CO4 3SQ
t: 01206 873666 f: 01206 874477
e: admit@essex.ac.uk
// www.essex.ac.uk

NN14 CertHE Business (Accounting, Finance and Management)
Duration: 1FT Cer
Entry Requirements: Contact the institution for details.

E77 EUROPEAN BUSINESS SCHOOL, LONDON
INNER CIRCLE
REGENT'S PARK
LONDON NW1 4NS
t: +44 (0)20 7487 7505 f: +44 (0)20 7487 7425
e: ebsl@regents.ac.uk
// www.ebslondon.ac.uk

N1L1 BA International Business with Economics and languages
Duration: 3FT/4FT Hon
Entry Requirements: *GCE:* 240-300.

N1LC BA International Business with Economics and two languages
Duration: 3FT/4FT Hon
Entry Requirements: *GCE:* 240-300.

N1N3 BA International Business with Finance and one language
Duration: 3FT/4FT Hon
Entry Requirements: *GCE:* 240-300.

N1NH BA International Business with Finance and two languages
Duration: 3FT/4FT Hon
Entry Requirements: *GCE:* 240-300.

E84 UNIVERSITY OF EXETER
LAVER BUILDING
NORTH PARK ROAD
EXETER
DEVON EX4 4QE
t: 01392 723044 f: 01392 722479
e: admissions@exeter.ac.uk
// www.exeter.ac.uk

NN41 BA Business and Accounting
Duration: 3FT Hon
Entry Requirements: *GCE:* AAA-AAB. *SQAH:* AAAAB-AAABB. *SQAAH:* AAB-ABB. *BTEC ExtDip:* DDD.

NN4C BA Business and Accounting with European Study (4 years)
Duration: 4FT Hon
Entry Requirements: *GCE:* AAA-AAB. *SQAH:* AAAAB-AAABB. *SQAAH:* AAB-ABB. *BTEC ExtDip:* DDD.

NND4 BA Business and Accounting with Industrial Experience (4 years)
Duration: 4FT Hon
Entry Requirements: *GCE:* AAA-AAB. *SQAH:* AAAAB-AAABB. *SQAAH:* AAB-ABB. *BTEC ExtDip:* DDD.

NN1L BA Business and Accounting with International Study (4 years)
Duration: 4FT Hon
Entry Requirements: *GCE:* AAA-AAB. *SQAH:* AAAAB-AAABB. *SQAAH:* AAB-ABB. *BTEC ExtDip:* DDD.

G14 UNIVERSITY OF GLAMORGAN, CARDIFF AND PONTYPRIDD
ENQUIRIES AND ADMISSIONS UNIT
PONTYPRIDD CF37 1DL
t: 08456 434030 f: 01443 654050
e: enquiries@glam.ac.uk
// www.glam.ac.uk

NNC4 BA Business and Accounting (Top-Up)
Duration: 1FT Hon
Entry Requirements: Contact the institution for details.

NNCK BA Business and Accounting (Top-Up) (February Start)
Duration: 1FT Hon
Entry Requirements: Contact the institution for details.

NN13 BA Business and Finance (Top-Up)
Duration: 1FT Hon
Entry Requirements: Contact the institution for details.

NN1H BA Business and Finance (Top-Up) (February Start)
Duration: 1FT Hon
Entry Requirements: Contact the institution for details.

G53 GLYNDWR UNIVERSITY
PLAS COCH
MOLD ROAD
WREXHAM LL11 2AW
t: 01978 293439 f: 01978 290008
e: sid@glyndwr.ac.uk
// www.glyndwr.ac.uk

NN14 BA Business Accounting
Duration: 3FT Hon
Entry Requirements: *GCE:* 240.

G70 UNIVERSITY OF GREENWICH
GREENWICH CAMPUS
OLD ROYAL NAVAL COLLEGE
PARK ROW
LONDON SE10 9LS
t: 020 8331 9000 f: 020 8331 8145
e: courseinfo@gre.ac.uk
// www.gre.ac.uk

N1NK BA Business Administration with Accounting & Finance (BITE)
Duration: 3FT/4SW Hon
Entry Requirements: *GCE:* 240-260.

N1NJ BA Business with Finance
Duration: 3FT Hon
Entry Requirements: *GCE:* 260. *IB:* 24.

N1NL FdA Business Administration with Accounting & Finance (BITE)
Duration: 2FT Fdg
Entry Requirements: *GCE:* 180-200.

G80 GRIMSBY INSTITUTE OF FURTHER AND HIGHER EDUCATION
NUNS CORNER
GRIMSBY
NE LINCOLNSHIRE DN34 5BQ
t: 0800 328 3631
e: headmissions@grimsby.ac.uk
// www.grimsby.ac.uk

N1N4 BA Business Management with Accounting
Duration: 3FT Hon
Entry Requirements: *GCE:* 120. Interview required. Portfolio required.

H36 UNIVERSITY OF HERTFORDSHIRE
UNIVERSITY ADMISSIONS SERVICE
COLLEGE LANE
HATFIELD
HERTS AL10 9AB
t: 01707 284800
// www.herts.ac.uk

NN4D BA Accounting/Business
Duration: 3FT/4SW Hon
Entry Requirements: *GCE:* 300. *IB:* 30.

NN13 BA Business with Finance
Duration: 3FT/4SW Hon
Entry Requirements: *GCE:* 300. *IB:* 30.

N1L1 BA Business/Economics
Duration: 3FT/4SW Hon
Entry Requirements: *GCE:* 260.

N1N3 FdA Business with Accounting
Duration: 2FT Fdg
Entry Requirements: *GCE:* 120.

H50 HOLBORN COLLEGE
WOOLWICH ROAD
LONDON SE7 8LN
t: 020 8317 6000 f: 020 8317 6001
e: UKAdmissions@kaplan.co.uk
// www.holborncollege.ac.uk

N1N4 BA Business Management with Accounting
Duration: 3FT Hon
Entry Requirements: *GCE:* 120. *IB:* 24.

NCN4 BA Business Management with Accounting (with Foundation Year)
Duration: 4FT Hon
Entry Requirements: Contact the institution for details.

H54 HOPWOOD HALL COLLEGE
ROCHDALE ROAD
MIDDLETON
MANCHESTER M24 6XH
t: 0161 643 7560 f: 0161 643 2114
e: admissions@hopwood.ac.uk
// www.hopwood.ac.uk

31NN HND Business and Finance
Duration: 2FT HND
Entry Requirements: *GCE:* 40. Interview required.

H60 THE UNIVERSITY OF HUDDERSFIELD
QUEENSGATE
HUDDERSFIELD HD1 3DH
t: 01484 473969 f: 01484 472765
e: admissionsandrecords@hud.ac.uk
// www.hud.ac.uk

N1N3 BA Business Studies with Financial Services
Duration: 3FT/4SW Hon
Entry Requirements: *GCE:* 300.

N1NH BA Business with Financial Services (Top-Up)
Duration: 1FT Hon
Entry Requirements: HND required.

NN50 BA(Hons) European Business
Duration: 3FT Hon
Entry Requirements: *GCE:* 300.

H72 THE UNIVERSITY OF HULL
THE UNIVERSITY OF HULL
COTTINGHAM ROAD
HULL HU6 7RX
t: 01482 466100 f: 01482 442290
e: admissions@hull.ac.uk
// www.hull.ac.uk

NN14 BA Business and Accounting
Duration: 3FT Hon
Entry Requirements: *GCE:* 300. *IB:* 30. *BTEC ExtDip:* DMM.

NNC4 BA Business and Accounting (International) (4 years)
Duration: 4FT Hon
Entry Requirements: *GCE:* 300. *IB:* 30. *BTEC ExtDip:* DMM.

NND4 BA Business and Accounting (with Professional Experience) (4 years)
Duration: 4FT Hon
Entry Requirements: *GCE:* 300. *IB:* 30. *BTEC ExtDip:* DMM.

NL11 BA Business and Business Economics
Duration: 3FT Hon
Entry Requirements: *GCE:* 300. *IB:* 30. *BTEC ExtDip:* DMM.

NLC1 BA Business and Business Economics (International) (4 years)
Duration: 4FT Hon
Entry Requirements: *GCE:* 300. *IB:* 30. *BTEC ExtDip:* DMM.

NL1C BA Business and Business Economics (with Professional Experience) (4 years)
Duration: 4FT Hon
Entry Requirements: *GCE:* 300. *IB:* 30. *BTEC ExtDip:* DMM.

NN13 BA Business and Financial Management
Duration: 3FT Hon
Entry Requirements: *GCE:* 300. *IB:* 30. *BTEC ExtDip:* DMM.

NNC3 BA Business and Financial Management (International) (4 years)
Duration: 4FT Hon
Entry Requirements: *GCE:* 300. *IB:* 30. *BTEC ExtDip:* DMM.

NND3 BA Business and Financial Management (with Professional Experience) (4 years)
Duration: 4FT Hon
Entry Requirements: *GCE:* 300. *IB:* 30. *BTEC ExtDip:* DMM.

K12 KEELE UNIVERSITY
KEELE UNIVERSITY
STAFFORDSHIRE ST5 5BG
t: 01782 734005 f: 01782 632343
e: undergraduate@keele.ac.uk
// www.keele.ac.uk

NN41 BA Accounting and International Business
Duration: 3FT Hon
Entry Requirements: *GCE:* ABB.

LN11 BA Economics and International Business
Duration: 3FT Hon
Entry Requirements: *GCE:* ABB.

NN31 BA Finance and International Business
Duration: 3FT Hon
Entry Requirements: *GCE:* ABB.

K15 KENSINGTON COLLEGE OF BUSINESS
WESLEY HOUSE
4 WILD COURT
HOLBORN
LONDON WC2B 4AU
t: 020 7404 6330 f: 020 7404 6708
e: kcb@kensingtoncoll.ac.uk
// www.kensingtoncoll.ac.uk

NN14 FdA Business and Accounts
Duration: 2FT Fdg
Entry Requirements: Contact the institution for details.

K24 THE UNIVERSITY OF KENT
RECRUITMENT & ADMISSIONS OFFICE
REGISTRY
UNIVERSITY OF KENT
CANTERBURY, KENT CT2 7NZ
t: 01227 827272 f: 01227 827077
e: information@kent.ac.uk
// www.kent.ac.uk

LN11 BA Business and Economics
Duration: 3FT Hon
Entry Requirements: *GCE:* ABB. *SQAH:* AABBB. *SQAAH:* ABB. *IB:* 33. *OCR ND:* D *OCR NED:* D2

3N1N HND Business (Finance)
Duration: 2FT HND
Entry Requirements: *GCE:* 80. *SQAH:* BC. *SQAAH:* C. *IB:* 24. *OCR ND:* M2 *OCR NED:* M3

K84 KINGSTON UNIVERSITY
STUDENT INFORMATION & ADVICE CENTRE
COOPER HOUSE
40-46 SURBITON ROAD
KINGSTON UPON THAMES KT1 2HX
t: 0844 8552177 f: 020 8547 7080
e: aps@kingston.ac.uk
// www.kingston.ac.uk

NL11 BA Business and Economics (Applied)
Duration: 3FT Hon
Entry Requirements: *GCE:* 240-320. *IB:* 25.

N1N4 BA Business with Accounting
Duration: 3FT/4SW Hon/Ord
Entry Requirements: *GCE:* 280. *SQAH:* BBCCC. *SQAAH:* BCC. *IB:* 25.

N1NK BA Business with Accounting
Duration: 4SW Hon
Entry Requirements: *GCE:* 280. *SQAH:* BBCCC. *SQAAH:* BCC. *IB:* 25.

N1NL BA Business with Accounting with year abroad
Duration: 4FT Hon
Entry Requirements: *GCE:* 280. *SQAH:* BBCCC. *SQAAH:* BCC. *IB:* 25.

L1N1 BSc Business Economics
Duration: 3FT Hon
Entry Requirements: *GCE:* 260. *IB:* 24.

L23 UNIVERSITY OF LEEDS
THE UNIVERSITY OF LEEDS
WOODHOUSE LANE
LEEDS LS2 9JT
t: 0113 343 3999
e: admissions@leeds.ac.uk
// www.leeds.ac.uk

LN11 BSc International Business and Economics
Duration: 3FT Hon
Entry Requirements: *GCE:* AAA. *SQAH:* AAAAA. *SQAAH:* AAA. *IB:* 36. Interview required.

NN13 BSc International Business and Finance
Duration: 3FT Hon
Entry Requirements: *GCE:* AAA. *SQAH:* AAAAA. *SQAAH:* AAA. *IB:* 36. Interview required.

L39 UNIVERSITY OF LINCOLN
ADMISSIONS
BRAYFORD POOL
LINCOLN LN6 7TS
t: 01522 886097 f: 01522 886146
e: admissions@lincoln.ac.uk
// www.lincoln.ac.uk

NN13 BA Business and Finance
Duration: 3FT Hon
Entry Requirements: *GCE:* 280.

L41 THE UNIVERSITY OF LIVERPOOL
THE FOUNDATION BUILDING
BROWNLOW HILL
LIVERPOOL L69 7ZX
t: 0151 794 2000 f: 0151 708 6502
e: ugrecruitment@liv.ac.uk
// www.liv.ac.uk

LN11 BA Business Economics
Duration: 3FT Hon
Entry Requirements: *GCE:* AAB. *SQAAH:* AAB. *IB:* 35.

L62 THE LONDON COLLEGE, UCK
VICTORIA GARDENS
NOTTING HILL GATE
LONDON W11 3PE
t: 020 7243 4000 f: 020 7243 1484
e: admissions@lcuck.ac.uk
// www.lcuck.ac.uk

41NN HND Business Accounting
Duration: 2FT HND
Entry Requirements: Contact the institution for details.

L68 LONDON METROPOLITAN UNIVERSITY
166-220 HOLLOWAY ROAD
LONDON N7 8DB
t: 020 7133 4200
e: admissions@londonmet.ac.uk
// www.londonmet.ac.uk

NNL1 BA Accounting and Business Management
Duration: 3FT Hon
Entry Requirements: Contact the institution for details.

NN31 BA Banking and Business Management
Duration: 3FT Hon
Entry Requirements: *GCE:* 240. *IB:* 28.

LN1C BA International Business and Economics
Duration: 3FT Hon
Entry Requirements: *GCE:* 240. *IB:* 28.

NNCH BSc International Business and Finance
Duration: 3FT Hon
Entry Requirements: Contact the institution for details.

M20 THE UNIVERSITY OF MANCHESTER
RUTHERFORD BUILDING
OXFORD ROAD
MANCHESTER M13 9PL
t: 0161 275 2077 f: 0161 275 2106
e: ug-admissions@manchester.ac.uk
// www.manchester.ac.uk

NL11 BA Business Studies and Economics
Duration: 3FT Hon
Entry Requirements: *GCE:* AAB. *SQAH:* AAABB. *SQAAH:* AAB. *IB:* 35.

M40 THE MANCHESTER METROPOLITAN UNIVERSITY
ADMISSIONS OFFICE
ALL SAINTS (GMS)
ALL SAINTS
MANCHESTER M15 6BH
t: 0161 247 2000
// www.mmu.ac.uk

NN13 BA Business/Financial Management
Duration: 3FT Hon
Entry Requirements: *GCE:* 280. *IB:* 28. *BTEC Dip:* D*D*. *BTEC ExtDip:* DMM.

LN1D BA Economics/International Business
Duration: 3FT Hon
Entry Requirements: *GCE:* 240-280. *IB:* 29.

LNC1 BA/BSc Business Economics/International Business
Duration: 3FT Hon
Entry Requirements: *GCE:* 240-280. *IB:* 29.

NL1D BA/BSc Business/Economics
Duration: 3FT Hon
Entry Requirements: **GCE:** 240-280. **IB:** 29.

N21 NEWCASTLE UNIVERSITY
KING'S GATE
NEWCASTLE UPON TYNE NE1 7RU
t: 01912083333
// www.ncl.ac.uk

NN14 BA Business Accounting and Finance (includes business placement) (4 years)
Duration: 4FT Hon
Entry Requirements: **GCE:** AAA-AAB. **SQAH:** AAAAA-AAABB. **BTEC ExtDip:** DDD. Interview required.

N37 UNIVERSITY OF WALES, NEWPORT
ADMISSIONS
LODGE ROAD
CAERLEON
NEWPORT NP18 3QT
t: 01633 432030 f: 01633 432850
e: admissions@newport.ac.uk
// www.newport.ac.uk

NN14 BA Business and Accounting
Duration: 3FT Hon
Entry Requirements: **GCE:** 240. **IB:** 24.

NL11 BA Business and Economics
Duration: 3FT Hon
Entry Requirements: **GCE:** 240. **IB:** 24.

N38 UNIVERSITY OF NORTHAMPTON
PARK CAMPUS
BOUGHTON GREEN ROAD
NORTHAMPTON NN2 7AL
t: 0800 358 2232 f: 01604 722083
e: admissions@northampton.ac.uk
// www.northampton.ac.uk

N4N1 BA Accounting/Business
Duration: 3FT Hon
Entry Requirements: **GCE:** 260-280. **SQAH:** AAA-BBBB. **IB:** 24. **BTEC Dip:** DD. **BTEC ExtDip:** DMM. **OCR ND:** D **OCR NED:** M2

NN13 BA Business Entrepreneurship
Duration: 3FT Hon
Entry Requirements: **GCE:** 260-280. **SQAH:** AAA-BBBB. **IB:** 24. **BTEC Dip:** DD. **BTEC ExtDip:** DMM. **OCR ND:** D **OCR NED:** M2

N1LC BA Business Entrepreneurship/Economics
Duration: 3FT Hon
Entry Requirements: **GCE:** 260-280. **SQAH:** AAA-BBBB. **IB:** 24. **BTEC Dip:** DD. **BTEC ExtDip:** DMM. **OCR ND:** D **OCR NED:** M2

N1N4 BA Business/Accounting
Duration: 3FT Hon
Entry Requirements: **GCE:** 260-280. **SQAH:** AAA-BBBB. **IB:** 24. **BTEC Dip:** DD. **BTEC ExtDip:** DMM. **OCR ND:** D **OCR NED:** M2

N1L1 BA Business/Economics
Duration: 3FT Hon
Entry Requirements: **GCE:** 260-280. **SQAH:** AAA-BBBB. **IB:** 24. **BTEC Dip:** DD. **BTEC ExtDip:** DMM. **OCR ND:** D **OCR NED:** M2

L1N1 BA Economics/Business
Duration: 3FT Hon
Entry Requirements: **GCE:** 260-280. **SQAH:** AAA-BBBB. **IB:** 24. **BTEC Dip:** DD. **BTEC ExtDip:** DMM. **OCR ND:** D **OCR NED:** M2

N77 NORTHUMBRIA UNIVERSITY
TRINITY BUILDING
NORTHUMBERLAND ROAD
NEWCASTLE UPON TYNE NE1 8ST
t: 0191 243 7420 f: 0191 227 4561
e: er.admissions@northumbria.ac.uk
// www.northumbria.ac.uk

N1L1 BA Business with Economics
Duration: 3FT Hon
Entry Requirements: **GCE:** 300. **SQAH:** BBBBC. **SQAAH:** BBC. **IB:** 26. **BTEC ExtDip:** DDM. **OCR NED:** D2

N1N3 BA Business with Finance Management
Duration: 3FT Hon
Entry Requirements: **GCE:** 280. **SQAH:** BBCCC. **SQAAH:** BCC. **IB:** 25. **BTEC ExtDip:** DMM. **OCR NED:** M2

P80 UNIVERSITY OF PORTSMOUTH
ACADEMIC REGISTRY
UNIVERSITY HOUSE
WINSTON CHURCHILL AVENUE
PORTSMOUTH PO1 2UP
t: 023 9284 8484 f: 023 9284 3082
e: admissions@port.ac.uk
// www.port.ac.uk

NN41 BA Accounting and Business
Duration: 3FT/4SW Hon
Entry Requirements: **GCE:** 280. **IB:** 28. **BTEC Dip:** D*D*. **BTEC ExtDip:** DMM.

L1N1 BA Economics with Business
Duration: 3FT/4SW Hon
Entry Requirements: **GCE:** 260-280. **IB:** 27. **BTEC Dip:** D*D. **BTEC ExtDip:** DMM.

NN31 BA Finance and Business
Duration: 3FT/4SW Hon
Entry Requirements: **GCE:** 280. **IB:** 28. **BTEC Dip:** D*D*. **BTEC ExtDip:** DMM.

N3N1 BA Finance with Business Communication
Duration: 1FT/2FT Hon
Entry Requirements: Contact the institution for details.

LN11 BA International Trade and Business Communication
Duration: 3FT Hon
Entry Requirements: Contact the institution for details.

LN1D BA International Trade, Logistics and Business Communication
Duration: 1FT Hon
Entry Requirements: Contact the institution for details.

R12 THE UNIVERSITY OF READING
THE UNIVERSITY OF READING
PO BOX 217
READING RG6 6AH
t: 0118 378 8619 f: 0118 378 8924
e: student.recruitment@reading.ac.uk
// www.reading.ac.uk

NN41 BA Accounting and Business
Duration: 4SW Hon
Entry Requirements: *GCE:* AAB. *SQAH:* AAABB. *SQAAH:* AAB.
BTEC Dip: DD. *BTEC ExtDip:* DDD.

R20 RICHMOND, THE AMERICAN INTERNATIONAL UNIVERSITY IN LONDON
QUEENS ROAD
RICHMOND
SURREY TW10 6JP
t: 020 8332 9000 f: 020 8332 1596
e: enroll@richmond.ac.uk
// www.richmond.ac.uk

NN13 BA Business Administration: Finance
Duration: 3FT/4FT Hon
Entry Requirements: *GCE:* 260. *IB:* 33.

S03 THE UNIVERSITY OF SALFORD
SALFORD M5 4WT
t: 0161 295 4545 f: 0161 295 4646
e: ug-admissions@salford.ac.uk
// www.salford.ac.uk

N1N3 BSc Business Studies with Financial Management
Duration: 3FT Hon
Entry Requirements: *GCE:* BBC. *IB:* 29. *BTEC ExtDip:* DMM.
OCR ND: D *OCR NED:* M2

N1NH BSc Business Studies with Financial Management with Professional Experience
Duration: 4SW Hon
Entry Requirements: *GCE:* 300. *IB:* 29. *OCR ND:* D

N1L1 BSc Business with Economics
Duration: 3FT Hon
Entry Requirements: *GCE:* BBC. *IB:* 28. *BTEC ExtDip:* DMM.
OCR ND: D *OCR NED:* M2

N1LC BSc Business with Economics (with Professional Experience)
Duration: 4SW Hon
Entry Requirements: *GCE:* 300. *IB:* 29. *OCR ND:* D

N1LD BSc Business with Economics (with Studies in Canada)
Duration: 3FT Hon
Entry Requirements: *GCE:* BBC. *IB:* 28. *BTEC ExtDip:* DMM.
OCR ND: D *OCR NED:* M2

NDL1 BSc Business with Economics with Studies in Canada with Professional Experience
Duration: 4SW Hon
Entry Requirements: *GCE:* 300. *IB:* 29. *OCR ND:* D

S21 SHEFFIELD HALLAM UNIVERSITY
CITY CAMPUS
HOWARD STREET
SHEFFIELD S1 1WB
t: 0114 225 5555 f: 0114 225 2167
e: admissions@shu.ac.uk
// www.shu.ac.uk

NN13 BA Business and Finance (2 year conversion)
Duration: 2FT Hon
Entry Requirements: Contact the institution for details.

NN1H BA Business and Financial Management
Duration: 3FT/4SW Hon
Entry Requirements: *GCE:* 300.

NN1I BA International Banking and Investment (Top-up)
Duration: 1FT Hon
Entry Requirements: HND required.

S30 SOUTHAMPTON SOLENT UNIVERSITY
EAST PARK TERRACE
SOUTHAMPTON
HAMPSHIRE SO14 0RT
t: +44 (0) 23 8031 9039 f: + 44 (0)23 8022 2259
e: admissions@solent.ac.uk
// www.solent.ac.uk/

N4N1 BA Accountancy (with Business Foundation)
Duration: 4FT Hon
Entry Requirements: *GCE:* 80.

NN13 BA Business and Finance (Top-Up)
Duration: 1FT Hon
Entry Requirements: HND required.

S72 STAFFORDSHIRE UNIVERSITY
COLLEGE ROAD
STOKE ON TRENT ST4 2DE
t: 01782 292753 f: 01782 292740
e: admissions@staffs.ac.uk
// www.staffs.ac.uk

NN41 BA Accounting and Business
Duration: 3FT Hon
Entry Requirements: *GCE:* BB-BCC. *IB:* 24. *BTEC Dip:* DD. *BTEC*
ExtDip: MMM. Interview required.

S75 THE UNIVERSITY OF STIRLING
STUDENT RECRUITMENT & ADMISSIONS SERVICE
UNIVERSITY OF STIRLING
STIRLING
SCOTLAND FK9 4LA
t: 01786 467044 f: 01786 466800
e: admissions@stir.ac.uk
// www.stir.ac.uk

LN11 BA Business Studies and Economics
Duration: 4FT Hon
Entry Requirements: *GCE:* BBC. *SQAH:* BBBB. *SQAAH:* AAA-CCC.
IB: 32. *BTEC ExtDip:* DMM.

NN13 BA Business Studies and Finance
Duration: 4FT Hon
Entry Requirements: *GCE:* BBC. *SQAH:* BBBB. *SQAAH:* AAA-CCC.
IB: 32. *BTEC ExtDip:* DMM.

S78 THE UNIVERSITY OF STRATHCLYDE
GLASGOW G1 1XQ
t: 0141 552 4400 f: 0141 552 0775
// www.strath.ac.uk

NN41 BA Accounting and Business Enterprise
Duration: 4FT Hon
Entry Requirements: *GCE:* AAA. *SQAH:* AAAAAB-AAAA. *IB:* 36.

NL11 BA Business Enterprise and Economics
Duration: 4FT Hon
Entry Requirements: *GCE:* AAB. *SQAH:* AAAABB-AAAB. *IB:* 36.

NN13 BA Business Enterprise and Finance
Duration: 4FT Hon
Entry Requirements: *GCE:* AAB. *SQAH:* AAAABB-AAAB. *IB:* 36.

NN14 BA International Business and Accounting
Duration: 4FT Hon
Entry Requirements: *GCE:* AAA. *SQAH:* AAAA-AAABB. *IB:* 36.

S84 UNIVERSITY OF SUNDERLAND
STUDENT HELPLINE
THE STUDENT GATEWAY
CHESTER ROAD
SUNDERLAND SR1 3SD
t: 0191 515 3000 f: 0191 515 3805
e: student.helpline@sunderland.ac.uk
// www.sunderland.ac.uk

NN1H BA Business and Financial Management
Duration: 3FT Hon
Entry Requirements: *OCR ND:* D *OCR NED:* M3

S85 UNIVERSITY OF SURREY
STAG HILL
GUILDFORD
SURREY GU2 7XH
t: +44(0)1483 689305 f: +44(0)1483 689388
e: ugteam@surrey.ac.uk
// www.surrey.ac.uk

LN11 BSc Business Economics (3 or 4 years)
Duration: 3FT/4SW Hon
Entry Requirements: *GCE:* AAA-AAB. *SQAH:* AAAAA-AAABB.
SQAAH: AAA-AAB.

S90 UNIVERSITY OF SUSSEX
UNDERGRADUATE ADMISSIONS
SUSSEX HOUSE
UNIVERSITY OF SUSSEX
BRIGHTON BN1 9RH
t: 01273 678416 f: 01273 678545
e: ug.applicants@sussex.ac.uk
// www.sussex.ac.uk

NN31 BSc Finance and Business
Duration: 3FT Hon
Entry Requirements: *GCE:* AAB. *SQAH:* AAABB. *IB:* 35. *BTEC*
SubDip: D. *BTEC Dip:* DD. *BTEC ExtDip:* DDD. *OCR ND:* D *OCR*
NED: D1

S93 SWANSEA UNIVERSITY
SINGLETON PARK
SWANSEA SA2 8PP
t: 01792 295111 f: 01792 295110
e: admissions@swansea.ac.uk
// www.swansea.ac.uk

N1NK BA Business Management (Accounting)
Duration: 3FT Hon
Entry Requirements: *GCE:* ABB-BBB. *IB:* 33.

N1N4 BSc Business Management (Accounting)
Duration: 3FT Hon
Entry Requirements: *GCE:* ABB-BBB. *IB:* 33.

N1N3 BSc Business Management (Finance)
Duration: 3FT Hon
Entry Requirements: *GCE:* ABB-BBB. *IB:* 33.

U20 UNIVERSITY OF ULSTER
COLERAINE
CO. LONDONDERRY
NORTHERN IRELAND BT52 1SA
t: 028 7012 4221 f: 028 7012 4908
e: online@ulster.ac.uk
// www.ulster.ac.uk

N1N4 BSc Business Studies with Accounting
Duration: 3FT Hon
Entry Requirements: *GCE:* 240. *IB:* 24.

N1NK BSc Business with Accounting
Duration: 4SW Hon
Entry Requirements: *GCE:* 240-280. *IB:* 24.

W05 THE UNIVERSITY OF WEST LONDON
ST MARY'S ROAD
EALING
LONDON W5 5RF
t: 0800 036 8888 f: 020 8566 1353
e: learning.advice@uwl.ac.uk
// www.uwl.ac.uk

N1N3 BA Business Studies with Finance
Duration: 3FT Hon
Entry Requirements: *GCE:* 200. *IB:* 28. Interview required.

W75 UNIVERSITY OF WOLVERHAMPTON
ADMISSIONS UNIT
MX207, CAMP STREET
WOLVERHAMPTON
WEST MIDLANDS WV1 1AD
t: 01902 321000 f: 01902 321896
e: admissions@wlv.ac.uk
// www.wlv.ac.uk

NN14 BA Business and Accounting
Duration: 3FT Hon
Entry Requirements: Contact the institution for details.

NN13 BA Business and Finance
Duration: 3FT Hon
Entry Requirements: Contact the institution for details.

W80 UNIVERSITY OF WORCESTER
HENWICK GROVE
WORCESTER WR2 6AJ
t: 01905 855111 f: 01905 855377
e: admissions@worc.ac.uk
// www.worcester.ac.uk

NNC6 BA Business, Accountancy & Human Resource Management
Duration: 3FT/4SW Hon
Entry Requirements: *GCE:* 280. *IB:* 25. *OCR ND:* D *OCR NED:* M3

N000 BA Business, Accountancy & Advertising
Duration: 3FT/4SW Hon
Entry Requirements: *GCE:* 280. *IB:* 25. *OCR ND:* D *OCR NED:* M3

NLC1 BA Business, Accountancy & Economics
Duration: 3FT/4SW Hon
Entry Requirements: *GCE:* 280. *IB:* 25. *OCR ND:* D *OCR NED:* M3

NNC5 BA Business, Accountancy & Marketing
Duration: 3FT/4SW Hon
Entry Requirements: *GCE:* 280. *IB:* 25. *OCR ND:* D *OCR NED:* M3

LN15 BA Business, Economics & Advertising
Duration: 3FT/4SW Hon
Entry Requirements: *GCE:* 280. *IB:* 25. *OCR ND:* D *OCR NED:* M3

NL11 BA Business, Economics & Finance
Duration: 3FT/4SW Hon
Entry Requirements: Contact the institution for details.

NN14 BA Business, Entrepreneurship & Accountancy
Duration: 3FT/4SW Hon
Entry Requirements: *GCE:* 280. *IB:* 25. *OCR ND:* D *OCR NED:* M3

NN1K BA Business, Finance & Accountancy
Duration: 3FT/4SW Hon
Entry Requirements: Contact the institution for details.

NN13 BA Business, Finance & Entrepreneurship
Duration: 3FT/4SW Hon
Entry Requirements: Contact the institution for details.

NN1M BA Business, Finance & Marketing
Duration: 3FT/4SW Hon
Entry Requirements: Contact the institution for details.

NN24 BA Business, Management & Accountancy
Duration: 3FT/4SW Hon
Entry Requirements: *GCE:* 280. *IB:* 25. *OCR ND:* D *OCR NED:* M3

NL21 BA Business, Management & Economics
Duration: 3FT/4SW Hon
Entry Requirements: *GCE:* 280. *IB:* 25. *OCR ND:* D *OCR NED:* M3

NN1H BA Business, Management & Finance
Duration: 3FT/4SW Hon
Entry Requirements: Contact the institution for details.

NL51 BA Business, Marketing & Economics
Duration: 3FT/4SW Hon
Entry Requirements: *GCE:* 280. *IB:* 25. *OCR ND:* D *OCR NED:* M3

W81 WORCESTER COLLEGE OF TECHNOLOGY
DEANSWAY
WORCESTER WR1 2JF
t: 01905 725555 f: 01905 28906
// www.wortech.ac.uk

N1N4 FdA Business with Accounting
Duration: 2FT Hon
Entry Requirements: *GCE:* 80. Interview required.

Y75 YORK ST JOHN UNIVERSITY
LORD MAYOR'S WALK
YORK YO31 7EX
t: 01904 876598 f: 01904 876940/876921
e: admissions@yorksj.ac.uk
// w3.yorksj.ac.uk

N1N4 BA Accounting and Business Management
Duration: 3FT Hon
Entry Requirements: Contact the institution for details.

COMPUTING AND COMPUTER SCIENCE
COMBINATIONS

A20 THE UNIVERSITY OF ABERDEEN
UNIVERSITY OFFICE
KING'S COLLEGE
ABERDEEN AB24 3FX
t: +44 (0) 1224 273504 f: +44 (0) 1224 272034
e: sras@abdn.ac.uk
// www.abdn.ac.uk/sras

N4G4 MA Accountancy with Computing
Duration: 4FT Hon
Entry Requirements: Contact the institution for details.

L1G4 MA Economics with Computing
Duration: 4FT Hon
Entry Requirements: Contact the institution for details.

N3G4 MA Finance with Computing
Duration: 4FT Hon
Entry Requirements: Contact the institution for details.

A40 ABERYSTWYTH UNIVERSITY
ABERYSTWYTH UNIVERSITY, WELCOME CENTRE
PENGLAIS CAMPUS
ABERYSTWYTH
CEREDIGION SY23 3FB
t: 01970 622021 f: 01970 627410
e: ug-admissions@aber.ac.uk
// www.aber.ac.uk

G5N4 BSc Business Information Technology with Accounting & Finance
Duration: 3FT Hon
Entry Requirements: *GCE:* 280. *IB:* 28.

N4G4 BScEcon Accounting & Finance with Computer Science
Duration: 3FT Hon
Entry Requirements: *GCE:* 300. *IB:* 27.

L1G4 BScEcon Business Economics with Computer Science
Duration: 3FT Hon
Entry Requirements: *GCE:* 300. *IB:* 27.

B90 THE UNIVERSITY OF BUCKINGHAM
YEOMANRY HOUSE
HUNTER STREET
BUCKINGHAM MK18 1EG
t: 01280 820313 f: 01280 822245
e: info@buckingham.ac.uk
// www.buckingham.ac.uk

G4N4 BSc Computing with Accounting & Finance
Duration: 2FT Hon
Entry Requirements: *GCE:* BBB-BBC. *SQAH:* ABBB-BBBB. *SQAAH:* BBB-BBC. *IB:* 34.

G4L1 BSc Computing with Economics
Duration: 2FT Hon
Entry Requirements: *GCE:* BBB-BBC. *SQAH:* ABBB-BBBB. *SQAAH:* BBB-BBC. *IB:* 34.

L1G5 BScEcon Economics with Information Systems
Duration: 2FT Hon
Entry Requirements: *GCE:* BBB. *SQAH:* ABBB. *SQAAH:* BBB. *IB:* 34.

C58 UNIVERSITY OF CHICHESTER
BISHOP OTTER CAMPUS
COLLEGE LANE
CHICHESTER
WEST SUSSEX PO19 6PE
t: 01243 816002 f: 01243 816161
e: admissions@chi.ac.uk
// www.chiuni.ac.uk

GN53 BA Information Technology Management for Business and Finance (Placement)
Duration: 4SW Hon
Entry Requirements: *GCE:* BCD-CCC. *SQAAH:* CCC. *IB:* 28. *BTEC SubDip:* M. *BTEC Dip:* DD.

D65 UNIVERSITY OF DUNDEE
NETHERGATE
DUNDEE DD1 4HN
t: 01382 383838 f: 01382 388150
e: contactus@dundee.ac.uk
// www.dundee.ac.uk/admissions/
undergraduate/

GN44 BSc Accountancy and Applied Computing
Duration: 4FT Hon
Entry Requirements: *GCE:* BCC. *SQAH:* ABBB. *IB:* 30.

GL41 BSc Applied Computing and Economics
Duration: 4FT Hon
Entry Requirements: *GCE:* BCC. *SQAH:* ABBB. *IB:* 30.

GLK1 BSc Applied Computing and Financial Economics
Duration: 4FT Hon
Entry Requirements: *GCE:* BCC. *SQAH:* ABBB. *IB:* 30.

E14 UNIVERSITY OF EAST ANGLIA
NORWICH NR4 7TJ
t: 01603 591515 f: 01603 591523
e: admissions@uea.ac.uk
// www.uea.ac.uk

GN54 BSc Business Information Systems
Duration: 3FT Hon   CRB Check: Required
Entry Requirements: *GCE:* ABB. *SQAH:* AAABB. *SQAAH:* ABB. *IB:* 32. *BTEC ExtDip:* DDM.

E28 UNIVERSITY OF EAST LONDON
DOCKLANDS CAMPUS
UNIVERSITY WAY
LONDON E16 2RD
t: 020 8223 3333 f: 020 8223 2978
e: study@uel.ac.uk
// www.uel.ac.uk

GL51 BA/BSc Business Information Systems/Business Economics
Duration: 3FT Hon
Entry Requirements: *GCE:* 240. *IB:* 24.

G28 UNIVERSITY OF GLASGOW
71 SOUTHPARK AVENUE
UNIVERSITY OF GLASGOW
GLASGOW G12 8QQ
t: 0141 330 6062 f: 0141 330 2961
e: student.recruitment@glasgow.ac.uk
// www.glasgow.ac.uk

GL41 BSc Computing Science/Economics
Duration: 4FT Hon
Entry Requirements: *GCE:* ABB. *SQAH:* AAAB-BBBB. *IB:* 32.

GLK1 MA Computing Science/Economics
Duration: 4FT Hon
Entry Requirements: *GCE:* ABB. *SQAH:* AAAA-AABB. *IB:* 36.

GLL1 MA Computing/Economics
Duration: 4FT Hon
Entry Requirements: *GCE:* ABB. *SQAH:* AAAB-ABBB. *IB:* 36.

H36 UNIVERSITY OF HERTFORDSHIRE
UNIVERSITY ADMISSIONS SERVICE
COLLEGE LANE
HATFIELD
HERTS AL10 9AB
t: 01707 284800
// www.herts.ac.uk

NG45 BA Accounting/Information Systems
Duration: 3FT/4SW Hon
Entry Requirements: *GCE:* 300. *IB:* 30.

LG15 BA Economics/Information Systems
Duration: 3FT/4SW Hon
Entry Requirements: *GCE:* 300. *IB:* 30.

K12 KEELE UNIVERSITY
KEELE UNIVERSITY
STAFFORDSHIRE ST5 5BG
t: 01782 734005 f: 01782 632343
e: undergraduate@keele.ac.uk
// www.keele.ac.uk

GN43 BSc Computer Science and Finance
Duration: 3FT Hon
Entry Requirements: *GCE:* ABB.

GN4H BSc Creative Computing and Finance
Duration: 3FT Hon
Entry Requirements: *GCE:* ABB.

NG34 BSc Finance and Information Systems
Duration: 3FT Hon
Entry Requirements: *GCE:* ABB.

K24 THE UNIVERSITY OF KENT
RECRUITMENT & ADMISSIONS OFFICE
REGISTRY
UNIVERSITY OF KENT
CANTERBURY, KENT CT2 7NZ
t: 01227 827272 f: 01227 827077
e: information@kent.ac.uk
// www.kent.ac.uk

L1G4 BSc Economics with Computing
Duration: 3FT Hon
Entry Requirements: *GCE:* ABB. *SQAH:* AABBB. *SQAAH:* ABB. *IB:* 33. *OCR ND:* D *OCR NED:* D2

L14 LANCASTER UNIVERSITY
THE UNIVERSITY
LANCASTER
LANCASHIRE LA1 4YW
t: 01524 592029 f: 01524 846243
e: ugadmissions@lancaster.ac.uk
// www.lancs.ac.uk

NG44 BSc Accounting, Finance and Computer Science
Duration: 3FT Hon
Entry Requirements: *GCE:* AAA-AAB. *SQAH:* AAABB-ABBBB. *SQAAH:* AAA-AAB.

www.ucas.com
www.cukas.ac.uk

at the heart of connecting people to higher education

L46 LIVERPOOL HOPE UNIVERSITY
HOPE PARK
LIVERPOOL L16 9JD
t: 0151 291 3331 f: 0151 291 3434
e: administration@hope.ac.uk
// www.hope.ac.uk

NI42 BA Accounting and Information Technology
Duration: 3FT Hon
Entry Requirements: *GCE:* 300-320. *IB:* 25.

N38 UNIVERSITY OF NORTHAMPTON
PARK CAMPUS
BOUGHTON GREEN ROAD
NORTHAMPTON NN2 7AL
t: 0800 358 2232 f: 01604 722083
e: admissions@northampton.ac.uk
// www.northampton.ac.uk

N4G5 BA Accounting/Business Computing Systems
Duration: 3FT Hon
Entry Requirements: *GCE:* 260-280. *SQAH:* AAA-BBBB. *IB:* 24.
BTEC Dip: DD. *BTEC ExtDip:* DMM. *OCR ND:* D *OCR NED:* M2

N4G4 BA Accounting/Computing
Duration: 3FT Hon
Entry Requirements: *GCE:* 260-280. *SQAH:* AAA-BBBB. *IB:* 24.
BTEC Dip: DD. *BTEC ExtDip:* DMM. *OCR ND:* D *OCR NED:* M2

N4GK BA Accounting/Web Design
Duration: 3FT Hon
Entry Requirements: *GCE:* 260-280. *SQAH:* AAA-BBBB. *IB:* 24.
BTEC Dip: DD. *BTEC ExtDip:* DMM. *OCR ND:* D *OCR NED:* M2

L1G4 BA Economics/Computing
Duration: 3FT Hon
Entry Requirements: *GCE:* 260-280. *SQAH:* AAA-BBBB. *IB:* 24.
BTEC Dip: DD. *BTEC ExtDip:* DMM. *OCR ND:* D *OCR NED:* M2

G5N4 BSc Business Computing Systems/Accounting
Duration: 3FT Hon
Entry Requirements: *GCE:* 260-280. *SQAH:* AAA-BBBB. *IB:* 24.
BTEC Dip: DD. *BTEC ExtDip:* DMM. *OCR ND:* D *OCR NED:* M2

G4N4 BSc Computing/Accounting
Duration: 3FT Hon
Entry Requirements: *GCE:* 260-280. *SQAH:* AAA-BBBB. *IB:* 24.
BTEC Dip: DD. *BTEC ExtDip:* DMM. *OCR ND:* D *OCR NED:* M2

G4L1 BSc Computing/Economics
Duration: 3FT Hon
Entry Requirements: *GCE:* 260-280. *SQAH:* AAA-BBBB. *IB:* 24.
BTEC Dip: DD. *BTEC ExtDip:* DMM. *OCR ND:* D *OCR NED:* M2

G4NK BSc Web Design/Accounting
Duration: 3FT Hon
Entry Requirements: *GCE:* 260-280. *SQAH:* AAA-BBBB. *IB:* 24.
BTEC Dip: DD. *BTEC ExtDip:* DMM. *OCR ND:* D *OCR NED:* M2

S36 UNIVERSITY OF ST ANDREWS
ST KATHARINE'S WEST
16 THE SCORES
ST ANDREWS
FIFE KY16 9AX
t: 01334 462150 f: 01334 463330
e: admissions@st-andrews.ac.uk
// www.st-andrews.ac.uk

GL41 BSc Computer Science and Economics
Duration: 4FT Hon
Entry Requirements: *GCE:* AAA. *SQAH:* AAAB. *IB:* 38.

LG14 BSc Economics-Internet Computer Science
Duration: 4FT Hon
Entry Requirements: *GCE:* AAA. *SQAH:* AAAA. *IB:* 38.

S93 SWANSEA UNIVERSITY
SINGLETON PARK
SWANSEA SA2 8PP
t: 01792 295111 f: 01792 295110
e: admissions@swansea.ac.uk
// www.swansea.ac.uk

G4L1 BSc Computing with Finance
Duration: 3FT Hon
Entry Requirements: *GCE:* ABB. *IB:* 33.

L1G4 BSc Financial Economics with Computing
Duration: 3FT Hon
Entry Requirements: *GCE:* 280.

U20 UNIVERSITY OF ULSTER
COLERAINE
CO. LONDONDERRY
NORTHERN IRELAND BT52 1SA
t: 028 7012 4221 f: 028 7012 4908
e: online@ulster.ac.uk
// www.ulster.ac.uk

G4NK BSc Computing with Accounting
Duration: 4SW Hon
Entry Requirements: *GCE:* 280. *IB:* 24. Interview required.
Admissions Test required.

GEOGRAPHY AND GEOLOGY COMBINATIONS

K12 KEELE UNIVERSITY
KEELE UNIVERSITY
STAFFORDSHIRE ST5 5BG
t: 01782 734005 f: 01782 632343
e: undergraduate@keele.ac.uk
// www.keele.ac.uk

NF46 BSc Accounting and Geology
Duration: 3FT Hon
Entry Requirements: *GCE:* ABB.

NF48 BSc Accounting and Physical Geography
Duration: 3FT Hon
Entry Requirements: *GCE:* ABB.

FL61 BSc Economics and Geology
Duration: 3FT Hon
Entry Requirements: *GCE:* ABB.

FL81 BSc Economics and Physical Geography
Duration: 3FT Hon
Entry Requirements: *GCE:* ABB.

FN63 BSc Finance and Geology
Duration: 3FT Hon
Entry Requirements: *GCE:* ABB.

L79 LOUGHBOROUGH UNIVERSITY
LOUGHBOROUGH
LEICESTERSHIRE LE11 3TU
t: 01509 223522 f: 01509 223905
e: admissions@lboro.ac.uk
// www.lboro.ac.uk

L1F8 BSc Economics with Geography
Duration: 3FT Hon
Entry Requirements: *GCE:* AAB. *SQAH:* AABBB. *SQAAH:* AB. *IB:* 34. *BTEC ExtDip:* DDD.

N38 UNIVERSITY OF NORTHAMPTON
PARK CAMPUS
BOUGHTON GREEN ROAD
NORTHAMPTON NN2 7AL
t: 0800 358 2232 f: 01604 722083
e: admissions@northampton.ac.uk
// www.northampton.ac.uk

N4F8 BA Accounting/Physical Geography
Duration: 3FT Hon
Entry Requirements: *GCE:* 260-280. *SQAH:* AAA-BBBB. *IB:* 24. *BTEC Dip:* DD. *BTEC ExtDip:* DMM. *OCR ND:* D *OCR NED:* M2

F8N4 BSc Physical Geography/Accounting
Duration: 3FT Hon
Entry Requirements: *GCE:* 260-280. *SQAH:* AAA-BBBB. *IB:* 24. *BTEC Dip:* DD. *BTEC ExtDip:* DMM. *OCR ND:* D *OCR NED:* M2

P60 PLYMOUTH UNIVERSITY
DRAKE CIRCUS
PLYMOUTH PL4 8AA
t: 01752 585858 f: 01752 588055
e: admissions@plymouth.ac.uk
// www.plymouth.ac.uk

L1FW BSc Economics with Geography
Duration: 3FT/4SW Hon
Entry Requirements: *GCE:* 240. *IB:* 24.

S36 UNIVERSITY OF ST ANDREWS
ST KATHARINE'S WEST
16 THE SCORES
ST ANDREWS
FIFE KY16 9AX
t: 01334 462150 f: 01334 463330
e: admissions@st-andrews.ac.uk
// www.st-andrews.ac.uk

LF16 BSc Economics-Environmental Geoscience
Duration: 4FT Hon
Entry Requirements: *GCE:* AAA. *SQAH:* AAAA. *IB:* 38.

FL61 BSc Economics-Geoscience
Duration: 4FT Hon
Entry Requirements: *GCE:* AAA. *SQAH:* AAAA. *IB:* 38.

LANGUAGE COMBINATIONS

A20 THE UNIVERSITY OF ABERDEEN
UNIVERSITY OFFICE
KING'S COLLEGE
ABERDEEN AB24 3FX
t: +44 (0) 1224 273504 f: +44 (0) 1224 272034
e: sras@abdn.ac.uk
// www.abdn.ac.uk/sras

NR41 MA Accountancy and French
Duration: 5FT Hon
Entry Requirements: *GCE:* BBB. *SQAH:* BBBB. *IB:* 30.

NR42 MA Accountancy and German
Duration: 5FT Hon
Entry Requirements: *GCE:* BBB. *SQAH:* BBBB. *IB:* 30.

NR44 MA Accountancy and Hispanic Studies
Duration: 5FT Hon
Entry Requirements: *GCE:* BBB. *SQAH:* BBBB. *IB:* 30.

N4R1 MA Accountancy with French
Duration: 4FT Hon
Entry Requirements: *GCE:* BBB. *SQAH:* BBBB. *IB:* 30.

N4R2 MA Accountancy with German
Duration: 4FT Hon
Entry Requirements: *GCE:* BBB. *SQAH:* BBBB. *IB:* 30.

LQ13 MA Economics and English
Duration: 4FT Hon
Entry Requirements: *GCE:* BBB. *SQAH:* BBBB. *IB:* 30.

LR11 MA Economics and French
Duration: 5FT Hon
Entry Requirements: *GCE:* BBB. *SQAH:* BBBB. *IB:* 30.

RL11 MA Economics and French
Duration: 4FT Hon
Entry Requirements: *GCE:* BBB. *SQAH:* BBBB. *IB:* 30.

QL51 MA Economics and Gaelic Studies
Duration: 4FT Hon
Entry Requirements: *GCE:* BBB. *SQAH:* BBBB. *IB:* 30.

LR12 MA Economics and German
Duration: 5FT Hon
Entry Requirements: *GCE:* BBB. *SQAH:* BBBB. *IB:* 30.

RL21 MA Economics and German
Duration: 4FT Hon
Entry Requirements: *GCE:* BBB. *SQAH:* BBBB. *IB:* 30.

LR14 MA Economics and Hispanic Studies
Duration: 5FT Hon
Entry Requirements: *GCE:* BBB. *SQAH:* BBBB. *IB:* 30.

RL41 MA Economics and Hispanic Studies
Duration: 4FT Hon
Entry Requirements: *GCE:* BBB. *SQAH:* BBBB. *IB:* 30.

LQ12 MA Economics and Literature in a World Context
Duration: 4FT Hon
Entry Requirements: *GCE:* BBB. *SQAH:* BBBB. *IB:* 30.

NQ33 MA English and Finance
Duration: 4FT Hon
Entry Requirements: *GCE:* BBB. *SQAH:* BBBB. *IB:* 30.

NR31 MA Finance and French
Duration: 5FT Hon
Entry Requirements: *GCE:* BBB. *SQAH:* BBBB. *IB:* 30.

RN13 MA Finance and French
Duration: 4FT Hon
Entry Requirements: *GCE:* BBB. *SQAH:* BBBB. *IB:* 30.

NR32 MA Finance and German
Duration: 5FT Hon
Entry Requirements: *GCE:* BBB. *SQAH:* BBBB. *IB:* 30.

RN23 MA Finance and German
Duration: 4FT Hon
Entry Requirements: *GCE:* BBB. *SQAH:* BBBB. *IB:* 30.

RN43 MA Finance and Hispanic Studies
Duration: 5FT Hon
Entry Requirements: *GCE:* BBB. *SQAH:* BBBB. *IB:* 30.

RNK3 MA Finance and Hispanic Studies
Duration: 4FT Hon
Entry Requirements: *GCE:* BBB. *SQAH:* BBBB. *IB:* 30.

NQ32 MA Finance and Literature in a World Context
Duration: 4FT Hon
Entry Requirements: *GCE:* BBB. *SQAH:* BBBB. *IB:* 30.

A40 ABERYSTWYTH UNIVERSITY
ABERYSTWYTH UNIVERSITY, WELCOME CENTRE
PENGLAIS CAMPUS
ABERYSTWYTH
CEREDIGION SY23 3FB
t: 01970 622021 f: 01970 627410
e: ug-admissions@aber.ac.uk
// www.aber.ac.uk

N4Q5 BScEcon Accounting & Finance with Cymraeg
Duration: 3FT Hon
Entry Requirements: *GCE:* 300. *IB:* 27.

N4R1 BScEcon Accounting & Finance with French (4 years)
Duration: 4FT Hon
Entry Requirements: *GCE:* 300. *IB:* 28.

NR41 BScEcon Accounting & Finance/French
Duration: 4FT Hon
Entry Requirements: *GCE:* 300. *IB:* 28.

NR44 BScEcon Accounting & Finance/Spanish
Duration: 4FT Hon
Entry Requirements: *GCE:* 300. *IB:* 28.

L1R1 BScEcon Economics with French (4 years)
Duration: 4FT Hon
Entry Requirements: *GCE:* 300. *IB:* 28.

LR11 BScEcon Economics/French
Duration: 4FT Hon
Entry Requirements: *GCE:* 280. *IB:* 28.

B06 BANGOR UNIVERSITY
BANGOR UNIVERSITY
BANGOR
GWYNEDD LL57 2DG
t: 01248 388484 f: 01248 370451
e: admissions@bangor.ac.uk
// www.bangor.ac.uk

NR43 BA Accounting/Italian (4 years)
Duration: 4FT Hon
Entry Requirements: *GCE:* 240-260. *IB:* 28.

NR44 BA Accounting/Spanish (4 years)
Duration: 4FT Hon
Entry Requirements: *GCE:* 240-260. *IB:* 28.

LR13 BA Economics/Italian (4 years)
Duration: 4FT Hon
Entry Requirements: *GCE:* 260-300. *IB:* 28.

LR14 BA Economics/Spanish (4 years)
Duration: 4FT Hon
Entry Requirements: *GCE:* 260-300. *IB:* 28.

NR41 BA French/Accounting (4 years)
Duration: 4FT Hon
Entry Requirements: *GCE:* 240-260. *IB:* 28.

LR11 BA French/Economics (4 years)
Duration: 4FT Hon
Entry Requirements: *GCE:* 240-260. *IB:* 28.

NR42 BA German/Accounting (4 years)
Duration: 4FT Hon
Entry Requirements: *GCE:* 240-260. *IB:* 28.

LR12 BA German/Economics (4 years)
Duration: 4FT Hon
Entry Requirements: *GCE:* 240-260. *IB:* 28.

B32 THE UNIVERSITY OF BIRMINGHAM
EDGBASTON
BIRMINGHAM B15 2TT
t: 0121 415 8900 f: 0121 414 7159
e: admissions@bham.ac.uk
// www.birmingham.ac.uk

L1R2 BSc Economics with German (4 years)
Duration: 4FT Hon
Entry Requirements: *GCE:* AAA. *SQAH:* AAABB. *SQAAH:* AA.

L1R3 BSc Economics with Italian (4 years)
Duration: 4FT Hon
Entry Requirements: *GCE:* AAA. *SQAH:* AAABB. *SQAAH:* AA.

L1T2 BSc Economics with Japanese (4 years)
Duration: 4FT Hon
Entry Requirements: *GCE:* AAA. *SQAH:* AAABB. *SQAAH:* AA.

L1R5 BSc Economics with Portuguese (4 years)
Duration: 4FT Hon
Entry Requirements: *GCE:* AAA. *SQAH:* AAABB. *SQAAH:* AA.

L1R4 BSc Economics with Spanish (4 years)
Duration: 4FT Hon
Entry Requirements: *GCE:* AAA. *SQAH:* AAABB. *SQAAH:* AA.

N3R2 BSc Money, Banking & Finance with German (4 years)
Duration: 4FT Hon
Entry Requirements: *GCE:* AAA. *SQAH:* AAABB. *SQAAH:* AA.

N3R3 BSc Money, Banking & Finance with Italian (4 years)
Duration: 4FT Hon
Entry Requirements: *GCE:* AAA. *SQAH:* AAABB. *SQAAH:* AA.

N3R5 BSc Money, Banking & Finance with Portuguese (4 years)
Duration: 4FT Hon
Entry Requirements: *GCE:* AAA. *SQAH:* AAABB. *SQAAH:* AA.

N3R4 BSc Money, Banking & Finance with Spanish (4 years)
Duration: 4FT Hon
Entry Requirements: *GCE:* AAA. *SQAH:* AAABB. *SQAAH:* AA.

B90 THE UNIVERSITY OF BUCKINGHAM
YEOMANRY HOUSE
HUNTER STREET
BUCKINGHAM MK18 1EG
t: 01280 820313 f: 01280 822245
e: info@buckingham.ac.uk
// www.buckingham.ac.uk

N4R1 BSc Accounting with French
Duration: 2FT Hon
Entry Requirements: *GCE:* BBB-BCC. *SQAH:* ABBB-BBBC. *SQAAH:* BBB-BCC. *IB:* 34.

N4R4 BSc Accounting with Spanish
Duration: 2FT Hon
Entry Requirements: *GCE:* BBB-BCC. *SQAH:* ABBB-BBBC. *SQAAH:* BBB-BCC. *IB:* 34.

L1QH BSc Economics with English Language Studies
Duration: 2FT Hon
Entry Requirements: *GCE:* BBB. *SQAH:* ABBB. *SQAAH:* BBB. *IB:* 34.

L1Q3 BSc Economics with English as a Foreign Language
Duration: 2FT Hon
Entry Requirements: *GCE:* BBB. *SQAH:* ABBB. *SQAAH:* BBB. *IB:* 34.

L1R1 BSc Economics with French
Duration: 2FT Hon
Entry Requirements: *GCE:* BBB. *SQAH:* ABBB. *SQAAH:* BBB. *IB:* 34.

L1R4 BSc Economics with Spanish
Duration: 2FT Hon
Entry Requirements: *GCE:* BBB. *SQAH:* ABBB. *SQAAH:* BBB. *IB:* 34.

C15 CARDIFF UNIVERSITY
PO BOX 927
30-36 NEWPORT ROAD
CARDIFF CF24 0DE
t: 029 2087 9999 f: 029 2087 6138
e: admissions@cardiff.ac.uk
// www.cardiff.ac.uk

RL11 BA Economics/French (4 years)
Duration: 4FT Hon
Entry Requirements: *GCE:* AAB. *SQAH:* AAABB. *SQAAH:* ABB. *IB:* 35.

RL21 BA Economics/German (4 years)
Duration: 4FT Hon
Entry Requirements: *GCE:* BBB. *SQAH:* AAABB-AABBB. *SQAAH:* AAB-BBB.

RL31 BA Economics/Italian (4 years)
Duration: 4FT Hon
Entry Requirements: *GCE:* BBB. *SQAH:* AAABB-AABBB. *SQAAH:* BBB. *OCR NED:* D2

LR14 BA Economics/Spanish (4 years)
Duration: 4FT Hon
Entry Requirements: *GCE:* AAB. *SQAH:* AAABB. *SQAAH:* AAB. *IB:* 35.

N4R2 BSc Accounting with a European Language (German)
Duration: 4FT Hon
Entry Requirements: *GCE:* AAB. *SQAH:* AAABB. *SQAAH:* AAB. *IB:* 35. *OCR NED:* D1 Interview required.

N4R4 BSc Accounting with a European Language (Spanish)
Duration: 4FT Hon
Entry Requirements: *GCE:* AAB. *SQAH:* AAABB. *SQAAH:* AAB. *IB:* 35. *OCR NED:* D1 Interview required.

L1R9 BSc Business Economics with a European Language (French)
Duration: 4FT Hon
Entry Requirements: *GCE:* AAB. *SQAH:* AAABB. *SQAAH:* AAB. *IB:* 35. *OCR NED:* D1 Interview required.

L1RX BSc Business Economics with a European Language (German)
Duration: 4FT Hon
Entry Requirements: *GCE:* AAB. *SQAH:* AAABB. *SQAAH:* AAB. *IB:* 35. *OCR NED:* D1 Interview required.

L1RY BSc Business Economics with a European Language (Spanish)
Duration: 4FT Hon
Entry Requirements: *GCE:* AAB. *SQAH:* AAABB. *SQAAH:* AAB. *IB:* 35. *OCR NED:* D1 Interview required.

L1R2 BSc Economics with a European Language (German)
Duration: 4FT Hon
Entry Requirements: *GCE:* AAB. *SQAH:* AAABB. *SQAAH:* AAB. *IB:* 35. *OCR NED:* D1 Interview required.

L1R4 BSc Economics with a European Language (Spanish)
Duration: 4FT Hon
Entry Requirements: *GCE:* AAB. *SQAH:* AAABB. *SQAAH:* AAB. *IB:* 35. *OCR NED:* D1 Interview required.

C58 UNIVERSITY OF CHICHESTER
BISHOP OTTER CAMPUS
COLLEGE LANE
CHICHESTER
WEST SUSSEX PO19 6PE
t: 01243 816002 f: 01243 816161
e: admissions@chi.ac.uk
// www.chiuni.ac.uk

N4Q3 BA Accounting & Finance with International English Studies
Duration: 3FT Hon
Entry Requirements: *GCE:* BCD-CCC. *SQAAH:* CCC. *IB:* 28. *BTEC SubDip:* M. *BTEC Dip:* DD.

NQ43 BA Accounting and International English Studies
Duration: 3FT Hon
Entry Requirements: *GCE:* BCD-CCC. *SQAAH:* CCC. *IB:* 28. *BTEC SubDip:* M. *BTEC Dip:* DD.

D39 UNIVERSITY OF DERBY
KEDLESTON ROAD
DERBY DE22 1GB
t: 01332 591167 f: 01332 597724
e: askadmissions@derby.ac.uk
// www.derby.ac.uk

NQ43 BA Accounting and English
Duration: 3FT Hon
Entry Requirements: *Foundation:* Distinction. *GCE:* 260-300. *IB:* 28. *BTEC Dip:* D*D*. *BTEC ExtDip:* DMM. *OCR NED:* M2

D65 UNIVERSITY OF DUNDEE
NETHERGATE
DUNDEE DD1 4HN
t: 01382 383838 f: 01382 388150
e: contactus@dundee.ac.uk
// www.dundee.ac.uk/admissions/undergraduate/

TLN0 MA American Studies and Business Economics with Marketing
Duration: 4FT Hon
Entry Requirements: *GCE:* BCC. *SQAH:* ABBB. *IB:* 30.

LNR0 MA Business Economics with Marketing and European Studies
Duration: 4FT Hon
Entry Requirements: *GCE:* BCC. *SQAH:* ABBB. *IB:* 30.

LRN0 MA Business Economics with Marketing with French
Duration: 4FT Hon
Entry Requirements: *GCE:* BCC. *SQAH:* ABBB. *IB:* 30.

RLN0 MA Business Economics with Marketing with German
Duration: 4FT Hon
Entry Requirements: *GCE:* BCC. *SQAH:* ABBB. *IB:* 30.

RNL0 MA Business Economics with Marketing with Spanish
Duration: 4FT Hon
Entry Requirements: *GCE:* BCC. *SQAH:* ABBB. *IB:* 30.

LR18 MA Economics and European Studies
Duration: 4FT Hon
Entry Requirements: *GCE:* BCC. *SQAH:* ABBB. *IB:* 30.

L1R1 MA Economics with French
Duration: 4FT Hon
Entry Requirements: *GCE:* BCC. *SQAH:* ABBB. *IB:* 30.

L1R2 MA Economics with German
Duration: 4FT Hon
Entry Requirements: *GCE:* BCC. *SQAH:* ABBB. *IB:* 30.

L1R4 MA Economics with Spanish
Duration: 4FT Hon
Entry Requirements: *GCE:* BCC. *SQAH:* ABBB. *IB:* 30.

L1RC MA Financial Economics with French
Duration: 4FT Hon
Entry Requirements: *GCE:* BCC. *SQAH:* ABBB. *IB:* 30.

L1RF MA Financial Economics with German
Duration: 4FT Hon
Entry Requirements: *GCE:* BCC. *SQAH:* ABBB. *IB:* 30.

L1RK MA Financial Economics with Spanish
Duration: 4FT Hon
Entry Requirements: *GCE:* BCC. *SQAH:* ABBB. *IB:* 30.

D86 DURHAM UNIVERSITY
DURHAM UNIVERSITY
UNIVERSITY OFFICE
DURHAM DH1 3HP
t: 0191 334 2000 f: 0191 334 6055
e: admissions@durham.ac.uk
// www.durham.ac.uk

L1R1 BA Economics with French
Duration: 4FT Hon
Entry Requirements: *GCE:* A*AA. *SQAH:* AAAAA. *SQAAH:* AAA. *IB:* 38.

E56 THE UNIVERSITY OF EDINBURGH
STUDENT RECRUITMENT & ADMISSIONS
57 GEORGE SQUARE
EDINBURGH EH8 9JU
t: 0131 650 4360 f: 0131 651 1236
e: sra.enquiries@ed.ac.uk
// www.ed.ac.uk/studying/undergraduate/

TL61 MA Arabic and Economics
Duration: 4FT Hon
Entry Requirements: *GCE:* AAA-BBB. *SQAH:* AABB-BBBB. *IB:* 34.

LT11 MA Economics and Chinese
Duration: 4FT Hon
Entry Requirements: *GCE:* AAA-BBB. *SQAH:* AAAA-BBBB. *IB:* 34.

E70 THE UNIVERSITY OF ESSEX
WIVENHOE PARK
COLCHESTER
ESSEX CO4 3SQ
t: 01206 873666 f: 01206 874477
e: admit@essex.ac.uk
// www.essex.ac.uk

L1R1 BA Economics with French
Duration: 3FT Hon
Entry Requirements: *GCE:* ABB. *SQAH:* AAAB. *IB:* 34.

L1RC BA Economics with French (Including Year Abroad)
Duration: 4FT Hon
Entry Requirements: *GCE:* ABB. *SQAH:* AAAB. *IB:* 34.

L1R2 BA Economics with German
Duration: 3FT Hon
Entry Requirements: *GCE:* ABB. *SQAH:* AAAB. *IB:* 34.

L1RF BA Economics with German (Including Year Abroad)
Duration: 4FT Hon
Entry Requirements: *GCE:* ABB. *SQAH:* AAAB. *IB:* 34.

L1R3 BA Economics with Italian
Duration: 3FT Hon
Entry Requirements: *GCE:* ABB. *SQAH:* AAAB. *IB:* 34.

L1RH BA Economics with Italian (Including Year Abroad)
Duration: 4FT Hon
Entry Requirements: *GCE:* ABB. *SQAH:* AAAB. *IB:* 34.

L1R5 BA Economics with Portuguese
Duration: 4FT Hon
Entry Requirements: *GCE:* ABB. *SQAH:* AAAB. *IB:* 34.

L1RM BA Economics with Portuguese (Including Year Abroad)
Duration: 4FT Hon
Entry Requirements: *GCE:* ABB. *SQAH:* AAAB. *IB:* 34.

L1R4 BA Economics with Spanish
Duration: 3FT Hon
Entry Requirements: *GCE:* ABB. *SQAH:* AAAB. *IB:* 34.

L1RK BA Economics with Spanish (Including Year Abroad)
Duration: 4FT Hon
Entry Requirements: *GCE:* ABB. *SQAH:* AAAB. *IB:* 34.

NR3Y BSc Banking and Finance with a Modern Language
Duration: 4FT Hon
Entry Requirements: *GCE:* ABB. *SQAH:* AAAB. *IB:* 34.

NR39 BSc Finance and Modern Languages
Duration: 4FT Hon
Entry Requirements: *GCE:* ABB. *SQAH:* AAAB. *IB:* 34.

N3R9 BSc Finance with a Modern Language
Duration: 4FT Hon
Entry Requirements: *GCE:* ABB. *SQAH:* AAAB. *IB:* 34.

G28 UNIVERSITY OF GLASGOW
71 SOUTHPARK AVENUE
UNIVERSITY OF GLASGOW
GLASGOW G12 8QQ
t: 0141 330 6062 f: 0141 330 2961
e: student.recruitment@glasgow.ac.uk
// www.glasgow.ac.uk

N4T9 BAcc Accountancy with Languages
Duration: 4FT Hon
Entry Requirements: *GCE:* A*AB-AAA. *SQAH:* AAAABB-AAABB. *IB:* 36.

R4L1 MA Business Economics with Spanish Language
Duration: 5FT Hon
Entry Requirements: *GCE:* ABB. *SQAH:* AAAA-AABB. *IB:* 36.

RL71 MA Central & East European Studies/Business Economics
Duration: 4FT Hon
Entry Requirements: *GCE:* ABB. *SQAH:* AAAA-AABB. *IB:* 36.

RL81 MA Central & East European Studies/Economics
Duration: 4FT Hon
Entry Requirements: *GCE:* ABB. *SQAH:* AAAA-AABB. *IB:* 36.

LQC2 MA Comparative Literature/Economics
Duration: 4FT Hon
Entry Requirements: *GCE:* ABB. *SQAH:* AAAB-ABBB. *IB:* 34.

L1R1 MA Economics with French Language
Duration: 5FT Hon
Entry Requirements: *GCE:* ABB. *SQAH:* AAAA-AABB. *IB:* 36.

L1R7 MA Economics with Russian Language
Duration: 5FT Hon
Entry Requirements: *GCE:* ABB. *SQAH:* AAAA-AABB. *IB:* 36.

L1RK MA Economics with Spanish
Duration: 5FT Hon
Entry Requirements: *GCE:* ABB. *SQAH:* AAAA-AABB. *IB:* 36.

LQ15 MA Economics/Celtic Civilisation
Duration: 4FT Hon
Entry Requirements: *GCE:* ABB. *SQAH:* AAAB-ABBB. *IB:* 36.

LQ1H MA Economics/English Language
Duration: 4FT Hon
Entry Requirements: *GCE:* ABB. *SQAH:* AAAB-ABBB. *IB:* 36.

LQD3 MA Economics/English Literature
Duration: 4FT Hon
Entry Requirements: *GCE:* ABB. *SQAH:* AAAB-ABBB. *IB:* 36.

LR11 MA Economics/French
Duration: 5FT Hon
Entry Requirements: *GCE:* ABB. *SQAH:* AAAB-ABBB. *IB:* 36.

LQ17 MA Economics/Greek
Duration: 4FT Hon
Entry Requirements: *GCE:* ABB. *SQAH:* AAAB-ABBB. *IB:* 36.

LQ16 MA Economics/Latin
Duration: 4FT Hon
Entry Requirements: *GCE:* ABB. *SQAH:* AAAB-ABBB. *IB:* 36.

LR17 MA Economics/Russian
Duration: 5FT Hon
Entry Requirements: *GCE:* ABB. *SQAH:* AAAB-ABBB. *IB:* 36.

LQ12 MA Economics/Scottish Literature
Duration: 4FT Hon
Entry Requirements: *GCE:* ABB. *SQAH:* AAAB-ABBB. *IB:* 36.

RL21 MA German/Economics
Duration: 5FT Hon
Entry Requirements: *GCE:* ABB. *SQAH:* AAAB-ABBB. *IB:* 36.

RL41 MA Spanish/Economics
Duration: 5FT Hon
Entry Requirements: *GCE:* ABB. *SQAH:* AAAB-ABBB. *IB:* 36.

G70 UNIVERSITY OF GREENWICH
GREENWICH CAMPUS
OLD ROYAL NAVAL COLLEGE
PARK ROW
LONDON SE10 9LS
t: 020 8331 9000 f: 020 8331 8145
e: courseinfo@gre.ac.uk
// www.gre.ac.uk

N3R9 BA Economics with Language
Duration: 3FT Hon
Entry Requirements: Contact the institution for details.

H36 UNIVERSITY OF HERTFORDSHIRE
UNIVERSITY ADMISSIONS SERVICE
COLLEGE LANE
HATFIELD
HERTS AL10 9AB
t: 01707 284800
// www.herts.ac.uk

NR41 BA Accounting with French
Duration: 3FT/4SW Hon
Entry Requirements: *GCE:* 300. *IB:* 30.

NR42 BA Accounting with German
Duration: 3FT/4SW Hon
Entry Requirements: *GCE:* 300. *IB:* 30.

NR43 BA Accounting with Italian
Duration: 3FT/4SW Hon
Entry Requirements: *GCE:* 300. *IB:* 30.

N4T1 BA Accounting with Mandarin Chinese
Duration: 3FT/4SW Hon
Entry Requirements: *GCE:* 300. *IB:* 30.

NR44 BA Accounting with Spanish
Duration: 3FT/4SW Hon
Entry Requirements: *GCE:* 300. *IB:* 30.

NR48 BA Accounting/European Studies
Duration: 3FT/4SW Hon
Entry Requirements: *GCE:* 300. *IB:* 30.

LR11 BA Economics with French
Duration: 3FT/4SW Hon
Entry Requirements: *GCE:* 260. *IB:* 30.

LR12 BA Economics with German
Duration: 3FT/4SW Hon
Entry Requirements: *GCE:* 260. *IB:* 30.

LR13 BA Economics with Italian
Duration: 3FT/4SW Hon
Entry Requirements: *GCE:* 300. *IB:* 30.

L1T1 BA Economics with Mandarin Chinese
Duration: 3FT/4SW Hon
Entry Requirements: *GCE:* 260.

LR14 BA Economics with Spanish
Duration: 3FT/4SW Hon
Entry Requirements: *GCE:* 300. *IB:* 30.

LR18 BA Economics/European Studies
Duration: 3FT/4SW Hon
Entry Requirements: *GCE:* 300. *IB:* 30.

R8N3 BA European Studies with Finance
Duration: 3FT/4SW Hon
Entry Requirements: *GCE:* 300. *IB:* 30.

L1Q1 BSc Economics/English Language & Communication
Duration: 3FT/4SW Hon
Entry Requirements: *GCE:* 300.

Q1L1 BSc English Language & Communication/Economics
Duration: 3FT/4SW Hon
Entry Requirements: *GCE:* 300.

K12 KEELE UNIVERSITY
KEELE UNIVERSITY
STAFFORDSHIRE ST5 5BG
t: 01782 734005 f: 01782 632343
e: undergraduate@keele.ac.uk
// www.keele.ac.uk

NQ43 BA Accounting and English
Duration: 3FT Hon
Entry Requirements: *GCE:* ABB.

NT37 BA American Studies and Finance
Duration: 3FT Hon
Entry Requirements: *GCE:* ABB.

LQ13 BA Economics and English
Duration: 3FT Hon
Entry Requirements: *GCE:* ABB.

NQ33 BA English and Finance
Duration: 3FT Hon
Entry Requirements: *GCE:* ABB.

K24 THE UNIVERSITY OF KENT
RECRUITMENT & ADMISSIONS OFFICE
REGISTRY
UNIVERSITY OF KENT
CANTERBURY, KENT CT2 7NZ
t: 01227 827272 f: 01227 827077
e: information@kent.ac.uk
// www.kent.ac.uk

L1R4 BSc Economics with a Language (Spanish)
Duration: 3FT Hon
Entry Requirements: *GCE:* ABB. *SQAH:* AABBB. *SQAAH:* ABB. *IB:* 33. *OCR ND:* D *OCR NED:* D2

K84 KINGSTON UNIVERSITY
STUDENT INFORMATION & ADVICE CENTRE
COOPER HOUSE
40-46 SURBITON ROAD
KINGSTON UPON THAMES KT1 2HX
t: 0844 8552177 f: 020 8547 7080
e: aps@kingston.ac.uk
// www.kingston.ac.uk

LQ13 BA Economics (Applied) and English Language & Communication
Duration: 3FT Hon
Entry Requirements: *GCE:* 240-320. *IB:* 24.

L1R1 BA Economics (Applied) with French
Duration: 3FT Hon
Entry Requirements: *GCE:* 240-320. *IB:* 24.

L1R4 BA Economics (Applied) with Spanish
Duration: 3FT Hon
Entry Requirements: *GCE:* 240-320. *IB:* 24.

L23 UNIVERSITY OF LEEDS
THE UNIVERSITY OF LEEDS
WOODHOUSE LANE
LEEDS LS2 9JT
t: 0113 343 3999
e: admissions@leeds.ac.uk
// www.leeds.ac.uk

LT13 BA Asia Pacific Studies and Economics
Duration: 3FT Hon
Entry Requirements: *GCE:* AAB. *SQAAH:* AAB. *IB:* 36.

LT11 BA Chinese and Economics
Duration: 4FT Hon
Entry Requirements: *GCE:* AAB. *SQAAH:* AAB. *IB:* 36.

RL11 BA Economics and French
Duration: 4FT Hon
Entry Requirements: *GCE:* AAA. *SQAAH:* AAA. *IB:* 37.

RL21 BA Economics and German
Duration: 4FT Hon
Entry Requirements: *GCE:* AAB. *SQAAH:* AAB. *IB:* 36.

LR13 BA Economics and Italian A
Duration: 4FT Hon
Entry Requirements: *GCE:* AAB. *SQAAH:* AAB. *IB:* 36.

LRC3 BA Economics and Italian B
Duration: 4FT Hon
Entry Requirements: *GCE:* AAB. *SQAAH:* AAB. *IB:* 36.

TL21 BA Economics and Japanese
Duration: 4FT Hon
Entry Requirements: *GCE:* AAB. *SQAAH:* AAB. *IB:* 36.

RL71 BA Economics and Russian A
Duration: 4FT Hon
Entry Requirements: *GCE:* AAB. *SQAAH:* AAB. *IB:* 36.

RLR1 BA Economics and Russian B
Duration: 4FT Hon
Entry Requirements: *GCE:* AAB. *SQAAH:* AAB. *IB:* 36.

RLT1 BA Economics and Russian Civilisation
Duration: 3FT Hon
Entry Requirements: *GCE:* AAB. *SQAAH:* AAB. *IB:* 36.

LT1H BA Economics and South East Asian Studies
Duration: 4FT Hon
Entry Requirements: *GCE:* AAB. *SQAAH:* AAB. *IB:* 36.

RL41 BA Economics and Spanish
Duration: 4FT Hon
Entry Requirements: *GCE:* AAB. *SQAAH:* AAB. *IB:* 36.

LT1J BA Economics and Thai & South East Asian Studies
Duration: 4FT Hon
Entry Requirements: *GCE:* AAB. *SQAAH:* AAB. *IB:* 36.

L46 LIVERPOOL HOPE UNIVERSITY
HOPE PARK
LIVERPOOL L16 9JD
t: 0151 291 3331 f: 0151 291 3434
e: administration@hope.ac.uk
// www.hope.ac.uk

NQ43 BA Accounting and English Language
Duration: 3FT Hon
Entry Requirements: *GCE:* 300-320. *IB:* 25.

N38 UNIVERSITY OF NORTHAMPTON
PARK CAMPUS
BOUGHTON GREEN ROAD
NORTHAMPTON NN2 7AL
t: 0800 358 2232 f: 01604 722083
e: admissions@northampton.ac.uk
// www.northampton.ac.uk

N4Q3 BA Accounting/English
Duration: 3FT Hon
Entry Requirements: *GCE:* 260-280. *SQAH:* AAA-BBBB. *IB:* 24.
BTEC Dip: DD. *BTEC ExtDip:* DMM. *OCR ND:* D *OCR NED:* M2

L1Q3 BA Economics/English
Duration: 3FT Hon
Entry Requirements: *GCE:* 260-280. *SQAH:* AAA-BBBB. *IB:* 24.
BTEC Dip: DD. *BTEC ExtDip:* DMM. *OCR ND:* D *OCR NED:* M2

L1R1 BA Economics/French
Duration: 3FT Hon
Entry Requirements: *GCE:* 260-280. *SQAH:* AAA-BBBB. *IB:* 24.
BTEC Dip: DD. *BTEC ExtDip:* DMM. *OCR ND:* D *OCR NED:* M2

Q3N4 BA English/Accounting
Duration: 3FT Hon
Entry Requirements: *GCE:* 260-280. *SQAH:* AAA-BBBB. *IB:* 24.
BTEC Dip: DD. *BTEC ExtDip:* DMM. *OCR ND:* D *OCR NED:* M2

Q3L1 BA English/Economics
Duration: 3FT Hon
Entry Requirements: *GCE:* 260-280. *SQAH:* AAA-BBBB. *IB:* 24.
BTEC Dip: DD. *BTEC ExtDip:* DMM. *OCR ND:* D *OCR NED:* M2

R1L1 BA French/Economics
Duration: 3FT Hon
Entry Requirements: *GCE:* 260-280. *SQAH:* AAA-BBBB. *IB:* 24.
BTEC Dip: DD. *BTEC ExtDip:* DMM. *OCR ND:* D *OCR NED:* M2

N84 THE UNIVERSITY OF NOTTINGHAM
THE ADMISSIONS OFFICE
THE UNIVERSITY OF NOTTINGHAM
UNIVERSITY PARK
NOTTINGHAM NG7 2RD
t: 0115 951 5151 f: 0115 951 4668
// www.nottingham.ac.uk

L1T1 BA Economics with Chinese Studies
Duration: 3FT Hon
Entry Requirements: *GCE:* A*AA-AABB. *SQAAH:* AAA. *IB:* 38.

L1R1 BA Economics with French
Duration: 4FT Hon
Entry Requirements: *GCE:* A*AA-AABB. *SQAAH:* AAA. *IB:* 38.

L1R2 BA Economics with German
Duration: 4FT Hon
Entry Requirements: *GCE:* A*AA-AABB. *SQAAH:* AAA. *IB:* 38.

L1R4 BA Economics with Hispanic Studies
Duration: 4FT Hon
Entry Requirements: *GCE:* A*AA-AABB. *SQAAH:* AAA. *IB:* 38.

L1R7 BA Economics with Russian
Duration: 4FT Hon
Entry Requirements: *GCE:* A*AA-AABB. *SQAAH:* AAA. *IB:* 38.

T135 MSci Accounting and Finance for Contemporary China
Duration: 4FT Hon
Entry Requirements: Contact the institution for details.

Q75 QUEEN'S UNIVERSITY BELFAST
UNIVERSITY ROAD
BELFAST BT7 1NN
t: 028 9097 3838 f: 028 9097 5151
e: admissions@qub.ac.uk
// www.qub.ac.uk

LQF5 BA International Studies and Irish
Duration: 3FT Hon
Entry Requirements: Contact the institution for details.

N4R1 BSc Accounting with French
Duration: 4FT Hon
Entry Requirements: *GCE:* AAB-ABBa. *SQAH:* AAAA-AAABB.
SQAAH: AAB. *IB:* 34.

N4R4 BSc Accounting with Spanish
Duration: 4FT Hon
Entry Requirements: *GCE:* AAB-ABBa. *SQAH:* AAAA-AAABB.
SQAAH: AAB. *IB:* 34.

L1R1 BSc Economics with French
Duration: 3FT Hon
Entry Requirements: *GCE:* ABB-BBBb. *SQAH:* ABBBB. *SQAAH:*
ABB. *IB:* 33.

L1R4 BSc Economics with Spanish
Duration: 3FT Hon
Entry Requirements: *GCE:* ABB-BBBb. *SQAH:* ABBBB. *SQAAH:*
ABB. *IB:* 33.

R12 THE UNIVERSITY OF READING
THE UNIVERSITY OF READING
PO BOX 217
READING RG6 6AH
t: 0118 378 8619 f: 0118 378 8924
e: student.recruitment@reading.ac.uk
// www.reading.ac.uk

LR11 BA French and Economics
Duration: 4FT Hon
Entry Requirements: *GCE:* ABC-BBB. *SQAH:* ABBBC-BBBBB.
SQAAH: ABC-BBB.

LR12 BA German and Economics
Duration: 4FT Hon
Entry Requirements: *GCE:* ABC-BBB. *SQAH:* ABBBC-BBBBB.
SQAAH: ABC-BBB.

LR13 BA Italian and Economics
Duration: 4FT Hon
Entry Requirements: *Foundation:* Pass. *GCE:* ABC-BBB. *SQAH:*
ABBBC-BBBBB. *SQAAH:* ABC-BBB.

R72 ROYAL HOLLOWAY, UNIVERSITY OF LONDON
ROYAL HOLLOWAY, UNIVERSITY OF LONDON
EGHAM
SURREY TW20 0EX
t: 01784 414944 f: 01784 473662
e: Admissions@rhul.ac.uk
// www.rhul.ac.uk

L1R1 BA Economics with French
Duration: 3FT Hon
Entry Requirements: *GCE:* AAA-ABB. *SQAH:* AAAAA-AABBB.
SQAAH: AAA-ABB. *IB:* 32.

L1R2 BA Economics with German
Duration: 3FT Hon
Entry Requirements: *GCE:* AAA-ABB. *SQAH:* AAAAA-AABBB.
SQAAH: AAA-ABB. *IB:* 32.

L1R3 BA Economics with Italian
Duration: 3FT Hon
Entry Requirements: *GCE:* AAA-ABB. *SQAH:* AAAAA-AABBB.
SQAAH: AAA-ABB. *IB:* 32.

L1R4 BA Economics with Spanish
Duration: 3FT Hon
Entry Requirements: *GCE:* AAA-ABB. *SQAH:* AAAAA-AABBB.
SQAAH: AAA-ABB. *IB:* 32.

S09 SCHOOL OF ORIENTAL AND AFRICAN STUDIES (UNIVERSITY OF LONDON)
THORNHAUGH STREET
RUSSELL SQUARE
LONDON WC1H 0XG
t: 020 7898 4301 f: 020 7898 4039
e: undergradadmissions@soas.ac.uk
// www.soas.ac.uk

TL51 BA Economics and African Studies
Duration: 3FT Hon
Entry Requirements: *GCE:* AAA.

LT16 BA Economics and Arabic
Duration: 4FT Hon
Entry Requirements: *GCE:* AAA.

LT1H BA Economics and Burmese
Duration: 3FT Hon
Entry Requirements: *GCE:* AAA.

LT11 BA Economics and Chinese
Duration: 4FT Hon
Entry Requirements: *GCE:* AAA.

LQ13 BA Economics and Linguistics
Duration: 3FT Hon
Entry Requirements: *GCE:* AAA.

TLJC BA Economics and South-East Asian Studies
Duration: 3FT Hon
Entry Requirements: *GCE:* AAA.

LT13 BA Economics and Tibetan
Duration: 3FT Hon
Entry Requirements: *GCE:* AAA.

LT1J BA Economics and Tibetan (including year abroad)
Duration: 4FT Hon
Entry Requirements: *GCE:* AAA.

LT19 BA Georgian and Economics
Duration: 3FT Hon
Entry Requirements: *GCE:* AAA.

LTC5 BA Hausa and Economics
Duration: 4FT Hon
Entry Requirements: *GCE:* AAA.

LQ14 BA Hebrew and Economics
Duration: 4FT Hon
Entry Requirements: *GCE:* AAA.

LTCH BA Indonesian and Economics
Duration: 3FT Hon
Entry Requirements: *GCE:* AAA.

TL21 BA Japanese Studies and Economics
Duration: 3FT Hon
Entry Requirements: *GCE:* AAA.

LT12 BA Japanese and Economics
Duration: 4FT Hon
Entry Requirements: Contact the institution for details.

LTCL BA Korean and Economics
Duration: 4FT Hon
Entry Requirements: *GCE:* AAA.

TL61 BA Middle Eastern Studies and Economics
Duration: 3FT Hon
Entry Requirements: *GCE:* AAA.

LTD6 BA Persian and Economics
Duration: 3FT Hon
Entry Requirements: *GCE:* AAA.

TLH1 BA South Asian Studies and Economics
Duration: 3FT Hon
Entry Requirements: *GCE:* AAA.

TL3C BA South Asian Studies and Economics (Including Year Abroad)
Duration: 4FT Hon
Entry Requirements: *GCE:* AAA.

LTD5 BA Swahili and Economics
Duration: 4FT Hon
Entry Requirements: *GCE:* AAA.

TL31 BA Thai and Economics
Duration: 3FT Hon
Entry Requirements: *GCE:* AAA.

LTC6 BA Turkish and Economics
Duration: 4FT Hon
Entry Requirements: *GCE:* AAA.

TL3D BA Vietnamese and Economics
Duration: 3FT Hon
Entry Requirements: *GCE:* AAA.

S18 THE UNIVERSITY OF SHEFFIELD
THE UNIVERSITY OF SHEFFIELD
LEVEL 2, ARTS TOWER
WESTERN BANK
SHEFFIELD S10 2TN
t: 0114 222 8030 f: 0114 222 8032
// www.sheffield.ac.uk

RL11 BA French and Economics
Duration: 4FT Hon
Entry Requirements: *GCE:* AAB. *SQAH:* AAABB. *SQAAH:* AB. *IB:* 35. *BTEC ExtDip:* DDD.

RL21 BA German and Economics
Duration: 4FT Hon
Entry Requirements: *GCE:* AAB. *SQAH:* AAABB. *SQAAH:* AB. *IB:* 35. *BTEC ExtDip:* DDD.

RL41 BA Hispanic Studies and Economics
Duration: 4FT Hon
Entry Requirements: *GCE:* AAB. *SQAH:* AAABB. *SQAAH:* AB. *IB:* 35. *BTEC ExtDip:* DDD.

RL71 BA Russian and Economics
Duration: 4FT Hon
Entry Requirements: *GCE:* AAB. *SQAH:* AAABB. *SQAAH:* AB. *IB:* 35. *BTEC ExtDip:* DDD.

S30 SOUTHAMPTON SOLENT UNIVERSITY
EAST PARK TERRACE
SOUTHAMPTON
HAMPSHIRE SO14 0RT
t: +44 (0) 23 8031 9039 f: + 44 (0)23 8022 2259
e: admissions@solent.ac.uk
// www.solent.ac.uk/

N4QH BA Accountancy (International only) IFY - (Jan)
Duration: 4FT Hon
Entry Requirements: Contact the institution for details.

N4Q3 BA Accountancy with IFY (International Only, Sept)
Duration: 4FT Hon
Entry Requirements: Contact the institution for details.

S36 UNIVERSITY OF ST ANDREWS
ST KATHARINE'S WEST
16 THE SCORES
ST ANDREWS
FIFE KY16 9AX
t: 01334 462150 f: 01334 463330
e: admissions@st-andrews.ac.uk
// www.st-andrews.ac.uk

LT16 MA Arabic and Economics
Duration: 4FT Hon
Entry Requirements: *GCE:* AAA. *SQAH:* AAAB. *IB:* 38.

TLP1 MA Arabic and Economics (year abroad)
Duration: 5FT Hon
Entry Requirements: *GCE:* AAA. *SQAH:* AAAB. *IB:* 38.

LQ13 MA Economics and English
Duration: 4FT Hon
Entry Requirements: *GCE:* AAA. *SQAH:* AAAB. *IB:* 38.

LR12 MA Economics and German
Duration: 4FT Hon
Entry Requirements: *GCE:* AAA. *SQAH:* AAAB. *IB:* 38.

LRC2 MA Economics and German (year abroad)
Duration: 5FT Hon
Entry Requirements: *GCE:* AAA. *SQAH:* AAAB. *IB:* 38.

LR13 MA Economics and Italian
Duration: 4FT Hon
Entry Requirements: *GCE:* AAA. *SQAH:* AAAB. *IB:* 38.

LRC3 MA Economics and Italian (year abroad)
Duration: 5FT Hon
Entry Requirements: *GCE:* AAA. *SQAH:* AAAB. *IB:* 38.

TL61 MA Economics and Middle East Studies
Duration: 4FT Hon
Entry Requirements: *GCE:* AAA. *SQAH:* AAAB. *IB:* 38.

LR17 MA Economics and Russian
Duration: 4FT Hon
Entry Requirements: *GCE:* AAA. *SQAH:* AAAB. *IB:* 38.

LRC7 MA Economics and Russian (year abroad)
Duration: 5FT Hon
Entry Requirements: *GCE:* AAA. *SQAH:* AAAB. *IB:* 38.

LR14 MA Economics and Spanish
Duration: 4FT Hon
Entry Requirements: *GCE:* AAA. *SQAH:* AAAB. *IB:* 38.

LRC4 MA Economics and Spanish (year abroad)
Duration: 5FT Hon
Entry Requirements: *GCE:* AAA. *SQAH:* AAAB. *IB:* 38.

L1R2 MA Economics with German
Duration: 4FT Hon
Entry Requirements: *GCE:* AAA. *SQAH:* AAAA. *IB:* 38.

L1RF MA Economics with German (year abroad)
Duration: 5FT Hon
Entry Requirements: *GCE:* AAA. *SQAH:* AAAA. *IB:* 38.

L1RT MA Economics with Russian
Duration: 4FT Hon
Entry Requirements: *GCE:* AAA. *SQAH:* AAAA. *IB:* 38.

L1RR MA Economics with Russian (year abroad)
Duration: 5FT Hon
Entry Requirements: *GCE:* AAA. *SQAH:* AAAA. *IB:* 38.

L1RK MA Economics with Spanish
Duration: 4FT Hon
Entry Requirements: *GCE:* AAA. *SQAH:* AAAA. *IB:* 38.

L1RL MA Economics with Spanish (year abroad)
Duration: 5FT Hon
Entry Requirements: *GCE:* AAA. *SQAH:* AAAA. *IB:* 38.

S75 THE UNIVERSITY OF STIRLING
STUDENT RECRUITMENT & ADMISSIONS SERVICE
UNIVERSITY OF STIRLING
STIRLING
SCOTLAND FK9 4LA
t: 01786 467044 f: 01786 466800
e: admissions@stir.ac.uk
// www.stir.ac.uk

NR44 BAcc Accountancy and Spanish
Duration: 4FT Hon
Entry Requirements: *GCE:* BBC. *SQAH:* BBBB. *SQAAH:* AAA-CCC.
IB: 32. *BTEC ExtDip:* DMM.

S78 THE UNIVERSITY OF STRATHCLYDE
GLASGOW G1 1XQ
t: 0141 552 4400 f: 0141 552 0775
// www.strath.ac.uk

RL11 BA French and Economics
Duration: 4FT Hon
Entry Requirements: *GCE:* ABB. *SQAH:* AAABB-AAAB. *IB:* 34.

RL31 BA Italian and Economics
Duration: 4FT Hon
Entry Requirements: *GCE:* ABB. *SQAH:* AAABB-AAAB. *IB:* 34.

RL41 BA Spanish and Economics
Duration: 4FT Hon
Entry Requirements: *GCE:* ABB. *SQAH:* AAABB-AAAB. *IB:* 34.

S93 SWANSEA UNIVERSITY
SINGLETON PARK
SWANSEA SA2 8PP
t: 01792 295111 f: 01792 295110
e: admissions@swansea.ac.uk
// www.swansea.ac.uk

LR11 BA Economics and French (4 years)
Duration: 4FT Hon
Entry Requirements: *GCE:* ABB. *IB:* 33.

LR12 BA Economics and German
Duration: 4FT Hon
Entry Requirements: *GCE:* ABB. *IB:* 33.

LR13 BA Economics and Italian
Duration: 4FT Hon
Entry Requirements: *GCE:* ABB. *IB:* 33.

LR14 BA Economics and Spanish
Duration: 4FT Hon
Entry Requirements: *GCE:* ABB. *IB:* 33.

LQ15 BA Economics and Welsh
Duration: 3FT Hon
Entry Requirements: *GCE:* ABB. *IB:* 33.

U80 UNIVERSITY COLLEGE LONDON (UNIVERSITY OF LONDON)
GOWER STREET
LONDON WC1E 6BT
t: 020 7679 3000 f: 020 7679 3001
// www.ucl.ac.uk

L1RR BA Economics & Business with East European Studies (with a Year Abroad) (4 years)
Duration: 4FT Hon
Entry Requirements: *GCE:* AAAe-AABe. *SQAAH:* AAA-AAB. *BTEC ExtDip:* DDD. Interview required.

L1R7 BA Economics and Business with East European Studies
Duration: 3FT Hon
Entry Requirements: *GCE:* AAAe-AABe. *SQAAH:* AAA-AAB. *BTEC ExtDip:* DDD. Interview required.

GLR0 BSc Statistics, Economics and a Language
Duration: 3FT Hon
Entry Requirements: *GCE:* A*AAe-AAAe. *SQAAH:* AAA. Interview required.

LAW COMBINATIONS

A40 ABERYSTWYTH UNIVERSITY
ABERYSTWYTH UNIVERSITY, WELCOME CENTRE
PENGLAIS CAMPUS
ABERYSTWYTH
CEREDIGION SY23 3FB
t: 01970 622021 f: 01970 627410
e: ug-admissions@aber.ac.uk
// www.aber.ac.uk

M1N4 BA Law with Accounting & Finance
Duration: 3FT Hon
Entry Requirements: *GCE:* 340. *IB:* 28.

M1L1 BA Law with Economics
Duration: 3FT Hon
Entry Requirements: *GCE:* 340. *IB:* 28.

N4M1 BScEcon Accounting & Finance with Law
Duration: 3FT Hon
Entry Requirements: *GCE:* 300. *IB:* 27.

L1M1 BScEcon Economics with Law
Duration: 3FT Hon
Entry Requirements: *GCE:* 300. *IB:* 27.

B06 BANGOR UNIVERSITY
BANGOR UNIVERSITY
BANGOR
GWYNEDD LL57 2DG
t: 01248 388484 f: 01248 370451
e: admissions@bangor.ac.uk
// www.bangor.ac.uk

M1N4 LLB Law with Accounting & Finance
Duration: 3FT Hon
Entry Requirements: *GCE:* 280. *IB:* 28.

B50 BOURNEMOUTH UNIVERSITY
TALBOT CAMPUS
FERN BARROW
POOLE
DORSET BH12 5BB
t: 01202 524111
// www.bournemouth.ac.uk

NM41 BA Accounting and Law
Duration: 3FT Hon
Entry Requirements: *GCE:* 320. *IB:* 32. *BTEC SubDip:* D. *BTEC Dip:* DD. *BTEC ExtDip:* DDM.

NM3C BA Finance and Law (Top-up)
Duration: 1FT Hon
Entry Requirements: HND required.

NM31 FdA Finance and Law
Duration: 2FT Fdg
Entry Requirements: *GCE:* 120. *IB:* 24. Interview required.

B60 BRADFORD COLLEGE: AN ASSOCIATE COLLEGE OF LEEDS METROPOLITAN UNIVERSITY
GREAT HORTON ROAD
BRADFORD
WEST YORKSHIRE BD7 1AY
t: 01274 433008 f: 01274 431652
e: heregistry@bradfordcollege.ac.uk
// www.bradfordcollege.ac.uk/
university-centre

NM41 BA Accountancy and Law
Duration: 3FT Hon
Entry Requirements: *GCE:* 240.

B90 THE UNIVERSITY OF BUCKINGHAM
YEOMANRY HOUSE
HUNTER STREET
BUCKINGHAM MK18 1EG
t: 01280 820313 f: 01280 822245
e: info@buckingham.ac.uk
// www.buckingham.ac.uk

L000 BA Politics, Economics and Law
Duration: 2FT Hon
Entry Requirements: *GCE:* BCC. *SQAH:* BBBC. *SQAAH:* BCC. *IB:* 31.

LM11 BSc Economics, Business and Law
Duration: 2FT Hon
Entry Requirements: *GCE:* BBB. *SQAH:* ABBB. *SQAAH:* BBB. *IB:* 34.

M1N3 LLB Law with Business Finance
Duration: 2FT Hon
Entry Requirements: *GCE:* 300. *SQAH:* ABBB. *SQAAH:* BBB. *IB:* 34. *OCR NED:* M2 Interview required.

M1L1 LLB Law with Economics
Duration: 2FT Hon
Entry Requirements: *GCE:* 300. *SQAH:* ABBB. *SQAAH:* BBB. *IB:* 34. *OCR NED:* M2 Interview required.

D26 DE MONTFORT UNIVERSITY
THE GATEWAY
LEICESTER LE1 9BH
t: 0116 255 1551 f: 0116 250 6204
e: enquiries@dmu.ac.uk
// www.dmu.ac.uk

ML21 BA Law and Economics
Duration: 3FT Hon
Entry Requirements: *GCE:* 280. *IB:* 28. *BTEC Dip:* D*D*. *BTEC ExtDip:* DMM. *OCR NED:* M2 Interview required.

D39 UNIVERSITY OF DERBY
KEDLESTON ROAD
DERBY DE22 1GB
t: 01332 591167 f: 01332 597724
e: askadmissions@derby.ac.uk
// www.derby.ac.uk

MN1K BA Accounting and Law
Duration: 3FT Hon
Entry Requirements: *Foundation:* Distinction. *GCE:* 260-300. *IB:* 28. *BTEC Dip:* D*D*. *BTEC ExtDip:* DMM. *OCR NED:* M2

E56 THE UNIVERSITY OF EDINBURGH
STUDENT RECRUITMENT & ADMISSIONS
57 GEORGE SQUARE
EDINBURGH EH8 9JU
t: 0131 650 4360 f: 0131 651 1236
e: sra.enquiries@ed.ac.uk
// www.ed.ac.uk/studying/undergraduate/

MN14 LLB Law and Accountancy
Duration: 4FT Hon
Entry Requirements: *GCE:* AAA-BBB. *SQAH:* AAAA-BBBB. *IB:* 34.

ML11 LLB Law and Economics
Duration: 4FT Hon
Entry Requirements: *GCE:* AAA-BBB. *SQAH:* AAAB-BBBB. *IB:* 34.

LM11 MA Economics and Law
Duration: 4FT Hon
Entry Requirements: *GCE:* AAA-BBB. *SQAH:* AAAA-BBBB. *IB:* 34.

E59 EDINBURGH NAPIER UNIVERSITY
CRAIGLOCKHART CAMPUS
EDINBURGH EH14 1DJ
t: +44 (0)8452 60 60 40 f: 0131 455 6464
e: info@napier.ac.uk
// www.napier.ac.uk

N4M1 BA Accounting with Law
Duration: 3FT/4FT Ord/Hon
Entry Requirements: *GCE:* 230.

M1N4 LLB Law with Accounting
Duration: 3FT/4FT Ord/Hon
Entry Requirements: Contact the institution for details.

G14 UNIVERSITY OF GLAMORGAN, CARDIFF AND PONTYPRIDD
ENQUIRIES AND ADMISSIONS UNIT
PONTYPRIDD CF37 1DL
t: 08456 434030 f: 01443 654050
e: enquiries@glam.ac.uk
// www.glam.ac.uk

MN14 BA Accounting and Law
Duration: 3FT Hon
Entry Requirements: *GCE:* 220-260. Interview required.

G28 UNIVERSITY OF GLASGOW
71 SOUTHPARK AVENUE
UNIVERSITY OF GLASGOW
GLASGOW G12 8QQ
t: 0141 330 6062 f: 0141 330 2961
e: student.recruitment@glasgow.ac.uk
// www.glasgow.ac.uk

ML11 LLB Law/Economics
Duration: 4FT Hon
Entry Requirements: *GCE:* AAB. *SQAH:* AAAAB. *IB:* 34.
Admissions Test required.

H24 HERIOT-WATT UNIVERSITY, EDINBURGH
EDINBURGH CAMPUS
EDINBURGH EH14 4AS
t: 0131 449 5111 f: 0131 451 3630
e: ugadmissions@hw.ac.uk
// www.hw.ac.uk

NM32 MA Accountancy and Business Law
Duration: 4FT Hon
Entry Requirements: *GCE:* BBB. *SQAH:* AAAB-BBBBC. *SQAAH:* BB. *IB:* 29.

LM12 MA Economics and Business Law
Duration: 4FT Hon
Entry Requirements: *GCE:* BBB. *SQAH:* AAAB-BBBBC. *SQAAH:* BB. *IB:* 29.

NMH2 MA Finance and Business Law
Duration: 4FT Hon
Entry Requirements: *GCE:* BBB. *SQAH:* AAAB-BBBBC. *SQAAH:* BB. *IB:* 29.

H36 UNIVERSITY OF HERTFORDSHIRE
UNIVERSITY ADMISSIONS SERVICE
COLLEGE LANE
HATFIELD
HERTS AL10 9AB
t: 01707 284800
// www.herts.ac.uk

L1M1 BSc Economics/Law
Duration: 3FT/4SW Hon
Entry Requirements: *GCE:* 320.

M1L1 BSc Law/Economics
Duration: 3FT/4SW Hon
Entry Requirements: *GCE:* 320.

H60 THE UNIVERSITY OF HUDDERSFIELD
QUEENSGATE
HUDDERSFIELD HD1 3DH
t: 01484 473969 f: 01484 472765
e: admissionsandrecords@hud.ac.uk
// www.hud.ac.uk

N4M1 BA(Hons) Accountancy with Law
Duration: 3FT/4SW Hon
Entry Requirements: *GCE:* 300.

K12 KEELE UNIVERSITY
KEELE UNIVERSITY
STAFFORDSHIRE ST5 5BG
t: 01782 734005 f: 01782 632343
e: undergraduate@keele.ac.uk
// www.keele.ac.uk

NM41 BA Accounting and Law
Duration: 3FT Hon
Entry Requirements: *GCE:* ABB.

LM11 BA Economics and Law
Duration: 3FT Hon
Entry Requirements: *GCE:* ABB.

K24 THE UNIVERSITY OF KENT
RECRUITMENT & ADMISSIONS OFFICE
REGISTRY
UNIVERSITY OF KENT
CANTERBURY, KENT CT2 7NZ
t: 01227 827272 f: 01227 827077
e: information@kent.ac.uk
// www.kent.ac.uk

NM41 BA Law and Accounting & Finance (4 years)
Duration: 4FT Hon
Entry Requirements: *GCE:* AAB. *SQAH:* AAAAB. *IB:* 33. *OCR ND:* D *OCR NED:* M1

ML11 BA Law and Economics
Duration: 3FT Hon
Entry Requirements: *GCE:* AAB. *SQAH:* AAAAB. *IB:* 33. *OCR ND:* D

K84 KINGSTON UNIVERSITY
STUDENT INFORMATION & ADVICE CENTRE
COOPER HOUSE
40-46 SURBITON ROAD
KINGSTON UPON THAMES KT1 2HX
t: 0844 8552177 f: 020 8547 7080
e: aps@kingston.ac.uk
// www.kingston.ac.uk

LM11 BA Economics (Applied) and Law
Duration: 3FT Hon
Entry Requirements: *GCE:* 240-320. *IB:* 25.

L39 UNIVERSITY OF LINCOLN
ADMISSIONS
BRAYFORD POOL
LINCOLN LN6 7TS
t: 01522 886097 f: 01522 886146
e: admissions@lincoln.ac.uk
// www.lincoln.ac.uk

NM31 LLB Law and Finance
Duration: 3FT Hon
Entry Requirements: *GCE:* 300.

L41 THE UNIVERSITY OF LIVERPOOL
THE FOUNDATION BUILDING
BROWNLOW HILL
LIVERPOOL L69 7ZX
t: 0151 794 2000 f: 0151 708 6502
e: ugrecruitment@liv.ac.uk
// www.liv.ac.uk

M101 LLB Law with Accounting and Finance
Duration: 3FT Hon
Entry Requirements: *GCE:* AAA. *SQAH:* AAAAA. *SQAAH:* AA. *IB:* 36. *OCR ND:* D *OCR NED:* D2

L63 LCA BUSINESS SCHOOL, LONDON
19 CHARTERHOUSE STREET
LONDON EC1N 6RA
t: 020 7400 6789
e: info@lcabusinessschool.com
// www.lcabusinessschool.com

NM41 BSc Accounting and Law
Duration: 3FT Hon
Entry Requirements: *GCE:* 260. *SQAH:* BBCCC. *IB:* 24. *OCR ND:* D *OCR NED:* M2 Interview required.

N37 UNIVERSITY OF WALES, NEWPORT
ADMISSIONS
LODGE ROAD
CAERLEON
NEWPORT NP18 3QT
t: 01633 432030 f: 01633 432850
e: admissions@newport.ac.uk
// www.newport.ac.uk

MN14 BSc Accounting and Law
Duration: 3FT Hon
Entry Requirements: *GCE:* 240. *IB:* 24.

LM11 BSc Economics and Law
Duration: 3FT Hon
Entry Requirements: *GCE:* 240. *IB:* 24.

N38 UNIVERSITY OF NORTHAMPTON
PARK CAMPUS
BOUGHTON GREEN ROAD
NORTHAMPTON NN2 7AL
t: 0800 358 2232 f: 01604 722083
e: admissions@northampton.ac.uk
// www.northampton.ac.uk

N4M1 BA Accounting/Law
Duration: 3FT Hon
Entry Requirements: *GCE:* 260-280. *SQAH:* AAA-BBBB. *IB:* 24. *BTEC Dip:* DD. *BTEC ExtDip:* DMM. *OCR ND:* D *OCR NED:* M2

L1M1 BA Economics/Law
Duration: 3FT Hon
Entry Requirements: *GCE:* 260-280. *SQAH:* AAA-BBBB. *IB:* 24. *BTEC Dip:* DD. *BTEC ExtDip:* DMM. *OCR ND:* D *OCR NED:* M2

M1N4 BA Law/Accounting
Duration: 3FT Hon
Entry Requirements: *GCE:* 260-280. *SQAH:* AAA-BBBB. *IB:* 24. *BTEC Dip:* DD. *BTEC ExtDip:* DMM. *OCR ND:* D *OCR NED:* M2

M1L1 BA Law/Economics
Duration: 3FT Hon
Entry Requirements: *GCE:* 260-280. *SQAH:* AAA-BBBB. *IB:* 24. *BTEC Dip:* DD. *BTEC ExtDip:* DMM. *OCR ND:* D *OCR NED:* M2

P60 PLYMOUTH UNIVERSITY
DRAKE CIRCUS
PLYMOUTH PL4 8AA
t: 01752 585858 f: 01752 588055
e: admissions@plymouth.ac.uk
// www.plymouth.ac.uk

L1MG BSc Economics with Law
Duration: 3FT/4SW Hon
Entry Requirements: *GCE:* 240. *IB:* 24.

P80 UNIVERSITY OF PORTSMOUTH
ACADEMIC REGISTRY
UNIVERSITY HOUSE
WINSTON CHURCHILL AVENUE
PORTSMOUTH PO1 2UP
t: 023 9284 8484 f: 023 9284 3082
e: admissions@port.ac.uk
// www.port.ac.uk

L1MF BA Economics with Law
Duration: 3FT/4SW Hon
Entry Requirements: *GCE:* 260-300. *IB:* 27. *BTEC Dip:* D*D. *BTEC ExtDip:* DMM.

S03 THE UNIVERSITY OF SALFORD

SALFORD M5 4WT
t: 0161 295 4545 f: 0161 295 4646
e: ug-admissions@salford.ac.uk
// www.salford.ac.uk

M1N3 LLB Law with Finance

Duration: 3FT Hon
Entry Requirements: *GCE:* 300. *IB:* 29. *OCR NED:* M2 Interview
required.

S09 SCHOOL OF ORIENTAL AND AFRICAN STUDIES (UNIVERSITY OF LONDON)

THORNHAUGH STREET
RUSSELL SQUARE
LONDON WC1H 0XG
t: 020 7898 4301 f: 020 7898 4039
e: undergradadmissions@soas.ac.uk
// www.soas.ac.uk

LM11 BA Law and Economics

Duration: 3FT Hon
Entry Requirements: *GCE:* AAA.

S75 THE UNIVERSITY OF STIRLING

STUDENT RECRUITMENT & ADMISSIONS SERVICE
UNIVERSITY OF STIRLING
STIRLING
SCOTLAND FK9 4LA
t: 01786 467044 f: 01786 466800
e: admissions@stir.ac.uk
// www.stir.ac.uk

MN24 BAcc Accountancy and Business Law

Duration: 4FT Hon
Entry Requirements: *GCE:* BBC. *SQAH:* BBBB. *SQAAH:* AAA-CCC.
IB: 32. *BTEC ExtDip:* DMM.

S78 THE UNIVERSITY OF STRATHCLYDE

GLASGOW G1 1XQ
t: 0141 552 4400 f: 0141 552 0775
// www.strath.ac.uk

NM42 BA Accounting and Business Law

Duration: 4FT Hon
Entry Requirements: *GCE:* AAA. *SQAH:* AAAAAB-AAAA. *IB:* 36.

LM12 BA Economics and Business Law

Duration: 4FT Hon
Entry Requirements: *GCE:* AAB. *SQAH:* AAAABB-AAAB. *IB:* 36.

NM32 BA Finance and Business Law

Duration: 4FT Hon
Entry Requirements: *GCE:* AAB. *SQAH:* AAAABB-AAAB. *IB:* 36.

ML11 BA Law and Economics

Duration: 4FT Hon
Entry Requirements: *GCE:* ABB. *SQAH:* AAABB-AAAB. *IB:* 34.

S90 UNIVERSITY OF SUSSEX

UNDERGRADUATE ADMISSIONS
SUSSEX HOUSE
UNIVERSITY OF SUSSEX
BRIGHTON BN1 9RH
t: 01273 678416 f: 01273 678545
e: ug.applicants@sussex.ac.uk
// www.sussex.ac.uk

M1L1 LLB Law with Politics

Duration: 3FT Hon
Entry Requirements: *GCE:* AAA-AAB. *SQAH:* AAAAA-AAABB. *IB:*
35. *BTEC SubDip:* D. *BTEC Dip:* DD. *BTEC ExtDip:* DDD. *OCR
ND:* D *OCR NED:* D1

S93 SWANSEA UNIVERSITY

SINGLETON PARK
SWANSEA SA2 8PP
t: 01792 295111 f: 01792 295110
e: admissions@swansea.ac.uk
// www.swansea.ac.uk

ML11 LLB Law and Economics

Duration: 3FT Hon
Entry Requirements: *GCE:* AAB. *IB:* 34.

U20 UNIVERSITY OF ULSTER

COLERAINE
CO. LONDONDERRY
NORTHERN IRELAND BT52 1SA
t: 028 7012 4221 f: 028 7012 4908
e: online@ulster.ac.uk
// www.ulster.ac.uk

NM41 BSc Accounting and Law

Duration: 4FT Hon
Entry Requirements: *GCE:* AAA. *SQAH:* AAAAA. *SQAAH:* AAA. *IB:*
39.

M1N4 LLB Law with Accounting

Duration: 3FT Hon
Entry Requirements: *GCE:* BBB. *SQAH:* AABCC. *SQAAH:* BBB. *IB:*
25.

W75 UNIVERSITY OF WOLVERHAMPTON

ADMISSIONS UNIT
MX207, CAMP STREET
WOLVERHAMPTON
WEST MIDLANDS WV1 1AD
t: 01902 321000 f: 01902 321896
e: admissions@wlv.ac.uk
// www.wlv.ac.uk

MN1L BA Accounting and Law

Duration: 3FT Hon
Entry Requirements: *GCE:* 160-220. *IB:* 28.

MANAGEMENT COMBINATIONS

A20 THE UNIVERSITY OF ABERDEEN
UNIVERSITY OFFICE
KING'S COLLEGE
ABERDEEN AB24 3FX
t: +44 (0) 1224 273504 f: +44 (0) 1224 272034
e: sras@abdn.ac.uk
// www.abdn.ac.uk/sras

NN24 MA Accountancy and Management Studies
Duration: 4FT Hon
Entry Requirements: *GCE:* BBB. *SQAH:* BBBB. *IB:* 30.

NK42 MA Accountancy and Real Estate
Duration: 4FT Hon
Entry Requirements: *GCE:* BBB. *SQAH:* BBBB. *IB:* 30.

LNC2 MA Economics and Management Studies
Duration: 4FT Hon
Entry Requirements: *GCE:* BBB. *SQAH:* BBBB. *IB:* 30.

NN32 MA Finance and Management Studies
Duration: 4FT Hon
Entry Requirements: *GCE:* BBB. *SQAH:* BBBB. *IB:* 30.

A40 ABERYSTWYTH UNIVERSITY
ABERYSTWYTH UNIVERSITY, WELCOME CENTRE
PENGLAIS CAMPUS
ABERYSTWYTH
CEREDIGION SY23 3FB
t: 01970 622021 f: 01970 627410
e: ug-admissions@aber.ac.uk
// www.aber.ac.uk

N4N2 BScEcon Accounting & Finance with Management
Duration: 3FT Hon
Entry Requirements: *GCE:* 300. *IB:* 27.

L1N2 BScEcon Economics with Management
Duration: 3FT Hon
Entry Requirements: *GCE:* 300. *IB:* 27.

A80 ASTON UNIVERSITY, BIRMINGHAM
ASTON TRIANGLE
BIRMINGHAM B4 7ET
t: 0121 204 4444 f: 0121 204 3696
e: admissions@aston.ac.uk (automatic response)
// www.aston.ac.uk/prospective-students/ug

LN12 BSc Economics and Management
Duration: 4SW Hon
Entry Requirements: *GCE:* AAA-AAB. *SQAH:* AAAAA-AAAAB. *SQAAH:* AAA-AAB. *IB:* 35. *OCR NED:* D1

B06 BANGOR UNIVERSITY
BANGOR UNIVERSITY
BANGOR
GWYNEDD LL57 2DG
t: 01248 388484 f: 01248 370451
e: admissions@bangor.ac.uk
// www.bangor.ac.uk

N2N4 BA Management with Accounting
Duration: 3FT Hon
Entry Requirements: *GCE:* 260-300. *IB:* 28.

N2NK BSc Management with Accounting
Duration: 3FT Hon
Entry Requirements: *GCE:* 260-300. *IB:* 28.

B72 UNIVERSITY OF BRIGHTON
MITHRAS HOUSE 211
LEWES ROAD
BRIGHTON BN2 4AT
t: 01273 644644 f: 01273 642607
e: admissions@brighton.ac.uk
// www.brighton.ac.uk

N2N3 BSc Business Management with Finance
Duration: 3FT/4SW Hon
Entry Requirements: *GCE:* BBB. *IB:* 30.

B78 UNIVERSITY OF BRISTOL
UNDERGRADUATE ADMISSIONS OFFICE
SENATE HOUSE
TYNDALL AVENUE
BRISTOL BS8 1TH
t: 0117 928 9000 f: 0117 331 7391
e: ug-admissions@bristol.ac.uk
// www.bristol.ac.uk

NN42 BSc Accounting and Management
Duration: 3FT Hon
Entry Requirements: *GCE:* AAA-AAB. *SQAH:* AAAA. *SQAAH:* AA-AB.

LN12 BSc Economics and Management
Duration: 3FT Hon
Entry Requirements: *GCE:* A*AA-AAA. *SQAH:* AAAA. *SQAAH:* AA. *IB:* 38.

B84 BRUNEL UNIVERSITY
UXBRIDGE
MIDDLESEX UB8 3PH
t: 01895 265265 f: 01895 269790
e: admissions@brunel.ac.uk
// www.brunel.ac.uk

N2NL BSc Business and Management (Accounting) (4 year Thick SW)
Duration: 4FT Hon
Entry Requirements: *GCE:* AAB. *SQAAH:* AAB. *IB:* 35. *BTEC Dip:* D*D*. *BTEC ExtDip:* D*D*D. *OCR NED:* D1

LNC2 BSc Economics and Management
Duration: 3FT Hon
Entry Requirements: **GCE:** ABB. **SQAAH:** ABB. **IB:** 33. **BTEC ExtDip:** D*DD.

LND2 BSc Economics and Management (4 year Thick SW)
Duration: 4SW Hon
Entry Requirements: **GCE:** ABB. **SQAAH:** ABB. **IB:** 33. **BTEC ExtDip:** D*DD.

C15 CARDIFF UNIVERSITY
PO BOX 927
30-36 NEWPORT ROAD
CARDIFF CF24 0DE
t: 029 2087 9999 f: 029 2087 6138
e: admissions@cardiff.ac.uk
// www.cardiff.ac.uk

NN23 BSc Finance and Management
Duration: 3FT Hon
Entry Requirements: **GCE:** AAB. **SQAH:** AAABB. **SQAAH:** AAB. **IB:** 35. **OCR NED:** D1 Interview required.

NN24 BScEcon Accounting and Management
Duration: 3FT Hon
Entry Requirements: **GCE:** AAB. **SQAH:** AAABB. **SQAAH:** AAB. **IB:** 35. **OCR NED:** D1 Interview required.

LN12 BScEcon Economics and Management Studies
Duration: 3FT Hon
Entry Requirements: **GCE:** AAB. **SQAH:** AAABB. **SQAAH:** AAB. **IB:** 35. **OCR NED:** D1 Interview required.

C30 UNIVERSITY OF CENTRAL LANCASHIRE
PRESTON
LANCS PR1 2HE
t: 01772 201201 f: 01772 894954
e: uadmissions@uclan.ac.uk
// www.uclan.ac.uk

NNF4 BA Accounting and International Business
Duration: 3FT Hon
Entry Requirements: **GCE:** 240-280. **SQAH:** AABB-BBBC. **IB:** 28. **OCR ND:** D

NN24 BA Accounting and Management
Duration: 3FT Hon
Entry Requirements: **GCE:** 240-280. **SQAH:** AABB-BBBC. **IB:** 28. **OCR ND:** D

NL21 BA International Business and Economics
Duration: 3FT Hon
Entry Requirements: **GCE:** 240-280. **SQAH:** AABB-BBBC. **IB:** 28. **OCR ND:** D

D26 DE MONTFORT UNIVERSITY
THE GATEWAY
LEICESTER LE1 9BH
t: 0116 255 1551 f: 0116 250 6204
e: enquiries@dmu.ac.uk
// www.dmu.ac.uk

NL21 BA Business Management and Economics
Duration: 3FT/4SW Hon
Entry Requirements: **GCE:** 280. **IB:** 28. **BTEC Dip:** D*D*. **BTEC ExtDip:** DMM. **OCR NED:** M2 Interview required.

D39 UNIVERSITY OF DERBY
KEDLESTON ROAD
DERBY DE22 1GB
t: 01332 591167 f: 01332 597724
e: askadmissions@derby.ac.uk
// www.derby.ac.uk

NN24 BA Accounting and Business Management
Duration: 3FT Hon
Entry Requirements: **Foundation:** Distinction. **GCE:** 260-300. **IB:** 28. **BTEC Dip:** D*D*. **BTEC ExtDip:** DMM. **OCR NED:** M2

D65 UNIVERSITY OF DUNDEE
NETHERGATE
DUNDEE DD1 4HN
t: 01382 383838 f: 01382 388150
e: contactus@dundee.ac.uk
// www.dundee.ac.uk/admissions/undergraduate/

NN24 BSc Business Management (Accounting and Finance)
Duration: 4FT Hon
Entry Requirements: **GCE:** BCC. **SQAH:** ABBB. **IB:** 30.

D86 DURHAM UNIVERSITY
DURHAM UNIVERSITY
UNIVERSITY OFFICE
DURHAM DH1 3HP
t: 0191 334 2000 f: 0191 334 6055
e: admissions@durham.ac.uk
// www.durham.ac.uk

NN42 BA Accounting and Management
Duration: 3FT/4SW Hon
Entry Requirements: **GCE:** ABB. **SQAH:** AABBB. **SQAAH:** ABB. **IB:** 34.

E14 UNIVERSITY OF EAST ANGLIA
NORWICH NR4 7TJ
t: 01603 591515 f: 01603 591523
e: admissions@uea.ac.uk
// www.uea.ac.uk

N4N2 BSc Accounting with Management
Duration: 3FT Hon   CRB Check: Required
Entry Requirements: *GCE:* ABB. *SQAAH:* ABB. *IB:* 32. *BTEC ExtDip:* DDM. Interview required.

E42 EDGE HILL UNIVERSITY
ORMSKIRK
LANCASHIRE L39 4QP
t: 01695 657000 f: 01695 584355
e: study@edgehill.ac.uk
// www.edgehill.ac.uk

NN24 BSc Business and Management (Accounting)
Duration: 3FT Hon
Entry Requirements: *GCE:* 280. *IB:* 26. *OCR ND:* D *OCR NED:* M2

E56 THE UNIVERSITY OF EDINBURGH
STUDENT RECRUITMENT & ADMISSIONS
57 GEORGE SQUARE
EDINBURGH EH8 9JU
t: 0131 650 4360 f: 0131 651 1236
e: sra.enquiries@ed.ac.uk
// www.ed.ac.uk/studying/undergraduate/

L1N2 MA Economics with Management Science
Duration: 4FT Hon
Entry Requirements: *GCE:* AAA-BBB. *SQAH:* AAAA-BBBB. *IB:* 34.

E59 EDINBURGH NAPIER UNIVERSITY
CRAIGLOCKHART CAMPUS
EDINBURGH EH14 1DJ
t: +44 (0)8452 60 60 40 f: 0131 455 6464
e: info@napier.ac.uk
// www.napier.ac.uk

N4N2 BA Accounting with Entrepreneurship
Duration: 3FT/4FT Ord/Hon
Entry Requirements: *GCE:* 230.

N2N4 BA Business Management with Accounting
Duration: 3FT/4FT Ord/Hon
Entry Requirements: *GCE:* 230.

N2L1 BA Business Management with Economics
Duration: 3FT Hon
Entry Requirements: *GCE:* 230.

N2N3 BA Business Management with Finance
Duration: 3FT/4FT Ord/Hon
Entry Requirements: *GCE:* 230.

N2NH BA Business Management with Financial Services
Duration: 3FT/4FT Ord/Hon
Entry Requirements: *GCE:* 230.

L1N2 BA Economics with Management
Duration: 3FT/4FT Ord/Hon
Entry Requirements: *GCE:* 230.

E70 THE UNIVERSITY OF ESSEX
WIVENHOE PARK
COLCHESTER
ESSEX CO4 3SQ
t: 01206 873666 f: 01206 874477
e: admit@essex.ac.uk
// www.essex.ac.uk

NN24 BA Accounting and Management
Duration: 3FT Hon
Entry Requirements: *GCE:* ABB. *SQAH:* AAAB. *IB:* 34.

NNK2 BA Accounting and Management (Including Year Abroad)
Duration: 4FT Hon
Entry Requirements: *GCE:* ABB. *SQAH:* AAAB. *IB:* 34.

NN42 BA Accounting and Management (including Foundation Year)
Duration: 4FT Hon
Entry Requirements: *GCE:* 180. *SQAH:* CCCD. *IB:* 24.

NGL0 BSc Management, Mathematics and Economics
Duration: 3FT Hon
Entry Requirements: *GCE:* ABB-BBB. *SQAH:* AAAB-AABB. *BTEC ExtDip:* DDM.

LGN0 BSc Management, Mathematics and Economics (Including Year Abroad)
Duration: 4FT Hon
Entry Requirements: *GCE:* ABB-BBB. *SQAH:* AAAB-AABB. *BTEC ExtDip:* DDM.

G28 UNIVERSITY OF GLASGOW
71 SOUTHPARK AVENUE
UNIVERSITY OF GLASGOW
GLASGOW G12 8QQ
t: 0141 330 6062 f: 0141 330 2961
e: student.recruitment@glasgow.ac.uk
// www.glasgow.ac.uk

LNC2 MA Business Economics/Business & Management
Duration: 4FT Hon
Entry Requirements: *GCE:* ABB. *SQAH:* AAAA-AABB. *IB:* 36.

LN12 MA Economics/Business & Management
Duration: 4FT Hon
Entry Requirements: *GCE:* ABB. *SQAH:* AAAA-AABB. *IB:* 36.

G50 THE UNIVERSITY OF GLOUCESTERSHIRE
PARK CAMPUS
THE PARK
CHELTENHAM GL50 2RH
t: 01242 714501 f: 01242 714869
e: admissions@glos.ac.uk
// www.glos.ac.uk

NN24 BA Business Management and Accounting & Financial Management
Duration: 3FT Hon
Entry Requirements: *GCE:* 280-300.

NNF3 BA Business Management and Accounting & Financial Management
Duration: 4SW Hon
Entry Requirements: *GCE:* 280-300.

G53 GLYNDWR UNIVERSITY
PLAS COCH
MOLD ROAD
WREXHAM LL11 2AW
t: 01978 293439 f: 01978 290008
e: sid@glyndwr.ac.uk
// www.glyndwr.ac.uk

N2N4 FdA Business Management with Accounting
Duration: 2FT Fdg
Entry Requirements: *GCE:* 120.

H24 HERIOT-WATT UNIVERSITY, EDINBURGH
EDINBURGH CAMPUS
EDINBURGH EH14 4AS
t: 0131 449 5111 f: 0131 451 3630
e: ugadmissions@hw.ac.uk
// www.hw.ac.uk

NN23 MA Business and Finance
Duration: 4FT Hon
Entry Requirements: *GCE:* BBB. *SQAH:* AAAB-BBBBC. *SQAAH:* BB.
IB: 29.

LN12 MA Economics and Business Management
Duration: 4FT Hon
Entry Requirements: *GCE:* BBB. *SQAH:* AAAB-BBBBC. *SQAAH:* BB.
IB: 29.

H50 HOLBORN COLLEGE
WOOLWICH ROAD
LONDON SE7 8LN
t: 020 8317 6000 f: 020 8317 6001
e: UKAdmissions@kaplan.co.uk
// www.holborncollege.ac.uk

NFL1 BA Business Management with Economics
Duration: 3FT Hon
Entry Requirements: *GCE:* 120. *IB:* 24.

N2L1 BA Business Management with Economics (with Foundation Year)
Duration: 4FT Hon
Entry Requirements: Contact the institution for details.

H60 THE UNIVERSITY OF HUDDERSFIELD
QUEENSGATE
HUDDERSFIELD HD1 3DH
t: 01484 473969 f: 01484 472765
e: admissionsandrecords@hud.ac.uk
// www.hud.ac.uk

N2N3 BA Business Management with Finance
Duration: 3FT/4SW Hon
Entry Requirements: *GCE:* 300.

H72 THE UNIVERSITY OF HULL
THE UNIVERSITY OF HULL
COTTINGHAM ROAD
HULL HU6 7RX
t: 01482 466100 f: 01482 442290
e: admissions@hull.ac.uk
// www.hull.ac.uk

NN24 BA Management and Accounting
Duration: 3FT Hon
Entry Requirements: *GCE:* 300. *IB:* 30. *BTEC ExtDip:* DMM.

NN2K BA Management and Accounting (International) (4 years)
Duration: 4FT Hon
Entry Requirements: *GCE:* 300. *IB:* 30. *BTEC ExtDip:* DMM.

NN2L BA Management and Accounting (with Professional Experience) (4 years)
Duration: 4FT Hon
Entry Requirements: *GCE:* 300. *IB:* 30. *BTEC ExtDip:* DMM.

LN12 BA Management and Business Economics
Duration: 3FT Hon
Entry Requirements: *GCE:* 300. *IB:* 30. *BTEC ExtDip:* DMM.

LND2 BA Management and Business Economics (International) (4 years)
Duration: 4FT Hon
Entry Requirements: *GCE:* 300. *IB:* 30. *BTEC ExtDip:* DMM.

LNCF BA Management and Business Economics (with Professional Experience) (4 years)
Duration: 4FT Hon
Entry Requirements: *GCE:* 300. *IB:* 30. *BTEC ExtDip:* DMM.

NN23 BA Management and Financial Management
Duration: 3FT Hon
Entry Requirements: *GCE:* 300. *IB:* 30. *BTEC ExtDip:* DMM.

NN2H BA Management and Financial Management (International) (4 years)
Duration: 4FT Hon
Entry Requirements: *GCE:* 300. *IB:* 30. *BTEC ExtDip:* DMM.

NN2J BA Management and Financial Management (with Professional Experience) (4 years)
Duration: 4FT Hon
Entry Requirements: *GCE:* 300. *IB:* 30. *BTEC ExtDip:* DMM.

NN32 BSc Financial Management and Supply Chain Management
Duration: 3FT Hon
Entry Requirements: *GCE:* 300. *IB:* 30. *BTEC ExtDip:* DMM.

NN3F BSc Financial Management and Supply Chain Management (International) (4 years)
Duration: 4FT Hon
Entry Requirements: *GCE:* 300. *IB:* 30. *BTEC ExtDip:* DMM.

NNH2 BSc Financial Management and Supply Chain Management (with Prof Exp) (4yrs)
Duration: 4FT Hon
Entry Requirements: *GCE:* 300. *IB:* 30. *BTEC ExtDip:* DMM.

K12 KEELE UNIVERSITY
KEELE UNIVERSITY
STAFFORDSHIRE ST5 5BG
t: 01782 734005 f: 01782 632343
e: undergraduate@keele.ac.uk
// www.keele.ac.uk

NN42 BA Accounting and Business Management
Duration: 3FT Hon
Entry Requirements: *GCE:* ABB.

K24 THE UNIVERSITY OF KENT
RECRUITMENT & ADMISSIONS OFFICE
REGISTRY
UNIVERSITY OF KENT
CANTERBURY, KENT CT2 7NZ
t: 01227 827272 f: 01227 827077
e: information@kent.ac.uk
// www.kent.ac.uk

NNC4 BA Accounting & Management
Duration: 3FT Hon
Entry Requirements: *GCE:* 320. *IB:* 33. *OCR ND:* D *OCR NED:* D2

NN2K BA Accounting & Management with a Year in Industry
Duration: 4FT Hon
Entry Requirements: *GCE:* 320. *IB:* 33. *OCR ND:* D *OCR NED:* D2

L14 LANCASTER UNIVERSITY
THE UNIVERSITY
LANCASTER
LANCASHIRE LA1 4YW
t: 01524 592029 f: 01524 846243
e: ugadmissions@lancaster.ac.uk
// www.lancs.ac.uk

NN24 BSc Accounting and Management Studies
Duration: 3FT Hon
Entry Requirements: *GCE:* AAA-AAB. *SQAH:* AAABB-ABBBB. *SQAAH:* AAA-AAB.

NN23 BSc Finance and Management Studies
Duration: 3FT Hon
Entry Requirements: *GCE:* AAA-AAB. *SQAH:* AAABB-ABBBB. *SQAAH:* AAA-AAB.

L23 UNIVERSITY OF LEEDS
THE UNIVERSITY OF LEEDS
WOODHOUSE LANE
LEEDS LS2 9JT
t: 0113 343 3999
e: admissions@leeds.ac.uk
// www.leeds.ac.uk

NN42 BSc Accounting and Management
Duration: 3FT Hon
Entry Requirements: *GCE:* AAA. *SQAH:* AAAAA. *SQAAH:* AAA. *IB:* 34.

LN12 BSc Economics and Management
Duration: 3FT Hon
Entry Requirements: *GCE:* AAA. *SQAH:* AAAAA. *SQAAH:* AAA. *IB:* 36. Interview required.

L34 UNIVERSITY OF LEICESTER
UNIVERSITY ROAD
LEICESTER LE1 7RH
t: 0116 252 5281 f: 0116 252 2447
e: admissions@le.ac.uk
// www.le.ac.uk

NL21 BA Management Studies and Economics
Duration: 3FT Hon
Entry Requirements: *GCE:* ABB. *SQAH:* AABBB. *SQAAH:* ABB. *IB:* 32.

L46 LIVERPOOL HOPE UNIVERSITY
HOPE PARK
LIVERPOOL L16 9JD
t: 0151 291 3331 f: 0151 291 3434
e: administration@hope.ac.uk
// www.hope.ac.uk

NN42 BA Accounting and Business Management
Duration: 3FT Hon
Entry Requirements: *GCE:* 300-320. *IB:* 25.

M20 THE UNIVERSITY OF MANCHESTER
RUTHERFORD BUILDING
OXFORD ROAD
MANCHESTER M13 9PL
t: 0161 275 2077 f: 0161 275 2106
e: ug-admissions@manchester.ac.uk
// www.manchester.ac.uk

NN24 BSc Management (Accounting and Finance)
Duration: 3FT Hon
Entry Requirements: *GCE:* AAB. *SQAAH:* AAB. *IB:* 35.

M40 THE MANCHESTER METROPOLITAN UNIVERSITY
ADMISSIONS OFFICE
ALL SAINTS (GMS)
ALL SAINTS
MANCHESTER M15 6BH
t: 0161 247 2000
// www.mmu.ac.uk

N2N3 BA Business Management with Financial Management
Duration: 3FT Hon
Entry Requirements: *GCE:* 280. *IB:* 28. *BTEC Dip:* D*D*. *BTEC ExtDip:* DMM.

N21 NEWCASTLE UNIVERSITY
KING'S GATE
NEWCASTLE UPON TYNE NE1 7RU
t: 01912083333
// www.ncl.ac.uk

LN12 BA Economics and Business Management
Duration: 3FT/4SW Hon
Entry Requirements: *GCE:* AAB. *SQAH:* AAABB. *IB:* 35. *BTEC ExtDip:* DDD.

N38 UNIVERSITY OF NORTHAMPTON
PARK CAMPUS
BOUGHTON GREEN ROAD
NORTHAMPTON NN2 7AL
t: 0800 358 2232 f: 01604 722083
e: admissions@northampton.ac.uk
// www.northampton.ac.uk

N4NG BA Accounting with Applied Management
Duration: 3FT Hon
Entry Requirements: *GCE:* 260-280. *SQAH:* AAA-BBBB. *IB:* 24. *BTEC Dip:* DD. *BTEC ExtDip:* DMM. *OCR ND:* D *OCR NED:* M2

N4N2 BA Accounting/Management
Duration: 3FT Hon
Entry Requirements: *GCE:* 260-280. *SQAH:* AAA-BBBB. *IB:* 24. *BTEC Dip:* DD. *BTEC ExtDip:* DMM. *OCR ND:* D *OCR NED:* M2

L1NA BA Economics with Applied Management
Duration: 3FT Hon
Entry Requirements: *GCE:* 260-280. *SQAH:* AAA-BBBB. *IB:* 24. *BTEC Dip:* DD. *BTEC ExtDip:* DMM. *OCR ND:* D *OCR NED:* M2

L1NF BA Economics/Business Entrepreneurship
Duration: 3FT Hon
Entry Requirements: *GCE:* 260-280. *SQAH:* AAA-BBBB. *IB:* 24. *BTEC Dip:* DD. *BTEC ExtDip:* DMM. *OCR ND:* D *OCR NED:* M2

L1N2 BA Economics/Management
Duration: 3FT Hon
Entry Requirements: *GCE:* 260-280. *SQAH:* AAA-BBBB. *IB:* 24. *BTEC Dip:* DD. *BTEC ExtDip:* DMM. *OCR ND:* D *OCR NED:* M2

N2N4 BA Management/Accounting
Duration: 3FT Hon
Entry Requirements: *GCE:* 260-280. *SQAH:* AAA-BBBB. *IB:* 24. *BTEC Dip:* DD. *BTEC ExtDip:* DMM. *OCR ND:* D *OCR NED:* M2

N2L1 BA Management/Economics
Duration: 3FT Hon
Entry Requirements: *GCE:* 260-280. *SQAH:* AAA-BBBB. *IB:* 24. *BTEC Dip:* DD. *BTEC ExtDip:* DMM. *OCR ND:* D *OCR NED:* M2

N91 NOTTINGHAM TRENT UNIVERSITY
DRYDEN BUILDING
BURTON STREET
NOTTINGHAM NG1 4BU
t: +44 (0) 115 848 4200 f: +44 (0) 115 848 8869
e: applications@ntu.ac.uk
// www.ntu.ac.uk

NN24 BA Business Management and Accounting & Finance
Duration: 4SW Hon
Entry Requirements: *GCE:* 300. *BTEC ExtDip:* DDM. *OCR NED:* D2

NNF3 BA Business Management and Accounting & Finance
Duration: 3FT Hon
Entry Requirements: *GCE:* 300. *BTEC ExtDip:* DDM. *OCR NED:* D2

NL21 BA Business Management and Economics
Duration: 3FT Hon
Entry Requirements: *GCE:* 300. *BTEC ExtDip:* DDM. *OCR NED:* D2

NL2C BA Business Management and Economics
Duration: 4SW Hon
Entry Requirements: *GCE:* 300. *BTEC ExtDip:* DDM. *OCR NED:* D2

NN23 BSc Property Finance and Investment
Duration: 3FT/4SW Hon
Entry Requirements: *GCE:* 280. *OCR NED:* M2

O33 OXFORD UNIVERSITY
UNDERGRADUATE ADMISSIONS OFFICE
UNIVERSITY OF OXFORD
WELLINGTON SQUARE
OXFORD OX1 2JD
t: 01865 288000 f: 01865 270212
e: undergraduate.admissions@admin.ox.ac.uk
// www.admissions.ox.ac.uk

LN12 BA Economics and Management
Duration: 3FT Hon
Entry Requirements: *GCE:* AAA. *SQAH:* AAAAA-AAAAB. *SQAAH:* AAB. Interview required. Admissions Test required.

HLN0 MEng Engineering, Economics and Management (4 years)
Duration: 4FT Hon
Entry Requirements: *GCE:* A*AA. *SQAH:* AAAAA-AAAAB. *SQAAH:* AAB. Interview required. Admissions Test required.

FLN0 MEng Materials, Economics and Management (4 years)
Duration: 4FT Hon
Entry Requirements: *GCE:* A*AA. *SQAH:* AAAAA-AAAAB. *SQAAH:* AAB. Interview required.

Q50 QUEEN MARY, UNIVERSITY OF LONDON
QUEEN MARY, UNIVERSITY OF LONDON
MILE END ROAD
LONDON E1 4NS
t: 020 7882 5555 f: 020 7882 5500
e: admissions@qmul.ac.uk
// www.qmul.ac.uk

LN12 BSc Economics, Finance and Management
Duration: 3FT Hon
Entry Requirements: *GCE:* AAB. *SQAAH:* AAB. *IB:* 36.

R12 THE UNIVERSITY OF READING
THE UNIVERSITY OF READING
PO BOX 217
READING RG6 6AH
t: 0118 378 8619 f: 0118 378 8924
e: student.recruitment@reading.ac.uk
// www.reading.ac.uk

NN24 BA Accounting and Management
Duration: 3FT/4SW Hon
Entry Requirements: *GCE:* AAB. *SQAH:* AAABB. *SQAAH:* AAB. *BTEC Dip:* DD. *BTEC ExtDip:* DDD.

R48 ROEHAMPTON UNIVERSITY
ROEHAMPTON LANE
LONDON SW15 5PU
t: 020 8392 3232 f: 020 8392 3470
e: enquiries@roehampton.ac.uk
// www.roehampton.ac.uk

NN24 BSc Business Management and Accounting
Duration: 3FT Hon
Entry Requirements: *GCE:* 320. *IB:* 27. *BTEC ExtDip:* DDM. *OCR NED:* D2 Interview required.

R72 ROYAL HOLLOWAY, UNIVERSITY OF LONDON
ROYAL HOLLOWAY, UNIVERSITY OF LONDON
EGHAM
SURREY TW20 0EX
t: 01784 414944 f: 01784 473662
e: Admissions@rhul.ac.uk
// www.rhul.ac.uk

LN12 BSc Economics and Management
Duration: 3FT Hon
Entry Requirements: *GCE:* AAA-ABB. *SQAH:* AAAAA-AABBB. *SQAAH:* AAA-ABB. *IB:* 32.

N2N4 BSc Management with Accounting
Duration: 3FT Hon
Entry Requirements: *GCE:* AAB. *SQAH:* AAABB. *SQAAH:* ABB. *IB:* 35.

NN24 BSc Management with Accounting (Year in Business)
Duration: 4FT Hon
Entry Requirements: Contact the institution for details.

NN23 BSc Management with Entrepreneurship
Duration: 3FT Hon
Entry Requirements: Contact the institution for details.

S18 THE UNIVERSITY OF SHEFFIELD
THE UNIVERSITY OF SHEFFIELD
LEVEL 2, ARTS TOWER
WESTERN BANK
SHEFFIELD S10 2TN
t: 0114 222 8030 f: 0114 222 8032
// www.sheffield.ac.uk

NL21 BA Business Management and Economics
Duration: 3FT Hon
Entry Requirements: *GCE:* AAB. *SQAH:* AAABB. *SQAAH:* AB. *IB:* 35. *BTEC ExtDip:* DDD.

S27 UNIVERSITY OF SOUTHAMPTON
HIGHFIELD
SOUTHAMPTON SO17 1BJ
t: 023 8059 4732 f: 023 8059 3037
e: admissions@soton.ac.uk
// www.southampton.ac.uk

NN24 BSc Management Sciences and Accounting
Duration: 3FT Hon
Entry Requirements: *GCE:* AAB. *SQAH:* AAABB. *SQAAH:* AB. *IB:* 34.

S36 UNIVERSITY OF ST ANDREWS
ST KATHARINE'S WEST
16 THE SCORES
ST ANDREWS
FIFE KY16 9AX
t: 01334 462150 f: 01334 463330
e: admissions@st-andrews.ac.uk
// www.st-andrews.ac.uk

LNC2 BSc Economics and Management
Duration: 4FT Hon
Entry Requirements: *GCE:* AAA. *SQAH:* AAAA. *IB:* 38.

LN12 BSc Economics and Management Science
Duration: 4FT Hon
Entry Requirements: *GCE:* AAA. *SQAH:* AAAA. *IB:* 38.

NL21 MA Economics and Management
Duration: 4FT Hon
Entry Requirements: *GCE:* AAA. *SQAH:* AAAA. *IB:* 38.

S75 THE UNIVERSITY OF STIRLING
STUDENT RECRUITMENT & ADMISSIONS SERVICE
UNIVERSITY OF STIRLING
STIRLING
SCOTLAND FK9 4LA
t: 01786 467044 f: 01786 466800
e: admissions@stir.ac.uk
// www.stir.ac.uk

NNF4 BAcc Accountancy and Business Studies
Duration: 4FT Hon
Entry Requirements: *GCE:* BBC. *SQAH:* BBBB. *SQAAH:* AAA-CCC. *IB:* 32. *BTEC ExtDip:* DMM.

S78 THE UNIVERSITY OF STRATHCLYDE
GLASGOW G1 1XQ
t: 0141 552 4400 f: 0141 552 0775
// www.strath.ac.uk

NN42 BA Accounting and Management
Duration: 4FT Hon
Entry Requirements: *GCE:* AAA. *SQAH:* AAAAAB-AAAA. *IB:* 36.

LN12 BA Economics and Management
Duration: 4FT Hon
Entry Requirements: *GCE:* AAB. *SQAH:* AAAABB-AAAB. *IB:* 36.

NN32 BA Finance and Management
Duration: 4FT Hon
Entry Requirements: *GCE:* AAB. *SQAH:* AAAABB-AAAB. *IB:* 36.

S82 UNIVERSITY CAMPUS SUFFOLK (UCS)
WATERFRONT BUILDING
NEPTUNE QUAY
IPSWICH
SUFFOLK IP4 1QJ
t: 01473 338833 f: 01473 339900
e: info@ucs.ac.uk
// www.ucs.ac.uk

N2N3 BA Business Management with Finance
Duration: 3FT Hon
Entry Requirements: *GCE:* 280. *IB:* 28. *BTEC ExtDip:* DMM.
Interview required.

S90 UNIVERSITY OF SUSSEX
UNDERGRADUATE ADMISSIONS
SUSSEX HOUSE
UNIVERSITY OF SUSSEX
BRIGHTON BN1 9RH
t: 01273 678416 f: 01273 678545
e: ug.applicants@sussex.ac.uk
// www.sussex.ac.uk

LN12 BSc Economics and Management Studies
Duration: 3FT Hon
Entry Requirements: *GCE:* AAB. *SQAH:* AAABB. *IB:* 35. *BTEC SubDip:* D. *BTEC Dip:* DD. *BTEC ExtDip:* DDD. *OCR ND:* D *OCR NED:* D1

S93 SWANSEA UNIVERSITY
SINGLETON PARK
SWANSEA SA2 8PP
t: 01792 295111 f: 01792 295110
e: admissions@swansea.ac.uk
// www.swansea.ac.uk

NL21 BSc Business Management and Economics
Duration: 3FT Hon
Entry Requirements: *GCE:* ABB. *IB:* 33.

N2N4 BSc Management Science (Accounting)
Duration: 3FT Hon
Entry Requirements: *GCE:* ABB-BBB. *IB:* 33.

N2N3 BSc Management Science (Finance)
Duration: 3FT Hon
Entry Requirements: *GCE:* ABB-BBB. *IB:* 33.

W36 WEST CHESHIRE COLLEGE
EATON ROAD
HANDBRIDGE
CHESTER
CHESHIRE CH4 7ER
t: 01244 656555 f: 01244 670687
e: info@west-cheshire.ac.uk
// www.west-cheshire.ac.uk

N4N2 FdA Accounting with Management
Duration: 2FT Fdg
Entry Requirements: Contact the institution for details.

W50 UNIVERSITY OF WESTMINSTER
2ND FLOOR, CAVENDISH HOUSE
101 NEW CAVENDISH STREET,
LONDON W1W 6XH
t: 020 7915 5511
e: course-enquiries@westminster.ac.uk
// www.westminster.ac.uk

NN24 BA Business Management (Accounting)
Duration: 3FT/4SW Hon
Entry Requirements: *GCE:* BCC. *IB:* 28.

NL21 BA Business Management (Economics)
Duration: 3FT/4SW Hon
Entry Requirements: *GCE:* BCC. *IB:* 28.

N3N2 BA Finance with Management
Duration: 3FT/4SW Hon
Entry Requirements: *GCE:* BBC. *SQAH:* BBBBB. *SQAAH:* BBB. *IB:* 28.

N4N2 BSc Accounting with Management
Duration: 3FT/4SW Hon
Entry Requirements: *GCE:* BBB. *SQAH:* BBBBB. *SQAAH:* BBB. *IB:* 28.

W76 UNIVERSITY OF WINCHESTER
WINCHESTER
HANTS SO22 4NR
t: 01962 827234 f: 01962 827288
e: course.enquiries@winchester.ac.uk
// www.winchester.ac.uk

NN42 BA Accounting and Management
Duration: 3FT Hon
Entry Requirements: *Foundation:* Distinction. *GCE:* 260-300. *IB:* 25. *OCR ND:* D *OCR NED:* M2

Y50 THE UNIVERSITY OF YORK
STUDENT RECRUITMENT AND ADMISSIONS
UNIVERSITY OF YORK
HESLINGTON
YORK YO10 5DD
t: 01904 324000 f: 01904 323538
e: ug-admissions@york.ac.uk
// www.york.ac.uk

NN4F BSc Accounting, Business Finance & Management with a Year in Industry
Duration: 4SW Hon
Entry Requirements: *GCE:* AAB. *SQAH:* AAAAB. *SQAAH:* AB. *IB:* 35. *BTEC ExtDip:* DDD.

NN42 BSc Accounting, Business Finance and Management
Duration: 3FT Hon
Entry Requirements: *GCE:* AAB. *SQAH:* AAAAB. *SQAAH:* AB. *IB:* 35. *BTEC ExtDip:* DDD.

Y75 YORK ST JOHN UNIVERSITY
LORD MAYOR'S WALK
YORK YO31 7EX
t: 01904 876598 f: 01904 876940/876921
e: admissions@yorksj.ac.uk
// w3.yorksj.ac.uk

NN23 BA Business Management and Finance
Duration: 3FT Hon
Entry Requirements: *Foundation:* Pass. *GCE:* 200-240. *IB:* 24.

MARKETING COMBINATIONS

A40 ABERYSTWYTH UNIVERSITY
ABERYSTWYTH UNIVERSITY, WELCOME CENTRE
PENGLAIS CAMPUS
ABERYSTWYTH
CEREDIGION SY23 3FB
t: 01970 622021 f: 01970 627410
e: ug-admissions@aber.ac.uk
// www.aber.ac.uk

N4N5 BScEcon Accounting & Finance with Marketing
Duration: 3FT Hon
Entry Requirements: *GCE:* 300. *IB:* 27.

LN15 BScEcon Economics/Marketing
Duration: 3FT Hon
Entry Requirements: *GCE:* 300. *IB:* 27.

N5N4 BScEcon Marketing with Accounting & Finance
Duration: 3FT Hon
Entry Requirements: *GCE:* 280. *IB:* 27.

N5L1 BScEcon Marketing with Economics
Duration: 3FT Hon
Entry Requirements: *GCE:* 280. *IB:* 27.

B56 THE UNIVERSITY OF BRADFORD
RICHMOND ROAD
BRADFORD
WEST YORKSHIRE BD7 1DP
t: 0800 073 1225 f: 01274 235585
e: course-enquiries@bradford.ac.uk
// www.bradford.ac.uk

L1N5 BSc Economics with Marketing
Duration: 3FT Hon
Entry Requirements: *GCE:* 260-300. *IB:* 25.

C10 CANTERBURY CHRIST CHURCH UNIVERSITY
NORTH HOLMES ROAD
CANTERBURY
KENT CT1 1QU
t: 01227 782900 f: 01227 782888
e: admissions@canterbury.ac.uk
// www.canterbury.ac.uk

N5N4 BSc Marketing with Accounting
Duration: 3FT Hon
Entry Requirements: *GCE:* 240. *IB:* 24.

C30 UNIVERSITY OF CENTRAL LANCASHIRE
PRESTON
LANCS PR1 2HE
t: 01772 201201 f: 01772 894954
e: uadmissions@uclan.ac.uk
// www.uclan.ac.uk

NN54 BA Accounting and Marketing
Duration: 3FT Hon
Entry Requirements: *GCE:* 240-280. *SQAH:* AABB-BBBC. *IB:* 28. *OCR ND:* D

C58 UNIVERSITY OF CHICHESTER
BISHOP OTTER CAMPUS
COLLEGE LANE
CHICHESTER
WEST SUSSEX PO19 6PE
t: 01243 816002 f: 01243 816161
e: admissions@chi.ac.uk
// www.chiuni.ac.uk

NN53 BA Marketing and Finance
Duration: 3FT Hon
Entry Requirements: *GCE:* BCD-CCC. *SQAAH:* CCC. *IB:* 28. *BTEC SubDip:* M. *BTEC Dip:* DD.

NN35 BA Marketing and Finance (Placement)
Duration: 4SW Hon
Entry Requirements: *GCE:* BCD-CCC. *SQAAH:* CCC. *IB:* 28. *BTEC SubDip:* M. *BTEC Dip:* DD.

D39 UNIVERSITY OF DERBY
KEDLESTON ROAD
DERBY DE22 1GB
t: 01332 591167 f: 01332 597724
e: askadmissions@derby.ac.uk
// www.derby.ac.uk

NN45 BA Accounting and Marketing
Duration: 3FT Hon
Entry Requirements: *Foundation:* Distinction. *GCE:* 260-300. *IB:* 28. *BTEC Dip:* D*D*. *BTEC ExtDip:* DMM. *OCR NED:* M2

D65 UNIVERSITY OF DUNDEE
NETHERGATE
DUNDEE DD1 4HN
t: 01382 383838 f: 01382 388150
e: contactus@dundee.ac.uk
// www.dundee.ac.uk/admissions/
undergraduate/

L1N5 BSc Business Economics with Marketing
Duration: 4FT Hon
Entry Requirements: *GCE:* BCC. *SQAH:* ABBB. *IB:* 30.

LN15 MA Business Economics with Marketing
Duration: 4FT Hon
Entry Requirements: *GCE:* BCC. *SQAH:* ABBB. *IB:* 30.

LLN0 MA Business Economics with Marketing and Geography
Duration: 4FT Hon
Entry Requirements: *GCE:* BCC. *SQAH:* ABBB. *IB:* 30.

LNV0 MA Business Economics with Marketing and History
Duration: 4FT Hon
Entry Requirements: *GCE:* BCC. *SQAH:* ABBB. *IB:* 30.

LNG0 MA Business Economics with Marketing and Mathematics
Duration: 4FT Hon
Entry Requirements: *GCE:* BCC. *SQAH:* ABBB. *IB:* 30.

L0N0 MA Business Economics with Marketing and Politics
Duration: 4FT Hon
Entry Requirements: *GCE:* BCC. *SQAH:* ABBB. *IB:* 30.

LNC0 MA Business Economics with Marketing and Psychology
Duration: 4FT Hon
Entry Requirements: *GCE:* BCC. *SQAH:* ABBB. *IB:* 30.

E59 EDINBURGH NAPIER UNIVERSITY
CRAIGLOCKHART CAMPUS
EDINBURGH EH14 1DJ
t: +44 (0)8452 60 60 40 f: 0131 455 6464
e: info@napier.ac.uk
// www.napier.ac.uk

N4N5 BA Accounting with Marketing Management
Duration: 3FT/4FT Ord/Hon
Entry Requirements: *GCE:* 230.

H24 HERIOT-WATT UNIVERSITY, EDINBURGH
EDINBURGH CAMPUS
EDINBURGH EH14 4AS
t: 0131 449 5111 f: 0131 451 3630
e: ugadmissions@hw.ac.uk
// www.hw.ac.uk

LN15 MA Economics and Marketing
Duration: 4FT Hon
Entry Requirements: *GCE:* BBB. *SQAH:* AAAB-BBBBC. *SQAAH:* BB. *IB:* 29.

H36 UNIVERSITY OF HERTFORDSHIRE
UNIVERSITY ADMISSIONS SERVICE
COLLEGE LANE
HATFIELD
HERTS AL10 9AB
t: 01707 284800
// www.herts.ac.uk

NN45 BA Accounting/Marketing
Duration: 3FT/4SW Hon
Entry Requirements: *GCE:* 300. *IB:* 30.

N5N3 BA Marketing with Finance
Duration: 3FT/4SW Hon
Entry Requirements: *GCE:* 300. *IB:* 30.

H72 THE UNIVERSITY OF HULL
THE UNIVERSITY OF HULL
COTTINGHAM ROAD
HULL HU6 7RX
t: 01482 466100 f: 01482 442290
e: admissions@hull.ac.uk
// www.hull.ac.uk

NN54 BA Marketing and Accounting
Duration: 3FT Hon
Entry Requirements: *GCE:* 300. *IB:* 30. *BTEC ExtDip:* DMM.

NN5K BA Marketing and Accounting (International) (4 years)
Duration: 4FT Hon
Entry Requirements: *GCE:* 300. *IB:* 30. *BTEC ExtDip:* DMM.

NNM4 BA Marketing and Accounting (with Professional Experience) (4 years)
Duration: 4FT Hon
Entry Requirements: *GCE:* 300. *IB:* 30. *BTEC ExtDip:* DMM.

NL51 BA Marketing and Business Economics
Duration: 3FT Hon
Entry Requirements: *GCE:* 300. *IB:* 30. *BTEC ExtDip:* DMM.

NLM1 BA Marketing and Business Economics (International) (4 years)
Duration: 4FT Hon
Entry Requirements: *GCE:* 300. *IB:* 30. *BTEC ExtDip:* DMM.

NL5D BA Marketing and Business Economics (with Professional Experience) (4 years)
Duration: 4FT Hon
Entry Requirements: *GCE:* 300. *IB:* 30. *BTEC ExtDip:* DMM.

NN53 BA Marketing and Financial Management
Duration: 3FT Hon
Entry Requirements: *GCE:* 300. *IB:* 30. *BTEC ExtDip:* DMM.

NNM3 BA Marketing and Financial Management (International) (4 years)
Duration: 4FT Hon
Entry Requirements: *GCE:* 300. *IB:* 30. *BTEC ExtDip:* DMM.

NNN3 BA Marketing and Financial Management (with Professional Experience) (4 years)
Duration: 4FT Hon
Entry Requirements: *GCE:* 300. *IB:* 30. *BTEC ExtDip:* DMM.

K12 KEELE UNIVERSITY
KEELE UNIVERSITY
STAFFORDSHIRE ST5 5BG
t: 01782 734005 f: 01782 632343
e: undergraduate@keele.ac.uk
// www.keele.ac.uk

NN45 BA Accounting and Marketing
Duration: 3FT Hon
Entry Requirements: *GCE:* ABB.

LN15 BA Economics and Marketing
Duration: 3FT Hon
Entry Requirements: *GCE:* ABB.

NN35 BA Finance and Marketing
Duration: 3FT Hon
Entry Requirements: *GCE:* ABB.

N38 UNIVERSITY OF NORTHAMPTON
PARK CAMPUS
BOUGHTON GREEN ROAD
NORTHAMPTON NN2 7AL
t: 0800 358 2232 f: 01604 722083
e: admissions@northampton.ac.uk
// www.northampton.ac.uk

N4NM BA Accounting/Advertising
Duration: 3FT Hon
Entry Requirements: *GCE:* 260-280. *SQAH:* AAA-BBBB. *IB:* 24.
BTEC Dip: DD. *BTEC ExtDip:* DMM. *OCR ND:* D *OCR NED:* M2

N4N5 BA Accounting/Marketing
Duration: 3FT Hon
Entry Requirements: *GCE:* 260-280. *SQAH:* AAA-BBBB. *IB:* 24.
BTEC Dip: DD. *BTEC ExtDip:* DMM. *OCR ND:* D *OCR NED:* M2

N5NK BA Advertising/Accounting
Duration: 3FT Hon
Entry Requirements: *GCE:* 260-280. *SQAH:* AAA-BBBB. *IB:* 24.
BTEC Dip: DD. *BTEC ExtDip:* DMM. *OCR ND:* D *OCR NED:* M2

N5LC BA Advertising/Economics
Duration: 3FT Hon
Entry Requirements: *GCE:* 260-280. *SQAH:* AAA-BBBB. *IB:* 24.
BTEC Dip: DD. *BTEC ExtDip:* DMM. *OCR ND:* D *OCR NED:* M2

L1NM BA Economics/Advertising
Duration: 3FT Hon
Entry Requirements: *GCE:* 260-280. *SQAH:* AAA-BBBB. *IB:* 24.
BTEC Dip: DD. *BTEC ExtDip:* DMM. *OCR ND:* D *OCR NED:* M2

L1N5 BA Economics/Marketing
Duration: 3FT Hon
Entry Requirements: *GCE:* 260-280. *SQAH:* AAA-BBBB. *IB:* 24.
BTEC Dip: DD. *BTEC ExtDip:* DMM. *OCR ND:* D *OCR NED:* M2

N5N4 BA Marketing/Accounting
Duration: 3FT Hon
Entry Requirements: *GCE:* 260-280. *SQAH:* AAA-BBBB. *IB:* 24.
BTEC Dip: DD. *BTEC ExtDip:* DMM. *OCR ND:* D *OCR NED:* M2

N5L1 BA Marketing/Economics
Duration: 3FT Hon
Entry Requirements: *GCE:* 260-280. *SQAH:* AAA-BBBB. *IB:* 24.
BTEC Dip: DD. *BTEC ExtDip:* DMM. *OCR ND:* D *OCR NED:* M2

P60 PLYMOUTH UNIVERSITY
DRAKE CIRCUS
PLYMOUTH PL4 8AA
t: 01752 585858 f: 01752 588055
e: admissions@plymouth.ac.uk
// www.plymouth.ac.uk

L1N5 BSc Business Economics with Marketing
Duration: 3FT/4SW Hon
Entry Requirements: *GCE:* 240. *IB:* 24.

S75 THE UNIVERSITY OF STIRLING
STUDENT RECRUITMENT & ADMISSIONS SERVICE
UNIVERSITY OF STIRLING
STIRLING
SCOTLAND FK9 4LA
t: 01786 467044 f: 01786 466800
e: admissions@stir.ac.uk
// www.stir.ac.uk

NL51 BA Economics and Marketing
Duration: 4FT Hon
Entry Requirements: *GCE:* BBC. *SQAH:* BBBB. *SQAAH:* AAA-CCC.
IB: 32. *BTEC ExtDip:* DMM.

NN45 BAcc Accountancy and Marketing
Duration: 4FT Hon
Entry Requirements: *GCE:* BBC. *SQAH:* BBBB. *SQAAH:* AAA-CCC.
IB: 32. *BTEC ExtDip:* DMM.

S78 THE UNIVERSITY OF STRATHCLYDE
GLASGOW G1 1XQ
t: 0141 552 4400 f: 0141 552 0775
// www.strath.ac.uk

NN45 BA Accounting and Marketing
Duration: 4FT Hon
Entry Requirements: *GCE:* AAA. *SQAH:* AAAAAB-AAAA. *IB:* 36.

LN15 BA Economics and Marketing
Duration: 4FT Deg
Entry Requirements: *GCE:* AAB. *SQAH:* AAAABB-AAAB. *IB:* 36.

NN35 BA Finance and Marketing
Duration: 4FT Hon
Entry Requirements: *GCE:* AAB. *SQAH:* AAAABB-AAAB. *IB:* 36.

U20 UNIVERSITY OF ULSTER
COLERAINE
CO. LONDONDERRY
NORTHERN IRELAND BT52 1SA
t: 028 7012 4221 f: 028 7012 4908
e: online@ulster.ac.uk
// www.ulster.ac.uk

NN4M BSc Accounting and Advertising
Duration: 4SW Hon
Entry Requirements: *GCE:* 240. *IB:* 24.

NN45 BSc Accounting and Marketing
Duration: 4SW Hon
Entry Requirements: *GCE:* 240. *IB:* 24.

N5N4 BSc Advertising with Accounting
Duration: 4FT Hon
Entry Requirements: *GCE:* 240. *IB:* 24.

MATHEMATICS AND STATISTICS
COMBINATIONS

A20 THE UNIVERSITY OF ABERDEEN
UNIVERSITY OFFICE
KING'S COLLEGE
ABERDEEN AB24 3FX
t: +44 (0) 1224 273504 f: +44 (0) 1224 272034
e: sras@abdn.ac.uk
// www.abdn.ac.uk/sras

LG11 MA Economics and Mathematics
Duration: 4FT Hon
Entry Requirements: *GCE:* BBB. *SQAH:* BBBB. *IB:* 30.

A40 ABERYSTWYTH UNIVERSITY
ABERYSTWYTH UNIVERSITY, WELCOME CENTRE
PENGLAIS CAMPUS
ABERYSTWYTH
CEREDIGION SY23 3FB
t: 01970 622021 f: 01970 627410
e: ug-admissions@aber.ac.uk
// www.aber.ac.uk

G1N4 BSc Mathematics with Accounting & Finance
Duration: 3FT Hon
Entry Requirements: *GCE:* 320. *IB:* 27.

G1L1 BSc Mathematics with Economics
Duration: 3FT Hon
Entry Requirements: *GCE:* 320. *IB:* 27.

N4G1 BScEcon Accounting & Finance with Mathematics
Duration: 3FT Hon
Entry Requirements: *GCE:* 300. *IB:* 27.

N4G3 BScEcon Accounting & Finance with Statistics
Duration: 3FT Hon
Entry Requirements: *GCE:* 300. *IB:* 27.

L1G1 BScEcon Economics with Mathematics
Duration: 3FT Hon
Entry Requirements: *GCE:* 300. *IB:* 27.

A80 ASTON UNIVERSITY, BIRMINGHAM
ASTON TRIANGLE
BIRMINGHAM B4 7ET
t: 0121 204 4444 f: 0121 204 3696
e: admissions@aston.ac.uk (automatic response)
// www.aston.ac.uk/prospective-students/ug

G1L1 BSc Mathematics with Economics
Duration: 4SW Hon
Entry Requirements: *GCE:* 320-340. *SQAH:* ABBBB. *SQAAH:* ABB. *IB:* 32.

B32 THE UNIVERSITY OF BIRMINGHAM
EDGBASTON
BIRMINGHAM B15 2TT
t: 0121 415 8900 f: 0121 414 7159
e: admissions@bham.ac.uk
// www.birmingham.ac.uk

LG13 BSc Mathematical Economics and Statistics
Duration: 3FT Hon
Entry Requirements: *GCE:* AAA. *SQAH:* AAABB. *SQAAH:* AA.

B72 UNIVERSITY OF BRIGHTON
MITHRAS HOUSE 211
LEWES ROAD
BRIGHTON BN2 4AT
t: 01273 644644 f: 01273 642607
e: admissions@brighton.ac.uk
// www.brighton.ac.uk

G1N3 BSc Mathematics with Finance
Duration: 3FT/4SW Hon
Entry Requirements: *GCE:* BBB. *IB:* 30.

B78 UNIVERSITY OF BRISTOL
UNDERGRADUATE ADMISSIONS OFFICE
SENATE HOUSE
TYNDALL AVENUE
BRISTOL BS8 1TH
t: 0117 928 9000 f: 0117 331 7391
e: ug-admissions@bristol.ac.uk
// www.bristol.ac.uk

LG11 BSc Economics and Mathematics
Duration: 3FT Hon
Entry Requirements: *GCE:* A*AA-AAA. *SQAH:* AAAA. *SQAAH:* AA. *IB:* 38.

B84 BRUNEL UNIVERSITY
UXBRIDGE
MIDDLESEX UB8 3PH
t: 01895 265265 f: 01895 269790
e: admissions@brunel.ac.uk
// www.brunel.ac.uk

GN13 BSc Financial Mathematics
Duration: 3FT Hon
Entry Requirements: *GCE:* ABB. *SQAAH:* ABB. *IB:* 33. *BTEC ExtDip:* D*DD.

GND3 BSc Financial Mathematics (4 year Thick SW)
Duration: 4SW Hon
Entry Requirements: *GCE:* ABB. *SQAAH:* ABB. *IB:* 33. *BTEC ExtDip:* D*DD.

GN1H MMath Financial Mathematics (4 years)
Duration: 4FT Hon
Entry Requirements: *GCE:* AAA. *SQAAH:* AAA. *IB:* 37.

GN1J MMath Financial Mathematics (5 year Thick SW)
Duration: 5FT Hon
Entry Requirements: *GCE:* AAA. *SQAAH:* AAA. *IB:* 37.

C60 CITY UNIVERSITY
NORTHAMPTON SQUARE
LONDON EC1V 0HB
t: 020 7040 5060 f: 020 7040 8995
e: ugadmissions@city.ac.uk
// www.city.ac.uk

G1L1 BSc Mathematical Science with Finance & Economics (3 years or 4 year SW)
Duration: 3FT Hon
Entry Requirements: *GCE:* 360. *IB:* 32.

GN13 BSc Mathematics and Finance (3 years or 4 year SW)
Duration: 3FT Hon
Entry Requirements: *GCE:* 360. *IB:* 32.

D39 UNIVERSITY OF DERBY
KEDLESTON ROAD
DERBY DE22 1GB
t: 01332 591167 f: 01332 597724
e: askadmissions@derby.ac.uk
// www.derby.ac.uk

GN14 BSc Accounting and Mathematics
Duration: 3FT Hon
Entry Requirements: *Foundation:* Distinction. *GCE:* 260-300. *IB:* 28. *BTEC Dip:* D*D*. *BTEC ExtDip:* DMM. *OCR NED:* M2

D65 UNIVERSITY OF DUNDEE
NETHERGATE
DUNDEE DD1 4HN
t: 01382 383838 f: 01382 388150
e: contactus@dundee.ac.uk
// www.dundee.ac.uk/admissions/undergraduate/

GN14 BSc Accountancy and Mathematics
Duration: 4FT Hon
Entry Requirements: *GCE:* BCC. *SQAH:* ABBB. *IB:* 30.

GL11 BSc Mathematics and Economics
Duration: 4FT Hon
Entry Requirements: *GCE:* BCC. *SQAH:* ABBB. *IB:* 30.

GLD1 BSc Mathematics and Financial Economics
Duration: 4FT Hon
Entry Requirements: *GCE:* BCC. *SQAH:* ABBB. *IB:* 30.

E28 UNIVERSITY OF EAST LONDON
DOCKLANDS CAMPUS
UNIVERSITY WAY
LONDON E16 2RD
t: 020 8223 3333 f: 020 8223 2978
e: study@uel.ac.uk
// www.uel.ac.uk

L1G1 BA Business Economics with Mathematics
Duration: 3FT Hon
Entry Requirements: *GCE:* 240. *IB:* 24. *OCR ND:* M1 *OCR NED:* P1 Interview required.

E56 THE UNIVERSITY OF EDINBURGH
STUDENT RECRUITMENT & ADMISSIONS
57 GEORGE SQUARE
EDINBURGH EH8 9JU
t: 0131 650 4360 f: 0131 651 1236
e: sra.enquiries@ed.ac.uk
// www.ed.ac.uk/studying/undergraduate/

LG11 MA Economics and Mathematics
Duration: 4FT Hon
Entry Requirements: *GCE:* AAA-ABC. *SQAH:* AAAA-ABBC. *IB:* 34.

LG13 MA Economics and Statistics
Duration: 4FT Hon
Entry Requirements: *GCE:* AAA-ABC. *SQAH:* AAAA-ABBC. *IB:* 34.

E70 THE UNIVERSITY OF ESSEX
WIVENHOE PARK
COLCHESTER
ESSEX CO4 3SQ
t: 01206 873666 f: 01206 874477
e: admit@essex.ac.uk
// www.essex.ac.uk

GN14 BSc Accounting and Mathematics
Duration: 3FT Hon
Entry Requirements: *GCE:* ABB-BBB. *SQAH:* AAAB-AABB. *BTEC ExtDip:* DDM.

GN1K BSc Accounting and Mathematics (Including Year Abroad)
Duration: 4FT Hon
Entry Requirements: *GCE:* ABB-BBB. *SQAH:* AAAB-AABB. *BTEC ExtDip:* DDM.

LG11 BSc Economics and Mathematics
Duration: 3FT Hon
Entry Requirements: *GCE:* ABB-BBB. *SQAH:* AAAB-AABB. *BTEC ExtDip:* DDM.

LG1C BSc Economics and Mathematics (Including Year Abroad)
Duration: 4FT Hon
Entry Requirements: *GCE:* ABB-BBB. *SQAH:* AAAB-AABB. *BTEC ExtDip:* DDM.

L1G1 BSc Economics with Mathematics
Duration: 3FT Hon
Entry Requirements: *GCE:* ABB. *SQAH:* AAAB. *IB:* 34.

GN13 BSc Finance and Mathematics
Duration: 3FT Hon
Entry Requirements: *GCE:* ABB-BBB. *SQAH:* AAAB-AABB. *BTEC ExtDip:* DDM.

GN1H BSc Finance and Mathematics (Including Year Abroad)
Duration: 4FT Hon
Entry Requirements: *GCE:* ABB-BBB. *SQAH:* AAAB-AABB. *BTEC ExtDip:* DDM.

NGL1 BSc Management, Mathematics and Economics (including Foundation Year)
Duration: 4FT Hon
Entry Requirements: *GCE:* 180. *SQAH:* CCCD. *IB:* 24.

G1L1 BSc Mathematics with Economics
Duration: 3FT Hon
Entry Requirements: *GCE:* ABB-BBB. *SQAH:* AAAB-AABB. *BTEC ExtDip:* DDM.

G1LC BSc Mathematics with Economics (Including Year Abroad)
Duration: 4FT Hon
Entry Requirements: *GCE:* ABB-BBB. *SQAH:* AAAB-AABB. *BTEC ExtDip:* DDM.

E84 UNIVERSITY OF EXETER
LAVER BUILDING
NORTH PARK ROAD
EXETER
DEVON EX4 4QE
t: 01392 723044 f: 01392 722479
e: admissions@exeter.ac.uk
// www.exeter.ac.uk

G1N4 BSc Mathematics with Accounting
Duration: 3FT Hon
Entry Requirements: *GCE:* A*AA-AAB. *SQAH:* AAAAA-AABBB. *SQAAH:* AAA-ABB.

G1L1 BSc Mathematics with Economics
Duration: 3FT Hon
Entry Requirements: *GCE:* A*AA-AAB. *SQAH:* AAAAA-AABBB. *SQAAH:* AAA-ABB.

G1N3 BSc Mathematics with Finance
Duration: 3FT Hon
Entry Requirements: *GCE:* A*AA-AAB. *SQAH:* AAAAA-AABBB. *SQAAH:* AAA-ABB.

www.ucas.com

at the heart of connecting people to higher education

G14 UNIVERSITY OF GLAMORGAN, CARDIFF AND PONTYPRIDD
ENQUIRIES AND ADMISSIONS UNIT
PONTYPRIDD CF37 1DL
t: 08456 434030 f: 01443 654050
e: enquiries@glam.ac.uk
// www.glam.ac.uk

G1N3 BSc Financial Mathematics
Duration: 3FT Hon
Entry Requirements: *GCE:* BBB. *IB:* 26. *BTEC SubDip:* M. *BTEC Dip:* MM. *BTEC ExtDip:* DDM. Interview required.

GN1K BSc Mathematics and Accounting
Duration: 3FT Hon
Entry Requirements: *GCE:* BBB. *IB:* 26. *BTEC SubDip:* M. *BTEC Dip:* DD. *BTEC ExtDip:* MMM. Interview required.

G1NK BSc Mathematics with Accounting
Duration: 3FT Hon
Entry Requirements: *GCE:* BBB. *IB:* 26. *BTEC SubDip:* M. *BTEC Dip:* MM. *BTEC ExtDip:* DDM. Interview required.

G28 UNIVERSITY OF GLASGOW
71 SOUTHPARK AVENUE
UNIVERSITY OF GLASGOW
GLASGOW G12 8QQ
t: 0141 330 6062 f: 0141 330 2961
e: student.recruitment@glasgow.ac.uk
// www.glasgow.ac.uk

NG41 BSc Accounting and Applied Mathematics
Duration: 4FT Hon
Entry Requirements: *GCE:* AAB. *SQAH:* AAAABB-AAABB. *IB:* 34.

NG4C BSc Accounting and Mathematics
Duration: 4FT Hon
Entry Requirements: *GCE:* AAB. *SQAH:* AAAABB-AAABB. *IB:* 34.

NG4D BSc Accounting and Pure Mathematics
Duration: 4FT Hon
Entry Requirements: *GCE:* AAB. *SQAH:* AAAABB-AAABB. *IB:* 34.

GN34 BSc Accounting and Statistics
Duration: 4FT Hon
Entry Requirements: *GCE:* AAB. *SQAH:* AAAABB-AAABB. *IB:* 34.

LG1C BSc Applied Mathematics and Economics
Duration: 3FT/4FT Deg/Hon
Entry Requirements: *GCE:* ABB. *SQAH:* AAAB-BBBB. *IB:* 32.

GN13 BSc Finance and Applied Mathematics
Duration: 4FT Hon
Entry Requirements: *GCE:* AAB. *SQAH:* AAAABB-AAABB. *IB:* 34.

NG3C BSc Finance and Mathematics
Duration: 4FT Hon
Entry Requirements: *GCE:* AAB. *SQAH:* AAAABB-AAABB. *IB:* 34.

NG31 BSc Finance and Pure Mathematics
Duration: 4FT Hon
Entry Requirements: *GCE:* AAB. *SQAH:* AAAABB-AAABB. *IB:* 34.

GN33 BSc Finance and Statistics
Duration: 4FT Hon
Entry Requirements: *GCE:* AAB. *SQAH:* AAAABB-AAABB. *IB:* 34.

LG1D BSc Mathematics/Economics
Duration: 4FT Hon
Entry Requirements: *GCE:* ABB. *SQAH:* AAAB-BBBB. *IB:* 32.

GL31 BSc Statistics and Economics
Duration: 4FT Hon
Entry Requirements: *GCE:* ABB. *SQAH:* AAAB-BBBB. *IB:* 32.

LG11 MA Business Economics/Mathematics
Duration: 4FT Hon
Entry Requirements: *GCE:* ABB. *SQAH:* AAAA-AABB. *IB:* 36.

GL11 MA Economics/Mathematics
Duration: 4FT Hon
Entry Requirements: *GCE:* ABB. *SQAH:* AAAA-AABB. *IB:* 36.

GLC1 MA Economics/Mathematics
Duration: 4FT Hon
Entry Requirements: *GCE:* ABB. *SQAH:* AAAB-ABBB. *IB:* 36.

G70 UNIVERSITY OF GREENWICH
GREENWICH CAMPUS
OLD ROYAL NAVAL COLLEGE
PARK ROW
LONDON SE10 9LS
t: 020 8331 9000 f: 020 8331 8145
e: courseinfo@gre.ac.uk
// www.gre.ac.uk

LG11 BSc Mathematics and Economics
Duration: 3FT Hon
Entry Requirements: *GCE:* 260. *IB:* 24.

G1L1 BSc Mathematics with Economics
Duration: 3FT Hon
Entry Requirements: *GCE:* 260. *IB:* 24.

H24 HERIOT-WATT UNIVERSITY, EDINBURGH
EDINBURGH CAMPUS
EDINBURGH EH14 4AS
t: 0131 449 5111 f: 0131 451 3630
e: ugadmissions@hw.ac.uk
// www.hw.ac.uk

G1N3 BSc Mathematics with Finance
Duration: 3FT/4FT Hon
Entry Requirements: *GCE:* BBB. *SQAH:* ABBBC. *SQAAH:* BBB. *IB:* 26.

H36 UNIVERSITY OF HERTFORDSHIRE
UNIVERSITY ADMISSIONS SERVICE
COLLEGE LANE
HATFIELD
HERTS AL10 9AB
t: 01707 284800
// www.herts.ac.uk

L1G1 BSc Economics/Mathematics
Duration: 3FT/4SW Hon
Entry Requirements: *GCE:* 280.

GN13 BSc Financial Mathematics
Duration: 3FT/4SW Hon
Entry Requirements: *GCE:* 260.

G1L1 BSc Mathematics/Economics
Duration: 3FT/4SW Hon
Entry Requirements: *GCE:* 280.

K12 KEELE UNIVERSITY
KEELE UNIVERSITY
STAFFORDSHIRE ST5 5BG
t: 01782 734005 f: 01782 632343
e: undergraduate@keele.ac.uk
// www.keele.ac.uk

NG41 BSc Accounting and Mathematics
Duration: 3FT Hon
Entry Requirements: *GCE:* ABB.

GL11 BSc Economics and Mathematics
Duration: 3FT Hon
Entry Requirements: *GCE:* ABB.

GN13 BSc Finance and Mathematics
Duration: 3FT Hon
Entry Requirements: *GCE:* ABB.

K24 THE UNIVERSITY OF KENT
RECRUITMENT & ADMISSIONS OFFICE
REGISTRY
UNIVERSITY OF KENT
CANTERBURY, KENT CT2 7NZ
t: 01227 827272 f: 01227 827077
e: information@kent.ac.uk
// www.kent.ac.uk

GN14 BA Mathematics and Accounting & Finance (3 or 4 years)
Duration: 3FT/4SW Hon
Entry Requirements: *GCE:* 300. *IB:* 33. *OCR ND:* D *OCR NED:* M2

GN13 BSc Financial Mathematics
Duration: 3FT/4SW Hon
Entry Requirements: *GCE:* 300. *IB:* 33. *OCR ND:* D *OCR NED:* M2

L14 LANCASTER UNIVERSITY
THE UNIVERSITY
LANCASTER
LANCASHIRE LA1 4YW
t: 01524 592029 f: 01524 846243
e: ugadmissions@lancaster.ac.uk
// www.lancs.ac.uk

GL11 BA Economics and Mathematics
Duration: 3FT Hon
Entry Requirements: *GCE:* AAB. *SQAH:* ABBBB. *SQAAH:* ABB. *IB:* 35.

NG41 BSc Accounting, Finance and Mathematics
Duration: 3FT Hon
Entry Requirements: *GCE:* AAA. *SQAH:* AAABB. *SQAAH:* AAA. *IB:* 36.

GN13 BSc Financial Mathematics
Duration: 3FT Hon
Entry Requirements: *GCE:* AAA. *SQAH:* AAABB. *SQAAH:* AAA. *IB:* 36.

L23 UNIVERSITY OF LEEDS
THE UNIVERSITY OF LEEDS
WOODHOUSE LANE
LEEDS LS2 9JT
t: 0113 343 3999
e: admissions@leeds.ac.uk
// www.leeds.ac.uk

NG31 BSc Actuarial Mathematics
Duration: 3FT Hon
Entry Requirements: *GCE:* AAB. *SQAAH:* AAB. *IB:* 34.

GL11 BSc Economics and Mathematics
Duration: 3FT Hon
Entry Requirements: *GCE:* AAB. *SQAAH:* AAB.

G1N3 BSc Mathematics with Finance
Duration: 3FT Hon
Entry Requirements: *GCE:* AAB. *SQAAH:* AAB. *IB:* 34.

L34 UNIVERSITY OF LEICESTER
UNIVERSITY ROAD
LEICESTER LE1 7RH
t: 0116 252 5281 f: 0116 252 2447
e: admissions@le.ac.uk
// www.le.ac.uk

GN13 BSc Financial Mathematics
Duration: 3FT Hon
Entry Requirements: *GCE:* AAB. *SQAH:* AAAAB-AAABB. *SQAAH:* AAB. *IB:* 34.

G1L1 BSc Mathematics with Economics
Duration: 3FT Hon
Entry Requirements: *GCE:* AAB. *SQAH:* AAAAB-AAABB. *SQAAH:* AAB. *IB:* 34.

L41 THE UNIVERSITY OF LIVERPOOL
THE FOUNDATION BUILDING
BROWNLOW HILL
LIVERPOOL L69 7ZX
t: 0151 794 2000 f: 0151 708 6502
e: ugrecruitment@liv.ac.uk
// www.liv.ac.uk

GL11 BA Economics and Mathematics
Duration: 3FT Hon
Entry Requirements: *GCE:* ABB. *SQAAH:* ABB. *IB:* 33. Interview required.

G1N3 BSc Mathematics with Finance
Duration: 3FT Hon
Entry Requirements: *GCE:* ABB. *SQAAH:* ABB. *IB:* 33. Interview required.

L46 LIVERPOOL HOPE UNIVERSITY
HOPE PARK
LIVERPOOL L16 9JD
t: 0151 291 3331 f: 0151 291 3434
e: administration@hope.ac.uk
// www.hope.ac.uk

NG41 BSc Accounting and Mathematics
Duration: 3FT Hon
Entry Requirements: *GCE:* 300-320. *IB:* 25.

L68 LONDON METROPOLITAN UNIVERSITY
166-220 HOLLOWAY ROAD
LONDON N7 8DB
t: 020 7133 4200
e: admissions@londonmet.ac.uk
// www.londonmet.ac.uk

NG31 BSc Financial Mathematics
Duration: 3FT Hon
Entry Requirements: *GCE:* 200. *IB:* 28.

L72 LONDON SCHOOL OF ECONOMICS AND POLITICAL SCIENCE (UNIVERSITY OF LONDON)
HOUGHTON STREET
LONDON WC2A 2AE
t: 020 7955 7125 f: 020 7955 6001
e: ug.admissions@lse.ac.uk
// www.lse.ac.uk

GL11 BSc Mathematics and Economics
Duration: 3FT Hon
Entry Requirements: *GCE:* A*AA. *SQAH:* AAAAA. *SQAAH:* AAA. *IB:* 38.

G1L1 BSc Mathematics with Economics
Duration: 3FT Hon
Entry Requirements: *GCE:* A*AA. *SQAH:* AAAAA. *SQAAH:* AAA. *IB:* 38.

G3N3 BSc Statistics with Finance
Duration: 3FT Hon
Entry Requirements: *GCE:* AAA. *SQAH:* AAAAA. *SQAAH:* AAA. *IB:* 38.

L79 LOUGHBOROUGH UNIVERSITY
LOUGHBOROUGH
LEICESTERSHIRE LE11 3TU
t: 01509 223522 f: 01509 223905
e: admissions@lboro.ac.uk
// www.lboro.ac.uk

GN13 BSc Financial Mathematics
Duration: 3FT Hon
Entry Requirements: *GCE:* AAA-AAB. *SQAH:* ABB. *SQAAH:* AA. *IB:* 36.

GNC3 BSc Financial Mathematics
Duration: 4SW Hon
Entry Requirements: *GCE:* AAA-AAB. *SQAH:* ABB. *SQAAH:* AA. *IB:* 36.

G1N4 BSc Mathematics and Accounting and Financial Management
Duration: 3FT Hon
Entry Requirements: *GCE:* AAA-AAB. *SQAH:* ABB. *SQAAH:* AA. *IB:* 36.

G1NK BSc Mathematics and Accounting and Financial Management
Duration: 4SW Hon
Entry Requirements: *GCE:* AAA-AAB. *SQAH:* ABB. *SQAAH:* AA. *IB:* 36.

G1L1 BSc Mathematics with Economics
Duration: 3FT Hon
Entry Requirements: *GCE:* AAA-AAB. *SQAH:* ABB. *SQAAH:* AA. *IB:* 36.

G1LC BSc Mathematics with Economics
Duration: 4SW Hon
Entry Requirements: *GCE:* AAA-AAB. *SQAH:* ABB. *SQAAH:* AA. *IB:* 36.

M20 THE UNIVERSITY OF MANCHESTER
RUTHERFORD BUILDING
OXFORD ROAD
MANCHESTER M13 9PL
t: 0161 275 2077 f: 0161 275 2106
e: ug-admissions@manchester.ac.uk
// www.manchester.ac.uk

NG31 BSc Actuarial Science and Mathematics
Duration: 3FT Hon
Entry Requirements: *GCE:* A*AB-AAB. *SQAH:* AAAAB. *SQAAH:* AAB. *IB:* 36. Interview required.

G1N3 BSc Mathematics with Finance
Duration: 3FT Hon
Entry Requirements: *GCE:* A*AB-AAB. *SQAH:* AAAAB. *SQAAH:* AAB. *IB:* 36. Interview required.

G1NH BSc Mathematics with Financial Mathematics
Duration: 3FT Hon
Entry Requirements: *GCE:* A*AB-AAB. *SQAH:* AAAAB. *SQAAH:* AAB. *IB:* 36. Interview required.

G1NJ MMath Mathematics with Financial Mathematics
Duration: 4FT Hon
Entry Requirements: *GCE:* A*AB-AAB. *SQAH:* AAAAB. *SQAAH:* AAB. *IB:* 36. Interview required.

M40 THE MANCHESTER METROPOLITAN UNIVERSITY
ADMISSIONS OFFICE
ALL SAINTS (GMS)
ALL SAINTS
MANCHESTER M15 6BH
t: 0161 247 2000
// www.mmu.ac.uk

GL11 BA/BSc Economics/Mathematics
Duration: 3FT Hon
Entry Requirements: *GCE:* 240-280. *IB:* 29.

N21 NEWCASTLE UNIVERSITY
KING'S GATE
NEWCASTLE UPON TYNE NE1 7RU
t: 01912083333
// www.ncl.ac.uk

NG41 BSc Accounting and Mathematics
Duration: 3FT Hon
Entry Requirements: *GCE:* AAB. *SQAH:* AAABB. *IB:* 35.

GL11 BSc Economics and Mathematics
Duration: 3FT Hon
Entry Requirements: *GCE:* AAB. *SQAH:* AAABB. *IB:* 35.

GN13 BSc Financial Mathematics
Duration: 3FT Hon
Entry Requirements: *GCE:* AAB. *SQAAH:* AB.

N84 THE UNIVERSITY OF NOTTINGHAM
THE ADMISSIONS OFFICE
THE UNIVERSITY OF NOTTINGHAM
UNIVERSITY PARK
NOTTINGHAM NG7 2RD
t: 0115 951 5151 f: 0115 951 4668
// www.nottingham.ac.uk

GL11 BSc Mathematics and Economics
Duration: 3FT Hon
Entry Requirements: *GCE:* AAA. *SQAAH:* AAA. *IB:* 38.

N91 NOTTINGHAM TRENT UNIVERSITY
DRYDEN BUILDING
BURTON STREET
NOTTINGHAM NG1 4BU
t: +44 (0) 115 848 4200 f: +44 (0) 115 848 8869
e: applications@ntu.ac.uk
// www.ntu.ac.uk

GN13 BSc Financial Mathematics
Duration: 3FT/4SW Hon
Entry Requirements: *GCE:* 280. *BTEC Dip:* D*D*. *BTEC ExtDip:* DMM. *OCR NED:* M2

P60 PLYMOUTH UNIVERSITY
DRAKE CIRCUS
PLYMOUTH PL4 8AA
t: 01752 585858 f: 01752 588055
e: admissions@plymouth.ac.uk
// www.plymouth.ac.uk

G1N3 BSc Mathematics with Finance
Duration: 3FT Hon
Entry Requirements: *GCE:* 320. *IB:* 30.

Q50 QUEEN MARY, UNIVERSITY OF LONDON
QUEEN MARY, UNIVERSITY OF LONDON
MILE END ROAD
LONDON E1 4NS
t: 020 7882 5555 f: 020 7882 5500
e: admissions@qmul.ac.uk
// www.qmul.ac.uk

G1N4 BSc Mathematics with Finance & Accounting
Duration: 3FT Hon
Entry Requirements: *GCE:* 340. *IB:* 36.

GN13 BSc Mathematics, Business Management and Finance
Duration: 3FT Hon
Entry Requirements: *GCE:* 340. *IB:* 36.

GL11 BSc Mathematics, Statistics and Financial Economics
Duration: 3FT Hon
Entry Requirements: *GCE:* AAB. *IB:* 36.

LG11 BScEcon Economics, Statistics and Mathematics
Duration: 3FT Hon
Entry Requirements: *GCE:* AAB. *SQAAH:* AAB. *IB:* 36.

Q75 QUEEN'S UNIVERSITY BELFAST
UNIVERSITY ROAD
BELFAST BT7 1NN
t: 028 9097 3838 f: 028 9097 5151
e: admissions@qub.ac.uk
// www.qub.ac.uk

G1N3 BSc Mathematics with Finance
Duration: 3FT Hon
Entry Requirements: Contact the institution for details.

R12 THE UNIVERSITY OF READING
THE UNIVERSITY OF READING
PO BOX 217
READING RG6 6AH
t: 0118 378 8619 f: 0118 378 8924
e: student.recruitment@reading.ac.uk
// www.reading.ac.uk

GL11 BSc Mathematics and Economics
Duration: 3FT Hon
Entry Requirements: *GCE:* 320-340.

G1N3 BSc Mathematics with Finance and Investment Banking
Duration: 3FT Hon
Entry Requirements: *GCE:* 360. *SQAH:* AAABB. *SQAAH:* AAB. *BTEC Dip:* DD. *BTEC ExtDip:* DDD. *OCR ND:* D *OCR NED:* M3

R72 ROYAL HOLLOWAY, UNIVERSITY OF LONDON
ROYAL HOLLOWAY, UNIVERSITY OF LONDON
EGHAM
SURREY TW20 0EX
t: 01784 414944 f: 01784 473662
e: Admissions@rhul.ac.uk
// www.rhul.ac.uk

LG11 BSc Economics and Mathematics
Duration: 3FT Hon
Entry Requirements: *GCE:* AAB. *IB:* 35.

NG31 BSc Finance and Mathematics
Duration: 3FT Hon
Entry Requirements: *GCE:* AAB. *IB:* 35.

S18 THE UNIVERSITY OF SHEFFIELD
THE UNIVERSITY OF SHEFFIELD
LEVEL 2, ARTS TOWER
WESTERN BANK
SHEFFIELD S10 2TN
t: 0114 222 8030 f: 0114 222 8032
// www.sheffield.ac.uk

NG41 BA Accounting & Financial Management and Mathematics
Duration: 3FT Hon
Entry Requirements: *GCE:* AAB. *SQAH:* AAABB. *SQAAH:* AB. *IB:* 35. *BTEC ExtDip:* DDD.

LG11 BSc Economics and Mathematics
Duration: 3FT Hon
Entry Requirements: *GCE:* AAB. *SQAH:* AAABB. *SQAAH:* AB. *IB:* 35. *BTEC Dip:* DD. *BTEC ExtDip:* DDD.

GN13 BSc Financial Mathematics
Duration: 3FT Hon
Entry Requirements: *GCE:* AAB. *SQAH:* AAABB. *SQAAH:* AB. *IB:* 35. *BTEC ExtDip:* DDD.

S27 UNIVERSITY OF SOUTHAMPTON
HIGHFIELD
SOUTHAMPTON SO17 1BJ
t: 023 8059 4732 f: 023 8059 3037
e: admissions@soton.ac.uk
// www.southampton.ac.uk

G1N3 BSc Mathematics with Actuarial Science
Duration: 3FT Hon
Entry Requirements: *GCE:* AAA-AAB. *SQAH:* AAAAA. *SQAAH:* AA. *IB:* 36.

G1NH BSc Mathematics with Finance
Duration: 3FT Hon
Entry Requirements: *GCE:* AAA-AAB. *SQAH:* AAAAA. *SQAAH:* AA. *IB:* 36.

GL12 BSc Mathematics, Operational Research, Statistics and Economics
Duration: 3FT Hon
Entry Requirements: *GCE:* AAA-AAB. *SQAH:* AAAAA. *SQAAH:* AA. *IB:* 36.

S36 UNIVERSITY OF ST ANDREWS
ST KATHARINE'S WEST
16 THE SCORES
ST ANDREWS
FIFE KY16 9AX
t: 01334 462150 f: 01334 463330
e: admissions@st-andrews.ac.uk
// www.st-andrews.ac.uk

GLC1 BSc Economics and Mathematics
Duration: 4FT Hon
Entry Requirements: *GCE:* AAA. *SQAH:* AAAB. *IB:* 38.

GL31 BSc Economics and Statistics
Duration: 4FT Hon
Entry Requirements: *GCE:* AAA. *SQAH:* AAAB. *IB:* 38.

GL11 MA Economics and Mathematics
Duration: 4FT Hon
Entry Requirements: *GCE:* AAA. *SQAH:* AAAB. *IB:* 38.

GLH1 MA Economics and Statistics
Duration: 4FT Hon
Entry Requirements: *GCE:* AAA. *SQAH:* AAAB. *IB:* 38.

S75 THE UNIVERSITY OF STIRLING

STUDENT RECRUITMENT & ADMISSIONS SERVICE
UNIVERSITY OF STIRLING
STIRLING
SCOTLAND FK9 4LA
t: 01786 467044 f: 01786 466800
e: admissions@stir.ac.uk
// www.stir.ac.uk

GL11 BA Economics and Mathematics
Duration: 4FT Hon
Entry Requirements: *GCE:* BBC. *SQAH:* BBBB. *SQAAH:* AAA-CCC.
IB: 32. *BTEC ExtDip:* DMM.

GN13 BA Finance and Mathematics
Duration: 4FT Hon
Entry Requirements: *GCE:* BBC. *SQAH:* BBBB. *SQAAH:* AAA-CCC.
IB: 32. *BTEC ExtDip:* DMM.

GN14 BAcc Accountancy and Mathematics
Duration: 4FT Hon
Entry Requirements: *GCE:* BBC. *SQAH:* BBBB. *SQAAH:* AAA-CCC.
IB: 32. *BTEC ExtDip:* DMM.

S78 THE UNIVERSITY OF STRATHCLYDE

GLASGOW G1 1XQ
t: 0141 552 4400 f: 0141 552 0775
// www.strath.ac.uk

NG42 BA Accounting and Business Technology
Duration: 4FT Hon
Entry Requirements: *GCE:* AAA. *SQAH:* AAAAAB-AAAA. *IB:* 36.

GN24 BA Accounting and Management Science
Duration: 4FT Hon
Entry Requirements: *GCE:* AAA. *SQAH:* AAAAAB-AAAA. *IB:* 36.

NG41 BA Accounting and Mathematics & Statistics
Duration: 4FT Hon
Entry Requirements: *GCE:* AAA. *SQAH:* AAAAAB-AAAA. *IB:* 36.

GL21 BA Business Technology and Economics
Duration: 4FT Hon
Entry Requirements: *GCE:* AAB. *SQAH:* AAAABB-AAAB. *IB:* 36.

GN23 BA Business Technology and Finance
Duration: 4FT Hon
Entry Requirements: *GCE:* AAB. *SQAH:* AAAABB-AAAB. *IB:* 36.

LG12 BA Economics and Management Science
Duration: 4FT Hon
Entry Requirements: *GCE:* AAB. *SQAH:* AAAABB-AAAB. *IB:* 36.

LG1C BA Economics, Mathematics and Statistics
Duration: 4FT Hon
Entry Requirements: *GCE:* AAB. *SQAH:* AAAABB-AAAB. *IB:* 36.

NG32 BA Finance and Management Science
Duration: 4FT Hon
Entry Requirements: *GCE:* AAB. *SQAH:* AAAABB-AAAB. *IB:* 36.

NG33 BA Finance, Mathematics and Statistics
Duration: 4FT Hon
Entry Requirements: *GCE:* AAB. *SQAH:* AAAABB-AAAB. *IB:* 36.

GN34 BSc Mathematics, Statistics and Accounting
Duration: 4FT Hon
Entry Requirements: *GCE:* AAB. *SQAH:* AAAABB-AAAA. *IB:* 36.

G1L1 BSc Mathematics, Statistics and Economics
Duration: 4FT Hon
Entry Requirements: *GCE:* AAB-BBB. *SQAH:* ABBBC-ABBB. *IB:* 32.

GN33 BSc Mathematics, Statistics and Finance
Duration: 4FT Hon
Entry Requirements: *GCE:* AAB-BBB. *SQAH:* ABBBC-ABBB. *IB:* 32.

S90 UNIVERSITY OF SUSSEX

UNDERGRADUATE ADMISSIONS
SUSSEX HOUSE
UNIVERSITY OF SUSSEX
BRIGHTON BN1 9RH
t: 01273 678416 f: 01273 678545
e: ug.applicants@sussex.ac.uk
// www.sussex.ac.uk

G1L1 BSc Mathematics with Economics
Duration: 3FT Hon
Entry Requirements: *GCE:* AAA-AAB. *SQAH:* AAAAA-AAABB.
SQAAH: AAB. *IB:* 35. *BTEC SubDip:* D. *BTEC Dip:* DD. *BTEC ExtDip:* DDD. *OCR ND:* D *OCR NED:* D1

G1LC MMath Mathematics with Economics
Duration: 4FT Hon
Entry Requirements: *GCE:* AAA. *SQAH:* AAAAA. *SQAAH:* AAA. *IB:* 35. *BTEC SubDip:* D. *BTEC Dip:* DD. *BTEC ExtDip:* DDD. *OCR ND:* D *OCR NED:* D1

S93 SWANSEA UNIVERSITY

SINGLETON PARK
SWANSEA SA2 8PP
t: 01792 295111 f: 01792 295110
e: admissions@swansea.ac.uk
// www.swansea.ac.uk

G3N3 BSc Actuarial Studies
Duration: 3FT Hon
Entry Requirements: *GCE:* ABB. *IB:* 33.

G3NH BSc Actuarial Studies (with a year abroad) (4 years)
Duration: 4FT Hon
Entry Requirements: *GCE:* ABB. *IB:* 33.

G3NK BSc Actuarial Studies with Accounting
Duration: 3FT Hon
Entry Requirements: *GCE:* ABB. *IB:* 33.

G3N4 BSc Actuarial Studies with Accounting with a year abroad
Duration: 4FT Hon
Entry Requirements: *GCE:* ABB. *IB:* 33.

GL11 BSc Economics and Mathematics
Duration: 3FT Hon
Entry Requirements: *GCE:* ABB. *IB:* 33.

U80 UNIVERSITY COLLEGE LONDON (UNIVERSITY OF LONDON)
GOWER STREET
LONDON WC1E 6BT
t: 020 7679 3000 f: 020 7679 3001
// www.ucl.ac.uk

G1L1 BSc Mathematics with Economics
Duration: 3FT Hon
Entry Requirements: *GCE:* A*A*Ae-A*AAe. *SQAAH:* AAA. Interview required. Admissions Test required.

GLN0 BSc Statistics, Economics and Finance
Duration: 3FT Hon
Entry Requirements: *GCE:* A*AAe-AAAe. *SQAAH:* AAA. Interview required.

LG13 BScEcon Economics and Statistics
Duration: 3FT Hon
Entry Requirements: *GCE:* A*AAe-AAAe. *SQAAH:* AAA. Interview required.

G1LC MSci Mathematics with Economics
Duration: 4FT Hon
Entry Requirements: *GCE:* A*A*Ae-A*AAe. *SQAAH:* AAA. Interview required. Admissions Test required.

W20 THE UNIVERSITY OF WARWICK
COVENTRY CV4 8UW
t: 024 7652 3723 f: 024 7652 4649
e: ugadmissions@warwick.ac.uk
// www.warwick.ac.uk

GL11 BSc Mathematics and Economics
Duration: 3FT Hon
Entry Requirements: *GCE:* A*A*Aa-A*AA. *SQAH:* AAABB. *SQAAH:* AA. *IB:* 39.

GLN0 BSc Mathematics, Operational Research, Statistics, Economics
Duration: 3FT Hon
Entry Requirements: *SQAAH:* AA. Interview required.

G0L0 BSc.MMORSE Mathematics, Operational Research, Statistics and Economics
Duration: 4FT Hon
Entry Requirements: *SQAAH:* AA. Interview required.

Y50 THE UNIVERSITY OF YORK
STUDENT RECRUITMENT AND ADMISSIONS
UNIVERSITY OF YORK
HESLINGTON
YORK YO10 5DD
t: 01904 324000 f: 01904 323538
e: ug-admissions@york.ac.uk
// www.york.ac.uk

LG11 BA/BSc Economics/Mathematics (Equal)
Duration: 3FT Hon
Entry Requirements: *GCE:* AAA-AAB. *SQAH:* AAAAA-AAAAB. *SQAAH:* AA-AB. *IB:* 36.

GL11 BSc Mathematics / Finance (Equal)
Duration: 3FT Hon
Entry Requirements: *GCE:* AAB. *SQAH:* AAAAB. *SQAAH:* AB. *IB:* 35.

POLITICS COMBINATIONS

A20 THE UNIVERSITY OF ABERDEEN
UNIVERSITY OFFICE
KING'S COLLEGE
ABERDEEN AB24 3FX
t: +44 (0) 1224 273504 f: +44 (0) 1224 272034
e: sras@abdn.ac.uk
// www.abdn.ac.uk/sras

LLC2 MA Economics and International Relations
Duration: 4FT Hon
Entry Requirements: *GCE:* BBB. *SQAH:* BBBB. *IB:* 30.

LL12 MA Economics and Politics
Duration: 4FT Hon
Entry Requirements: *GCE:* BBB. *SQAH:* BBBB. *IB:* 30.

NLH2 MA Finance and International Relations
Duration: 4FT Hon
Entry Requirements: *GCE:* BBB. *SQAH:* BBBB. *IB:* 30.

NL32 MA Finance and Politics
Duration: 4FT Hon
Entry Requirements: *GCE:* BBB. *SQAH:* BBBB. *IB:* 30.

A40 ABERYSTWYTH UNIVERSITY
ABERYSTWYTH UNIVERSITY, WELCOME CENTRE
PENGLAIS CAMPUS
ABERYSTWYTH
CEREDIGION SY23 3FB
t: 01970 622021 f: 01970 627410
e: ug-admissions@aber.ac.uk
// www.aber.ac.uk

L1LF BScEcon Economics with International Politics
Duration: 3FT Hon
Entry Requirements: *GCE:* 300. *IB:* 27.

L1L2 BScEcon Economics with Politics
Duration: 3FT Hon
Entry Requirements: *GCE:* 300. *IB:* 27.

L2L1 BScEcon International Politics with Economics
Duration: 3FT Hon
Entry Requirements: *GCE:* 300. *IB:* 30.

B16 UNIVERSITY OF BATH
CLAVERTON DOWN
BATH BA2 7AY
t: 01225 383019 f: 01225 386366
e: admissions@bath.ac.uk
// www.bath.ac.uk

LL12 BSc Economics and Politics
Duration: 3FT Hon
Entry Requirements: *GCE:* A*AA. *SQAAH:* AAB. *IB:* 38.

LLC2 BSc Economics and Politics (Sandwich)
Duration: 4SW Hon
Entry Requirements: *GCE:* A*AA. *SQAAH:* AAB. *IB:* 38.

L2L1 BSc Politics with Economics
Duration: 3FT Hon
Entry Requirements: *GCE:* AAA. *SQAAH:* AAB. *IB:* 38.

L2LC BSc Politics with Economics (Sandwich)
Duration: 4SW Hon
Entry Requirements: *GCE:* AAA. *SQAAH:* AAB. *IB:* 38.

B32 THE UNIVERSITY OF BIRMINGHAM
EDGBASTON
BIRMINGHAM B15 2TT
t: 0121 415 8900 f: 0121 414 7159
e: admissions@bham.ac.uk
// www.birmingham.ac.uk

LL21 BA International Relations with Economics
Duration: 3FT Hon
Entry Requirements: *GCE:* AAB. *SQAH:* AABBB. *SQAAH:* AA.

LL12 BSc Economics and Political Science
Duration: 3FT Hon
Entry Requirements: *GCE:* AAA. *SQAH:* AAABB. *SQAAH:* AA.

LL2C BSc European Politics, Society and Economics
Duration: 3FT Hon
Entry Requirements: *GCE:* AAB-ABB. *SQAH:* AABBB-ABBBB. *SQAAH:* AA-AB.

B56 THE UNIVERSITY OF BRADFORD
RICHMOND ROAD
BRADFORD
WEST YORKSHIRE BD7 1DP
t: 0800 073 1225 f: 01274 235585
e: course-enquiries@bradford.ac.uk
// www.bradford.ac.uk

L1L2 BSc Economics with International Relations
Duration: 3FT Hon
Entry Requirements: *GCE:* 260-300. *IB:* 25.

B78 UNIVERSITY OF BRISTOL
UNDERGRADUATE ADMISSIONS OFFICE
SENATE HOUSE
TYNDALL AVENUE
BRISTOL BS8 1TH
t: 0117 928 9000 f: 0117 331 7391
e: ug-admissions@bristol.ac.uk
// www.bristol.ac.uk

LL12 BSc Economics and Politics
Duration: 3FT Hon
Entry Requirements: *GCE:* AAB. *SQAH:* AAAA. *SQAAH:* AA-AB.

B84 BRUNEL UNIVERSITY
UXBRIDGE
MIDDLESEX UB8 3PH
t: 01895 265265 f: 01895 269790
e: admissions@brunel.ac.uk
// www.brunel.ac.uk

LLC2 BSc Politics and Economics
Duration: 3FT Hon
Entry Requirements: *GCE:* AAB. *SQAAH:* AAB. *IB:* 35. *BTEC ExtDip:* D*D*D.

LL12 BSc Politics and Economics (4 year Thick SW)
Duration: 4SW Hon
Entry Requirements: *GCE:* AAB. *SQAAH:* AAB. *IB:* 35. *BTEC ExtDip:* D*D*D.

B90 THE UNIVERSITY OF BUCKINGHAM
YEOMANRY HOUSE
HUNTER STREET
BUCKINGHAM MK18 1EG
t: 01280 820313 f: 01280 822245
e: info@buckingham.ac.uk
// www.buckingham.ac.uk

LL21 BA Politics and Economics
Duration: 2FT Hon
Entry Requirements: *GCE:* BCC. *SQAH:* BBBC. *SQAAH:* BCC. *IB:* 31.

L1L2 BSc Economics with Politics
Duration: 2FT Hon
Entry Requirements: *GCE:* BBB. *SQAH:* ABBB. *SQAAH:* BBB. *IB:* 34.

C15 CARDIFF UNIVERSITY
PO BOX 927
30-36 NEWPORT ROAD
CARDIFF CF24 0DE
t: 029 2087 9999 f: 029 2087 6138
e: admissions@cardiff.ac.uk
// www.cardiff.ac.uk

LL12 BScEcon Politics and Economics
Duration: 3FT Hon
Entry Requirements: *GCE:* AAB. *SQAH:* AAABB. *SQAAH:* AAB. *IB:* 35. *OCR NED:* D2

D26 DE MONTFORT UNIVERSITY
THE GATEWAY
LEICESTER LE1 9BH
t: 0116 255 1551 f: 0116 250 6204
e: enquiries@dmu.ac.uk
// www.dmu.ac.uk

LL12 BA Economics and Politics
Duration: 3FT/4SW Hon
Entry Requirements: *GCE:* 280. *IB:* 28. *BTEC Dip:* D*D*. *BTEC ExtDip:* DMM. *OCR NED:* M2 Interview required.

D65 UNIVERSITY OF DUNDEE
NETHERGATE
DUNDEE DD1 4HN
t: 01382 383838 f: 01382 388150
e: contactus@dundee.ac.uk
// www.dundee.ac.uk/admissions/undergraduate/

LLD2 MA Economics and International Relations
Duration: 4FT Hon
Entry Requirements: *GCE:* BCC. *SQAH:* ABBB. *IB:* 30.

LL12 MA Economics and Politics
Duration: 4FT Hon
Entry Requirements: *GCE:* BCC. *SQAH:* ABBB. *IB:* 30.

D86 DURHAM UNIVERSITY
DURHAM UNIVERSITY
UNIVERSITY OFFICE
DURHAM DH1 3HP
t: 0191 334 2000 f: 0191 334 6055
e: admissions@durham.ac.uk
// www.durham.ac.uk

LL12 BA Economics and Politics
Duration: 3FT Hon
Entry Requirements: *GCE:* AAA. *SQAH:* AAAAB. *SQAAH:* AAA. *IB:* 37.

E14 UNIVERSITY OF EAST ANGLIA
NORWICH NR4 7TJ
t: 01603 591515 f: 01603 591523
e: admissions@uea.ac.uk
// www.uea.ac.uk

L2L1 BA International Development with Economics
Duration: 3FT Hon   CRB Check: Required
Entry Requirements: *GCE:* ABB. *SQAH:* ABB. *IB:* 32. *BTEC ExtDip:* DDM. Interview required.

L2LC BA International Development with Economics with Overseas Experience
Duration: 3FT Hon   CRB Check: Required
Entry Requirements: *GCE:* ABB. *SQAH:* ABB. *IB:* 32. *BTEC ExtDip:* DDM. Interview required.

L0V0 BA Philosophy, Politics and Economics
Duration: 3FT Hon   CRB Check: Required
Entry Requirements: *GCE:* ABB. *SQAH:* ABB. *IB:* 32. *BTEC ExtDip:* DDM. Interview required.

LL12 BSc Politics and Economics
Duration: 3FT Hon   CRB Check: Required
Entry Requirements: *GCE:* ABB. *SQAH:* ABB. *IB:* 32. *BTEC ExtDip:* DDM. Interview required.

E28 UNIVERSITY OF EAST LONDON
DOCKLANDS CAMPUS
UNIVERSITY WAY
LONDON E16 2RD
t: 020 8223 3333 f: 020 8223 2978
e: study@uel.ac.uk
// www.uel.ac.uk

L1L2 BA Business Economics with International Politics
Duration: 3FT Hon
Entry Requirements: *GCE:* 240. *IB:* 24.

LL12 BA Business Economics/International Politics
Duration: 3FT Hon
Entry Requirements: *GCE:* 240. *IB:* 24.

L2L1 BA International Politics with Business Economics
Duration: 3FT Hon
Entry Requirements: *GCE:* 240. *IB:* 24.

E56 THE UNIVERSITY OF EDINBURGH
STUDENT RECRUITMENT & ADMISSIONS
57 GEORGE SQUARE
EDINBURGH EH8 9JU
t: 0131 650 4360 f: 0131 651 1236
e: sra.enquiries@ed.ac.uk
// www.ed.ac.uk/studying/undergraduate/

LL12 MA Economics and Politics
Duration: 4FT Hon
Entry Requirements: *GCE:* AAA-BBB. *SQAH:* AAAA-BBBB. *IB:* 34.

E70 THE UNIVERSITY OF ESSEX
WIVENHOE PARK
COLCHESTER
ESSEX CO4 3SQ
t: 01206 873666 f: 01206 874477
e: admit@essex.ac.uk
// www.essex.ac.uk

LL12 BA Economics and Politics
Duration: 3FT Hon
Entry Requirements: *GCE:* AAB-ABB. *SQAH:* AAAA-AAAB.

LL1F BA Economics and Politics (Including Year Abroad)
Duration: 4FT Hon
Entry Requirements: *GCE:* AAB-ABB. *SQAH:* AAAA-AAAB.

L0VA BA Philosophy, Politics and Economics (Including Year Abroad)
Duration: 4SW Hon
Entry Requirements: *GCE:* AAB-ABB. *SQAH:* AAAA-AAAB.

E84 UNIVERSITY OF EXETER
LAVER BUILDING
NORTH PARK ROAD
EXETER
DEVON EX4 4QE
t: 01392 723044 f: 01392 722479
e: admissions@exeter.ac.uk
// www.exeter.ac.uk

LL12 BA Economics and Politics
Duration: 3FT Hon
Entry Requirements: *GCE:* A*AA-AAB. *SQAH:* AAAAA-AAABB.
SQAAH: AAA-ABB.

LL1F BA Economics and Politics with European Study (4 years)
Duration: 4FT Hon
Entry Requirements: *GCE:* A*AA-AAB. *SQAH:* AAAAA-AAABB.
SQAAH: AAA-ABB.

LL1G BA Economics and Politics with Industrial Experience (4 years)
Duration: 4FT Hon
Entry Requirements: *GCE:* A*AA-AAB. *SQAH:* AAAAA-AAABB.
SQAAH: AAA-ABB.

LLCF BA Economics and Politics with International Study (4 years)
Duration: 4FT Hon
Entry Requirements: *GCE:* A*AA-AAB. *SQAH:* AAAAA-AAABB.
SQAAH: AAA-ABB.

G28 UNIVERSITY OF GLASGOW
71 SOUTHPARK AVENUE
UNIVERSITY OF GLASGOW
GLASGOW G12 8QQ
t: 0141 330 6062 f: 0141 330 2961
e: student.recruitment@glasgow.ac.uk
// www.glasgow.ac.uk

LLC2 MA Business Economics/Politics
Duration: 4FT Hon
Entry Requirements: *GCE:* ABB. *SQAH:* AAAA-AABB. *IB:* 36.

LL12 MA Economics/Politics
Duration: 4FT Hon
Entry Requirements: *GCE:* ABB. *SQAH:* AAAA-AABB. *IB:* 36.

G56 GOLDSMITHS, UNIVERSITY OF LONDON
GOLDSMITHS, UNIVERSITY OF LONDON
NEW CROSS
LONDON SE14 6NW
t: 020 7048 5300 f: 020 7919 7509
e: admissions@gold.ac.uk
// www.gold.ac.uk

LL12 BA Economics, Politics and Public Policy
Duration: 3FT Hon
Entry Requirements: *GCE:* BBB. *SQAH:* BBBBC. *SQAAH:* BBC.
Interview required.

K12 KEELE UNIVERSITY
KEELE UNIVERSITY
STAFFORDSHIRE ST5 5BG
t: 01782 734005 f: 01782 632343
e: undergraduate@keele.ac.uk
// www.keele.ac.uk

NL42 BA Accounting and International Relations
Duration: 3FT Hon
Entry Requirements: *GCE:* ABB.

NL4F BA Accounting and Politics
Duration: 3FT Hon
Entry Requirements: *GCE:* ABB.

LLC2 BA Economics and International Relations
Duration: 3FT Hon
Entry Requirements: **GCE:** ABB.

LL12 BA Economics and Politics
Duration: 3FT Hon
Entry Requirements: **GCE:** ABB.

LN23 BA Finance and Politics
Duration: 3FT Hon
Entry Requirements: **GCE:** ABB.

K24 THE UNIVERSITY OF KENT
RECRUITMENT & ADMISSIONS OFFICE
REGISTRY
UNIVERSITY OF KENT
CANTERBURY, KENT CT2 7NZ
t: 01227 827272 f: 01227 827077
e: information@kent.ac.uk
// www.kent.ac.uk

LL12 BA Economics and Politics
Duration: 3FT Hon
Entry Requirements: **GCE:** ABB. **SQAH:** AABBB. **SQAAH:** ABB. **IB:** 33. **OCR ND:** D **OCR NED:** D2

K84 KINGSTON UNIVERSITY
STUDENT INFORMATION & ADVICE CENTRE
COOPER HOUSE
40-46 SURBITON ROAD
KINGSTON UPON THAMES KT1 2HX
t: 0844 8552177 f: 020 8547 7080
e: aps@kingston.ac.uk
// www.kingston.ac.uk

LL12 BA Economics (Applied) and Human Rights
Duration: 3FT Hon
Entry Requirements: **GCE:** 240-360. **IB:** 24.

LLC2 BA Economics (Applied) and Politics
Duration: 3FT Hon
Entry Requirements: **GCE:** 240-360. **IB:** 24.

LLD2 BSc Economics (Applied) and International Relations
Duration: 3FT Hon
Entry Requirements: **GCE:** 220-320.

L14 LANCASTER UNIVERSITY
THE UNIVERSITY
LANCASTER
LANCASHIRE LA1 4YW
t: 01524 592029 f: 01524 846243
e: ugadmissions@lancaster.ac.uk
// www.lancs.ac.uk

LL12 BA Economics and International Relations
Duration: 3FT Hon
Entry Requirements: **GCE:** AAB. **SQAH:** ABBBB. **SQAAH:** AAB. **IB:** 35.

LL21 BA Economics and Politics
Duration: 3FT Hon
Entry Requirements: **GCE:** AAB. **SQAH:** ABBBB. **SQAAH:** AAB. **IB:** 35.

L23 UNIVERSITY OF LEEDS
THE UNIVERSITY OF LEEDS
WOODHOUSE LANE
LEEDS LS2 9JT
t: 0113 343 3999
e: admissions@leeds.ac.uk
// www.leeds.ac.uk

LL12 BA Economics and Politics
Duration: 3FT Hon
Entry Requirements: **GCE:** AAB. **SQAAH:** AAB. **IB:** 36.

L34 UNIVERSITY OF LEICESTER
UNIVERSITY ROAD
LEICESTER LE1 7RH
t: 0116 252 5281 f: 0116 252 2447
e: admissions@le.ac.uk
// www.le.ac.uk

LL12 BA Politics and Economics
Duration: 3FT Hon
Entry Requirements: **GCE:** ABB. **SQAH:** AABBB. **SQAAH:** ABB. **IB:** 32.

L46 LIVERPOOL HOPE UNIVERSITY
HOPE PARK
LIVERPOOL L16 9JD
t: 0151 291 3331 f: 0151 291 3434
e: administration@hope.ac.uk
// www.hope.ac.uk

NL42 BA Accounting and International Relations
Duration: 3FT Hon
Entry Requirements: **GCE:** 300-320. **IB:** 25.

NL24 BA Accounting and Politics
Duration: 3FT Hon
Entry Requirements: **GCE:** 300-320. **IB:** 25.

L72 LONDON SCHOOL OF ECONOMICS AND POLITICAL SCIENCE (UNIVERSITY OF LONDON)
HOUGHTON STREET
LONDON WC2A 2AE
t: 020 7955 7125 f: 020 7955 6001
e: ug.admissions@lse.ac.uk
// www.lse.ac.uk

LL12 BSc Government and Economics
Duration: 3FT Hon
Entry Requirements: *GCE:* AAA. *SQAH:* AAAAA. *SQAAH:* AAA. *IB:* 38.

L79 LOUGHBOROUGH UNIVERSITY
LOUGHBOROUGH
LEICESTERSHIRE LE11 3TU
t: 01509 223522 f: 01509 223905
e: admissions@lboro.ac.uk
// www.lboro.ac.uk

L1L2 BSc Economics with Politics
Duration: 3FT Hon
Entry Requirements: *GCE:* AAB. *SQAH:* AABBB. *SQAAH:* AB. *IB:* 34. *BTEC ExtDip:* DDD.

M20 THE UNIVERSITY OF MANCHESTER
RUTHERFORD BUILDING
OXFORD ROAD
MANCHESTER M13 9PL
t: 0161 275 2077 f: 0161 275 2106
e: ug-admissions@manchester.ac.uk
// www.manchester.ac.uk

LL12 BA Economics and Politics
Duration: 3FT Hon
Entry Requirements: *GCE:* AAB. *SQAH:* AAABB. *SQAAH:* AAB.

M40 THE MANCHESTER METROPOLITAN UNIVERSITY
ADMISSIONS OFFICE
ALL SAINTS (GMS)
ALL SAINTS
MANCHESTER M15 6BH
t: 0161 247 2000
// www.mmu.ac.uk

LL1G BA Economics/Politics
Duration: 3FT Hon
Entry Requirements: *GCE:* 240-280. *IB:* 29.

N21 NEWCASTLE UNIVERSITY
KING'S GATE
NEWCASTLE UPON TYNE NE1 7RU
t: 01912083333
// www.ncl.ac.uk

LL21 BA Politics and Economics
Duration: 3FT Hon
Entry Requirements: *GCE:* AAB-ABB. *SQAH:* AAABB-AABBB.

N38 UNIVERSITY OF NORTHAMPTON
PARK CAMPUS
BOUGHTON GREEN ROAD
NORTHAMPTON NN2 7AL
t: 0800 358 2232 f: 01604 722083
e: admissions@northampton.ac.uk
// www.northampton.ac.uk

N4L2 BA Accounting/Politics
Duration: 3FT Hon
Entry Requirements: *GCE:* 260-280. *SQAH:* AAA-BBBB. *IB:* 24. *BTEC Dip:* DD. *BTEC ExtDip:* DMM. *OCR ND:* D *OCR NED:* M2

L2N4 BA Politics/Accounting
Duration: 3FT Hon
Entry Requirements: *GCE:* 260-280. *SQAH:* AAA-BBBB. *IB:* 24. *BTEC Dip:* DD. *BTEC ExtDip:* DMM. *OCR ND:* D *OCR NED:* M2

N84 THE UNIVERSITY OF NOTTINGHAM
THE ADMISSIONS OFFICE
THE UNIVERSITY OF NOTTINGHAM
UNIVERSITY PARK
NOTTINGHAM NG7 2RD
t: 0115 951 5151 f: 0115 951 4668
// www.nottingham.ac.uk

LL21 BA Politics and Economics
Duration: 3FT Hon
Entry Requirements: *GCE:* AAA. *SQAAH:* AAA. *IB:* 36.

O33 OXFORD UNIVERSITY
UNDERGRADUATE ADMISSIONS OFFICE
UNIVERSITY OF OXFORD
WELLINGTON SQUARE
OXFORD OX1 2JD
t: 01865 288000 f: 01865 270212
e: undergraduate.admissions@admin.ox.ac.uk
// www.admissions.ox.ac.uk

L0V0 BA Philosophy, Politics and Economics
Duration: 3FT Hon
Entry Requirements: *GCE:* AAA. *SQAH:* AAAAA-AAAAB. *SQAAH:* AAB. Interview required. Admissions Test required.

O66 OXFORD BROOKES UNIVERSITY
ADMISSIONS OFFICE
HEADINGTON CAMPUS
GIPSY LANE
OXFORD OX3 0BP
t: 01865 483040 f: 01865 483983
e: admissions@brookes.ac.uk
// www.brookes.ac.uk

LL21 BA Economics, Politics and International Relations
Duration: 3FT Hon
Entry Requirements: *GCE:* BBC. *IB:* 30. *BTEC ExtDip:* DMM.

LN13 BSc Economics, Finance and International Business
Duration: 3FT/4SW Hon
Entry Requirements: *GCE:* BBC.

P60 PLYMOUTH UNIVERSITY
DRAKE CIRCUS
PLYMOUTH PL4 8AA
t: 01752 585858 f: 01752 588055
e: admissions@plymouth.ac.uk
// www.plymouth.ac.uk

L1LA BSc Economics with International Relations
Duration: 3FT/4SW Hon
Entry Requirements: *GCE:* 240. *IB:* 24.

L1LB BSc Economics with Politics
Duration: 3FT/4SW Hon
Entry Requirements: *GCE:* 240. *IB:* 24.

L2LD BSc International Relations with Economics
Duration: 3FT Hon
Entry Requirements: *GCE:* 240. *IB:* 24.

Q50 QUEEN MARY, UNIVERSITY OF LONDON
QUEEN MARY, UNIVERSITY OF LONDON
MILE END ROAD
LONDON E1 4NS
t: 020 7882 5555 f: 020 7882 5500
e: admissions@qmul.ac.uk
// www.qmul.ac.uk

LL12 BScEcon Economics and Politics
Duration: 3FT Hon
Entry Requirements: *GCE:* AAB. *SQAAH:* AAB. *IB:* 36.

Q75 QUEEN'S UNIVERSITY BELFAST
UNIVERSITY ROAD
BELFAST BT7 1NN
t: 028 9097 3838 f: 028 9097 5151
e: admissions@qub.ac.uk
// www.qub.ac.uk

LV00 BA Politics, Philosophy and Economics
Duration: 3FT Hon
Entry Requirements: *GCE:* AAB-ABBa. *SQAH:* AAABB. *SQAAH:* AAB. *IB:* 35.

R12 THE UNIVERSITY OF READING
THE UNIVERSITY OF READING
PO BOX 217
READING RG6 6AH
t: 0118 378 8619 f: 0118 378 8924
e: student.recruitment@reading.ac.uk
// www.reading.ac.uk

LL21 BA International Relations and Economics
Duration: 3FT Hon
Entry Requirements: *GCE:* ABC-BBB. *SQAH:* ABBBC-BBBBB. *SQAAH:* ABC-BBB.

LL12 BA Politics and Economics
Duration: 3FT Hon
Entry Requirements: *GCE:* ABC-BBB. *SQAH:* ABBBC-BBBBB. *SQAAH:* ABC-BBB.

R72 ROYAL HOLLOWAY, UNIVERSITY OF LONDON
ROYAL HOLLOWAY, UNIVERSITY OF LONDON
EGHAM
SURREY TW20 0EX
t: 01784 414944 f: 01784 473662
e: Admissions@rhul.ac.uk
// www.rhul.ac.uk

L1L2 BA Economics with Political Studies
Duration: 3FT Hon
Entry Requirements: *GCE:* AAA-ABB. *SQAH:* AAAAA-AABBB. *SQAAH:* AAA-ABB. *IB:* 32.

L0V0 BA/BSc Politics, Philosophy and Economics
Duration: 3FT Hon
Entry Requirements: *GCE:* AAA-AAB. *SQAH:* AAAAA-AABBB. *SQAAH:* AAA-AAB. *IB:* 35.

LL12 BSc Economics, Politics & International Relations
Duration: 3FT Hon
Entry Requirements: *GCE:* AAA-ABB. *SQAH:* AAAAA-AABBB. *SQAAH:* AAA-ABB. *IB:* 32.

R90 RUSKIN COLLEGE OXFORD
WALTON STREET
OXFORD OX1 2HE
t: 01865 759604 f: 01865 759640
e: admissions@ruskin.ac.uk
// www.ruskin.ac.uk

L001 BA Social and Political Studies
Duration: 3FT Ord
Entry Requirements: Contact the institution for details.

S09 SCHOOL OF ORIENTAL AND AFRICAN STUDIES (UNIVERSITY OF LONDON)
THORNHAUGH STREET
RUSSELL SQUARE
LONDON WC1H 0XG
t: 020 7898 4301 f: 020 7898 4039
e: undergradadmissions@soas.ac.uk
// www.soas.ac.uk

LL12 BA Politics and Economics
Duration: 3FT Hon
Entry Requirements: *GCE:* AAA.

S18 THE UNIVERSITY OF SHEFFIELD
THE UNIVERSITY OF SHEFFIELD
LEVEL 2, ARTS TOWER
WESTERN BANK
SHEFFIELD S10 2TN
t: 0114 222 8030 f: 0114 222 8032
// www.sheffield.ac.uk

LL12 BA Economics and Politics
Duration: 3FT Hon
Entry Requirements: *GCE:* AAB. *SQAH:* AAABB. *SQAAH:* AB. *IB:* 35. *BTEC ExtDip:* DDD.

S27 UNIVERSITY OF SOUTHAMPTON
HIGHFIELD
SOUTHAMPTON SO17 1BJ
t: 023 8059 4732 f: 023 8059 3037
e: admissions@soton.ac.uk
// www.southampton.ac.uk

LL12 BSc Politics and Economics
Duration: 3FT Hon
Entry Requirements: *GCE:* AAB. *SQAH:* AAABB. *SQAAH:* AB. *IB:* 34.

S36 UNIVERSITY OF ST ANDREWS
ST KATHARINE'S WEST
16 THE SCORES
ST ANDREWS
FIFE KY16 9AX
t: 01334 462150 f: 01334 463330
e: admissions@st-andrews.ac.uk
// www.st-andrews.ac.uk

LL12 MA Economics and International Relations
Duration: 4FT Hon
Entry Requirements: *GCE:* AAA. *SQAH:* AAAA. *IB:* 38.

S75 THE UNIVERSITY OF STIRLING
STUDENT RECRUITMENT & ADMISSIONS SERVICE
UNIVERSITY OF STIRLING
STIRLING
SCOTLAND FK9 4LA
t: 01786 467044 f: 01786 466800
e: admissions@stir.ac.uk
// www.stir.ac.uk

LL12 BA Economics and Politics
Duration: 4FT Hon
Entry Requirements: *GCE:* BBC. *SQAH:* BBBB. *SQAAH:* AAA-CCC. *IB:* 32. *BTEC ExtDip:* DMM.

L0V0 BA Politics, Philosophy and Economics
Duration: 4FT Hon
Entry Requirements: *GCE:* BBC. *SQAH:* BBBB. *SQAAH:* AAA-CCC. *IB:* 32. *BTEC ExtDip:* DMM.

S78 THE UNIVERSITY OF STRATHCLYDE
GLASGOW G1 1XQ
t: 0141 552 4400 f: 0141 552 0775
// www.strath.ac.uk

LL21 BA Politics and Economics
Duration: 4FT Hon
Entry Requirements: *GCE:* ABB. *SQAH:* AAABB-AAAB. *IB:* 34.

S85 UNIVERSITY OF SURREY
STAG HILL
GUILDFORD
SURREY GU2 7XH
t: +44(0)1483 689305 f: +44(0)1483 689388
e: ugteam@surrey.ac.uk
// www.surrey.ac.uk

LL12 BSc Politics and Economics
Duration: 3FT/4SW Hon
Entry Requirements: *GCE:* AAA. *BTEC ExtDip:* DDD.

S90 UNIVERSITY OF SUSSEX
UNDERGRADUATE ADMISSIONS
SUSSEX HOUSE
UNIVERSITY OF SUSSEX
BRIGHTON BN1 9RH
t: 01273 678416 f: 01273 678545
e: ug.applicants@sussex.ac.uk
// www.sussex.ac.uk

LLC2 BA Economics and International Relations
Duration: 3FT Hon
Entry Requirements: *GCE:* AAB. *SQAH:* AAABB. *IB:* 35. *BTEC SubDip:* D. *BTEC Dip:* DD. *BTEC ExtDip:* DDD. *OCR ND:* D *OCR NED:* D1

LL12 BA Economics and Politics
Duration: 3FT Hon
Entry Requirements: *GCE:* AAB. *SQAH:* AAABB. *IB:* 35. *BTEC SubDip:* D. *BTEC Dip:* DD. *BTEC ExtDip:* DDD. *OCR ND:* D *OCR NED:* D1

L0V0 BA Philosophy, Politics and Economics
Duration: 3FT Hon
Entry Requirements: *GCE:* AAA. *SQAH:* AAAAA. *IB:* 36. *BTEC SubDip:* D. *BTEC Dip:* DD. *BTEC ExtDip:* DDD. *OCR ND:* D *OCR NED:* D1

S93 SWANSEA UNIVERSITY
SINGLETON PARK
SWANSEA SA2 8PP
t: 01792 295111 f: 01792 295110
e: admissions@swansea.ac.uk
// www.swansea.ac.uk

LL12 BA Economics and Politics
Duration: 3FT Hon
Entry Requirements: *GCE:* ABB. *IB:* 33.

L0V0 BA Philosophy, Politics and Economics
Duration: 3FT Hon
Entry Requirements: *GCE:* AAB. *IB:* 34.

W20 THE UNIVERSITY OF WARWICK
COVENTRY CV4 8UW
t: 024 7652 3723 f: 024 7652 4649
e: ugadmissions@warwick.ac.uk
// www.warwick.ac.uk

LLD2 BA Economics, Politics and International Studies
Duration: 3FT Hon
Entry Requirements: *GCE:* A*AAB-A*AAa. *SQAAH:* AA. *IB:* 38.

L0V0 BA/BSc Philosophy, Politics and Economics
Duration: 3FT Hon
Entry Requirements: *GCE:* AAAb. *SQAAH:* AA.

W50 UNIVERSITY OF WESTMINSTER
2ND FLOOR, CAVENDISH HOUSE
101 NEW CAVENDISH STREET,
LONDON W1W 6XH
t: 020 7915 5511
e: course-enquiries@westminster.ac.uk
// www.westminster.ac.uk

LL12 BA Development Studies and International Relations
Duration: 3FT Hon
Entry Requirements: *GCE:* BCC. *SQAH:* BBCCC. *SQAAH:* BCC. *IB:* 28.

Y50 THE UNIVERSITY OF YORK
STUDENT RECRUITMENT AND ADMISSIONS
UNIVERSITY OF YORK
HESLINGTON
YORK YO10 5DD
t: 01904 324000 f: 01904 323538
e: ug-admissions@york.ac.uk
// www.york.ac.uk

LL12 BA Economics/Politics (Equal)
Duration: 3FT Hon
Entry Requirements: *GCE:* AAA. *SQAH:* AAAAA. *SQAAH:* AA. *IB:* 36.

L0V0 BA Philosophy, Politics and Economics
Duration: 3FT Hon
Entry Requirements: *GCE:* A*AA-AAA. *SQAH:* AAAAA. *SQAAH:* AA. *IB:* 36. *BTEC ExtDip:* DDD.

SCIENCE COMBINATIONS

A20 THE UNIVERSITY OF ABERDEEN
UNIVERSITY OFFICE
KING'S COLLEGE
ABERDEEN AB24 3FX
t: +44 (0) 1224 273504 f: +44 (0) 1224 272034
e: sras@abdn.ac.uk
// www.abdn.ac.uk/sras

F1N4 BSc Chemistry with Accountancy
Duration: 4FT Hon
Entry Requirements: *GCE:* BBB. *SQAH:* BBBB. *IB:* 30.

LC18 MA Economics and Psychology
Duration: 4FT Hon
Entry Requirements: *GCE:* BBB. *SQAH:* BBBB. *IB:* 30.

B94 BUCKINGHAMSHIRE NEW UNIVERSITY
QUEEN ALEXANDRA ROAD
HIGH WYCOMBE
BUCKINGHAMSHIRE HP11 2JZ
t: 0800 0565 660 f: 01494 605 023
e: admissions@bucks.ac.uk
// bucks.ac.uk

CN63 BA Football Business and Finance
Duration: 3FT Hon
Entry Requirements: *GCE:* 200-240. *IB:* 24. *OCR ND:* M1 *OCR NED:* M3

D39 UNIVERSITY OF DERBY
KEDLESTON ROAD
DERBY DE22 1GB
t: 01332 591167 f: 01332 597724
e: askadmissions@derby.ac.uk
// www.derby.ac.uk

NC48 BA/BSc Accounting and Psychology
Duration: 3FT Hon
Entry Requirements: *Foundation:* Distinction. *GCE:* 260-300. *IB:* 28. *BTEC Dip:* D*D*. *BTEC ExtDip:* DMM. *OCR NED:* M2

E28 UNIVERSITY OF EAST LONDON
DOCKLANDS CAMPUS
UNIVERSITY WAY
LONDON E16 2RD
t: 020 8223 3333 f: 020 8223 2978
e: study@uel.ac.uk
// www.uel.ac.uk

LC18 BA Business Economics and Psychosocial Studies
Duration: 3FT Hon
Entry Requirements: *GCE:* 240.

E56 THE UNIVERSITY OF EDINBURGH
STUDENT RECRUITMENT & ADMISSIONS
57 GEORGE SQUARE
EDINBURGH EH8 9JU
t: 0131 650 4360 f: 0131 651 1236
e: sra.enquiries@ed.ac.uk
// www.ed.ac.uk/studying/undergraduate/

L1F9 MA Economics with Environmental Studies
Duration: 4FT Hon
Entry Requirements: *GCE:* AAA-BBB. *SQAH:* AAAA-BBBB. *IB:* 34.

G28 UNIVERSITY OF GLASGOW
71 SOUTHPARK AVENUE
UNIVERSITY OF GLASGOW
GLASGOW G12 8QQ
t: 0141 330 6062 f: 0141 330 2961
e: student.recruitment@glasgow.ac.uk
// www.glasgow.ac.uk

LC18 MA Business Economics/Psychology
Duration: 4FT Hon
Entry Requirements: *GCE:* ABB. *SQAH:* AAAA-AABB. *IB:* 36.

CL81 MA Economics/Psychology
Duration: 4FT Hon
Entry Requirements: *GCE:* ABB. *SQAH:* AAAA-AABB. *IB:* 36.

H36 UNIVERSITY OF HERTFORDSHIRE
UNIVERSITY ADMISSIONS SERVICE
COLLEGE LANE
HATFIELD
HERTS AL10 9AB
t: 01707 284800
// www.herts.ac.uk

L1B9 BSc Economics/Health Studies
Duration: 3FT/4SW Hon
Entry Requirements: *GCE:* 280.

L1B1 BSc Economics/Human Biology
Duration: 3FT/4SW Hon
Entry Requirements: *GCE:* 280.

L1C6 BSc Economics/Sports Studies
Duration: 3FT/4SW Hon
Entry Requirements: *GCE:* 280.

B9L1 BSc Health Studies/Economics
Duration: 3FT/4SW Hon
Entry Requirements: *GCE:* 280.

B1L1 BSc Human Biology/Economics
Duration: 3FT/4SW Hon
Entry Requirements: *GCE:* 280. *IB:* 25.

C6L1 BSc Sports Studies/Economics
Duration: 3FT/4SW Hon
Entry Requirements: *GCE:* 280.

K12 KEELE UNIVERSITY
KEELE UNIVERSITY
STAFFORDSHIRE ST5 5BG
t: 01782 734005 f: 01782 632343
e: undergraduate@keele.ac.uk
// www.keele.ac.uk

NC48 BSc Accounting and Applied Psychology
Duration: 4FT Hon
Entry Requirements: *GCE:* ABB.

NF45 BSc Accounting and Astrophysics
Duration: 3FT Hon
Entry Requirements: *GCE:* ABB.

NC47 BSc Accounting and Biochemistry
Duration: 3FT Hon
Entry Requirements: *GCE:* ABB.

NC41 BSc Accounting and Biology
Duration: 3FT Hon
Entry Requirements: *GCE:* ABB.

NF44 BSc Accounting and Forensic Science
Duration: 3FT Hon
Entry Requirements: *GCE:* ABB.

NB41 BSc Accounting and Neuroscience
Duration: 3FT Hon
Entry Requirements: *GCE:* ABB.

NF43 BSc Accounting and Physics
Duration: 3FT Hon
Entry Requirements: *GCE:* ABB.

NC4V BSc Accounting and Psychology
Duration: 3FT Hon
Entry Requirements: *GCE:* ABB.

FNX3 BSc Applied Environmental Science and Finance
Duration: 3FT Hon
Entry Requirements: *GCE:* ABB.

CL8C BSc Applied Psychology and Economics
Duration: 4FT Deg
Entry Requirements: *GCE:* ABB.

FL51 BSc Astrophysics and Economics
Duration: 3FT Hon
Entry Requirements: *GCE:* ABB.

CL71 BSc Biochemistry and Economics
Duration: 3FT Hon
Entry Requirements: *GCE:* ABB.

CN73 BSc Biochemistry and Finance
Duration: 3FT Hon
Entry Requirements: *GCE:* ABB.

CL11 BSc Biology and Economics
Duration: 3FT Hon
Entry Requirements: *GCE:* ABB.

CN13 BSc Biology and Finance
Duration: 3FT Hon
Entry Requirements: *GCE:* ABB.

FNC3 BSc Chemistry and Finance
Duration: 3FT Hon
Entry Requirements: *GCE:* ABB.

FL41 BSc Economics and Forensic Science
Duration: 3FT Hon
Entry Requirements: *GCE:* ABB.

LC1C BSc Economics and Human Biology
Duration: 3FT Hon
Entry Requirements: *GCE:* ABB.

BL11 BSc Economics and Neuroscience
Duration: 3FT Hon
Entry Requirements: *GCE:* ABB.

FL31 BSc Economics and Physics
Duration: 3FT Hon
Entry Requirements: *GCE:* ABB.

CL81 BSc Economics and Psychology
Duration: 3FT Hon
Entry Requirements: *GCE:* ABB.

NC3C BSc Finance and Human Biology
Duration: 3FT Hon
Entry Requirements: *GCE:* ABB.

FN13 BSc Finance and Medicinal Chemistry
Duration: 3FT Hon
Entry Requirements: *GCE:* ABB.

BN13 BSc Finance and Neuroscience
Duration: 3FT Hon
Entry Requirements: *GCE:* ABB.

K84 KINGSTON UNIVERSITY
STUDENT INFORMATION & ADVICE CENTRE
COOPER HOUSE
40-46 SURBITON ROAD
KINGSTON UPON THAMES KT1 2HX
t: 0844 8552177 f: 020 8547 7080
e: aps@kingston.ac.uk
// www.kingston.ac.uk

L1F9 BA Economics (Applied) with Environmental Studies
Duration: 3FT Hon
Entry Requirements: *GCE:* 220-320. *IB:* 24.

L46 LIVERPOOL HOPE UNIVERSITY
HOPE PARK
LIVERPOOL L16 9JD
t: 0151 291 3331 f: 0151 291 3434
e: administration@hope.ac.uk
// www.hope.ac.uk

N4C8 BA Accounting and Psychology
Duration: 3FT Hon
Entry Requirements: *GCE:* 300-320. *IB:* 25.

NC41 BSc Accounting and Biology
Duration: 3FT Hon
Entry Requirements: *GCE:* 300-320. *IB:* 25.

L72 LONDON SCHOOL OF ECONOMICS AND POLITICAL SCIENCE (UNIVERSITY OF LONDON)
HOUGHTON STREET
LONDON WC2A 2AE
t: 020 7955 7125 f: 020 7955 6001
e: ug.admissions@lse.ac.uk
// www.lse.ac.uk

F9L1 BSc Environmental Policy with Economics
Duration: 3FT Hon
Entry Requirements: *GCE:* AAB. *SQAH:* AAAAA-AAAAB. *SQAAH:* AAA-AAB. *IB:* 37.

M40 THE MANCHESTER METROPOLITAN UNIVERSITY
ADMISSIONS OFFICE
ALL SAINTS (GMS)
ALL SAINTS
MANCHESTER M15 6BH
t: 0161 247 2000
// www.mmu.ac.uk

NC36 BA/BSc Financial Management/Sport
Duration: 3FT Hon
Entry Requirements: *GCE:* 280. *IB:* 28. *BTEC Dip:* D*D*. *BTEC ExtDip:* DMM.

N38 UNIVERSITY OF NORTHAMPTON
PARK CAMPUS
BOUGHTON GREEN ROAD
NORTHAMPTON NN2 7AL
t: 0800 358 2232 f: 01604 722083
e: admissions@northampton.ac.uk
// www.northampton.ac.uk

N4C1 BA Accounting/Biological Conservation
Duration: 3FT Hon
Entry Requirements: *GCE:* 260-280. *SQAH:* AAA-BBBB. *IB:* 24. *BTEC Dip:* DD. *BTEC ExtDip:* DMM. *OCR ND:* D *OCR NED:* M2

N4C8 BA Accounting/Psychology
Duration: 3FT Hon
Entry Requirements: *GCE:* 260-280. *SQAH:* AAA-BBBB. *IB:* 24. *BTEC Dip:* DD. *BTEC ExtDip:* DMM. *OCR ND:* D *OCR NED:* M2

N4C6 BA Accounting/Sport Studies
Duration: 3FT Hon
Entry Requirements: *GCE:* 260-280. *SQAH:* AAA-BBBB. *IB:* 24. *BTEC Dip:* DD. *BTEC ExtDip:* DMM. *OCR ND:* D *OCR NED:* M2

N4FV BA Accounting/Wastes Management
Duration: 3FT Hon
Entry Requirements: *GCE:* 260-280. *SQAH:* AAA-BBBB. *IB:* 24. *BTEC Dip:* DD. *BTEC ExtDip:* DMM. *OCR ND:* D *OCR NED:* M2

L1C1 BA Economics/Biological Conservation
Duration: 3FT Hon
Entry Requirements: *GCE:* 260-280. *SQAH:* AAA-BBBB. *IB:* 24. *BTEC Dip:* DD. *BTEC ExtDip:* DMM. *OCR ND:* D *OCR NED:* M2

L1B1 BA Economics/Human Bioscience
Duration: 3FT Hon
Entry Requirements: *GCE:* 260-280. *SQAH:* AAA-BBBB. *IB:* 24. *BTEC Dip:* DD. *BTEC ExtDip:* DMM. *OCR ND:* D *OCR NED:* M2

L1C6 BA Economics/Sport Studies
Duration: 3FT Hon
Entry Requirements: *GCE:* 260-280. *SQAH:* AAA-BBBB. *IB:* 24. *BTEC Dip:* DD. *BTEC ExtDip:* DMM. *OCR ND:* D *OCR NED:* M2

C8N4 BA Psychology/Accounting
Duration: 3FT Hon
Entry Requirements: *GCE:* 260-280. *SQAH:* AAA-BBBB. *IB:* 24. *BTEC Dip:* DD. *BTEC ExtDip:* DMM. *OCR ND:* D *OCR NED:* M2

C6N4 BA Sport Studies/Accounting
Duration: 3FT Hon
Entry Requirements: *GCE:* 260-280. *SQAH:* AAA-BBBB. *IB:* 24. *BTEC Dip:* DD. *BTEC ExtDip:* DMM. *OCR ND:* D *OCR NED:* M2

C6L1 BA Sport Studies/Economics
Duration: 3FT Hon
Entry Requirements: *GCE:* 260-280. *SQAH:* AAA-BBBB. *IB:* 24. *BTEC Dip:* DD. *BTEC ExtDip:* DMM. *OCR ND:* D *OCR NED:* M2

C1N4 BSc Biological Conservation/Accounting
Duration: 3FT Hon
Entry Requirements: *GCE:* 260-280. *SQAH:* AAA-BBBB. *IB:* 24. *BTEC Dip:* DD. *BTEC ExtDip:* DMM. *OCR ND:* D *OCR NED:* M2

C1L1 BSc Biological Conservation/Economics
Duration: 3FT Hon
Entry Requirements: *GCE:* 260-280. *SQAH:* AAA-BBBB. *IB:* 24. *BTEC Dip:* DD. *BTEC ExtDip:* DMM. *OCR ND:* D *OCR NED:* M2

B1L1 BSc Human Bioscience/Economics
Duration: 3FT Hon
Entry Requirements: *GCE:* 260-280. *SQAH:* AAA-BBBB. *IB:* 24. *BTEC Dip:* DD. *BTEC ExtDip:* DMM. *OCR ND:* D *OCR NED:* M2

F8NK BSc Wastes Management/Accounting
Duration: 3FT Hon
Entry Requirements: *GCE:* 260-280. *SQAH:* AAA-BBBB. *IB:* 24. *BTEC Dip:* DD. *BTEC ExtDip:* DMM. *OCR ND:* D *OCR NED:* M2

Q50 QUEEN MARY, UNIVERSITY OF LONDON
QUEEN MARY, UNIVERSITY OF LONDON
MILE END ROAD
LONDON E1 4NS
t: 020 7882 5555 f: 020 7882 5500
e: admissions@qmul.ac.uk
// www.qmul.ac.uk

FL71 BA Global Change: Environment, Economy & Development
Duration: 3FT Hon
Entry Requirements: *GCE:* 320-340. *IB:* 32.

Q75 QUEEN'S UNIVERSITY BELFAST
UNIVERSITY ROAD
BELFAST BT7 1NN
t: 028 9097 3838 f: 028 9097 5151
e: admissions@qub.ac.uk
// www.qub.ac.uk

F3N3 BSc Physics with Financial Mathematics
Duration: 3FT Hon
Entry Requirements: Contact the institution for details.

S36 UNIVERSITY OF ST ANDREWS
ST KATHARINE'S WEST
16 THE SCORES
ST ANDREWS
FIFE KY16 9AX
t: 01334 462150 f: 01334 463330
e: admissions@st-andrews.ac.uk
// www.st-andrews.ac.uk

CL11 BSc Biology and Economics
Duration: 4FT Hon
Entry Requirements: *GCE:* AAA. *SQAH:* AAAB. *IB:* 38.

LC18 BSc Economics and Psychology
Duration: 4FT Hon
Entry Requirements: *GCE:* AAA. *SQAH:* AAAB. *IB:* 38.

CL81 MA Economics and Psychology
Duration: 4FT Hon
Entry Requirements: *GCE:* AAA. *SQAH:* AAAB. *IB:* 38.

S75 THE UNIVERSITY OF STIRLING
STUDENT RECRUITMENT & ADMISSIONS SERVICE
UNIVERSITY OF STIRLING
STIRLING
SCOTLAND FK9 4LA
t: 01786 467044 f: 01786 466800
e: admissions@stir.ac.uk
// www.stir.ac.uk

FL91 BA Economics and Environmental Science
Duration: 4FT Hon
Entry Requirements: *GCE:* BBC. *SQAH:* BBBB. *SQAAH:* AAA-CCC. *IB:* 32. *BTEC ExtDip:* DMM.

NC46 BAcc Accountancy and Sports Studies
Duration: 4FT Hon
Entry Requirements: *GCE:* BBC. *SQAH:* BBBB. *SQAAH:* AAA-CCC. *IB:* 32. *BTEC ExtDip:* DMM.

S78 THE UNIVERSITY OF STRATHCLYDE
GLASGOW G1 1XQ
t: 0141 552 4400 f: 0141 552 0775
// www.strath.ac.uk

LC18 BA Economics and Psychology
Duration: 4FT Hon
Entry Requirements: *GCE:* AAB. *SQAH:* AAAABB-AAAB. *IB:* 36.

CL81 BA Psychology and Economics
Duration: 4FT Hon
Entry Requirements: *GCE:* ABB. *SQAH:* AAABB-AAAB. *IB:* 34.

S85 UNIVERSITY OF SURREY
STAG HILL
GUILDFORD
SURREY GU2 7XH
t: +44(0)1483 689305 f: +44(0)1483 689388
e: ugteam@surrey.ac.uk
// www.surrey.ac.uk

F3N3 BSc Physics with Finance (3 or 4 years)
Duration: 3FT Hon
Entry Requirements: *GCE:* ABB. *SQAH:* BBBBB. Interview required.

F3NH MPhys Physics with Finance (4 years)
Duration: 4FT Hon
Entry Requirements: *GCE:* AAB. *SQAH:* BBBBB. Interview required.

SOCIOLOGY AND SOCIAL SCIENCE
COMBINATIONS

A20 THE UNIVERSITY OF ABERDEEN
UNIVERSITY OFFICE
KING'S COLLEGE
ABERDEEN AB24 3FX
t: +44 (0) 1224 273504 f: +44 (0) 1224 272034
e: sras@abdn.ac.uk
// www.abdn.ac.uk/sras

LN64 MA Accountancy and Anthropology
Duration: 4FT Hon
Entry Requirements: *GCE:* BBB. *SQAH:* BBBB. *IB:* 30.

NL43 MA Accountancy and Sociology
Duration: 4FT Hon
Entry Requirements: *GCE:* BBB. *SQAH:* BBBB. *IB:* 30.

LL61 MA Anthropology and Economics
Duration: 4FT Hon
Entry Requirements: *GCE:* BBB. *SQAH:* BBBB. *IB:* 30.

LN63 MA Anthropology and Finance
Duration: 4FT Hon
Entry Requirements: *GCE:* BBB. *SQAH:* BBBB. *IB:* 30.

LL13 MA Economics and Sociology
Duration: 4FT Hon
Entry Requirements: *GCE:* BBB. *SQAH:* BBBB. *IB:* 30.

NL33 MA Finance and Sociology
Duration: 4FT Hon
Entry Requirements: *GCE:* BBB. *SQAH:* BBBB. *IB:* 30.

B06 BANGOR UNIVERSITY
BANGOR UNIVERSITY
BANGOR
GWYNEDD LL57 2DG
t: 01248 388484 f: 01248 370451
e: admissions@bangor.ac.uk
// www.bangor.ac.uk

LL14 BA Social Policy/Economics
Duration: 3FT Hon
Entry Requirements: *GCE:* 240-280. *IB:* 28.

LL13 BA Sociology/Economics
Duration: 3FT Hon
Entry Requirements: *GCE:* 240-280. *IB:* 28.

B16 UNIVERSITY OF BATH
CLAVERTON DOWN
BATH BA2 7AY
t: 01225 383019 f: 01225 386366
e: admissions@bath.ac.uk
// www.bath.ac.uk

LL19 BSc Economics and International Development
Duration: 3FT Hon
Entry Requirements: *GCE:* A*AA. *SQAAH:* AAB. *IB:* 38.

LLC9 BSc Economics and International Development (Sandwich)
Duration: 4SW Hon
Entry Requirements: *GCE:* A*AA. *SQAAH:* AAB. *IB:* 38.

B24 BIRKBECK, UNIVERSITY OF LONDON
MALET STREET
LONDON WC1E 7HX
t: 020 7631 6316
e: webform: www.bbk.ac.uk/ask
// www.bbk.ac.uk/ask

LL14 BSc Economics and Social Policy
Duration: 3FT Hon
Entry Requirements: *GCE:* ABB. *SQAH:* AAAA-AABB. *IB:* 36.
Admissions Test required.

B56 THE UNIVERSITY OF BRADFORD
RICHMOND ROAD
BRADFORD
WEST YORKSHIRE BD7 1DP
t: 0800 073 1225 f: 01274 235585
e: course-enquiries@bradford.ac.uk
// www.bradford.ac.uk

L1L9 BSc Economics with Development Studies
Duration: 3FT Hon
Entry Requirements: *GCE:* 260-300. *IB:* 25.

E28 UNIVERSITY OF EAST LONDON
DOCKLANDS CAMPUS
UNIVERSITY WAY
LONDON E16 2RD
t: 020 8223 3333 f: 020 8223 2978
e: study@uel.ac.uk
// www.uel.ac.uk

L1L9 BA Business Economics with Third World Development
Duration: 3FT Hon
Entry Requirements: *GCE:* 240. *IB:* 24.

LLC3 BA Business Economics/Sociology
Duration: 3FT Hon
Entry Requirements: *GCE:* 240. *IB:* 24.

LL19 BA Business Economics/Third World Development
Duration: 3FT Hon
Entry Requirements: *GCE:* 240. *IB:* 24.

L3L1 BA Sociology with Business Economics
Duration: 3FT Hon
Entry Requirements: *GCE:* 240. *IB:* 24.

E56 THE UNIVERSITY OF EDINBURGH
STUDENT RECRUITMENT & ADMISSIONS
57 GEORGE SQUARE
EDINBURGH EH8 9JU
t: 0131 650 4360 f: 0131 651 1236
e: sra.enquiries@ed.ac.uk
// www.ed.ac.uk/studying/undergraduate/

LL13 MA Economics and Sociology
Duration: 4FT Hon
Entry Requirements: *GCE:* AAA-BBB. *SQAH:* AAAA-BBBB. *IB:* 34.

LL41 MA Social Policy and Economics
Duration: 4FT Hon
Entry Requirements: *GCE:* BBB. *SQAH:* BBBB. *IB:* 34.

G28 UNIVERSITY OF GLASGOW
71 SOUTHPARK AVENUE
UNIVERSITY OF GLASGOW
GLASGOW G12 8QQ
t: 0141 330 6062 f: 0141 330 2961
e: student.recruitment@glasgow.ac.uk
// www.glasgow.ac.uk

LLC4 MA Business Economics/Public Policy
Duration: 4FT Hon
Entry Requirements: *GCE:* ABB. *SQAH:* AAAA-AABB. *IB:* 36.

LL14 MA Economics/Public Policy
Duration: 4FT Hon
Entry Requirements: *GCE:* ABB. *SQAH:* AAAA-AABB. *IB:* 36.

LLP1 MA Sociology/Business Economics
Duration: 4FT Hon
Entry Requirements: *GCE:* ABB. *SQAH:* AAAA-AABB. *IB:* 36.

LL61 MA Sociology/Economics
Duration: 4FT Hon
Entry Requirements: *GCE:* ABB. *SQAH:* AAAA-AABB. *IB:* 36.

K12 KEELE UNIVERSITY
KEELE UNIVERSITY
STAFFORDSHIRE ST5 5BG
t: 01782 734005 f: 01782 632343
e: undergraduate@keele.ac.uk
// www.keele.ac.uk

NL4H BA Accounting and Sociology
Duration: 3FT Hon
Entry Requirements: *GCE:* ABB.

L1L3 BA Business Economics with Social Science Foundation Year
Duration: 4FT Hon
Entry Requirements: *GCE:* 160.

LL13 BA Economics and Sociology
Duration: 3FT Hon
Entry Requirements: *GCE:* ABB.

LLC3 BA Economics with Social Science Foundation Year
Duration: 4FT Hon
Entry Requirements: *GCE:* CC.

LN33 BA Finance and Sociology
Duration: 3FT Hon
Entry Requirements: *GCE:* ABB.

N3L3 BA Finance with Social Science Foundation Year
Duration: 4FT Hon
Entry Requirements: *GCE:* CC.

K24 THE UNIVERSITY OF KENT
RECRUITMENT & ADMISSIONS OFFICE
REGISTRY
UNIVERSITY OF KENT
CANTERBURY, KENT CT2 7NZ
t: 01227 827272 f: 01227 827077
e: information@kent.ac.uk
// www.kent.ac.uk

LL16 BA Social Anthropology and Economics
Duration: 3FT Hon
Entry Requirements: *GCE:* AAB. *SQAH:* AAABB. *SQAAH:* AAB. *IB:* 33. *OCR ND:* D *OCR NED:* D1

LL13 BA Sociology and Economics
Duration: 3FT Hon
Entry Requirements: *GCE:* ABB. *SQAH:* AABBB. *SQAAH:* ABB. *IB:* 33. *OCR ND:* D *OCR NED:* D2

K84 KINGSTON UNIVERSITY
STUDENT INFORMATION & ADVICE CENTRE
COOPER HOUSE
40-46 SURBITON ROAD
KINGSTON UPON THAMES KT1 2HX
t: 0844 8552177 f: 020 8547 7080
e: aps@kingston.ac.uk
// www.kingston.ac.uk

LL31 BA Criminology and Economics (Applied)
Duration: 3FT Hon
Entry Requirements: *GCE:* 240-320. *SQAH:* BBCCC. *SQAAH:* BBC.

LL13 BA Economics (Applied) and Sociology
Duration: 3FT Hon
Entry Requirements: *GCE:* 240-320. *IB:* 24.

L72 LONDON SCHOOL OF ECONOMICS AND POLITICAL SCIENCE (UNIVERSITY OF LONDON)
HOUGHTON STREET
LONDON WC2A 2AE
t: 020 7955 7125 f: 020 7955 6001
e: ug.admissions@lse.ac.uk
// www.lse.ac.uk

LLK1 BSc Social Policy and Economics
Duration: 3FT Hon
Entry Requirements: *GCE:* ABB. *SQAH:* AAABB-AABBB. *SQAAH:* ABB. *IB:* 37.

M20 THE UNIVERSITY OF MANCHESTER
RUTHERFORD BUILDING
OXFORD ROAD
MANCHESTER M13 9PL
t: 0161 275 2077 f: 0161 275 2106
e: ug-admissions@manchester.ac.uk
// www.manchester.ac.uk

LL91 BA Development Studies and Economics
Duration: 3FT Hon
Entry Requirements: *GCE:* AAB. *SQAH:* AAABB. *SQAAH:* AAB. *IB:* 35.

LL13 BA Economics and Sociology
Duration: 3FT Hon
Entry Requirements: *GCE:* AAB. *SQAH:* AAABB. *SQAAH:* AAB.

N38 UNIVERSITY OF NORTHAMPTON
PARK CAMPUS
BOUGHTON GREEN ROAD
NORTHAMPTON NN2 7AL
t: 0800 358 2232 f: 01604 722083
e: admissions@northampton.ac.uk
// www.northampton.ac.uk

N4L4 BA Accounting/Health Studies
Duration: 3FT Hon
Entry Requirements: *GCE:* 260-280. *SQAH:* AAA-BBBB. *IB:* 24.
BTEC Dip: DD. *BTEC ExtDip:* DMM. *OCR ND:* D *OCR NED:* M2

N4LX BA Accounting/International Development
Duration: 3FT Hon
Entry Requirements: *GCE:* 260-280. *SQAH:* AAA-BBBB. *IB:* 24.
BTEC Dip: DD. *BTEC ExtDip:* DMM. *OCR ND:* D *OCR NED:* M2

N4L3 BA Accounting/Sociology
Duration: 3FT Hon
Entry Requirements: *GCE:* 260-280. *SQAH:* AAA-BBBB. *IB:* 24.
BTEC Dip: DD. *BTEC ExtDip:* DMM. *OCR ND:* D *OCR NED:* M2

L1L4 BA Economics/Health Studies
Duration: 3FT Hon
Entry Requirements: *GCE:* 260-280. *SQAH:* AAA-BBBB. *IB:* 24.
BTEC Dip: DD. *BTEC ExtDip:* DMM. *OCR ND:* D *OCR NED:* M2

L1LX BA Economics/International Development
Duration: 3FT Hon
Entry Requirements: *GCE:* 260-280. *SQAH:* AAA-BBBB. *IB:* 24.
BTEC Dip: DD. *BTEC ExtDip:* DMM. *OCR ND:* D *OCR NED:* M2

L1L5 BA Economics/Social Care
Duration: 3FT Hon
Entry Requirements: *GCE:* 260-280. *SQAH:* AAA-BBBB. *IB:* 24.
BTEC Dip: DD. *BTEC ExtDip:* DMM. *OCR ND:* D *OCR NED:* M2

L1L3 BA Economics/Sociology
Duration: 3FT Hon
Entry Requirements: *GCE:* 260-280. *SQAH:* AAA-BBBB. *IB:* 24.
BTEC Dip: DD. *BTEC ExtDip:* DMM. *OCR ND:* D *OCR NED:* M2

L4N4 BA Health Studies/Accounting
Duration: 3FT Hon
Entry Requirements: *GCE:* 260-280. *SQAH:* AAA-BBBB. *IB:* 24.
BTEC Dip: DD. *BTEC ExtDip:* DMM. *OCR ND:* D *OCR NED:* M2

L4L1 BA Health Studies/Economics
Duration: 3FT Hon
Entry Requirements: *GCE:* 260-280. *SQAH:* AAA-BBBB. *IB:* 24.
BTEC Dip: DD. *BTEC ExtDip:* DMM. *OCR ND:* D *OCR NED:* M2

L9NK BA International Development/Accounting
Duration: 3FT Hon
Entry Requirements: *GCE:* 260-280. *SQAH:* AAA-BBBB. *IB:* 24.
BTEC Dip: DD. *BTEC ExtDip:* DMM. *OCR ND:* D *OCR NED:* M2

L9LC BA International Development/Economics
Duration: 3FT Hon
Entry Requirements: *GCE:* 260-280. *SQAH:* AAA-BBBB. *IB:* 24.
BTEC Dip: DD. *BTEC ExtDip:* DMM. *OCR ND:* D *OCR NED:* M2

L5L1 BA Social Care/Economics
Duration: 3FT Hon
Entry Requirements: *GCE:* 260-280. *SQAH:* AAA-BBBB. *IB:* 24.
BTEC Dip: DD. *BTEC ExtDip:* DMM. *OCR ND:* D *OCR NED:* M2

L3N4 BA Sociology/Accounting
Duration: 3FT Hon
Entry Requirements: *GCE:* 260-280. *SQAH:* AAA-BBBB. *IB:* 24.
BTEC Dip: DD. *BTEC ExtDip:* DMM. *OCR ND:* D *OCR NED:* M2

L3L1 BA Sociology/Economics
Duration: 3FT Hon
Entry Requirements: *GCE:* 260-280. *SQAH:* AAA-BBBB. *IB:* 24.
BTEC Dip: DD. *BTEC ExtDip:* DMM. *OCR ND:* D *OCR NED:* M2

Q50 QUEEN MARY, UNIVERSITY OF LONDON
QUEEN MARY, UNIVERSITY OF LONDON
MILE END ROAD
LONDON E1 4NS
t: 020 7882 5555 f: 020 7882 5500
e: admissions@qmul.ac.uk
// www.qmul.ac.uk

LL31 BA Cities, Economies and Social Change
Duration: 3FT Hon
Entry Requirements: *GCE:* 320-340. *IB:* 32.

S09 SCHOOL OF ORIENTAL AND AFRICAN STUDIES (UNIVERSITY OF LONDON)
THORNHAUGH STREET
RUSSELL SQUARE
LONDON WC1H 0XG
t: 020 7898 4301 f: 020 7898 4039
e: undergradadmissions@soas.ac.uk
// www.soas.ac.uk

LL91 BA Economics and Development Studies
Duration: 3FT Hon
Entry Requirements: *GCE:* AAA.

LL16 BA Social Anthropology and Economics
Duration: 3FT Hon
Entry Requirements: *GCE:* AAA.

S36 UNIVERSITY OF ST ANDREWS
ST KATHARINE'S WEST
16 THE SCORES
ST ANDREWS
FIFE KY16 9AX
t: 01334 462150 f: 01334 463330
e: admissions@st-andrews.ac.uk
// www.st-andrews.ac.uk

LL16 MA Economics and Social Anthropology
Duration: 4FT Hon
Entry Requirements: *GCE:* AAA. *SQAH:* AAAB. *IB:* 38.

L1L6 MA Economics with Social Anthropology
Duration: 4FT Hon
Entry Requirements: *GCE:* AAA. *SQAH:* AAAA. *IB:* 38.

S90 UNIVERSITY OF SUSSEX
UNDERGRADUATE ADMISSIONS
SUSSEX HOUSE
UNIVERSITY OF SUSSEX
BRIGHTON BN1 9RH
t: 01273 678416 f: 01273 678545
e: ug.applicants@sussex.ac.uk
// www.sussex.ac.uk

LL19 BA Economics and International Development
Duration: 3FT Hon
Entry Requirements: *GCE:* AAB. *SQAH:* AAABB. *IB:* 35. *BTEC SubDip:* D. *BTEC Dip:* DD. *BTEC ExtDip:* DDD. *OCR ND:* D *OCR NED:* D1

S93 SWANSEA UNIVERSITY
SINGLETON PARK
SWANSEA SA2 8PP
t: 01792 295111 f: 01792 295110
e: admissions@swansea.ac.uk
// www.swansea.ac.uk

LL41 BA Economics and Social Policy
Duration: 3FT Hon
Entry Requirements: *GCE:* ABB. *IB:* 33.

Y50 THE UNIVERSITY OF YORK
STUDENT RECRUITMENT AND ADMISSIONS
UNIVERSITY OF YORK
HESLINGTON
YORK YO10 5DD
t: 01904 324000 f: 01904 323538
e: ug-admissions@york.ac.uk
// www.york.ac.uk

LL13 BA Economics/Sociology (Equal)
Duration: 3FT Hon
Entry Requirements: *GCE:* AAB. *SQAH:* AAAAB. *IB:* 35. *BTEC ExtDip:* DDD.

ECONOMICS AND OTHER COMBINATIONS

A20 THE UNIVERSITY OF ABERDEEN
UNIVERSITY OFFICE
KING'S COLLEGE
ABERDEEN AB24 3FX
t: +44 (0) 1224 273504 f: +44 (0) 1224 272034
e: sras@abdn.ac.uk
// www.abdn.ac.uk/sras

VL61 MA Divinity and Economics
Duration: 4FT Hon
Entry Requirements: Contact the institution for details.

LL17 MA Economics and Geography
Duration: 4FT Hon
Entry Requirements: *GCE:* BBB. *SQAH:* BBBB. *IB:* 30.

LV11 MA Economics and History
Duration: 4FT Hon
Entry Requirements: *GCE:* BBB. *SQAH:* BBBB. *IB:* 30.

LM19 MA Economics and Legal Studies
Duration: 4FT Hon
Entry Requirements: *GCE:* BBB. *SQAH:* BBBB. *IB:* 30.

LV15 MA Economics and Philosophy
Duration: 4FT Hon
Entry Requirements: *GCE:* BBB. *SQAH:* BBBB. *IB:* 30.

LK12 MA Economics and Real Estate
Duration: 4FT Hon
Entry Requirements: *GCE:* BBB. *SQAH:* BBBB. *IB:* 30.

A40 ABERYSTWYTH UNIVERSITY
ABERYSTWYTH UNIVERSITY, WELCOME CENTRE
PENGLAIS CAMPUS
ABERYSTWYTH
CEREDIGION SY23 3FB
t: 01970 622021 f: 01970 627410
e: ug-admissions@aber.ac.uk
// www.aber.ac.uk

L7L1 BA Human Geography with Economics
Duration: 3FT Hon
Entry Requirements: *GCE:* 300-320.

LN14 BScEcon Accounting & Finance/Economics
Duration: 3FT Hon
Entry Requirements: *GCE:* 300. *IB:* 27.

L1V3 BScEcon Economics with Economic & Social History
Duration: 3FT Hon
Entry Requirements: *GCE:* 300. *IB:* 27.

L1L7 BScEcon Economics with Human Geography
Duration: 3FT Hon
Entry Requirements: *GCE:* 300. *IB:* 28.

B06 BANGOR UNIVERSITY
BANGOR UNIVERSITY
BANGOR
GWYNEDD LL57 2DG
t: 01248 388484 f: 01248 370451
e: admissions@bangor.ac.uk
// www.bangor.ac.uk

LV11 BA History/Economics
Duration: 3FT Hon
Entry Requirements: *GCE:* 240-280. *IB:* 28.

B25 BIRMINGHAM CITY UNIVERSITY
PERRY BARR
BIRMINGHAM B42 2SU
t: 0121 331 5595 f: 0121 331 7994
// www.bcu.ac.uk

LK12 BSc Construction Management and Economics
Duration: 3FT Hon
Entry Requirements: *GCE:* 260. *IB:* 28.

B32 THE UNIVERSITY OF BIRMINGHAM
EDGBASTON
BIRMINGHAM B15 2TT
t: 0121 415 8900 f: 0121 414 7159
e: admissions@bham.ac.uk
// www.birmingham.ac.uk

LL71 BSc Geography and Economics
Duration: 3FT Hon
Entry Requirements: *GCE:* AAA. *SQAH:* AAABB. *SQAAH:* AA.

KL41 BSc Urban & Regional Planning and Economics
Duration: 3FT Hon
Entry Requirements: *GCE:* ABB. *SQAH:* ABBBB. *SQAAH:* AB.

B56 THE UNIVERSITY OF BRADFORD
RICHMOND ROAD
BRADFORD
WEST YORKSHIRE BD7 1DP
t: 0800 073 1225 f: 01274 235585
e: course-enquiries@bradford.ac.uk
// www.bradford.ac.uk

VL31 BA Economics and History
Duration: 3FT Hon
Entry Requirements: *GCE:* 240. *IB:* 24.

L160 BSc Economics and International Economics
Duration: 3FT Hon
Entry Requirements: *GCE:* 260-300. *IB:* 25.

B78 UNIVERSITY OF BRISTOL
UNDERGRADUATE ADMISSIONS OFFICE
SENATE HOUSE
TYNDALL AVENUE
BRISTOL BS8 1TH
t: 0117 928 9000 f: 0117 331 7391
e: ug-admissions@bristol.ac.uk
// www.bristol.ac.uk

VL51 BSc Philosophy and Economics
Duration: 3FT Hon
Entry Requirements: *GCE:* AAA. *SQAH:* AAAAA. *SQAAH:* AAA. *IB:* 37.

B90 THE UNIVERSITY OF BUCKINGHAM
YEOMANRY HOUSE
HUNTER STREET
BUCKINGHAM MK18 1EG
t: 01280 820313 f: 01280 822245
e: info@buckingham.ac.uk
// www.buckingham.ac.uk

VL21 BA History and Economics
Duration: 2FT Hon
Entry Requirements: *GCE:* BCC. *SQAH:* BBBC. *SQAAH:* BCC. *IB:* 31.

V2L1 BA History with Economics
Duration: 2FT Hon
Entry Requirements: *GCE:* BCC. *SQAH:* BBBC. *SQAAH:* BCC. *IB:* 31.

L1V1 BSc Economics with History
Duration: 2FT Hon
Entry Requirements: *GCE:* BBB. *SQAH:* ABBB. *SQAAH:* BBB. *IB:* 34.

L1P5 BSc Economics with Journalism
Duration: 2FT Hon
Entry Requirements: *GCE:* BBB. *SQAH:* ABBB. *SQAAH:* BBB. *IB:* 34.

C05 UNIVERSITY OF CAMBRIDGE
CAMBRIDGE ADMISSIONS OFFICE
FITZWILLIAM HOUSE
32 TRUMPINGTON STREET
CAMBRIDGE CB2 1QY
t: 01223 333 308 f: 01223 746 868
e: admissions@cam.ac.uk
// www.study.cam.ac.uk/undergraduate/

KL41 BA Land Economy
Duration: 3FT Hon
Entry Requirements: *GCE:* A*AA. *SQAAH:* AAA-AAB. Interview required.

C15 CARDIFF UNIVERSITY
PO BOX 927
30-36 NEWPORT ROAD
CARDIFF CF24 0DE
t: 029 2087 9999 f: 029 2087 6138
e: admissions@cardiff.ac.uk
// www.cardiff.ac.uk

VL11 BA Economics/History
Duration: 3FT Hon
Entry Requirements: *GCE:* AAB. *SQAH:* AAABB. *SQAAH:* AAB. *IB:* 35.

VL51 BA Economics/Philosophy
Duration: 3FT Hon
Entry Requirements: *GCE:* AAB. *SQAH:* AAABB. *SQAAH:* AAB. *IB:* 35.

C60 CITY UNIVERSITY
NORTHAMPTON SQUARE
LONDON EC1V 0HB
t: 020 7040 5060 f: 020 7040 8995
e: ugadmissions@city.ac.uk
// www.city.ac.uk

LP15 BA Journalism and Economics (3 years or 4 year SW)
Duration: 3FT Hon
Entry Requirements: *GCE:* AAA. *IB:* 35.

D65 UNIVERSITY OF DUNDEE
NETHERGATE
DUNDEE DD1 4HN
t: 01382 383838 f: 01382 388150
e: contactus@dundee.ac.uk
// www.dundee.ac.uk/admissions/undergraduate/

LV11 MA Economics and History
Duration: 4FT Hon
Entry Requirements: *GCE:* BCC. *SQAH:* ABBB. *IB:* 30.

LK14 MA Spatial Economics and Development
Duration: 4FT Hon
Entry Requirements: *GCE:* BCC. *SQAH:* ABBB. *IB:* 30.

E28 UNIVERSITY OF EAST LONDON
DOCKLANDS CAMPUS
UNIVERSITY WAY
LONDON E16 2RD
t: 020 8223 3333 f: 020 8223 2978
e: study@uel.ac.uk
// www.uel.ac.uk

LP13 BA Business Economics/Film Studies
Duration: 3FT Hon
Entry Requirements: *GCE:* 240. *IB:* 24.

LV11 BA Business Economics/History
Duration: 3FT Hon
Entry Requirements: *GCE:* 240. *IB:* 24.

PL31 BA Business Economics/Media Studies
Duration: 3FT Hon
Entry Requirements: *GCE:* 240. *IB:* 24.

E56 THE UNIVERSITY OF EDINBURGH
STUDENT RECRUITMENT & ADMISSIONS
57 GEORGE SQUARE
EDINBURGH EH8 9JU
t: 0131 650 4360 f: 0131 651 1236
e: sra.enquiries@ed.ac.uk
// www.ed.ac.uk/studying/undergraduate/

LV13 MA Economics and Economic History
Duration: 4FT Hon
Entry Requirements: *GCE:* AAA-BBB. *SQAH:* AAAA-BBBB. *IB:* 34.

LL71 MA Geography and Economics
Duration: 4FT Hon
Entry Requirements: *GCE:* AAA-ABB. *SQAH:* AAAA-ABBB.

VL51 MA Philosophy and Economics
Duration: 4FT Hon
Entry Requirements: *GCE:* AAA-BBB. *SQAH:* AAAA-BBBB. *IB:* 34.

E70 THE UNIVERSITY OF ESSEX
WIVENHOE PARK
COLCHESTER
ESSEX CO4 3SQ
t: 01206 873666 f: 01206 874477
e: admit@essex.ac.uk
// www.essex.ac.uk

LV11 BA History and Economics
Duration: 3FT Hon
Entry Requirements: *GCE:* ABB. *SQAH:* AAAB. *IB:* 34.

VL11 BA History and Economics (Including Year Abroad)
Duration: 4FT Hon
Entry Requirements: Contact the institution for details.

E84 UNIVERSITY OF EXETER
LAVER BUILDING
NORTH PARK ROAD
EXETER
DEVON EX4 4QE
t: 01392 723044 f: 01392 722479
e: admissions@exeter.ac.uk
// www.exeter.ac.uk

L190 BA Economics with Econometrics
Duration: 3FT Hon
Entry Requirements: *GCE:* A*AA-AAB. *SQAH:* AAAAA-AAABB. *SQAAH:* AAA-ABB.

L191 BA Economics with Econometrics with European Study (4 years)
Duration: 4FT Hon
Entry Requirements: *GCE:* A*AA-AAB. *SQAH:* AAAAA-AAABB. *SQAAH:* AAA-ABB.

L193 BA Economics with Econometrics with Industrial Experience (4 years)
Duration: 4FT Hon
Entry Requirements: *GCE:* A*AA-AAB. *SQAH:* AAAAA-AAABB. *SQAAH:* AAA-ABB.

VL51 BA Philosophy and Political Economy
Duration: 3FT Hon
Entry Requirements: *GCE:* AAA-AAB. *SQAH:* AAAAB-AAABB. *SQAAH:* AAB-ABB. *BTEC ExtDip:* DDD.

VL5C BA Philosophy and Political Economy with Study Abroad (4 years)
Duration: 4FT Hon
Entry Requirements: *GCE:* AAA-AAB. *SQAH:* AAAAB-AAABB. *SQAAH:* AAB-ABB. *BTEC ExtDip:* DDD.

G28 UNIVERSITY OF GLASGOW
71 SOUTHPARK AVENUE
UNIVERSITY OF GLASGOW
GLASGOW G12 8QQ
t: 0141 330 6062 f: 0141 330 2961
e: student.recruitment@glasgow.ac.uk
// www.glasgow.ac.uk

LN16 MA Archaeology/Business Economics
Duration: 4FT Hon
Entry Requirements: *GCE:* ABB. *SQAH:* AAAA-AABB. *IB:* 36.

LV14 MA Archaeology/Economics
Duration: 4FT Hon
Entry Requirements: *GCE:* ABB. *SQAH:* AAAB-ABBB. *IB:* 34.

VL41 MA Archaeology/Economics
Duration: 4FT Hon
Entry Requirements: *GCE:* ABB. *SQAH:* AAAA-AABB. *IB:* 36.

LV13 MA Business Economics/Economic & Social History
Duration: 4FT Hon
Entry Requirements: *GCE:* ABB. *SQAH:* AAAA-AABB. *IB:* 36.

LLC7 MA Business Economics/Geography
Duration: 4FT Hon
Entry Requirements: *GCE:* ABB. *SQAH:* AAAA-AABB. *IB:* 36.

LV15 MA Business Economics/Philosophy
Duration: 4FT Hon
Entry Requirements: *GCE:* ABB. *SQAH:* AAAA-AABB. *IB:* 36.

LVD2 MA Business Economics/Scottish History
Duration: 4FT Hon
Entry Requirements: *GCE:* ABB. *SQAH:* AAAA-AABB. *IB:* 36.

LVC3 MA Economic & Social History/Economics
Duration: 4FT Hon
Entry Requirements: *GCE:* ABB. *SQAH:* AAAA-AABB. *IB:* 36.

LL17 MA Economics/Geography
Duration: 4FT Hon
Entry Requirements: *GCE:* ABB. *SQAH:* AAAA-AABB. *IB:* 36.

LV11 MA Economics/History
Duration: 4FT Hon
Entry Requirements: *GCE:* ABB. *SQAH:* AAAA-AABB. *IB:* 36.

LVC1 MA Economics/History
Duration: 4FT Hon
Entry Requirements: *GCE:* ABB. *SQAH:* AAAB-ABBB. *IB:* 36.

LW13 MA Economics/Music
Duration: 4FT Hon
Entry Requirements: *GCE:* ABB. *SQAH:* AAAB-ABBB. *IB:* 36.

LVC5 MA Economics/Philosophy
Duration: 4FT Hon
Entry Requirements: *GCE:* ABB. *SQAH:* AAAA-AABB. *IB:* 36.

LVD5 MA Economics/Philosophy
Duration: 4FT Hon
Entry Requirements: *GCE:* ABB. *SQAH:* AAAB-ABBB. *IB:* 36.

LVC2 MA Economics/Scottish History
Duration: 4FT Hon
Entry Requirements: *GCE:* ABB. *SQAH:* AAAA-AABB. *IB:* 36.

LVD1 MA Economics/Scottish History
Duration: 4FT Hon
Entry Requirements: *GCE:* ABB. *SQAH:* AAAB-ABBB. *IB:* 36.

LW14 MA Economics/Theatre Studies
Duration: 4FT Hon
Entry Requirements: *GCE:* ABB. *SQAH:* AAAB-ABBB. *IB:* 36.

LV16 MA Economics/Theology & Religious Studies
Duration: 4FT Hon
Entry Requirements: *GCE:* ABB. *SQAH:* AAAB-ABBB. *IB:* 36.

H36 UNIVERSITY OF HERTFORDSHIRE
UNIVERSITY ADMISSIONS SERVICE
COLLEGE LANE
HATFIELD
HERTS AL10 9AB
t: 01707 284800
// www.herts.ac.uk

L1L7 BSc Economics/Human Geography
Duration: 3FT/4SW Hon
Entry Requirements: *GCE:* 280.

L1V5 BSc Economics/Philosophy
Duration: 3FT/4SW Hon
Entry Requirements: *GCE:* 300.

L7L1 BSc Human Geography/Economics
Duration: 3FT/4SW Hon
Entry Requirements: *GCE:* 280.

V5L1 BSc Philosophy/Economics
Duration: 3FT/4SW Hon
Entry Requirements: *GCE:* 300.

H72 THE UNIVERSITY OF HULL
THE UNIVERSITY OF HULL
COTTINGHAM ROAD
HULL HU6 7RX
t: 01482 466100 f: 01482 442290
e: admissions@hull.ac.uk
// www.hull.ac.uk

LJ19 BA Business Economics and Supply Chain Management
Duration: 3FT Hon
Entry Requirements: **GCE:** 300. **IB:** 30. **BTEC ExtDip:** DMM.

LJD9 BA Business Economics and Supply Chain Management (International) (4 years)
Duration: 4FT Hon
Entry Requirements: **GCE:** 300. **IB:** 30. **BTEC ExtDip:** DMM.

LJC9 BA Business Economics and Supply Chain Management (with Prof Experience) (4 years)
Duration: 4FT Hon
Entry Requirements: **GCE:** 300. **IB:** 30. **BTEC ExtDip:** DMM.

V1L1 BA History with Economics
Duration: 3FT Hon
Entry Requirements: **GCE:** 280-320. **IB:** 30. **BTEC ExtDip:** DMM.

K12 KEELE UNIVERSITY
KEELE UNIVERSITY
STAFFORDSHIRE ST5 5BG
t: 01782 734005 f: 01782 632343
e: undergraduate@keele.ac.uk
// www.keele.ac.uk

LN19 BA Business Management and Economics
Duration: 3FT Hon
Entry Requirements: **GCE:** ABB.

LM19 BA Criminology and Economics
Duration: 3FT Hon
Entry Requirements: **GCE:** ABB.

LP13 BA Economics and Film Studies
Duration: 3FT Hon
Entry Requirements: **GCE:** ABB.

LLC7 BA Economics and Geography
Duration: 3FT Hon
Entry Requirements: **GCE:** ABB.

LV11 BA Economics and History
Duration: 3FT Hon
Entry Requirements: **GCE:** ABB.

LLD7 BA Economics and Human Geography
Duration: 3FT Hon
Entry Requirements: **GCE:** ABB.

LN16 BA Economics and Human Resource Management
Duration: 3FT Hon
Entry Requirements: **GCE:** ABB.

LW13 BA Economics and Music
Duration: 3FT Hon
Entry Requirements: **GCE:** ABB.

LWC3 BA Economics and Music Technology
Duration: 3FT Hon
Entry Requirements: **GCE:** ABB.

LV15 BA Economics and Philosophy
Duration: 3FT Hon
Entry Requirements: **GCE:** ABB.

K84 KINGSTON UNIVERSITY
STUDENT INFORMATION & ADVICE CENTRE
COOPER HOUSE
40-46 SURBITON ROAD
KINGSTON UPON THAMES KT1 2HX
t: 0844 8552177 f: 020 8547 7080
e: aps@kingston.ac.uk
// www.kingston.ac.uk

WL81 BA Creative Writing and Economics (Applied)
Duration: 3FT Hon
Entry Requirements: **GCE:** 240-320. **IB:** 30.

LV11 BA Economics (Applied) and History
Duration: 3FT Hon
Entry Requirements: **GCE:** 220-320. **IB:** 24.

LP15 BA Economics (Applied) and Journalism
Duration: 3FT Hon
Entry Requirements: **GCE:** 340.

LP13 BA Economics (Applied) and Media & Cultural Studies
Duration: 3FT Hon
Entry Requirements: **GCE:** 260-360. **IB:** 24.

LPC3 BA Economics (Applied) and Television & New Broadcasting Media
Duration: 3FT Hon
Entry Requirements: **GCE:** 240-320. **IB:** 24.

L14 LANCASTER UNIVERSITY
THE UNIVERSITY
LANCASTER
LANCASHIRE LA1 4YW
t: 01524 592029 f: 01524 846243
e: ugadmissions@lancaster.ac.uk
// www.lancs.ac.uk

LL71 BA Economics and Geography
Duration: 3FT Hon
Entry Requirements: **GCE:** AAB. **SQAH:** ABBBB. **SQAAH:** AAB. **IB:** 35.

L23 UNIVERSITY OF LEEDS
THE UNIVERSITY OF LEEDS
WOODHOUSE LANE
LEEDS LS2 9JT
t: 0113 343 3999
e: admissions@leeds.ac.uk
// www.leeds.ac.uk

LL17 BA Economics and Geography
Duration: 3FT Hon
Entry Requirements: *GCE:* AAA. *SQAAH:* AAA. *IB:* 36.

VL11 BA Economics and History
Duration: 3FT Hon
Entry Requirements: *GCE:* AAA. *SQAAH:* AAA. *IB:* 38.

VL51 BA Economics and Philosophy
Duration: 3FT Hon
Entry Requirements: *GCE:* AAB. *SQAAH:* AAB. *IB:* 36.

L1N9 BSc Economics with Transport Studies
Duration: 3FT Hon
Entry Requirements: *GCE:* AAA. *SQAH:* AAAAA. *SQAAH:* AAA. *IB:* 36. Interview required.

L72 LONDON SCHOOL OF ECONOMICS AND POLITICAL SCIENCE (UNIVERSITY OF LONDON)
HOUGHTON STREET
LONDON WC2A 2AE
t: 020 7955 7125 f: 020 7955 6001
e: ug.admissions@lse.ac.uk
// www.lse.ac.uk

V3L1 BSc Economic History with Economics
Duration: 3FT Hon
Entry Requirements: *GCE:* AAB. *SQAH:* AAAAA-AAABB. *SQAAH:* AAA-AAB. *IB:* 37.

VL31 BSc Economics and Economic History
Duration: 3FT Hon
Entry Requirements: *GCE:* AAB. *SQAH:* AAAAA-AAABB. *SQAAH:* AAA-AAB. *IB:* 37.

L1V3 BSc Economics with Economic History
Duration: 3FT Hon
Entry Requirements: *GCE:* A*AA. *SQAH:* AAAAA. *SQAAH:* AAA. *IB:* 38.

L7L1 BSc Geography with Economics
Duration: 3FT Hon
Entry Requirements: *GCE:* AAB. *SQAH:* AAAAA-AAABB. *SQAAH:* AAA-AAB. *IB:* 37.

LV15 BSc Philosophy and Economics
Duration: 3FT Hon
Entry Requirements: *GCE:* AAA. *SQAH:* AAAAA. *SQAAH:* AAA. *IB:* 38.

L79 LOUGHBOROUGH UNIVERSITY
LOUGHBOROUGH
LEICESTERSHIRE LE11 3TU
t: 01509 223522 f: 01509 223905
e: admissions@lboro.ac.uk
// www.lboro.ac.uk

LL17 BSc Geography with Economics
Duration: 3FT Hon
Entry Requirements: *GCE:* AAB. *SQAAH:* AA-AB.

M20 THE UNIVERSITY OF MANCHESTER
RUTHERFORD BUILDING
OXFORD ROAD
MANCHESTER M13 9PL
t: 0161 275 2077 f: 0161 275 2106
e: ug-admissions@manchester.ac.uk
// www.manchester.ac.uk

LV15 BA Econ Economics and Philosophy
Duration: 3FT Hon
Entry Requirements: *GCE:* AAB. *SQAH:* AAABB. *SQAAH:* AAB.

LM19 BAEcon Economics and Criminology
Duration: 3FT Hon
Entry Requirements: *GCE:* AAB. *SQAH:* AAABB. *SQAAH:* AAB. *IB:* 35.

N38 UNIVERSITY OF NORTHAMPTON
PARK CAMPUS
BOUGHTON GREEN ROAD
NORTHAMPTON NN2 7AL
t: 0800 358 2232 f: 01604 722083
e: admissions@northampton.ac.uk
// www.northampton.ac.uk

M9L1 BA Criminology/Economics
Duration: 3FT Hon
Entry Requirements: *GCE:* 260-280. *SQAH:* AAA-BBBB. *IB:* 24. *BTEC Dip:* DD. *BTEC ExtDip:* DMM. *OCR ND:* D *OCR NED:* M2

W5L1 BA Dance/Economics
Duration: 3FT Hon
Entry Requirements: *GCE:* 260-280. *SQAH:* AAA-BBBB. *IB:* 24. *BTEC Dip:* DD. *BTEC ExtDip:* DMM. *OCR ND:* D *OCR NED:* M2
Interview required.

W4L1 BA Drama/Economics
Duration: 3FT Hon
Entry Requirements: *GCE:* 260-280. *SQAH:* AAA-BBBB. *IB:* 24. *BTEC Dip:* DD. *BTEC ExtDip:* DMM. *OCR ND:* D *OCR NED:* M2
Interview required.

L1M9 BA Economics/Criminology
Duration: 3FT Hon
Entry Requirements: *GCE:* 260-280. *SQAH:* AAA-BBBB. *IB:* 24. *BTEC Dip:* DD. *BTEC ExtDip:* DMM. *OCR ND:* D *OCR NED:* M2

L1W5 BA Economics/Dance
Duration: 3FT Hon
Entry Requirements: *GCE:* 260-280. *SQAH:* AAA-BBBB. *IB:* 24.
BTEC Dip: DD. *BTEC ExtDip:* DMM. *OCR ND:* D *OCR NED:* M2
Interview required.

L1W4 BA Economics/Drama
Duration: 3FT Hon
Entry Requirements: *GCE:* 260-280. *SQAH:* AAA-BBBB. *IB:* 24.
BTEC Dip: DD. *BTEC ExtDip:* DMM. *OCR ND:* D *OCR NED:* M2
Interview required.

L1X3 BA Economics/Education Studies
Duration: 3FT Hon
Entry Requirements: *GCE:* 260-280. *SQAH:* AAA-BBBB. *IB:* 24.
BTEC Dip: DD. *BTEC ExtDip:* DMM. *OCR ND:* D *OCR NED:* M2

L1NV BA Economics/Events Management
Duration: 3FT Hon
Entry Requirements: *GCE:* 260-280. *SQAH:* AAA-BBBB. *IB:* 24.
BTEC Dip: DD. *BTEC ExtDip:* DMM. *OCR ND:* D *OCR NED:* M2

L1W6 BA Economics/Film & Television Studies
Duration: 3FT Hon
Entry Requirements: *GCE:* 260-280. *SQAH:* AAA-BBBB. *IB:* 24.
BTEC Dip: DD. *BTEC ExtDip:* DMM. *OCR ND:* D *OCR NED:* M2

L1W1 BA Economics/Fine Art Painting & Drawing
Duration: 3FT Hon
Entry Requirements: *GCE:* 260-280. *SQAH:* AAA-BBBB. *IB:* 24.
BTEC Dip: DD. *BTEC ExtDip:* DMM. *OCR ND:* D *OCR NED:* M2

L1V1 BA Economics/History
Duration: 3FT Hon
Entry Requirements: *GCE:* 260-280. *SQAH:* AAA-BBBB. *IB:* 24.
BTEC Dip: DD. *BTEC ExtDip:* DMM. *OCR ND:* D *OCR NED:* M2

L1L7 BA Economics/Human Geography
Duration: 3FT Hon
Entry Requirements: *GCE:* 260-280. *SQAH:* AAA-BBBB. *IB:* 24.
BTEC Dip: DD. *BTEC ExtDip:* DMM. *OCR ND:* D *OCR NED:* M2

L1N6 BA Economics/Human Resource Management
Duration: 3FT Hon
Entry Requirements: *GCE:* 260-280. *SQAH:* AAA-BBBB. *IB:* 24.
BTEC Dip: DD. *BTEC ExtDip:* DMM. *OCR ND:* D *OCR NED:* M2

L1P5 BA Economics/Journalism
Duration: 3FT Hon
Entry Requirements: *GCE:* 260-280. *SQAH:* AAA-BBBB. *IB:* 24.
BTEC Dip: DD. *BTEC ExtDip:* DMM. *OCR ND:* D *OCR NED:* M2

L1PH BA Economics/Media Production
Duration: 3FT Hon
Entry Requirements: *GCE:* 260-280. *SQAH:* AAA-BBBB. *IB:* 24.
BTEC Dip: DD. *BTEC ExtDip:* DMM. *OCR ND:* D *OCR NED:* M2

L1N8 BA Economics/Tourism
Duration: 3FT Hon
Entry Requirements: *GCE:* 260-280. *SQAH:* AAA-BBBB. *IB:* 24.
BTEC Dip: DD. *BTEC ExtDip:* DMM. *OCR ND:* D *OCR NED:* M2

X3L1 BA Education Studies/Economics
Duration: 3FT Hon
Entry Requirements: *GCE:* 260-280. *SQAH:* AAA-BBBB. *IB:* 24.
BTEC Dip: DD. *BTEC ExtDip:* DMM. *OCR ND:* D *OCR NED:* M2

N8LC BA Events Management/Economics
Duration: 3FT Hon
Entry Requirements: *GCE:* 260-280. *SQAH:* AAA-BBBB. *IB:* 24.
BTEC Dip: DD. *BTEC ExtDip:* DMM. *OCR ND:* D *OCR NED:* M2

W6L1 BA Film & Television Studies/Economics
Duration: 3FT Hon
Entry Requirements: *GCE:* 260-280. *SQAH:* AAA-BBBB. *IB:* 24.
BTEC Dip: DD. *BTEC ExtDip:* DMM. *OCR ND:* D *OCR NED:* M2

W1L1 BA Fine Art Painting & Drawing/Economics
Duration: 3FT Hon
Entry Requirements: *GCE:* 260-280. *SQAH:* AAA-BBBB. *IB:* 24.
BTEC Dip: DD. *BTEC ExtDip:* DMM. *OCR ND:* D *OCR NED:* M2

V1L1 BA History/Economics
Duration: 3FT Hon
Entry Requirements: *GCE:* 260-280. *SQAH:* AAA-BBBB. *IB:* 24.
BTEC Dip: DD. *BTEC ExtDip:* DMM. *OCR ND:* D *OCR NED:* M2

L7L1 BA Human Geography/Economics
Duration: 3FT Hon
Entry Requirements: *GCE:* 260-280. *SQAH:* AAA-BBBB. *IB:* 24.
BTEC Dip: DD. *BTEC ExtDip:* DMM. *OCR ND:* D *OCR NED:* M2

N6L1 BA Human Resource Management/Economics
Duration: 3FT Hon
Entry Requirements: *GCE:* 260-280. *SQAH:* AAA-BBBB. *IB:* 24.
BTEC Dip: DD. *BTEC ExtDip:* DMM. *OCR ND:* D *OCR NED:* M2

P5L1 BA Journalism/Economics
Duration: 3FT Hon
Entry Requirements: *GCE:* 260-280. *SQAH:* AAA-BBBB. *IB:* 24.
BTEC Dip: DD. *BTEC ExtDip:* DMM. *OCR ND:* D *OCR NED:* M2

P3LC BA Media Production/Economics
Duration: 3FT Hon
Entry Requirements: *GCE:* 260-280. *SQAH:* AAA-BBBB. *IB:* 24.
BTEC Dip: DD. *BTEC ExtDip:* DMM. *OCR ND:* D *OCR NED:* M2

X3LC BA Special Educational Needs & Inclusion/Economics
Duration: 3FT Hon
Entry Requirements: *GCE:* 260-280. *SQAH:* AAA-BBBB. *IB:* 24.
BTEC Dip: DD. *BTEC ExtDip:* DMM. *OCR ND:* D *OCR NED:* M2

N8L1 BA Tourism/Economics
Duration: 3FT Hon
Entry Requirements: *GCE:* 260-280. *SQAH:* AAA-BBBB. *IB:* 24.
BTEC Dip: DD. *BTEC ExtDip:* DMM. *OCR ND:* D *OCR NED:* M2

N84 THE UNIVERSITY OF NOTTINGHAM
THE ADMISSIONS OFFICE
THE UNIVERSITY OF NOTTINGHAM
UNIVERSITY PARK
NOTTINGHAM NG7 2RD
t: 0115 951 5151 f: 0115 951 4668
// www.nottingham.ac.uk

L160 BA Economics and International Economics
Duration: 3FT Hon
Entry Requirements: *GCE:* A*AA-AABB. *SQAAH:* AAA. *IB:* 38.

LV15 BA Economics and Philosophy
Duration: 3FT Hon
Entry Requirements: *GCE:* A*AA-AABB. *SQAAH:* AAA. *IB:* 38.

O33 OXFORD UNIVERSITY
UNDERGRADUATE ADMISSIONS OFFICE
UNIVERSITY OF OXFORD
WELLINGTON SQUARE
OXFORD OX1 2JD
t: 01865 288000 f: 01865 270212
e: undergraduate.admissions@admin.ox.ac.uk
// www.admissions.ox.ac.uk

LV11 BA History and Economics
Duration: 3FT Hon
Entry Requirements: *GCE:* AAA. *SQAH:* AAAAA-AAAAB. *SQAAH:* AAB. Interview required. Admissions Test required.

Q50 QUEEN MARY, UNIVERSITY OF LONDON
QUEEN MARY, UNIVERSITY OF LONDON
MILE END ROAD
LONDON E1 4NS
t: 020 7882 5555 f: 020 7882 5500
e: admissions@qmul.ac.uk
// www.qmul.ac.uk

LL71 BScEcon Geography and Economics
Duration: 3FT Hon
Entry Requirements: *GCE:* 340. *IB:* 36.

R12 THE UNIVERSITY OF READING
THE UNIVERSITY OF READING
PO BOX 217
READING RG6 6AH
t: 0118 378 8619 f: 0118 378 8924
e: student.recruitment@reading.ac.uk
// www.reading.ac.uk

LV11 BA History and Economics
Duration: 3FT Hon
Entry Requirements: *Foundation:* Pass. *GCE:* AAC-ABB. *SQAH:* AAACC-ABBBB. *SQAAH:* AAC-ABB.

DL61 BSc Food Marketing and Business Economics with Industrial Training
Duration: 4FT Hon
Entry Requirements: *GCE:* 300.

LL17 BSc Geography and Economics (Regional Science)
Duration: 3FT Hon
Entry Requirements: *GCE:* 320-340.

R72 ROYAL HOLLOWAY, UNIVERSITY OF LONDON
ROYAL HOLLOWAY, UNIVERSITY OF LONDON
EGHAM
SURREY TW20 0EX
t: 01784 414944 f: 01784 473662
e: Admissions@rhul.ac.uk
// www.rhul.ac.uk

L1W3 BA Economics with Music
Duration: 3FT Hon
Entry Requirements: *GCE:* AAA-ABB. *SQAH:* AAAAA-AABBB. *SQAAH:* AAA-ABB. *IB:* 32.

S09 SCHOOL OF ORIENTAL AND AFRICAN STUDIES (UNIVERSITY OF LONDON)
THORNHAUGH STREET
RUSSELL SQUARE
LONDON WC1H 0XG
t: 020 7898 4301 f: 020 7898 4039
e: undergradadmissions@soas.ac.uk
// www.soas.ac.uk

LL17 BA Geography and Economics
Duration: 3FT Hon
Entry Requirements: *GCE:* AAA.

LV11 BA History and Economics
Duration: 3FT Hon
Entry Requirements: *GCE:* AAA.

LV16 BA Study of Religions and Economics
Duration: 3FT Hon
Entry Requirements: *GCE:* AAA.

S18 THE UNIVERSITY OF SHEFFIELD
THE UNIVERSITY OF SHEFFIELD
LEVEL 2, ARTS TOWER
WESTERN BANK
SHEFFIELD S10 2TN
t: 0114 222 8030 f: 0114 222 8032
// www.sheffield.ac.uk

LV15 BA Economics and Philosophy
Duration: 3FT Hon
Entry Requirements: *GCE:* AAB. *SQAH:* AAABB. *SQAAH:* AB. *IB:* 35. *BTEC ExtDip:* DDD.

S27 UNIVERSITY OF SOUTHAMPTON
HIGHFIELD
SOUTHAMPTON SO17 1BJ
t: 023 8059 4732 f: 023 8059 3037
e: admissions@soton.ac.uk
// www.southampton.ac.uk

VL51 BA Economics and Philosophy
Duration: 3FT Hon
Entry Requirements: *GCE:* AAB. *IB:* 34.

S36 UNIVERSITY OF ST ANDREWS
ST KATHARINE'S WEST
16 THE SCORES
ST ANDREWS
FIFE KY16 9AX
t: 01334 462150 f: 01334 463330
e: admissions@st-andrews.ac.uk
// www.st-andrews.ac.uk

LVD1 MA Ancient History and Economics
Duration: 4FT Hon
Entry Requirements: *GCE:* AAA. *SQAH:* AAAB. *IB:* 38.

LV16 MA Biblical Studies and Economics
Duration: 4FT Hon
Entry Requirements: *GCE:* AAA. *SQAH:* AAAB. *IB:* 36.

LP13 MA Economics and Film Studies
Duration: 4FT Hon
Entry Requirements: *GCE:* AAA. *SQAH:* AAAB. *IB:* 38.

LL17 MA Economics and Geography
Duration: 4FT Hon
Entry Requirements: *GCE:* AAA. *SQAH:* AAAB. *IB:* 38.

LVC1 MA Economics and Mediaeval History
Duration: 4FT Hon
Entry Requirements: *GCE:* AAA. *SQAH:* AAAB. *IB:* 38.

LV11 MA Economics and Modern History
Duration: 4FT Hon
Entry Requirements: *GCE:* AAA. *SQAH:* AAAB. *IB:* 38.

LV15 MA Economics and Philosophy
Duration: 4FT Hon
Entry Requirements: *GCE:* AAA. *SQAH:* AAAB. *IB:* 38.

S78 THE UNIVERSITY OF STRATHCLYDE
GLASGOW G1 1XQ
t: 0141 552 4400 f: 0141 552 0775
// www.strath.ac.uk

LN18 BA Economics and Hospitality & Tourism
Duration: 4FT Hon
Entry Requirements: *GCE:* AAB. *SQAH:* AAAABB-AAAB. *IB:* 36.

LN16 BA Economics and Human Resource Management
Duration: 4FT Hon
Entry Requirements: *GCE:* AAB. *SQAH:* AAAABB-AAAB. *IB:* 36.

XL31 BA Education and Economics
Duration: 4FT Hon
Entry Requirements: Contact the institution for details.

LV11 BA History and Economics
Duration: 4FT Hon
Entry Requirements: *GCE:* ABB. *SQAH:* AAABB-AAAB. *IB:* 34.

PL51 BA Journalism & Creative Writing and Economics
Duration: 4FT Hon
Entry Requirements: *GCE:* ABB. *SQAH:* AAABB-AAAB. *IB:* 34.
Portfolio required.

S93 SWANSEA UNIVERSITY
SINGLETON PARK
SWANSEA SA2 8PP
t: 01792 295111 f: 01792 295110
e: admissions@swansea.ac.uk
// www.swansea.ac.uk

LL17 BA Economics and Geography
Duration: 3FT Hon
Entry Requirements: *GCE:* ABB. *IB:* 33.

LV11 BA Economics and History
Duration: 3FT Hon
Entry Requirements: *GCE:* ABB. *IB:* 33.

LL71 BSc Economics and Geography
Duration: 3FT Hon
Entry Requirements: *GCE:* ABB. *IB:* 33.

U80 UNIVERSITY COLLEGE LONDON (UNIVERSITY OF LONDON)
GOWER STREET
LONDON WC1E 6BT
t: 020 7679 3000 f: 020 7679 3001
// www.ucl.ac.uk

VL51 BA Philosophy and Economics
Duration: 3FT Hon
Entry Requirements: *GCE:* AAAe. *SQAAH:* AAA. *IB:* 38. Interview required.

LL17 BScEcon Economics and Geography
Duration: 3FT Hon
Entry Requirements: *GCE:* AAAe-AABe. *SQAAH:* AAA-AAB. Interview required.

W20 THE UNIVERSITY OF WARWICK
COVENTRY CV4 8UW
t: 024 7652 3723 f: 024 7652 4649
e: ugadmissions@warwick.ac.uk
// www.warwick.ac.uk

G0L0 BSc.MMORSE Mathematics, Operational Research, Statistics and Economics option - Operational Research and Statistics
Duration: 4FT Hon
Entry Requirements: *GCE:* A*AA-AABa. *SQAAH:* AA. *IB:* 39.
Interview required.

G0L0 BSc.MMORSE Mathematics, Operational Research, Statistics and Economics option - Econometrics and Mathematical Economics
Duration: 4FT Hon
Entry Requirements: *GCE:* A*AA-AABa. *SQAAH:* AA. *IB:* 39.
Interview required.

G0L0 BSc.MMORSE Mathematics, Operational Research, Statistics and Economics option - Statistics with Mathematics
Duration: 4FT Hon
Entry Requirements: *GCE:* A*AA-AABa. *SQAAH:* AA. *IB:* 39.
Interview required.

G0L0 BSc.MMORSE Mathematics, Operational Research, Statistics and Economics option - Actuarial and Financial Mathematics
Duration: 4FT Hon
Entry Requirements: *GCE:* A*AA-AABa. *SQAAH:* AA. *IB:* 39.
Interview required.

Y50 THE UNIVERSITY OF YORK
STUDENT RECRUITMENT AND ADMISSIONS
UNIVERSITY OF YORK
HESLINGTON
YORK YO10 5DD
t: 01904 324000 f: 01904 323538
e: ug-admissions@york.ac.uk
// www.york.ac.uk

LV13 BA Economics/Economic History (Equal)
Duration: 3FT Hon
Entry Requirements: *GCE:* AAA-AAB. *SQAH:* AAAAB. *SQAAH:* AB.
IB: 36.

LV15 BA Economics/Philosophy (Equal)
Duration: 3FT Hon
Entry Requirements: *GCE:* AAA. *SQAH:* AAAAA. *SQAAH:* AA. *IB:* 36.

VL11 BA History and Economics
Duration: 3FT Hon
Entry Requirements: *GCE:* AAA. *SQAH:* AAAAA. *SQAAH:* AA. *IB:* 36. *BTEC ExtDip:* DDD.

FINANCE AND OTHER COMBINATIONS

A20 THE UNIVERSITY OF ABERDEEN
UNIVERSITY OFFICE
KING'S COLLEGE
ABERDEEN AB24 3FX
t: +44 (0) 1224 273504 f: +44 (0) 1224 272034
e: sras@abdn.ac.uk
// www.abdn.ac.uk/sras

NV36 MA Divinity and Finance
Duration: 4FT Hon
Entry Requirements: *GCE:* BBB. *SQAH:* BBBB. *IB:* 30.

LN73 MA Finance and Geography
Duration: 4FT Hon
Entry Requirements: *GCE:* BBB. *SQAH:* BBBB. *IB:* 30.

NV31 MA Finance and History
Duration: 4FT Hon
Entry Requirements: *GCE:* BBB. *SQAH:* BBBB. *IB:* 30.

NVH3 MA Finance and History of Art
Duration: 4FT Hon
Entry Requirements: *GCE:* BBB. *SQAH:* BBBB. *IB:* 30.

NM31 MA Finance and Legal Studies
Duration: 4FT Hon
Entry Requirements: *GCE:* BBB. *SQAH:* BBBB. *IB:* 30.

NV35 MA Finance and Philosophy
Duration: 4FT Hon
Entry Requirements: *GCE:* BBB. *SQAH:* BBBB. *IB:* 30.

NK32 MA Finance and Real Estate
Duration: 4FT Hon
Entry Requirements: *GCE:* BBB. *SQAH:* BBBB. *IB:* 30.

A40 ABERYSTWYTH UNIVERSITY
ABERYSTWYTH UNIVERSITY, WELCOME CENTRE
PENGLAIS CAMPUS
ABERYSTWYTH
CEREDIGION SY23 3FB
t: 01970 622021 f: 01970 627410
e: ug-admissions@aber.ac.uk
// www.aber.ac.uk

N4P1 BScEcon Accounting & Finance with Information Management
Duration: 3FT Hon
Entry Requirements: *GCE:* 300. *IB:* 27.

B72 UNIVERSITY OF BRIGHTON
MITHRAS HOUSE 211
LEWES ROAD
BRIGHTON BN2 4AT
t: 01273 644644 f: 01273 642607
e: admissions@brighton.ac.uk
// www.brighton.ac.uk

N390 BSc Finance and Investment
Duration: 3FT/4SW Hon
Entry Requirements: *GCE:* BBB. *IB:* 30.

C58 UNIVERSITY OF CHICHESTER
BISHOP OTTER CAMPUS
COLLEGE LANE
CHICHESTER
WEST SUSSEX PO19 6PE
t: 01243 816002 f: 01243 816161
e: admissions@chi.ac.uk
// www.chiuni.ac.uk

NN8J BA Event Management and Finance - Placement
Duration: 4SW Hon
Entry Requirements: *GCE:* BCD-CCC. *SQAAH:* CCC. *IB:* 28. *BTEC SubDip:* M. *BTEC Dip:* DD.

NN36 BA Human Resource Management and Finance
Duration: 3FT Hon
Entry Requirements: *GCE:* BCD-CCC. *SQAAH:* CCC. *IB:* 28. *BTEC SubDip:* M. *BTEC Dip:* DD.

NN8H BA Tourism Management and Finance
Duration: 3FT Hon
Entry Requirements: *GCE:* BCD-CCC. *SQAAH:* CCC. *IB:* 28. *BTEC SubDip:* M. *BTEC Dip:* DD.

C85 COVENTRY UNIVERSITY
THE STUDENT CENTRE
COVENTRY UNIVERSITY
1 GULSON RD
COVENTRY CV1 2JH
t: 024 7615 2222 f: 024 7615 2223
e: studentenquiries@coventry.ac.uk
// www.coventry.ac.uk

N390 FYr Finance and Investment (Foundation Year)
Duration: 1FT FYr
Entry Requirements: *GCE:* 100. *IB:* 24. *BTEC Dip:* MP. *BTEC ExtDip:* PPP. *OCR ND:* P2 *OCR NED:* P3

09JN HND Investment with Operational Risk and Global Securities Operations
Duration: 2FT HND
Entry Requirements: *GCE:* 200. *IB:* 24. *BTEC Dip:* DM. *BTEC ExtDip:* MMP. *OCR ND:* M1 *OCR NED:* P1

G42 GLASGOW CALEDONIAN UNIVERSITY
STUDENT RECRUITMENT & ADMISSIONS SERVICE
CITY CAMPUS
COWCADDENS ROAD
GLASGOW G4 0BA
t: 0141 331 3000 f: 0141 331 8676
e: undergraduate@gcu.ac.uk
// www.gcu.ac.uk

N390 BA Finance, Investment & Risk
Duration: 4FT Hon
Entry Requirements: *GCE:* CCC. *SQAH:* BBCC. *IB:* 24.

K12 KEELE UNIVERSITY
KEELE UNIVERSITY
STAFFORDSHIRE ST5 5BG
t: 01782 734005 f: 01782 632343
e: undergraduate@keele.ac.uk
// www.keele.ac.uk

NN39 BA Business Management and Finance
Duration: 3FT Hon
Entry Requirements: *GCE:* ABB.

MNX3 BA Criminology and Finance
Duration: 3FT Hon
Entry Requirements: *GCE:* ABB.

NX33 BA Educational Studies and Finance
Duration: 3FT Hon
Entry Requirements: *GCE:* ABB.

NV31 BA Finance and History
Duration: 3FT Hon
Entry Requirements: *GCE:* ABB.

NN36 BA Finance and Human Resource Management
Duration: 3FT Hon
Entry Requirements: *GCE:* ABB.

PN33 BA Finance and Media, Communications & Culture
Duration: 3FT Hon
Entry Requirements: *GCE:* ABB.

NW33 BA Finance and Music
Duration: 3FT Hon
Entry Requirements: *GCE:* ABB.

NWH3 BA Finance and Music Technology
Duration: 3FT Hon
Entry Requirements: *GCE:* ABB.

NV35 BA Finance and Philosophy
Duration: 3FT Hon
Entry Requirements: *GCE:* ABB.

GN73 BSc Smart Systems and Finance
Duration: 3FT Hon
Entry Requirements: *GCE:* ABB.

L41 THE UNIVERSITY OF LIVERPOOL
THE FOUNDATION BUILDING
BROWNLOW HILL
LIVERPOOL L69 7ZX
t: 0151 794 2000 f: 0151 708 6502
e: ugrecruitment@liv.ac.uk
// www.liv.ac.uk

WN23 BA Communication, Media and Popular Music
Duration: 3FT Hon
Entry Requirements: *GCE:* ABB. *SQAAH:* ABB. *IB:* 33.

M40 THE MANCHESTER METROPOLITAN UNIVERSITY
ADMISSIONS OFFICE
ALL SAINTS (GMS)
ALL SAINTS
MANCHESTER M15 6BH
t: 0161 247 2000
// www.mmu.ac.uk

WN33 BA Creative Music Production/Financial Management
Duration: 3FT Hon
Entry Requirements: *GCE:* 280. *IB:* 28. *BTEC Dip:* D*D*. *BTEC ExtDip:* DMM. Interview required.

NN36 BA Financial Management/Human Resource Management
Duration: 3FT Hon
Entry Requirements: *GCE:* 280. *IB:* 28. *BTEC Dip:* D*D*. *BTEC ExtDip:* DMM.

NV35 BA Financial Management/Philosophy
Duration: 3FT Hon
Entry Requirements: *GCE:* 280. *IB:* 28. *BTEC Dip:* D*D*. *BTEC ExtDip:* DMM.

N38 UNIVERSITY OF NORTHAMPTON
PARK CAMPUS
BOUGHTON GREEN ROAD
NORTHAMPTON NN2 7AL
t: 0800 358 2232 f: 01604 722083
e: admissions@northampton.ac.uk
// www.northampton.ac.uk

JN93 BSc International Logistics & Trade Finance (top-up)
Duration: 1FT Hon
Entry Requirements: HND required.

N77 NORTHUMBRIA UNIVERSITY
TRINITY BUILDING
NORTHUMBERLAND ROAD
NEWCASTLE UPON TYNE NE1 8ST
t: 0191 243 7420 f: 0191 227 4561
e: er.admissions@northumbria.ac.uk
// www.northumbria.ac.uk

N390 BA Finance and Investment Management
Duration: 3FT Hon
Entry Requirements: *GCE:* 300. *SQAH:* BBBBC. *SQAAH:* BBC. *IB:* 26. *BTEC ExtDip:* DDM. *OCR NED:* D2

Q75 QUEEN'S UNIVERSITY BELFAST
UNIVERSITY ROAD
BELFAST BT7 1NN
t: 028 9097 3838 f: 028 9097 5151
e: admissions@qub.ac.uk
// www.qub.ac.uk

N323 BSc Actuarial Science and Risk Management
Duration: 4SW Hon
Entry Requirements: *GCE:* AAAa. *SQAAH:* AAA.

R12 THE UNIVERSITY OF READING
THE UNIVERSITY OF READING
PO BOX 217
READING RG6 6AH
t: 0118 378 8619 f: 0118 378 8924
e: student.recruitment@reading.ac.uk
// www.reading.ac.uk

N302 BSc Finance and Investment Banking
Duration: 3FT Hon
Entry Requirements: *GCE:* AAB. *SQAH:* AAABB. *SQAAH:* AAB. *BTEC Dip:* DD. *BTEC ExtDip:* DDD.

S03 THE UNIVERSITY OF SALFORD
SALFORD M5 4WT
t: 0161 295 4545 f: 0161 295 4646
e: ug-admissions@salford.ac.uk
// www.salford.ac.uk

K4N3 BSc Property Management and Investment
Duration: 3FT Hon
Entry Requirements: *GCE:* 300.

S21 SHEFFIELD HALLAM UNIVERSITY
CITY CAMPUS
HOWARD STREET
SHEFFIELD S1 1WB
t: 0114 225 5555 f: 0114 225 2167
e: admissions@shu.ac.uk
// www.shu.ac.uk

N391 BA International Finance and Fund Management
Duration: 3FT/4SW Hon
Entry Requirements: *GCE:* 300.

S78 THE UNIVERSITY OF STRATHCLYDE
GLASGOW G1 1XQ
t: 0141 552 4400 f: 0141 552 0775
// www.strath.ac.uk

NN38 BA Finance and Hospitality & Tourism
Duration: 4FT Hon
Entry Requirements: *GCE:* AAB. *SQAH:* AAAABB-AAAB. *IB:* 36.

NN36 BA Finance and Human Resource Management
Duration: 4FT Hon
Entry Requirements: *GCE:* AAB. *SQAH:* AAAABB-AAAB. *IB:* 36.

H3N3 MEng Mechanical Engineering with Financial Management (d)
Duration: 5FT Hon
Entry Requirements: *GCE:* A*A*A-AAA. *SQAH:* AAAAAB-AAAAB. *IB:* 36. Interview required.

U80 UNIVERSITY COLLEGE LONDON (UNIVERSITY OF LONDON)
GOWER STREET
LONDON WC1E 6BT
t: 020 7679 3000 f: 020 7679 3001
// www.ucl.ac.uk

H1N3 BEng Engineering with Business Finance
Duration: 3FT Hon
Entry Requirements: *GCE:* AAAe-AABe. *SQAAH:* AAA-AAB. Interview required.

H1NH MEng Engineering with Business Finance
Duration: 4FT Hon
Entry Requirements: *GCE:* A*AAe-AAAe. *SQAAH:* AAA. Interview required.

ACCOUNTANCY AND OTHER COMBINATIONS

A20 THE UNIVERSITY OF ABERDEEN
UNIVERSITY OFFICE
KING'S COLLEGE
ABERDEEN AB24 3FX
t: +44 (0) 1224 273504 f: +44 (0) 1224 272034
e: sras@abdn.ac.uk
// www.abdn.ac.uk/sras

NV46 MA Accountancy and Divinity
Duration: 4FT Hon
Entry Requirements: *GCE:* BBB. *SQAH:* BBBB. *IB:* 30.

NL47 MA Accountancy and Geography
Duration: 4FT Hon
Entry Requirements: *GCE:* BBB. *SQAH:* BBBB. *IB:* 30.

NM49 MA Accountancy and Legal Studies
Duration: 4FT Hon
Entry Requirements: *GCE:* BBB. *SQAH:* BBBB. *IB:* 30.

NV45 MA Accountancy and Philosophy
Duration: 4FT Hon
Entry Requirements: *GCE:* BBB. *SQAH:* BBBB. *IB:* 30.

B90 THE UNIVERSITY OF BUCKINGHAM
YEOMANRY HOUSE
HUNTER STREET
BUCKINGHAM MK18 1EG
t: 01280 820313 f: 01280 822245
e: info@buckingham.ac.uk
// www.buckingham.ac.uk

N4P9 BSc Accounting with Communication Studies (EFL)
Duration: 2FT Hon
Entry Requirements: *GCE:* BBB-BCC. *SQAH:* ABBB-BBBC. *SQAAH:* BBB-BCC. *IB:* 34.

C58 UNIVERSITY OF CHICHESTER
BISHOP OTTER CAMPUS
COLLEGE LANE
CHICHESTER
WEST SUSSEX PO19 6PE
t: 01243 816002 f: 01243 816161
e: admissions@chi.ac.uk
// www.chiuni.ac.uk

NN84 BA Event Management and Accounting & Finance
Duration: 3FT Hon
Entry Requirements: *GCE:* BCD-CCC. *SQAAH:* CCC. *IB:* 28. *BTEC SubDip:* M. *BTEC Dip:* DD.

D39 UNIVERSITY OF DERBY
KEDLESTON ROAD
DERBY DE22 1GB
t: 01332 591167 f: 01332 597724
e: askadmissions@derby.ac.uk
// www.derby.ac.uk

NM49 BA Accounting and Applied Criminology
Duration: 3FT Hon
Entry Requirements: *Foundation:* Distinction. *GCE:* 260-300. *IB:* 28. *BTEC Dip:* D*D*. *BTEC ExtDip:* DMM. *OCR NED:* M2

NN46 BA Accounting and Human Resource Management
Duration: 3FT Hon
Entry Requirements: *Foundation:* Distinction. *GCE:* 260-300. *IB:* 28. *BTEC Dip:* D*D*. *BTEC ExtDip:* DMM. *OCR NED:* M2

E59 EDINBURGH NAPIER UNIVERSITY
CRAIGLOCKHART CAMPUS
EDINBURGH EH14 1DJ
t: +44 (0)8452 60 60 40 f: 0131 455 6464
e: info@napier.ac.uk
// www.napier.ac.uk

N4N6 BA Accounting with Human Resource Management
Duration: 3FT/4FT Ord/Hon
Entry Requirements: *GCE:* 230.

H72 THE UNIVERSITY OF HULL
THE UNIVERSITY OF HULL
COTTINGHAM ROAD
HULL HU6 7RX
t: 01482 466100 f: 01482 442290
e: admissions@hull.ac.uk
// www.hull.ac.uk

NJ49 BSc Accounting and Supply Chain Management
Duration: 3FT Hon
Entry Requirements: *GCE:* 300. *IB:* 30. *BTEC ExtDip:* DMM.

NJ4X BSc Accounting and Supply Chain Management (International) (4years)
Duration: 4FT Hon
Entry Requirements: *GCE:* 300. *IB:* 30. *BTEC ExtDip:* DMM.

NJK9 BSc Accounting and Supply Chain Management (with Professional Experience) (4years)
Duration: 4FT Hon
Entry Requirements: *GCE:* 300. *IB:* 30. *BTEC ExtDip:* DMM.

K12 KEELE UNIVERSITY
KEELE UNIVERSITY
STAFFORDSHIRE ST5 5BG
t: 01782 734005 f: 01782 632343
e: undergraduate@keele.ac.uk
// www.keele.ac.uk

NM49 BA Accounting and Criminology
Duration: 3FT Hon
Entry Requirements: *GCE:* ABB.

NP43 BA Accounting and Film Studies
Duration: 3FT Hon
Entry Requirements: *GCE:* ABB.

NL47 BA Accounting and Geography
Duration: 3FT Hon
Entry Requirements: *GCE:* ABB.

NV41 BA Accounting and History
Duration: 3FT Hon
Entry Requirements: *GCE:* ABB.

NL4R BA Accounting and Human Geography
Duration: 3FT Hon
Entry Requirements: *GCE:* ABB.

NN46 BA Accounting and Human Resource Management
Duration: 3FT Hon
Entry Requirements: *GCE:* ABB.

NW43 BA Accounting and Music
Duration: 3FT Hon
Entry Requirements: *GCE:* ABB.

NJ49 BA Accounting and Music Technology
Duration: 3FT Hon
Entry Requirements: *GCE:* ABB.

NV45 BA Accounting and Philosophy
Duration: 3FT Hon
Entry Requirements: *GCE:* ABB.

L46 LIVERPOOL HOPE UNIVERSITY
HOPE PARK
LIVERPOOL L16 9JD
t: 0151 291 3331 f: 0151 291 3434
e: administration@hope.ac.uk
// www.hope.ac.uk

NX43 BA Accounting and Education
Duration: 3FT Hon   CRB Check: Required
Entry Requirements: *GCE:* 300-320. *IB:* 25.

NP43 BA Accounting and Media & Communication
Duration: 3FT Hon
Entry Requirements: *GCE:* 300-320. *IB:* 25. Interview required.

NN48 BA Accounting and Tourism
Duration: 3FT Hon
Entry Requirements: *GCE:* 300-320. *IB:* 25.

N38 UNIVERSITY OF NORTHAMPTON
PARK CAMPUS
BOUGHTON GREEN ROAD
NORTHAMPTON NN2 7AL
t: 0800 358 2232 f: 01604 722083
e: admissions@northampton.ac.uk
// www.northampton.ac.uk

N4D4 BA Accounting with Applied Equine Studies
Duration: 3FT Hon
Entry Requirements: *GCE:* 260-280. *SQAH:* AAA-BBBB. *IB:* 24.
BTEC Dip: DD. *BTEC ExtDip:* DMM. *OCR ND:* D *OCR NED:* M2

N4W8 BA Accounting/Creative Writing
Duration: 3FT Hon
Entry Requirements: *GCE:* 260-280. *SQAH:* AAA-BBBB. *IB:* 24.
BTEC Dip: DD. *BTEC ExtDip:* DMM. *OCR ND:* D *OCR NED:* M2

N4WK BA Accounting/Drama
Duration: 3FT Hon
Entry Requirements: *GCE:* 260-280. *SQAH:* AAA-BBBB. *IB:* 24.
BTEC Dip: DD. *BTEC ExtDip:* DMM. *OCR ND:* D *OCR NED:* M2
Interview required.

N4X3 BA Accounting/Education Studies
Duration: 3FT Hon
Entry Requirements: *GCE:* 260-280. *SQAH:* AAA-BBBB. *IB:* 24.
BTEC Dip: DD. *BTEC ExtDip:* DMM. *OCR ND:* D *OCR NED:* M2

N4NV BA Accounting/Events Management
Duration: 3FT Hon
Entry Requirements: *GCE:* 260-280. *SQAH:* AAA-BBBB. *IB:* 24.
BTEC Dip: DD. *BTEC ExtDip:* DMM. *OCR ND:* D *OCR NED:* M2

N4W6 BA Accounting/Film & Television Studies
Duration: 3FT Hon
Entry Requirements: *GCE:* 260-280. *SQAH:* AAA-BBBB. *IB:* 24.
BTEC Dip: DD. *BTEC ExtDip:* DMM. *OCR ND:* D *OCR NED:* M2

N4P3 BA Accounting/Media Production
Duration: 3FT Hon
Entry Requirements: *GCE:* 260-280. *SQAH:* AAA-BBBB. *IB:* 24.
BTEC Dip: DD. *BTEC ExtDip:* DMM. *OCR ND:* D *OCR NED:* M2

N4W3 BA Accounting/Popular Music
Duration: 3FT Hon
Entry Requirements: *GCE:* 260-280. *SQAH:* AAA-BBBB. *IB:* 24.
BTEC Dip: DD. *BTEC ExtDip:* DMM. *OCR ND:* D *OCR NED:* M2
Interview required.

N4N8 BA Accounting/Tourism
Duration: 3FT Hon
Entry Requirements: *GCE:* 260-280. *SQAH:* AAA-BBBB. *IB:* 24.
BTEC Dip: DD. *BTEC ExtDip:* DMM. *OCR ND:* D *OCR NED:* M2

W8N4 BA Creative Writing/Accounting
Duration: 3FT Hon
Entry Requirements: *GCE:* 260-280. *SQAH:* AAA-BBBB. *IB:* 24.
BTEC Dip: DD. *BTEC ExtDip:* DMM. *OCR ND:* D *OCR NED:* M2

W4N4 BA Drama/Accounting
Duration: 3FT Hon
Entry Requirements: *GCE:* 260-280. *SQAH:* AAA-BBBB. *IB:* 24.
BTEC Dip: DD. *BTEC ExtDip:* DMM. *OCR ND:* D *OCR NED:* M2
Interview required.

X3N4 BA Education Studies/Accounting
Duration: 3FT Hon
Entry Requirements: *GCE:* 260-280. *SQAH:* AAA-BBBB. *IB:* 24.
BTEC Dip: DD. *BTEC ExtDip:* DMM. *OCR ND:* D *OCR NED:* M2

N8NK BA Events Management/Accounting
Duration: 3FT Hon
Entry Requirements: *GCE:* 260-280. *SQAH:* AAA-BBBB. *IB:* 24.
BTEC Dip: DD. *BTEC ExtDip:* DMM. *OCR ND:* D *OCR NED:* M2

W6N4 BA Film & Television Studies/Accounting
Duration: 3FT Hon
Entry Requirements: *GCE:* 260-280. *SQAH:* AAA-BBBB. *IB:* 24.
BTEC Dip: DD. *BTEC ExtDip:* DMM. *OCR ND:* D *OCR NED:* M2

P3NK BA Media Production/Accounting
Duration: 3FT Hon
Entry Requirements: *GCE:* 260-280. *SQAH:* AAA-BBBB. *IB:* 24.
BTEC Dip: DD. *BTEC ExtDip:* DMM. *OCR ND:* D *OCR NED:* M2

W3N4 BA Popular Music/Accounting
Duration: 3FT Hon
Entry Requirements: *GCE:* 260-280. *SQAH:* AAA-BBBB. *IB:* 24.
BTEC Dip: DD. *BTEC ExtDip:* DMM. *OCR ND:* D *OCR NED:* M2

XN34 BA Special Educational Needs & Inclusion/Accounting
Duration: 3FT Hon
Entry Requirements: *GCE:* 260-280. *SQAH:* AAA-BBBB. *IB:* 24.
BTEC Dip: DD. *BTEC ExtDip:* DMM. *OCR ND:* D *OCR NED:* M2

N8N4 BA Tourism/Accounting
Duration: 3FT Hon
Entry Requirements: *GCE:* 260-280. *SQAH:* AAA-BBBB. *IB:* 24.
BTEC Dip: DD. *BTEC ExtDip:* DMM. *OCR ND:* D *OCR NED:* M2

S18 THE UNIVERSITY OF SHEFFIELD
THE UNIVERSITY OF SHEFFIELD
LEVEL 2, ARTS TOWER
WESTERN BANK
SHEFFIELD S10 2TN
t: 0114 222 8030 f: 0114 222 8032
// www.sheffield.ac.uk

NP41 BA Accounting and Financial Management and Informatics
Duration: 3FT Hon
Entry Requirements: *GCE:* ABB. *SQAH:* AAABB. *IB:* 33. *BTEC ExtDip:* DDM.

S78 THE UNIVERSITY OF STRATHCLYDE
GLASGOW G1 1XQ
t: 0141 552 4400 f: 0141 552 0775
// www.strath.ac.uk

NN48 BA Accounting and Hospitality & Tourism
Duration: 4FT Hon
Entry Requirements: *GCE:* AAA. *SQAH:* AAAAAB-AAAA. *IB:* 36.

NN46 BA Accounting and Human Resource Management
Duration: 4FT Hon
Entry Requirements: *GCE:* AAA. *SQAH:* AAAAAB-AAAA. *IB:* 36.

U20 UNIVERSITY OF ULSTER
COLERAINE
CO. LONDONDERRY
NORTHERN IRELAND BT52 1SA
t: 028 7012 4221 f: 028 7012 4908
e: online@ulster.ac.uk
// www.ulster.ac.uk

NN46 BSc Accounting and Human Resource Management
Duration: 4SW Hon
Entry Requirements: *GCE:* 240. *IB:* 24.

PS